Great Britain and her world, 1750–1914

W. O. HENDERSON

Edited by Barrie M. Ratcliffe

GREAT BRITAIN
AND HER WORLD
1750–1914
Essays in honour of W. O. Henderson

MANCHESTER UNIVERSITY PRESS

© 1975 Manchester University Press
Published by
Manchester University Press
Oxford Road, Manchester M13 9PL
UK ISBN 0 7190 0581 7

Printed in Great Britain by
Western Printing Services Ltd, Bristol

Contents

Preface

On the occasion of W. O. Henderson's retirement a group of his colleagues and friends have written the following collection of essays in his honour. The essays are all original with the exception of François Crouzet's which first appeared in *Annales*. This now appears in English. Though the essays are all different in style and approach they all deal with international and comparative aspects of the British economy between 1750 and 1914, a theme and a period central to W. O. Henderson's work and interests. Most of the essays, indeed, take up problems that he raised and studied. Thus D. A. Farnie's contribution takes up points raised in W. O. Henderson's first published work, *The Lancashire Cotton Famine*, while four of the essays discuss problems in the transfer of technology between Great Britain and Continental Europe, a field where he did pioneering work, as shown most notably by his *Britain and Industrial Europe, 1750–1870*. The essay on the origins of the 1860 Anglo-French commercial treaty treats of an aspect of nineteenth-century tariff history to which W. O. Henderson contributed not merely his works on the Zollverein and on the genesis of the EEC but a number of important articles. He also worked on economic aspects of the German colonial empire of 1884–1918, and three of the contributions here deal with imperial problems.

The bibliography of his published works gives an indication of his contribution to learning. It is hoped that the broad scope of these essays is at least some reflection of the wide range of his scholarship and the inspiration he has given to others. They are affectionately and respectfully dedicated to him.

BARRIE M. RATCLIFFE

Bibliography of the works of W. O. Henderson

BOOKS

1934
The Lancashire Cotton Famine, 1861–5 (Manchester University Press: first edition, 1934; second edition with two additional chapters, 1969; American edition of the second edition published by Augustus M. Kelley, New York).

1938
The Zollverein (Cambridge University Press, 1939, with a preface by Sir John Clapham; second edition, with an introduction by the author, published by Frank Cass & Co. Ltd, 1959; American edition published by Quadrangle Books, Chicago).

1954
Britain and Industrial Europe, 1750–1870 (first edition, Liverpool University Press, 1954; second edition, Leicester University Press, 1965; third edition (paperback), Leicester University Press, 1972).

1958
The State and the Industrial Revolution in Prussia, 1740–1870 (Liverpool University Press, 1958).

1961
The Industrial Revolution on the Continent: Germany, France, Russia, 1800–1914 (Frank Cass & Co. Ltd, 1961; new edition, 1967). An American edition was published under the title *The Industrial Revolution in Europe: Germany, France, Russia, 1815–1914* (Quadrangle Books, Chicago, 1968).

1962
The Genesis of the Common Market (Frank Cass & Co. Ltd, 1962; American edition, Quadrangle Books, Chicago).
Studies in German Colonial History (Frank Cass & Co. Ltd, 1962; American edition, Quadrangle Books, Chicago).

1963
Studies in the Economic Policy of Frederick the Great (Frank Cass & Co. Ltd, 1963).

1966
J. C. Fischer and his Diary of Industrial England, 1814–51 (Frank Cass & Co. Ltd, 1966).

1967
Engels: Selected Writings, edited and introduced by W. O. Henderson (Penguin Books, 1967). Translations appeared in Spanish and Catalan.

1968
Industrial Britain under the Regency: the Diaries of Escher, Bodmer, May and de Gallois, 1814–18 (Frank Cass & Co. Ltd, 1968).

1969
The Industrialization of Europe, 1790–1914 (Thames & Hudson, 1969). Translations of this book have appeared in French (by Henri Delgove), German (by Wolfgang Haüser), Dutch and Portuguese.

1975
Life of Friedrich Engels (Frank Cass & Co. Ltd, two volumes, 1975).
The Rise of German Industrial Power, (Maurice Temple Smith, 1975).

ATLAS

In collaboration with S. de Vries and T. Luykx, *An Atlas of World History* (Nelson, 1965).

ARTICLES

1928
'Chap Books', *Cambridge Review*, vol. L, 1928–29, pp.31–3.

1931
'The Public Works Act, 1863', *Economic History* (supplement), vol. II, January 1931, pp.312–21.

1932
'Empire cotton during the cotton famine, 1861–64', *Empire Cotton Growing Review*, vol. IX, January 1932, pp.53–8.
'The Cotton Supply Association, 1857–72', *Empire Cotton Growing Review*, vol. IX, April 1932, pp.132–5.

1933
'The Cotton Famine in Lancashire', *Transactions of the Historic Society of Lancashire and Cheshire for the Year 1932*, vol. LXXXIV, 1933, pp.1–26.
'The Liverpool Office in London', *Economia*, vol. XIII, 1933, pp.473–9.
'John Bright and Indian cotton', *Empire Cotton Growing Review*, vol. X, July 1933, pp.189–94.
'The cotton famine on the Continent, 1861–65', *Economic History Review*, vol. IV, 1932–34, April 1933, pp.195–207.
'Trade cycle in the nineteenth century', *History*, new series, vol. XVIII, 1933–34, July 1933, pp.147–53.

1934
'The Zollverein', *History*, new series, vol. XIX, June 1934, pp.1–20.

1935
'The German colonial empire, 1884–1918', *History*, new series, vol. xx,
    1935–36, September 1935, pp.151–8.
'The rise of German industry' (review article), *Economic History Review*,
    vol. v, 1934–35, April 1935, pp.120–4.
'The American Chamber of Commerce of the Port of Liverpool, 1801–
    1908', *Transactions of the Historic Society of Lancashire and Cheshire for the
    Year 1933*, vol. lxxxv, 1935, pp.1–61.

1937
'German colonisation', *German Life and Letters*, vol. i, No. 4, July 1937,
    pp.241–54.

1938
'Germany and Mitteleuropa', *German Life and Letters*, vol. ii, No. 3,
    April 1938, pp.161–74.
'Germany's trade with her colonies, 1884–1914', *Economic History
    Review*, vol. ix (1938–9), November 1938, pp.1–16.
'Economic aspects of German imperial colonisation', *Scottish Geographi-
    cal Magazine*, vol. liv, No. 3, May 1938, pp.150–61.

1939
'Some economic aspects of national socialism in Germany', *German Life
    and Letters*, vol. iii, No. 2, January 1939, pp.81–93.

1940
'Twenty years of mandate government: some aspects of the develop-
    ment of the former German colonies, 1919–39', *The Highway*, vol.
    xxxii, February 1940, pp.109–11.

1941
'The peace settlement, 1919', *History*, new series, vol. xxvi, June 1941,
    pp.60–9.
'The pan-German movement', *History*, new series, vol. xxvi, December
    1941, pp.188–98.

1942
'The conquest of the German colonies, 1914–18', *History*, new series,
    vol. xxvii, September 1942, pp.124–39.

1943
'The war economy of German East Africa, 1914–17', *Economic History
    Review*, vol. xiii, 1943, pp.104–10.

1944
Chapter iii, section 4, 'Economic development 1815–71' and chapter
    iv, section 2, 'Germany's economic development 1871–1914', in

Germany, vol. II, *History and Administration* (Naval Intelligence Division; Geographical Handbook series), March 1944.

Chapter I, 'The economic development of Germany, 1918–39' and appendix I (Chief towns and cities), in *Germany*, vol. III, *Economic Geography* (Naval Intelligence Division; Geographical Handbook series), November 1944.

1945

Historical introductions to roads, inland waterways and ports in chapters I and II of *Germany*, vol. IV, '*Ports and communications* (Naval Intelligence Division; Geographical Handbook series), May 1945.

'British economic activity in the German colonies, 1884–1914', *Economic History Review*, vol. XV, Nos. 1–2, 1945, pp.56–66.

1947

Introduction to G. B. Henderson, *Crimean War Diplomacy and Other Historical Essays* (Glasgow, 1947), pp.v–x.

'Technical colleges and adult education', *Further Education*, vol. I, No. 2, 1947, pp.34–5.

1948

'The origins of technical education in Wolverhampton' (Wolverhampton and Staffordshire Technical College: *College Studies in Local History*, No. 1, 1948) (pamphlet).

'Wolverhampton as the site of the first Newcomen engine', *Transactions of the Newcomen Society*, vol. XXVI, 1947–48 and 1948–49, pp.155–9.

'German economic penetration in the Middle East, 1870–1914', *Economic History Review*, vol. XVIII (1948), pp.54–64.

1950

'Prince Smith and free trade in Germany', *Economic History Review*, second series, vol. II, No. 3, 1950, pp.295–302.

1951

'Walther Rathenau, a pioneer of the planned economy', *Economic History Review*, second series, vol. IV, No. 1, 1951, pp.98–108.

'The Cotton Famine in Scotland and the relief of distress, 1862–64', *Scottish Historical Review*, vol. XXX, 1951, pp.154–64.

1952

'Economic progress in Western Germany, 1945–51', *German Life and Letters*, new series, vol. V, January 1952, pp.85–94.

'Charles Pelham Villiers', *History*, new series, vol. XXXVII, 1952, pp.25–39.

'Manchester and the Lancashire Cotton Famine', in C. R. Fay, *Round about Industrial Britain 1830–60* (Toronto, 1952), pp.101–14.

'England und die Industrialisierung Deutschlands', *Zeitschrift für die Gesamte Staatswissenschaft*, vol. CVIII (part 2), 1952, pp.264–94.

1953
'Der englische Einfluss auf die Entwicklung der französischen Textil-industrie', *Zeitschrift für die Gesamte Staatswissenschaft*, vol. CVIII (part 4), 1952, pp.717–42.
'William Thomas Mulvany: an Irish pioneer in the Ruhr', *Explorations in Entrepreneurial History*, vol. V, 1953, pp.107–20.

1954
'England und die Entwicklung der Eisenindustrie und des Transport-wesens in Frankreich, 1750–1850', *Zeitschrift für die Gesamte Staats-wissenschaft*, vol. CX (part 2), 1954, pp.312–45.

1955
'Peter Beuth and the rise of Prussian industry, 1810–45', *Economic History Review*, vol. VIII (1955), pp.222–31 (reprinted in T. P. Hughes, *The Development of Western Technology since 1500*, New York, 1964, pp. 113–20).

1956
'The genesis of the industrial revolution in France and Germany in the 18th century', *Kyklos*, fasc. 2, 1956, pp.190–206 (reprinted in *The Economic Development of Western Europe: the Eighteenth and Early Nineteenth Centuries*, edited by W. C. Scoville and J. C. Laforce, Lexington, Mass., 1969, pp.194–208).
'Christian von Rother als Beamter, Finanzmann und Unternehmer in Dienste des preussischen Staats', *Zeitschrift für die Gesamte Staatswissenschaft*, vol. CXII (part 3), 1956, pp.523–50.

1957
'A nineteenth century approach to a West European common market', *Kyklos*, fasc. 4, 1957, pp.448–56.
'The Anglo–French commercial treaty of 1786', *Economic History Review*, vol. X, 1957, pp.104–12.
'The evolution of modern industrial organization' in Arthur Roberts (ed), *Management Notebook* (Newman Neame, 1957), pp.13–51.

1959
'The rise of the Berlin silk and porcelain industries', *Business History*, vol. I, No. 2, June 1959, pp.84–98.

1961
'The rise of the metal and armament industries in Berlin and Brandenburg, 1712–95', *Business History*, vol. III, No. 2, June 1961, pp.63–74.
'Die Struktur der preussischen Wirtschaft um 1786', *Zeitschrift für die Gesamte Staatswissenschaft*, vol. CXVII (part 2), 1961, pp.292–319.

'L'Unione doganale tedesca del secolo XIX. I problemi del MEC egli insengnamenti dello Zollverein', *Mercurio*, vol. IV, No. 2, February 1961.

1962
'The Cotton Famine of 1862', *Journal of the Textile Institute, Proceedings*, vol. LIII, June 1962, pp.349–51.
'The Berlin commercial crisis of 1763', *Economic History Review*, second series, vol. XV, No. 1, August 1962, pp.89–102.

1963
'J. C. Fischer, a Swiss industrial pioneer', *Zeitschrift für die Gesamte Staatswissenschaft*, vol. CXIX, part 2, April 1963, pp.361–76.
'Europäische Zollpolitik. Zur Vorgeschichte des Gemeinsamen Marktes', *Europäischegemeinschaft*, June, 1963.
'Steelmaking at Sanderson's 130 Years Ago', *The Sanderson Kayser Magazine*, vol. I, No. 6, 1963, pp.2–6.
'La politica economica di Frederico il grande', *Mercurio*, November 1963, pp.33–8.

1964
'Castlereagh and Europe', in *The Congress of Vienna and Europe* (Pergamon Press, 1964).
'J. C. Fischers Reisen durch die Industriegebiete Englands 1814–51', *Tradition*, vol. IX, 1964, pp.113–32.
'Deutscher Zollverein', in *Handwörterbuch der Sozialwissenschaften*, Lieferung 52, 1964, pp.268–73.

1965
Introduction to F. Engels, *Die Lage der arbeitenden Klasse in England* (J. H. W. Dietz Nachfolger, GmbH, Hanover, 1965), pp.xi–xxvii.
'Wirtschaftsarchivarbeit in England', *Tradition*, vol. X (parts 5 and 6), December 1965, pp.271–6.
'German East Africa, 1884–1918', in *History of East Africa*, vol. II, edited by Vincent Harlow and E. M. Chilver (Oxford, 1965), ch. 3, pp. 123–62.

1966
'Die Entstehung der preussischen Eisenbahnen, 1815–48', in Karl Erich Born (ed.), *Moderne deutsche Wirtschaftsgeschichte* (1966), pp. 137–50.
'Mitteleuropäische Zollvereinspläne, 1840–1940', *Zeitschrift für die Gesamte Staatswissenschaft*, vol. CXXII (part 1), 1966, pp.130–62.
'Die Wassertransport in England während der industriellen Revolution', *Wissenschaftliche Zeitschrift der Hochschule für Verkehrswesen* (Dresden, 1967), pp.281–6 and pp.443–51.

'Der englische Bergbau während der industriellen Revolution', *Freiberger Forschungshefte*, Heft D. 52, July 1966, pp.23–56.

1967
'J. C. Fischers Besuche in London zwischen 1794 und 1851' (in two parts), *Tradition*, vol. XII, 1967, pp.349–64 and pp.416–26.
Articles on Celle, Cuxhaven, Hanover (town), Hildesheim etc. in *Chambers Encyclopaedia* (edition of 1967).

1969
'The growth of technical education in France and the activities of French mining engineers on the Continent in the age of Napoleon', in Karl Heinz Manegold (ed.), *Wissenschaft, Wirtschaft und Technik. Studien zur Geschichte (Wilhelm Treue zum 60. Geburtstag)* (1969), pp.358–62.

1970
'William Thomas Mulvany—ein irischer Unternehmer im Ruhrgebiet 1806–85', *Kölner Vorträge zur Sozial und Wirtschaftsgeschichte*, Heft 12, 1970 (pamphlet).

1971
'Bismarck's Germany' in *History of the English Speaking Peoples*, 1971, pp. 3362–5.
'The firm of Ermen and Engels in Manchester', *Internationale Wissenschaftliche Korrespondenz zur Geschichte der Deutschen Arbeiterbewegung*, vol. XI–XII, April 1971, pp.1–10.
'Friedrich Engels in Manchester', *Friedrich Engels 1820–1970* (Schriftenreihe des Forschungsinstituts der Friedrich-Ebert-Stiftung, vol. LXXXV, 1971, pp.27–38).

1972
'W. H. B. Court', Downing College Association, *News Letter*, 1972, pp. 25–6.

In Collaboration with W. H. Chaloner
'Aaron Manby, builder of the first iron steamship', *Transactions of the Newcomen Society*, vol. XXIX, 1953–4 and 1954–5, pp.77–91.
'The Manbys and the Industrial Revolution in France', *Transactions of the Newcomen Society*, vol. XXX, 1955–7, pp.63–75.
'Friedrich Engels and the England of the 1840s', *History Today*, vol. VI, 1956, pp.448–56.
'Friedrich Engels in Manchester', *Memoirs and Proceedings of the Manchester Literary and Philosophical Society*, session 1956–7, vol. XCVIII, pp. 1–17.
'Some aspects of the early history of automation', *Research*, vol. X, No. 9, September 1957, pp.334–9.

Introduction to F. Engels, *The Condition of the Working Class in England* (translated and edited by W. O. Henderson and W. H. Chaloner: Basil Blackwell, Oxford, 1958; revised introduction to second edition, 1971).

Introduction to *Engels as Military Critic* (Manchester University Press, 1959).

'Friedrich Engels and the England of the "hungry forties" ', in *The Long Debate on Poverty*, edited by the Institute of Economic Affairs, London, 1972, pp.169–86. German translation in *Ordo, Jahrbuch für die Ordnung von Wirtschaft und Gesellschaft*, 1974, pp.261–81.

In Collaboration with E. J. Passant

E. J. Passant, *A Short History of Germany 1815–45*: economic sections by W. O. Henderson (Cambridge University Press, 1959).

TRANSLATIONS

in collaboration with W. H. Chaloner

W. Schlote, *British Overseas Trade* (Basil Blackwell, 1952).

W. G. Hoffmann, *British Industry 1700–1950* (Basil Blackwell, 1955).

L. Drescher, 'The development of agricultural production in Great Britain and Ireland from the early eighteenth century' in *Manchester School*, May 1955, pp.153–83.

F. Pollock, *The Economic and Social Consequences of Automation* (Basil Blackwell, 1957).

F. Engels, *The Condition of the Working Class in Engl and* (Basil Blackwell, first edition, 1958; second edition, 1971). An American edition was published by the Stanford University Press in 1968.

W. G. Hoffmann, *The Growth of Industrial Economies* (Manchester University Press, 1958).

Eric Robinson

I

The transference of British technology to Russia, 1760–1820: a preliminary enquiry

I

The problem of backwardness in economic development, the failure to industrialise on a sufficient scale or with an adequately developed technology, which seems to have characterised the history of Russia at a time when other nations of the Western world were pressing forward with urgency to a modern economic structure, has long fascinated both political and economic historians. Alexander Gerschenkron, in examining 'The problem of economic development in Russian intellectual history of the nineteenth century',[1] sees 'the specific *Weltanschauung* of Russian intellectuals, with its deep and immediate concern for the welfare of the peasantry and its unwillingness to accept industrialisation', as arising out of Russia's economic backwardness in comparison with more advanced countries in the West. The longer economic development was deferred, the greater the gap between Russia and its European neighbours, the greater the costliness of industrialisation and the greater the sacrifices which would have to be borne so that the leap forward might be made. Viewed in this way, Russia is the ideal centre for the study of 'the late-comer thesis',[2] by which it is sometimes argued that Soviet Russia, having been the last great nation of the West to industrialise fully, is now in the position to employ the most recent technology and once more take the lead. The study of Russian economic development seems to some to have peculiar importance for the assessment of the possibilities of modernisation in underdeveloped countries today. On the one hand it may suggest the hope that the frog which leaps last may leap farthest: on the other hand, it may provide useful warnings about the political and economic costs of hope too long deferred. In addition it has become a commonplace for economic historians to compare and contrast the progress of industrialisation or the lack of it in Britain, Russia and the USA, so that the three nations are seen to be playing traditional roles almost like characters from some classical Chinese play. On this stage Britain industrialises first, races to world supremacy in the manufacture of cotton textiles, iron and steel production and heavy machinery; the USA, once freed from the shackles of British imperialism, absorbs the technology of Britain and, quickly improving on it, particularly with the 'American system', soon begins to challenge and then finally assumes the leadership; Russia, lost in darkness and autocratic oppression, though immensely rich in natural resources, loiters in the wings until the revolution of 1917 and then is involved in a frantic effort to catch up with its main international rival, the USA. In this drama Russia has hardly any lines for the first two acts. It seems worthwhile, therefore, to enquire a little more closely into what she was doing off-stage.

The impetus given by Peter the Great to the adoption of Western technology was certainly not lost during the eighteenth century and with the accession of Catherine II seems actually to have been strengthened. Though the 1763 manifesto seems to have 'attracted no new industries or enterprises of any great importance',[3] it underlined a clear intention on the part of the Russian government to recruit British entrepreneurs and British craftsmen, as well as others, whenever and wherever possible. The official English-language version of the manifesto of 1763 declared:

> If any of those Foreigners that have settled themselves in Russia shall erect Fabricks or Works, and manufacture there such Merchandizes, as have not been made yet in Russia: We do allow and give leave to sell and export the said Merchandizes out of our Empire for ten Years, without paying any inland Tolls, Port duties or Customs on the Borders. 10) If any Foreign Capitalist will erect Fabricks, Manufactures or Works in Russia, We allow him to purchase for the said Fabricks, Manufactures and Works a requisite Numbre [sic] of Bond-People and Peasants. 11) To those Foreigners which have settled themselves in Our Empire by Colonies or Places, we do allow and give leave to appoint such Markets and Fairs, as they themselves shall think most proper, without paying any Toll or Custom into Our Treasury.[4]

Not only were the terms clear and generous, but the manifesto provided a statement of policy that could be referred to in any future negotiations that might take place. A few persons were attracted even in the 'sixties. Two Englishmen, Kelly and Bury, proposed to introduce 'semi-silk and woollen English materials' not then manufactured in Russia and a resolution was made to set them up with a manufactory in Russia;[5] Francis Gardner, an Englishman, established a porcelain factory near Moscow in 1765, though it is suggested that he did not transfer British technology to Russia, because the porcelain which he proceeded to make was hard paste, such as had not been made in Britain at that date;[6] while the tradition of Scottish physicians at the imperial court was already well established independently of the new encouragement provided in the manifesto. The most attractive area of settlement for skilled foreigners seems to have been St Petersburg itself and its environs, where there soon grew up an important British settlement, composed of merchants, tanners, shipwrights and mechanics of several kinds, soon to be joined by masons, plasterers, instrument-makers and others. How were such persons recruited and how did the transfer of technology take place?

II

The grand tour of the English *milord* to visit the capitals of Europe, and particularly the antiquities of Rome, was mirrored by the constant flow of visitors to Britain in the eighteenth century to view the marvels—the machines, the crafts and the manufactories—of the most advanced industrial nation that men had ever known. Prussian, Bavarian, Hanoverian nobles, Russian princes and counts, French marquises, merchants from all nations, and a medley of Swedes, Danes, Portuguese and Spanish notables pushed their way into Birmingham button factories and Lancashire cotton mills, swooped elegantly round chemical works, paper mills, munition foundries or shipyards and reported their findings back to their Ministers at home. Espionage against industry is as old as industry itself[7] and Britain, as the centre of the industrial revolution, was the focus for this sort of work. Among the entourages of the visitors to Britain were secretaries with suspiciously horny hands or valets with a quick eye and a ready skill with a pencil. Dr W. O. Henderson has been a pioneer in relating their activities, but much still remains to be told.[8] Yet even when the British manufacturer surmised that his foreign visitor was a spy he was sometimes reluctant to cause offence, either because he anticipated business from his visitor or because he hesitated to offend his visitor's friends and connections.

Russian visitors to Britain were many in the later half of the eighteenth century. They ranged from members of the imperial Romanov family through aristocrats and Ministers of state down to ordinary mechanics. These visitors seem to have maintained close contact with the Russian embassy in London and often brought with them letters of introduction from M. Moussin Pouschkin, Count Chernayevsky, Count Vorontzov or whoever happened to be the Russian ambassador to the Court of St James's at the time. Assistance and guidance from the embassy are a more marked characteristic with Russians at this period than with visitors from other countries. Some few came to pursue university studies, such as Simon Desnitskii and John Tretiakov, who attended Dr Joseph Black's lectures on chemistry at the University of Glasgow in the winter of 1764–5 and who knew James Watt at that time,[9] or later the mathematical students of John Robison at Edinburgh, but the majority were bureaucrats and intellectuals in search of general education and useful information.

Such visitors early came to visit Boulton & Fothergill's manufactory of Birmingham wares at Soho in Handsworth, perhaps because the firm had already some trade with Russia, but possibly also because the secret had leaked out that Boulton might be capable of being enticed away from Britain.[10] In any event Boulton was visited in 1765 by a Russian merchant of the firm of 'Ivan Pastichoff *et fils*' at St Petersburg[11] and in October the same year John Gomme, Russian merchant, visited Soho in Boulton's absence.[12] The latter was a person of more than everyday consequence, as we learn from Lord MacCartney:

> All the great Discoveries and Improvements made in this Empire have been imagined and conducted by foreigners . . . The creation of a new port at Onega in the White Sea, utterly unknown a few Years ago, but now annually frequented by near 30,000 Ton of Shipping, is intirely owing to the Genius and Industry of Mr. Gomm[e], an English Merchant at St. Petersburg . . .[13]

As Boulton's & Fothergill's trade to Russia extended through the 1770s and 1780s the number of visitors also grew. In 1780–1 Boulton & Fothergill were doing business with at least eleven firms in St Petersburg as well as with John Tamesz & Co.[14] and with G. Thompson Rowand & Co. of Moscow. The value of the trade ran into several thousand pounds a year. It was, of course, in luxuries, but even things of ornament such as buttons, buckles and badges had a practical and even a military use when it came to uniforming soldiers. Moreover Birmingham was also a centre for the small arms trade and had the earliest proof house outside London. Peter Capper junior, the son of a Birmingham button manufacturer, established himself in St Petersburg, probably in the 1760s, and John Major, another Birmingham button manufacturer, was also in business there by the 1780s. Fothergill himself visited St Petersburg in 1767 for about three months, so that the avenues of introduction to Birmingham manufacturers were quite open.

From a letter written by Boulton to Lord Cathcart in October 1771 we know that Count Chemisev had visited Soho some time earlier.[15] In subsequent years Count Simon Vorontsov (1744–1822), his son and daughter, the Princess Dashkov (1744–1810), Count Grigor Orlov (1734–83), Prince Michael Golitzin, Count Zenovieff, Count Samoilov[16] and M. de Hoechel were among the aristocrats and officers of the imperial court who visited Soho. To them must be added men of science, both Russian-born and immigrants to Russia, who visited Boulton & Watt, or their sons—men such as Novosiltzov or Dr Rogerson, or industrialists like Baron Demidov and Mr Schlatter, or a future technocrat of some standing like A. Deriabin, or simple craftsmen and artisans of whom we shall have more to say later. The visits continued in the first decade of the nineteenth century with Major Nicholas Sabloukov, his brother Alexander, Prince Bariatinsky,[17] M. de

Kacheleff, General Koschelov, General de Kretov and his wife, M. de Bacounin, who had been educated at Glasgow, General de Hitrov, Colonel Poltoratsky,[18] Count Chreptowitch and several others. Some of them enter our story again, but it is sufficient here to list their names as an indication of the number and consequence of Boulton's Russian visitors. Though there is little doubt that Boulton was indeed charming and entertaining company, it was his industrial and commercial contacts that drew Russians to visit him.[19]

The usefulness of those contacts may be shown by a letter from A. Deriabin, who had been training in Boulton's works in order to supervise the mint which Boulton was building in St Petersburg, to Boulton in 1798. Deriabin set out in April 1798 for a tour of Cornwall with Gregory Watt, studying geology and visiting Cornish copper mines. From Cornwall he proceeded to Swansea in order to visit Holbrook, a friend of Boulton, who was a copper smelter. Deriabin writes: 'I have seen some of the other Copper Works, Copper mill[s] and some other very interesting things in the Neighbourhood of Swansea.'[20] From south Wales Deriabin intended to travel north to Scotland, first visiting William Wilkinson's ironworks at Bersham, and then travelling via Liverpool and Manchester. In the letter just quoted Deriabin refers to:

The list of the places and Gentlemen You were so kind as to promise to write to—

Liverpool
Prescot to see the looking Glass Manufactory, which is near Prescot
Keswick
Leadhills
Glasgow Mr. [Gilbert] Hamilton (Concerning the Carron Iron Works) and Mr. Miller Newcastle Mr [Thomas] Barnes Agent to —— Brandling Esqr
         Messrs Walker and Gishwick [for Fishwick]
Leeds   Messrs Fountain Wormald and Gott
Sheffield
Rotherham Messrs Walkers
MRB [Matthew Robinson Boulton] Backwell [for Bakewell] Mr Barker
         Derby Dr. Darwin
If you will be so kind as to give those letters to Mr. Gregory Watt, he will take the trouble to direct and send them all to me.

To this list Boulton has added a few names, which include 'Richardson Esqr Merchant Liverpool', 'Mr Benjamin Withers Merchant in Sheffield' and 'Messrs Walkers of Rotherham'. The above list includes some of the most famous firms of the period in looking-glass manufacture, woollen and cotton textiles, but particularly in metal manufacture. Since by this period, moreover, many manufacturers, including Boulton & Watt themselves, were restricting access to their business

premises, letters of introduction from Boulton would have been of outstanding value. On an earlier occasion we know that Boulton himself
accompanied the young Vorontsov and a friend to the Darbys' ironworks at Coalbrookdale.[21] When it is recalled that Deriabin became
head of all the imperial mines, mints and ordnance factories, this early
experience must have been very useful. It might be contended that
Boulton's aristocratic visitors knew too little of industry and engineering
to profit from his advice and introductions, but this could hardly be
maintained in connection with people like Deriabin, Novosiltzov and
L. F. Sabakin, all of whom were assisted by Boulton. What is more, it is
far from likely that Boulton was an isolated source of British help to
inquiring Russians. Indeed, we know that Charles Gascoigne of the
Carron Company was only too ready to assist them, and other manufacturers were anxious to sell to the Russian market.

III

Above and beyond the active social contacts mentioned above was the
persistent policy on the part of the Russian government of attempting to
recruit specialists in all sorts of arts and crafts. It is true that many
people approached with an invitation to go to Russia do not seem to
have responded too eagerly, but this does not seem to have deterred the
Russian authorities from issuing further invitations both to the same
people and to others.

Dr William Small, Boulton's physician and erstwhile tutor to Thomas
Jefferson and friend of Benjamin Franklin, received an invitation in
1765 to go to Russia through Dr Heberden,[22] but, finding that his
practice in Birmingham was beginning to thrive, decided not to accept.
Small, like other physicians of the period, was not restricted to medicine
but had an excellent grounding in mathematics and chemistry, and had
an inventive turn of mind.[23] Where the Russians failed with Small they
succeeded with Dr John Rogerson, another Scot, who went to Russia
and remained there for fifty years, often being consulted in other
matters than medical. Rogerson's uncle, Dr James Mounsey, had
been chief royal physician to the empress Elizabeth and to the emperor
Peter. Dr Matthew Guthrie, physician to the Imperial Cadet Corps,
was in Russia for over forty years. He was a man of wide scientific
interests[24] and corresponded with, among others, Dr Joseph Black, on
matters of such industrial importance as methods of making iron into
steel.[25] In this particular instance he was enquiring on behalf of a
friend, a Siberian ironmaster with the British name of Hill.[26]

If the industrial and scientific interests of physicians recruited to work
in Russia were a bonus incidental to their primary duties, the same
cannot be said of engineers and entrepreneurs to whom in a similar

manner offers were often made. James Watt was first approached in 1771 through his old friend John Robison, who, having gone to Russia as secretary to Admiral Sir Charles Knowles, himself the most senior British naval officer hired by the Russians, obtained employment as Professor of Natural Philosophy in the Imperial Naval Academy at St Petersburg. Robison invited Watt to accept the position of 'Master Founder of Iron Ordnance to Her Imperial Majesty', saying: 'I made no hesitation in recommending my friend, because I was well acquainted with your knowledge in Metallurgy and Mechanics, and your intimate acquaintance with all the process as carry'd on at Carron.'[27] The Russian ambassador, Moussin Pouschkin, at the same time assured Watt that 'there is no country I dare say where merits and knowledge are at this day more effectually acknowledged and encouraged, than in Russia. The Empress is herself as great a judge of them, as she is a warm Protectrice.'[28] Watt's many-sidedness would have appealed to the Russians. Certainly he knew the processes of ordnance manufacture at Carron, but he had also invented a new steam engine, as Robison well knew, and Robison was at that very time discussing it with J. G. Model, Professor of Pharmacy in St Petersburg, Franz Aepinas, the mathematician, and Dr Kruse, 'a Gentleman eminent in that country for Steel Works and great Knowledge in Chemistry, Magnetism etc.'[29] In addition Watt was an experienced canal engineer and must have considered the invitation fairly easily, for there is still in existence a document in his hand entitled 'Directions for making Preparatory Surveys for the Russian Canals by J. Watt'.[30] It is incomplete, not very technical but full of that strong common sense that characterised Watt's mind. Finally, James Watt was, of course, an accomplished maker and inventor of scientific instruments. In 1775 a further invitation was made by Moussin Pouschkin to recruit Watt and was again declined by Watt in a letter of great humility.[31] Erasmus Darwin rejoiced at his decision:

Lord how frightened I was, when I heard a Russian bear had laid hold of you with his great paw, and was dragging you to Russia—Pray don't go, if you can help it. Russia is like the Den of Cacus, you see the Footsteps of many Beasts going thither but of few returning. I hope your fire-machines will keep you here.[32]

Thus by a hair's breadth the Russians failed to recruit the most famous engineer of the day. Instead they hired Robert McKell, who had partnered Watt in building a few Newcomen engines and also some canal works, for a period of three years at a fee of £3,000.[33]

Other canal engineers were also approached, though apparently with few consequences of importance for Russian waterways. John Phillips senior, in recounting the history of the plan for uniting the Caspian to the Baltic by waterways, a project in which Löwitz was engaged in 1774 when murdered in the Pugachev uprising, says:

> The author of this history was sent in 1783, to push on this work, and had 700 men ordered to dig, and cut down timber, &c. but after being there nineteen months with often not 100 men, and as no carpenters were sent him, nor were other artificers to be had, while every possible obstacle was made by the Boyars to hinder the work; he returned to Petersburg, without doing anything but cutting down a few thousand timber trees.[34]

On the title page of the fourth edition of this work, dated 1803, Phillips describes himself as 'Sometime Surveyor to the Canals in Russia under Mr Cameron, Architect to the late Empress Catherine II'.

Charles Cameron has not usually been associated with canal engineering in Russia, but his involvement is an indication of the importance of such work. It may even be that the failure to improve the Russian transport system was of greater consequence to the economic development of the nation than the comparative backwardness of Russian metal-working techniques. The post system of travelling, so vividly described in 1852 by Werner von Siemens,[35] may have been sufficient for passenger travel but would clearly have impeded the movement of goods. Internal travel by water was the key to the transport problem, and without improved transportation the industrialisation of the country must have been badly obstructed.[36]

What types of British skill and goods were imported? First there was an interest in cannon founders and moulders. In November 1771 Lord Cathcart reported from St Petersburg that two men, one called Adam Ramage and the other Powell, had been given a contract by Moussin Pouschkin to serve in Russia as cannon founders and moulders at a salary of £100 per annum. They had been employed previously at the Carron ironworks at Falkirk and subsequently found themselves in St Petersburg without subsistence.[37] From this time onwards the Carron Company proved to be of great interest to Russia because of its production of 'carronades' and other munitions. (It is ironic that one partner in the Carron Company was a principal opponent of the seduction of British artificers abroad. This was Samuel Garbett.) The port of Leith was excellently situated for exporting men and goods to the Baltic; the Scots had already established a strong migratory pattern; and the Carron Company had a technological lead in the production of cannon. The Scottish naval officer in the service of Russia, Sir Samuel Greig, proved an excellent go-between. The Carron Company in the earlier 'eighties was principally under the management of Charles Gascoigne, Garbett's son-in-law, an active, ambitious and knowledgeable if not too scrupulous executive. Carron had obtained from the British government permission to export cannon to several foreign countries, including

Russia, and the business proved a paying one. One order for cannon from Greig mentions 432 guns wanted for four ships of 108 guns each.[38] But Gascoigne was persuaded by Greig not simply to export guns, which was legal, but also to export the cannon-founding and cannon-boring machinery, together with artisans to work them, which was contrary to law. Gascoigne and Garbett were in conflict over the finances and management of Carron,[39] and Garbett now informed the government of Gascoigne's intentions, with the result that the company was warned not to export any prohibited articles of machinery to Russia at a time when it had orders from Greig for machinery including '153 Racks with their Pinions and spindles 22 Lever Boxes and Gigger parts Commonly called Shifting Boxes 8 Collar Stools with their Brasses',[40] etc, together with 'the component parts of a Fire Engine, Cylinders for a Blowing Machine, Cranes for raising heavy weights and the Modell of a Water Engine'.[41] All these were to go to the Russian naval base at Kronstadt. The Carron Company's remonstrance to the objection by the Commissioners of Customs at Edinburgh to their exporting a model, made after Smeaton's design, for experiments upon wind and water power is particularly interesting:

> How can it be conceived that the exportation of this Machine should in any respects be detrimental to the arts or manufactures of this Country; or how is it possible to suppose that they should be ignorant of this subject at Petersburgh, in the first Mathematical School in the world, where the celebrated Bernoulli and Euler so long presided, who were members of the Royal Society . . .[42]

In addition Carron intended to export gun pigs for the cannon to be made at Kronstadt,[43] an axis for a water-wheel,[44] thousands of fire bricks, cast-iron kitchen utensils for Lieutenant General Toutalmin, Governor General of the Provinces of Olonetz and Archangel,[45] copying presses,[46] the model of an engine used by Smeaton in making his experiments referred to above, [47] and a new plough invented by Small.[48] Garbett made it perfectly clear to the British government that Carron intended to supply to Russia all the machinery requisite for blast furnaces, cannon-boring mills, casting and repair shops. Such was the wide range of machinery that Russia was obtaining from Carron, despite Garbett's representations to the government. It was his belief that, though Gascoigne was summoned to London for questioning, the government did not intend to enforce its own legislation as far as Russia was concerned, and so Gascoigne was allowed to leave London in peace, whereupon he immediately emigrated to Russia. On the other hand, it is clear that some of the articles were legally exportable—as, for example, steam engines and water-wheels. As early as 1773 Carron had exported to Kronstadt a steam engine of John Smeaton's design at

Catherine II's request. It was invoiced in September 1774 at £2,037
11s 6d.[49] A group of workmen under the direction of one Fifer, Adam
Smith and his son, John, went to Russia to install the engine and supervise its working. Construction must have proceeded slowly, since in
April–May 1776 there was correspondence about some engine drawings
still required by Adam Smith.[50] On this occasion, as later, the agent by
whom the order was received was Alexander Baxter, the Russian
consul general in London.

More important than the machines, models and manufactures, if we
accept the thesis that face-to-face encounters are necessary in the trans-
mission of technology at this period, were the men. We have already
enumerated Ramage, Powell, Fifer, Adam Smith, John Smith and
Gascoigne himself, all of whom had emigrated to Russia from Carron.
Now Gascoigne sought to entice over still others. In a letter to William
Pitt dated 14 July 1786 Garbett names other Carron artisans with
Gascoigne in Russia—Russell, Brown, MacSwan, Baird and Clarke.[51]
Later the same year Andrew Tibbats of Carron informed William
Cadell, a magistrate, that 'a brig called the *Empress of Russia* was going
to ship out to Russia four Carron moulders—James Harley, James
Heugh, John Eadie and William Muirhead.[52] The men were taken off
and Archibald Heugh, an employee of Carron, who had been asked by
Gascoigne to engage a dozen moulders, was prosecuted.

These attempts were by no means sporadic or isolated. Garbett drew
the attention of the Commercial Committee in Birmingham in 1784 to
the insufficiency of the laws which were intended to prevent English
workmen being enticed abroad.[53] He estimated that between 1784 and
1786 no fewer than 170 artisans and their families had emigrated to
Russia.[54] He warned of the imminent danger of a colony of nailers being
recruited from the Birmingham area,[55] and a month later, in August
1786, wrote to Matthew Boulton:

> Since you left home I have certain intelligence that many Articles in Hardware
> are establishing in Russia, and particularly Cabinet Furniture in Brass, vizt.
> Handles and Escutcheons, Buckles and Bath Metal Rings, various Articles in
> Metal Silvered—many common Steel Articles and different Sort of Iron
> Wares—[56]

As a consequence Garbett was of the opinion that 'in a few Years the
Russians will certainly be the considerable Manufacturers of Iron-
mongery and whether it is judicious in France and England by the
Treaty of Commerce now depending to open their Ports to them (by
indirect Commerce) ought to be considered'.[57] Many skilled artisans
were certainly recruited by the architect Charles Cameron in 1784 as a
result of a detailed advertisement in the Edinburgh newspapers. He
enlisted masons, plasterers, carpenters, bricklayers and a variety of men

skilled in the building trades.[58] The success of his recruiting drive is testified to by Samuel Bentham who was in Russia at the time:

> I have just receiv'd news from Petersburg of the arrival of men women and children to the amount of 139 from Scotland. The Prince [Potemkin] was pleas'd to hear it and will take good care of them in the Crimea which it seems is the place of their destination[59]

Potemkin's efforts to recruit skilled personnel from Britain are described in the same correspondence. Among the artisans mentioned in Samuel Bentham's letters to his brother Jeremy—that is, artisans required for work in the Crimea—are Mosberry, a shipwright; Burkett, also probably a shipwright, though he is referred to as a 'mechanician'; Peake, a shipwright; James Anderson, the Scots writer on agriculture; Logan Henderson, formerly an engineer for Boulton & Watt; Dinwiddie, the itinerant lecturer in science; Mears, John Clarke, shipwrights; John Varley, bricklayer and plasterer, and others. Not all these people actually went to Russia, nor did they in any event fulfil all the local needs.

Samuel Bentham lists and describes his needs in skilled labour. First, a practical shipwright, to supplement Bentham himself; second, a timber measurer with experience in shipwrighting; third, a millwright capable of erecting windmills for flourgrinding and for timber sawing, and finally a private secretary.[60] Elsewhere he speaks of the need for an English botanist, an English dairy lady with two assistants, a distiller, a shoemaker, a surgeon and physician, an architect, a man experienced in building corn mills, a bricklayer, a sailor, a barge- or boat-builder and a man experienced in weaving sailcloth.[61] These were to supplement two English craftsmen already at Krichev—James Nolman, a Quaker tanner from Newcastle upon Tyne, and a currier, Matthew Robson. By 1785 there were at Krichev a Scot called James Love, only son of Alexander Love of Gemeston; a blacksmith, John Aiton; a gardener, nephew of William Aiton, George III's gardener at Kew; Anthony Young, a millwright; John Bell, a ship's captain and master rigger; Robert Beattie, a master heckler, and two brickmakers, a sail-maker and a joiner. It is also known that William Statter, who was educated at William Turner's school in Newcastle, a young man of a mechanical turn, became director of Potemkin's possessions in the Ukraine and resided there till his death in 1813,[62] but this must have been after Samuel Bentham's departure.

The Russian government also managed to recruit some instrument makers. Morgan, a London instrument maker, was appointed 'Her Majesty's and her Fleets and Admiralty Mathematical and Optical Instrument Maker'.[63] Morgan brought with him two workmen, one of whom was Daniel McMillan, a fellow apprentice with James Watt at

Morgan's.[64] This would suggest that the Morgan with whom McMillan emigrated was Watt's former master, John Morgan, but the Morgan in Russia is named Francis[65] and therefore may have been a brother or a son of John Morgan. Morgan's daughter married Charles Baird, who had emigrated with Gascoigne from Carron, and Morgan and Baird for some time ran an iron foundry together. McMillan broke away from Morgan and set up on his own, and it was for this reason that he wrote to Watt asking Watt's help in finding notable customers and in persuading John Dollond, the London instrument maker, to supply him with goods. McMillan refers to a Russian, Karsakov, governor of the Crimea, who also visited Boulton & Watt at Soho, and complains about 'Idle English Mechanicks Who is in the Service here & hates to See a person Endeavour to get forward through Industry'. Samuel Bentham speaks of calling on McMillan, on 13 October 1782 in St Petersburg to see a spirit level,[66] and it is clear that he and Hynam, the watchmaker, were friends. One well known instrument maker, George Donisthorpe of Birmingham, offered his services to Matthew Boulton in connection with the mint at St Petersburg but does not appear to have gone there.[67]

By far the most important persons to emigrate, however, were Gascoigne and his associates, Charles Baird, James Baird and Adam Armstrong, since it is clear that these men played a leading part in such technological advances as were made during the period. Armstrong became house tutor to Samuel Greig's family and emigrated with him to Russia. He later played a part in recruiting Gascoigne, and after experience in the Alexandrovskii works and in the College of Mines he succeeded Gascoigne, except for a brief directorship by Poltoratsky, as director of the Olonets and Petersburg works, where he remained till his death. He has been credited with improvements in iron furnaces, discovering deposits of fireclay, concern for the ironworkers under his control and for casting some important bridges. His son, Roman Adamovitch Armstrong, also worked at Olonets, at the St Petersburg mint and elsewhere, and seems to have been a competent engineer, introducing wire-drawing machines, automatic weighing and trimming machines, and replacing platinum vessels with cheaper iron ones at the mint.

Charles Baird (1766–1843) was the second of the seven sons of Nicol Baird, superintendent of the Forth and Clyde canal.[68] He was apprenticed at Carron and then rose to be manager of the casting and finishing ordnance there, until in 1786 he left for Russia with Gascoigne. Between 1786 and 1789 he reorganised the Alexandrovskii gun works and the Konchezersk iron foundry near by. In 1792 he established a partnership with Francis Morgan and married Morgan's daughter, Sophia. Separating from Morgan, he set up his own famous Baird ironworks in St Petersburg, from which originated a phrase still remembered in

Leningrad today and describing something running smoothly: 'kak u Berda na zavode'—'like at Baird's works'.[69] The business thrived and established a lead in machine building and metallurgy. Baird trained many Russian mining and metallurgical experts, built the Admiralty's Izhova works and in 1804 restored the Kolpino works founded by Peter the Great. There is a very interesting account of him in a letter by Zacchaeus Walker to his uncle, Matthew Boulton:

in all the List of those worth notice, I can hear of no one so well adapted either by Character, knowledge, or Property, to promote your Interests and Views in Russia as Mr. Charles Baird.

I d'ont [sic] know whether you are acquainted with any branch of his family, but, he has an elder Brother in Edinburgh, and a younger one here whom probably Mr. James Watt may recollect having seen at Soho about 3 Years ago. He came to this Country originally for account of Sir Charles Gascoigne (as most of the Projectors have done) and in company with Mr. Roebuck of Birmingham, both of them having been employed in the Carron-Iron-Works; and about 14 Years ago had acquired sufficient property and knowledge of the Country under Mr. Gascoigne to venture setting up for himself as founder, forger, Steam-Engine-Maker etc etc but has chiefly been connected with the Board of Admiralty. He also undertakes all the Iron-work for the Mint-Department, and has done a good deal for us there, (at least as much as they have paid above £1,000 Sterling for, tho' I understood on arrival scarcely any thing in that way remained to be made.) Mr. Baird is supposed a Man of very noted property at present, tho' from the expensive mode of living necessarily adopted by all the English in business here, it is not easy to attain a precise knowledge of those facts without experiment; for mere appearances would indicate many to be rich who are overwhelmed with Debts. He is about 40 Years of age,—certainly very active and intelligent,—knows the Russian Language well,—which, rest assured is a very essential point and a work of time:—is pretty intimately acquainted with the Mechanical Professors in general, both Russian and Foreigners—also with many of the principal Nobility; and with the proper mode of applying the Key to the private Doors of the Chief Officers in most of the Government Departments; and as you will have observed, comes from the North side of the Tweed which is the best recommendation a man can bring to this City, the Caledonian Phalanx being the strongest and most numerous, and moving always in the closest Union. If not secured as a friend, he is in my estimation, the person who by his experience and address might in the event of your engaging extensively in this Country, become the most troublesome Opponent.[70]

Baird's younger brother referred to in the letter above was probably James Baird, who had also been a manager in the ordnance department at Carron. Another brother, Hugh Baird, of the canal basin near Glasgow, was an ironfounder and steam engine maker. He had worked in London with John Rennie on Boulton & Watt engines. In July 1802 Hugh and Robert Baird of Glasgow, engineers, sought 'leave to export from Grangemouth to St Petersburg, the Materials of Two small Steam Engines'.[71] Charles Baird himself soon went into the production of steam engines and by 1825 had produced 141. He had built Russia's first steamship, the *Elizaveta*, in 1815 and had a valuable monopoly of the steam ferry running between Kronstadt and St Petersburg.[72] Since there was a bar in the harbour necessitating the transhipment of goods to smaller vessels, this monopoly proved very lucrative. His interests in chemistry led him to sugar refining, which he managed to do without the use of bullocks' blood and was thus able to sell his product during Lent. From time to time he visited Britain, coming, for example, to Soho in 1807 to learn about the manufacture of dies for the St Petersburg mint.[73] He is said to have engaged in saw-milling and to have improved upon the vases made by the imperial porcelain works.[74] It is hardly surprising perhaps to find Zacchaeus Walker's praise of Baird tempered with the remark that he believed Baird to be 'guided by no particular attachments of blood, or friendship, or indeed strongly moved by any feelings except those of a most profound veneration for the God Plutus'.[75]

Charles Baird was succeeded by his son, Francis, and the firm continued into the nineteenth century. When Russia eventually began industrialisation in earnest in the 1870s George Baird joined with the French Terrenoire Company to form the Alexandrovskii steel company, and then in 1880 amalgamated with two firms from the Lyons area, modernising in the process George Baird's small shipyard, which still worked mainly for the Russian navy.[76] In this way the Usines Franco-Russes (Baird) carried the tradition of technology diffusion into still another century. Yet little is still known about the actual technological and administrative problems faced by this important firm during its history.

Charles Gascoigne, Baird's patron, who survived only until 1806, made an unparalleled contribution to Russian technology during the mere twenty years that he was the principal adviser on technology to the Russian government. At Alexandrovsk, Konchezersk, Izhora (Kolpino), Lugan and at the Russian mint he was a leading figure. Much as he was envied and disliked by British and Russians alike,[77] his energy and his technical 'know-how' were respected, and he was known to have a hand in every mechanical development worth mentioning during his twenty years in Russia. As 'the Baron' he occurs constantly in Zacchaeus Walker's letters to Boulton. His intellectual energy is reflected in an extensive correspondence concerning iron smelting and founding, though it is somewhat doubtful how successfully British ironfounding techniques were transplanted. (Baird is actually praised in the official biographical account for having replaced expensive coke-smelted iron with cheaper charcoal-smelted iron.) Yet surely it must be said that the arming of the Russian forces in this period would have been far less efficient had it not been for Gascoigne's expertise in cannon production, and the savings to the exchequer from the use of Russian iron must also have been important. While making a considerable fortune for himself, he was also indefatigable in the service of the Russian nation and seems to have been particularly capable in establishing systems of business administration that worked.

Another interesting, though less significant, figure was the millwright George Sheriff,[78] whose father, Thomas Sheriff, had also been employed at Carron. The precise date of his emigration to Russia is not known, but he had already had one tour of duty there by 1799, in the service of the architect Alexis Olenin. Returning to Scotland in that year, he was employed by the Clyde Iron Works near Glasgow, on whose behalf he ordered a 60 h.p. blowing engine from Boulton & Watt, and soon after a 72 h.p. engine for Morton Dalrymple of the Omoa Iron Works.[79] He still carried out commissions for Russia, however, and Boulton & Watt received from him an enquiry for a rotative steam engine for the use of John Major, the former Birmingham button maker, in St Petersburg.[80] In January 1800 he visited Soho, bringing with him a letter of introduction to Count Woronzow[81] and one from Mr Edington of the Clyde Iron Works.[82] Boulton & Watt introduced him in turn to Wright & Jessons, the famous boiler makers at Barnets Leasowe, so that he could see the blowing engine there. There followed a typical piece of Matthew Boulton intrigue, in which Boulton drafted a letter for Sheriff to send back to St Petersburg praising the machinery that Boulton was making for Russia. This draft includes the words:

> However I wish it not to be mentioned, so as to come to Mr. Boultons knowledge least he should take it amiss but I could not forbear giving you this information as I thought it would afford some satisfaction that you will soon have the compleatest Mint in the World without plague Vexation or risk of disappointment.[83]

After doing some survey work of a road in the Black Country,[84] Sheriff made his way to Manchester, calling on Ewart and Lee, who showed him some other Boulton & Watt engines at work. He delivered a confidential Russian document into Lee's hands, while saying that he had still others that he dared not send through the post. This document contained a plan, presumably of the mint in St Petersburg, 'made by a Russian in the year 1795 when Government proposed to buy Mr Bairds Engine for to work it as you see with Cranks and Rods, the presses showen are the same as at present used in the old mint in the fortress, only they work them by hand . . .'.[85]

In these ways Sheriff, although he had worked with Gascoigne, won Boulton's confidence, and when he returned to Russia in April 1802, just in time to receive Boulton's craftsmen who had arrived to set up the mint machinery, it seemed probable that he would be employed in some capacity by Boulton. The Birmingham workmen did not care for Sheriff's condescension to them and sowed doubts in Boulton's mind about his reliability. In 1804 Sheriff returned to Scotland once again and purchased Dalderse Foundry, near Falkirk, where he manufactured a variety of hardware. In 1822 he returned to Russia again and was employed in the bank for making the paper for currency notes and had charge of a 40 h.p. engine. In 1833 he wrote enquiring about an engine for a timber mill in Swedish Finland. Here, then, is still another Carron artisan who played a significant part in facilitating communication between Britain and Russia. From what we know of the Bairds, Sheriff, Armstrong and several other Scots, it would be wise to treat with reserve Tugan-Baranovsky's strictures on foreign workmen.[86]

We do not claim to have described the work of more than a fraction of the British artisans in Russia at the end of the eighteenth century and the beginning of the nineteenth,[87] but even so there is evidence of a thriving intercommunication, promoted and assisted by the conscious policies of the Russian government. Some at least of the workmen who emigrated were capable men well experienced in the technology of their period. They were not all fly-by-nights, for some of them settled in Russia, married the daughters of other emigrants and learnt the Russian language. In addition they preserved contacts with their home country and returned from time to time to refresh their knowledge. As for those of higher education, such as Professor John Robison, or the several physicians, they were far from being fossilised or uninterested in practical matters. Moreover if others who were invited to Russia had accepted—such men as Dr Joseph Black, Dr John Brown, James Watt, Dr William Small—the intellectual level of Russian life would have been still higher than it was, and besides its native and imported German mathematical genius would have received some of the best practical minds of the age. In addition, men like Gascoigne, Baird, Armstrong and others were men capable of administering industrial works on a large scale. It seems therefore very doubtful that it was on account of lack of 'know-how' that Russia failed to industrialise earlier.

IV

What of the state, however, of Russian native labour? Was this so backward that it hindered and obstructed the application of new technology? What attitude did the government adopt towards the training of domestic labour? I am here at a disadvantage in not yet having been able to work with Russian archives.[88]

Let it be said, first of all, that comments by European visitors are often extremely condescending. Zacchaeus Walker treats with scorn the officials, the craftsmen and the labourers whom he encounters during his stay in Russia:

> The interference of a whole Host of Saints on whose Name-days it was absolutely requisite for the Salvation of the Peoples Souls to get drunk, has been a principal cause of this delay.[89]
>
> Any thing requiring either accuracy or attention in its use here will soon be destroyed . . .[90]
>
> I have however insisted as far as prudence and decorum would admit with the Count [Vasiliev] in their not sending any more Slaves of the Crown, as numerous Precedents in this Country prove the improbability of their ever doing much good;—not that a great deal of ingenuity may not exist among them:—it would be a libel on human-nature to suppose the contrary . . .[91]

Such comments, however, are not in themselves basically different from the comments often made upon the work force in Britain by employers. Drunkenness and inattention were two of the principal charges laid against Boulton & Watt's employees at Soho, and there is no basic distinction to be made between a fair day and a saint's day. Mechanical ingenuity there was, and some able Russian mechanics had been sent to Britain for training. One Birmingham manufacturer, for example, commented in the following way upon the mechanics sent to Soho:

> Recollecting what you communicate to me from Mr. B respecting the Russian lads Mr. Whitmore was ask'd if He knew them. He replied that they had frequently been at his Manufactory and that one of them was as compleat a Mechanic as He had ever met with.[92]

We cannot be sure which of the Russian craftsmen is referred to here. When negotiations were seriously entered into in 1796 for the purchase by the Russian government of a Boulton mint, the problem of training Russian workmen immediately arose, since it would be difficult to find British workmen prepared to emigrate, as 'honest and good Workmen are generally settled and not easily prevailed upon to leave their establishments'.[93] Boulton, at that time, did not have a totally critical view of Russian skills, since he added that it was unnecessary to send British artisans to St Petersburg to repair some presses in the then existing mint, as he believed 'that many Men may be found in St Petersburg or in Her Imperial Majesty's Foundries who are capable of making such repairs'. Almost immediately thereafter Russian workmen began to arrive in Birmingham. In January 1797 Count Vorontzov sent Schlatter, a German from the Russian mint, Demetrius Outzin, Alexis Izvolsky, Hass (a medallionist), and Reinhard (a worker in iron).[94] One notices, however, that some of the names are German. Schlatter returned to Russia to speak with the empress and then came back to England in June 1797. Schlatter and the other workmen were shown

Boulton's method of re-smelting copper waste, the laminating mill at
Soho, and one of the steam engines, which was used for rolling sheet
copper, iron or steel, grinding and boring musket barrels, and working
a tilt hammer.[95] Four more workers were sent in October 1797.
Boulton has short comments on them in his notebook:

> Mr Touginoff a good man and is returned 1 Sep 1801
> Mr Liezel a German has made a Ram; a Model of a Steam Engine etc (Viena)
> Mr Grezin honest and slow
> Sobakin Junior deranged.[96]

Both Sabakin senior and Sabakin junior were there, and Sabakin senior
actually died in Birmingham. It is puzzling to see Boulton's comment on
Sabakin junior (L. F. Sabakin) in the light of F. N. Zagorskii's recent
life of him,[97] yet it is clear that Boulton's workers also found him
difficult:

> We hear that Mr. Sabacian is on his way from Siberia—Comeing to be along
> with us but we had much rather he had stayed there; as I ame afraid we Can
> not agree Long with him hear, and poor Grezen that we wished to have they
> will not Let Come[98]

However, Sabakin junior had the support of the Russian ambassador in
London. Smirnove, the ambassador's chaplain, wrote to Boulton:

> I am writing to Day to young Sobakin desiring him to come immediately to
> Town. The Count means to send him to Scotland, there to attend Lectures on
> Philosophy, Chemistry and whatever else you will advise him to do in that
> way. if you have any Scientific friends there may I beg the favor of you to
> furnish Mr Sobakin with a Letter of Introduction, as I am not well acquainted
> with any person at Edinburgh.[99]

Boulton obliged by giving Sabakin letters of introduction to Dr Joseph
Black and to John Robison,[100] and it was probably on this trip that
Sabakin saw steam engines at work in the Newcastle area,[101] as Thomas
Barnes, an experienced engineer, was an agent for Boulton & Watt in
that area.

Of the other workers we know less than of Sabakin. Touganoff was
trained as a surgical instrument maker, probably with Jonathan Deakin
in Birmingham, and then returned to that work in Russia. Grezin was
employed in making dies, was poorly paid and often in hard straits upon
his return.[102] Lizel, who came from Austria, had considerable abilities,
and while at Soho made models of Boulton's hydraulic ram, steam
engine and coinage press, much to the annoyance of Boulton,[103] who,
however, got his own back by telling the embassy that he suspected
Lizel of making them for use in *Austria*. Also at Boulton's at this time
was a mechanic called Kakoushkin, who had already been studying in

England for four years. Kakoushkin was friendly with Dick Dyas, one of the Soho workmen, but had already tried to view Boulton & Watt engines in London without success[104] Almost as soon as he arrived in Birmingham he began some industrial snooping so that Boulton demanded that he should be sent back to London.[105] Even so, he continued to get Lizel's models out of the factory and then pawned them with his landlady in London, from whom Smirnove tried to recover them. When he returned to Russia he became an engineman with Gascoigne's engines at Kronstadt until discharged on suspicion of stealing the brasses. He later turns up in the mint, arousing Walker's suspicions by sketching the machinery.[105] He was in fact at this time a Russian official under the control of Count Vassiliev.

Zagorskii makes mention of other Russian mechanics such as I. P. Kulibin, F. P. Borzov, and A. M. Sumin, who learnt technology from Britain, but as yet I have nothing to add on these people. Samuel Bentham writes of Russian shipwrights being trained in England, including one under his own tutelage, and there were also several Russian students at Edinburgh and Glasgow in the later eighteenth-century; Arthur Young had Russian pupils in agriculture, and there were clearly other points of contact between Russian mechanics and Britain, but much requires to be done in this area.[107] Nevertheless the evidence adduced suffices to suggest that there were Russian mechanics who had been trained in Britain and were able to instruct others in the most recent technology. If, on the other hand, there were conservative attitudes in Russia, something must be laid at the feet of ignorant administrators, something to the dead hand of serfdom, which rendered labour-saving machinery less attractive, and something to the necessity for adapting British technology to Russian conditions.

V

British visitors to Russia in the period are often contemptuous of the state of local technology even when introduced by their fellow country-men. For example, Zacchaeus Walker comments on an invention by John Major:

> I have previously alluded to Novelty as the grand source Action amongst the Russian *Sçavans*, who, in that, as in too many other qualifications, copy closely after their great Models the French, and as a proof of its force I cannot refrain from mentioning a new Phenomenon in the mechanical World. A Mr Major, originally from Birmingham, and whose History I believe will easily recur to Mr Boulton's recollection, after long roving about like a wandering Arab thro' Austria, Poland etc. etc. has pitched his Tent for these 3 or 3½ Years past in Siberia, in which philosophic retreat he has had leisure to contemplate uninterruptedly the profoundest depths of Mechanics, and has at last brought

forth a new Steam-Engine which for simplicity and cheapness in proportion to its' power is to set all that has hitherto been done or thought of at nought.[108]

According to Walker, Major had erected an engine in Siberia which had only worked for about half an hour at a time, which worked with the expansive force of steam but without a separate condenser, and which had the cylinder situated in the boiler to prevent it from freezing. It is the absence of the separate condenser that puzzles one here, but Major's attempt at least highlights the problem of adjusting British technology to Russian conditions. Samuel Bentham at first comments on the fact that the Russians have no conception that they can erect an iron foundry at any other place where there is a river to operate the bellows,[109] but later comes to the opinion:

> As to Steam Engines I have no immediate use for them although it is certain they would have their use, as for the raising of water for the working machines: But I should have no hopes of getting a man capable of erecting them for any Salary I could at present offer.[110]

He stresses the lack of trained enginemen but makes no mention of the availability of coal. Yet in St Petersburg, as on the eastern coast of the USA, steam engines were fuelled by imported British coal.[111] Could it be, as Chandler has suggested for the USA,[112] that the development of steam technology in Russia was hampered not so much by the absence of skilled personnel, though that was a factor, as by the lack of easily available coal supplies? Information about steam engines was, after all, available in Sabakin's translation of James Ferguson's lectures[113] and other publications as well as from British immigrants who had worked on steam engines. Moreover the Kronstadt, Baird and other engines provided working examples. In parts of the interior difficulties of adaptation may also have arisen from the climatic extremes.

The French experience demonstrates that the diffusion of steam technology in the form of Watt's double-acting rotative engine could be delayed for twenty years by the weaknesses of French ironfounders in producing accurately bored cylinders, despite a welter of advice from such experts as William Wilkinson and the Perier brothers.[114] Only the arrival in France of the English engineer Humphry Edwards seems to have overcome the problems, but one wonders even then whether the efforts of a single unaided individual are ever enough, in the face of backwardness in the supporting technology or a lack of appropriate fuels, to create a major break-through. Watt's steam engine may have been theoretically only an improvement upon Newcomen's engine, but from the point of view of precision engineering, despite its many defects to modern eyes, it was in a different category from anything that had preceded it. Landes finds the obstacles to Continental emulation of British industrialisation in institutional restrictions—internal custom barriers, restricted domestic markets, class prejudices against trade and mercantilist and guild restrictions on the scale and technique of production—and in 'social and psychological attitudes unfavorable to entrepreneurship'.[115] It is clear that half a century or more elapsed before other nations began to emulate the British, so that in this respect Russia does not provide an exception to the general trend.

It is true that in serfdom Russia had a special institutional limitation of her own. Peter Capper junior, the Birmingham hardware merchant in St Petersburg, wrote to Boulton:

> Doctor Rogerson the Court Physician lately put into my hands the Papers relating to your fire Engine, which he received from Mr. Rowland. The Doctor gave them to a person in Power who returned a general Answer that they wou'd not do in this country but I cou'd get no Reasons.
>
> I have lately had some discourse with a great Iron Master he tells me that little Power for drawing Mines is wanted as the ore is in such Abundance that they work none but what is cleared by a Level and if I understand him right that they work horizontally into the Mountains not sink Pitts and as one great Object of your Engine is a saving of Labor that as the Workmen are all Slaves, this advantage is of no Moment— (NB. I dont comprehend the Sense of this Objection).[116]

Here, in addition to a difference in mining techniques, is an allusion to the cheapness of labour, though Capper perfectly correctly senses the objections to this argument, and in fact tried not only to establish his own steam-driven slitting mill but also to obtain a privilege to monopolise the sale of Boulton & Watt engines in Russia.[117] Certainly there were several mine owners and textile manufacturers, as well as saw-mill owners, who were interested in steam engines. Besides Russian engines, such as those of I. I. Polzinov and L. F. Sabakin, there was Russian interest in steam engines designed by Major, Baird, Blakey,[118] Murray and others, though only Baird's and Murray's engines seem to have had practical significance.

Zacchaeus Walker, enquiring in 1805 about Boulton & Watt's interest in a more general sale of their engines to Russia, stressed the difficulty in obtaining payment from Russian customers and in getting satisfaction in the courts of law (objections which also deterred Boulton & Watt from extensive trade with the United States). We also emphasised the need for a permanently based agent in Russia familiar with the Russian language and customs, who might have to undertake long and expensive journeys. Another difficulty was that the Crown or the principal nobles were 'directly or indirectly Proprietors of nearly all Establishments of magnitude', and he believed that Boulton 'will easily admit these two Classes are too far removed in most Countries from the Mass of Society to be the best adapted for a proper choice and accomplishment of useful Works: in this Empire I make no scruple of saying they are the very worst'. He also anticipated obstruction from Gascoigne. In addition he found the mercantile class too small and too lacking in 'enterprize, Talents, and Industry'. In general he agreed with Charles Baird that 'the commercial and manufacturing state of this Country is not sufficiently ripe as yet to admit a uniform and regular business of that kind'.[119] Yet the principal reason for Boulton & Watt's failure to push their Russian market in steam engines had nothing to do with Russia at all. The fact was that they could not produce sufficient engines to meet the domestic British demand and, in any event, their ventures in Holland, France and Italy proved to be too troublesome to be really profitable in the face of their lack of managerial and productive capacity.

Despite clear evidence of institutional and social obstructions to technological advance in Russia at this period, it may well be that broader economic considerations concerned with fuel resources and transport may be at the root of the slow development experienced in changing over to a coal-burning economy, considerations such as those described in Chandler's paper on American industrialisation. But such matters, together with the investigation of the Russian point of view about technical exchanges with Britain, must await further study. In the interim this paper is presented as a preliminary enquiry.[120]

NOTES

[1] See E. J. Simmons (ed.), *Continuity and Change in Russian and Soviet Thought* (Harvard, 1955), pp.11–39.

[2] But see E. Ames and N. Rosenberg, 'Changing technological leadership and industrial growth', *Economic Journal*, March 1963, pp.13–31.

[3] Roger P. Bartlett,'Foreign settlement in Russia, 1762–1804: aspects of government policy and its implementation' (University of Oxford, Ph.D. thesis, 1972), p.238. Dr Bartlett and I propose to publish together an account of Charles Gascoigne's activities in Russia.

[4] *Ibid.*, appendix I.

[5] *Ibid.*, p.199.

[6] Private communication from J. V. G. Mallett, deputy keeper of ceramics, Victoria and Albert Museum. See also Marvin C. Ross, *Russian Porcelains* (Oklahoma, 1968).

[7] See P. Hamilton, *Espionage and Subversion in an Industrial Society* (London, 1967), p. xi and *passim*.

[8] W. O. Henderson, *Britain and Industrial Europe, 1750–1870* (Leicester, 1965).

[9] See E. Robinson and D. McKie, *Partners in Science: James Watt and Joseph Black* (London and Harvard, 1970), p.84, also James Watt to Daniel MacMillan, 18 October 1784, James Watt Private Letter Book, 1782–89, Dolowlod (hereafter abbreviated to Dol.). The author again wishes to express his deepest thanks to Major David Gibson-Watt, MC, MP.

[10] See an account of his dealings with Sweden in A. E. Musson and Eric Robinson, *Science and Technology in the Industrial Revolution* (Manchester, 1969), pp.225–7.

[11] M. Boulton to J. Motteux, 27 April 1765, Letter Book 1764–66, Assay Office Library, Birmingham.

[12] *Ibid.*, 31 October 1765.

[13] MacCartney's comment on the state of manufactures in Russia, 1766–67, BM Add. MS 33,764. Allowances should be made for MacCartney's chauvinism, a constant feature of foreign visitors' comments on Russia in this period.

[14] In 1793 the head of the house of Tamez was an Englishman named Dickenson. See

John Parkinson, *A Tour of Russia, Siberia and the Crimea, 1792–94*, ed. W. Collier (London, 1971), pp. 102–3.

[15] M. Boulton to Lord Cathcart, 30 October 1771, Letter Book 177–73, Assay Office Library, Birmingham (hereafter abbreviated to AOLB). The author wishes to express his thanks to Mr A. Westwood, MBE, the Director of the Assay Office, Birmingham, for permission to quote from the documents in his care. The name appears to be given as 'Chemisev' in the above document but is probably intended to be 'Chernisev'. Count Ivan Grigor'yevitch Chernishev (1726–97) was president of the Admiralty.

[16] Probably General Count Aleksandr Nikolayevitch Samoilov (1744–1814).

[17] Perhaps Prince Ivan Ivanovich Bariatinsky (1772–1825).

[18] Aleksandr Markovitch Poltoratsky (1766–1839) married Mary, daughter of Charles Gascoigne.

[19] In one of his notebooks which contains several references to Russia, Boulton has a list of tools etc. which almost certainly refers to the things desired at that time, 1800, by the Russians: 'Anvills, Hammers, Vices, Lathes, Presses, Dies and Collers, Cutters Beds and Punches, Rolls and flatters, Casting Moulds, Ingots, Die sinking Tools, *Workmen of every description*, Stamps, Screws, Levers, Carding tools and Millers, Casting pots, Crucibles, Pincers, Drills, Chissells, White Bricks, Stourbridge [fire clay]' (Notebook 86, p.23, AOLB). The italics are mine.

[20] A. Deriabin to M. Boulton, 12 April 1798, AOLB. It is probable that Deriabin also visited Humphreys's ironworks at Merthyr Tydfil.

[21] S. Vorontzov to M. Boulton, 30 April 1800, Russian Mint Box II, AOLB.

[22] John Baskerville to M. Boulton, 9 December 1765, AOLB.

[23] See R. E. Schofield, *The Lunar Society of Birmingham* (Oxford, 1963), *passim*; H. L. Ganter, 'William Small, Jefferson's beloved teacher', *William and Mary College Quarterly*, IV (third series, 1947) pp.505–11; G. W. Ewing, 'Early teaching of science at the College of William and Mary in Virginia', *ibid.*, XXXII, 4, 1938, pp.7–9.

[24] See A. G. Cross, 'Arcticus and *The Bee* (1790–4): an episode in Anglo-Russian cultural relations', *Oxford Slavonic Papers*, new series, II, 1969, pp.68 ff.

[25] Dr M. Guthrie to Dr Joseph Black, 22 September 1783, Black papers, University of Edinburgh, Gen. 783/IV/7–8. See also Guthrie to Black, 20 October 1781, Gen. 783/II/276–9, and draft of Black's reply.

[26] Could this possibly be Watt's and Joseph Black's friend, Ninian Hill, a physician and surgeon?

[27] John Robinson to James Watt, 22 April 1771 OS, *Partners in Science*, p.24,

[28] Moussin Pouschkin to James Watt, 16 July 1771, Boulton & Watt collection, Birmingham Reference Library (hereafter referred to as BRL).

[29] *Partners in Science*, pp.248–9.

[30] Dol. No date.

[31] H. W. Dickinson, *James Watt: Craftsman and Engineer* (Newton Abbot, 1967), p.74.

[32] E. Darwin to J. Watt, 29 March 1775, Dol. M. Boulton was naturally also relieved. See letter quoted by V. P. Muirhead, *The Life of James Watt* (London, 1858), pp. 262–3, where Boulton regrets 'sounding your trumpet at the Ambassadors'.

[33] J. Hutton to J. Watt, 1774, Dol.

[34] John Phillips, *A General History of Inland Navigation, Foreign and Domestic* (5th edition, 1805), pp.36–7. This reference was supplied to me by Dr W. H. Chaloner.

[35] *Inventor and Entrepreneur: Recollections of Werner von Siemens* (London and Munich, 1966), pp.97–9.

[36] Difficulties in recruiting canal engineers and in organising the labour resources for canal-construction are frequently mentioned in correspondence. Waxsell, a Russian visiting England to view the canals, was introduced to Boulton by William Vaughan, 29 January 1805, AOLB.

[37] PRO SP 91/8 f. 283, Lord Cathcart to Lord Suffolk, 26 November/6 December 1771. This reference was kindly given to me by Dr R. P. Bartlett who intends to publish something of greater length on the subject.

[38] Carron Company papers, GD 58/16/24 Ordnance Book, Edinburgh Register House.

[39] R. H. Campbell, *The Carron Company* (Edinburgh and London, 1961), ch. v, 'The finances', pp.123–53.

[40] Carron Company papers, GD 58/1/2 Carron Company Letter Book 1786/87. Letter to the Honble the Commissioners of the Customs, Edinburgh, August 1786.

[41] *Ibid.*, Carron Company Book No. 2, pp. 40–5, July, 1786.

[42] Carron Company Letter Book, 1784–6 (GD 58/1/20), pp.679–80. In 1798 James Watt junior was warning Richard Dearman that Russia would soon push Britain *out* of the European market for nails. See Boulton & Watt Letter Book (Office), July 1797–July 1798, BRL.

[43] *Ibid.*, resolutions 841–2.

[44] *Ibid.*, GD 58/1/21, Carron Company Letter Book, 1786–7, to Alexander Cumming, Bo'ness, 16 August 1786.

[45] *Ibid.*, to Adams Armstrong, Kronstadt, 17 April 1787.

[46] *Ibid.*, GD 58/1/20, to Ten Cate and Vollenhoven, Amsterdam, 27 April 1786.

[47] *Ibid.*, pp.679–80.

[48] *Ibid.*, GD 58/1/2, to Admiral Greig, 29 August 1787.

[49] Campbell, *op. cit.*, p.74.

[50] Carron Company Papers, GD 58/1/16, Letter Book 1775–6, pp.216, 302 ff., and 433.

[51] Garbett Correspondence, vol. 2, fo. 18, Birmingham Reference Library. Clarke may have been the George Clarke at Carron who made a replica of Smeaton's model machine.

[52] *Ibid.*, fo. 33, Tibbats to the Lord Advocate, 3 September 1786; petition of the Carron Company to the JPs of Stirling, 31 August 1786; fo. 34, affadavit of William Cadell, JP, 31 August 1786.

[53] Garbett correspondence, vol. 2, fos. 72, 76, 104, 126, 151.

[54] *Ibid.*, vol. 22, fos. 7–8, S. Garbett to the Marquis of Lansdowne, 16 June 1786.

[55] *Ibid.*, vol. 2, fo. 13, Garbett to the Marquis of Lansdowne, 31 July 1786. It should be noted that the imposition of duties upon nails by the Americans at this date caused considerable unemployment in Birmingham and thus encouraged emigration.

[56] S. Garbett to M. Boulton, 31 August 1786, Garbett Box II, AOLB.

[57] *Ibid.*, S. Garbett to M. Boulton, 19 November 1786.

[58] I. Rae, *Charles Cameron, Architect to the Court of Russia* (London, 1971), pp.50–4, cites also a letter from St Petersburg by William and John Lyon to their mother.

[59] BM Add. MS 33,539. But see also S. Bentham to J. Bentham, 18/29 July 1784, in which Samuel Bentham says that the Scots 'are all settled according to their destination in the new town of Sophia near Zarsco-Sella [Tsarskoye Selo] 20 versts from Petersburgh'.

[60] BM Add. MS 33,539, vol. IV, fos. 70–2.

[61] I. R. Christie, 'Samuel Bentham and the western colony at Krichev, 1784–7', *Slavonic and East European Review*, XLVIII, 3, pp.232–47. See also M. S. Bentham, *Life of Brigadier-General Sir Samuel Bentham* (London, 1862); M. S. Anderson, 'Great Britain and the growth of the Russian navy in the eighteenth century', *Slavonic and East European Review*, XLII, 2, pp.132–46; T. L. S. Spriggs (ed.), *The Correspondence of Jeremy Bentham*, vols. I and II (London, 1968); W. Kirchner, 'Samuel Bentham and Siberia', *Slavonic and East European Review*, XXXVI, 1958, pp.471–80; M. S. Anderson, 'Samuel Bentham in Russia, 1779–91', *American Slavonic and East European Review*, XV, 2, 1956.

[62] Private information from Mr F. G. J. Robinson. Source: MS register of pupils at William Turner's School.

[63] PRO, SP91/98, fo. 289. Information from Dr R. P. Bartlett.

[64] Daniel McMillan (St Petersburg) to James Watt ('To the Care of Mr Bolton, Birmingham'), 6 July 1784, Dol.

[65] Information from Dr A. G. Cross, University of East Anglia.

[66] BM Add. MS 33,564.

[67] G. Donisthorpe to M. Boulton, 15 March 1799, AOLB.

[68] T. Tower, *Memoir of the late Charles Baird, Esq.*, etc (London, 1867).

[69] Dr R. P. Bartlett, *op. cit.*, p.241.

[70] Z. Walker to M. Boulton, 4 April 1805, BRL. The 'Mr. Roebuck' referred to is probably John Roebuck junior.

[71] PRO PC/2/161, p.112.

72 This same monopoly had been sought by Robert Fulton. See J. W. Oliver, *History of American Technology* (New York, 1956), p.139.
73 See M. R. Boulton to Charles Baird, 30 June 1807; Charles Baird to M. R. Boulton, 17 July 1807; Rev James Smirnove to M. R. Boulton, 12 November 1807; Rev James Smirnove to M. R. Boulton, 14 November 1807; M. R. Boulton to John Woodward, 30 June 1807: Russian Mint Box I, AOLB.
74 See J. G. Kohl, *Russia, St Petersburg, Moscow, Kharkoff, Riga, Odessa, the German Provinces on the Baltic, the Steppes, the Crimea, and the Interior of the Empire* (London, 1844), pp.128–9. Kohl spells Baird's name 'Berth'. I owe this reference to Mr S. E. Wimbush, whose undergraduate essay stimulated me to undertake further research.
75 Z. Walker to M. Boulton, 5 October 1805, Russian Mint Box I, AOLB.
76 J. P. McKay, *Pioneers for Profit: Foreign Entrepreneurship and Russian Industrialization, 1885–1913* (Chicago, 1970), pp.41 and 114.
77 'All his Countrymen have the utmost Abhorrence of the Motive that brought him here, at least as it now appears, both towards him and the Admiral [Greig], who was the cause of his coming over': Peter Capper (St Petersburg) to Samuel Garbett, 23 June 1786, Garbett correspondence, vol. 2, BRL. Such remarks must of course be taken with a pinch of salt.
78 The account of him in J. C. Gibson, *Lands and Lairds of Larbert and Dunipace Parishes* (Glasgow, 1908), pp.80–1, is wildly inaccurate.
79 G. Sheriff to Boulton & Watt, 15 December 1833, OS, Box 5 ix, Boulton & Watt Collection, BRL. See also Boulton & Watt Letter Book (Office), May 1799–March 1800, BRL.
80 'Estimate delivered to Mr Sheriff for J. Major Esq. of Petersburg', 26 December 1799, Boulton & Watt Letter Book (Office), May 1799–March 1800, BRL.
81 G. Sheriff to Boulton & Watt, 15 December 1833, OS.
82 J. Watt junior to James Lawson, 16 January 1800, Boulton & Watt Letter Book (Office), May 1799–March 1800, BRL: 'We found Mr S. a very sensible, well-informed man. He has been long in Russia, and if he returns there I should think it not impossible that Mr [Boulton] may avail himself of his Services in the New Mint'.
83 'A Sketch for Mr Sheriff to write to St Petersburg, Jan. 1800', AOLB.
84 Thomas Loxdale to M. Boulton, 4 May 1800, AOLB: 'Mr Sheriff has completed his Survey of a line of road from Finger Post to Wednesbury'.
85 George Sheriff to M. Boulton, 16 January 1800, AOLB.
86 M. I. Tugan-Baranovsky, *The Russian Factory in the Nineteenth Century*, translated from the third Russian edition by A. and C. S. Levin under the supervision of Gregory Grossman (Homewood, Ill., 1970, published for the American Economic Association) by R. D. Irwin), pp.36 and 297.
87 In particular we do not here deal with the workmen sent out by Boulton to construct the mint machinery in St Petersburg. One, James Harley, who may have been the apprentice of that name who attempted to emigrate from Carron and was taken off the *Empress of Russia*, remained in Russia after the termination of his duties for Boulton in connection with the mint. An early sketch of Boulton's enterprise is provided by E. Robinson, 'Birmingham capitalists and Russian workers', *History Today*, VI, 10, October 1956, but the author intends to publish a much fuller account of this affair in a forthcoming paper.
88 The author wishes to acknowledge the grant of a Guggenheim Fellowship to assist him in this enquiry.
89 Z. Walker to M. Boulton, 21 September 1803, OS, Russian Mint Box I, AOLB.
90 Z. Walker to M. Boulton, 23 June 1803, Z. Walker Junior, AOLB.
91 Z. Walker to M. Boulton, 25 October 1803, Russian Mint Box I, AOLB.
92 William Wallis to Heneage Legge, 21 June 1800, Russian Mint Box I, AOLB.
93 M. Boulton to A. Baxter, 15 August 1796, Russian Mint Box II, AOLB.
94 Vorontzov to Bolton, 9/20 January 1797, *ibid.*
95 M. Boulton to Vorontzov, 20 February 1797, *ibid.*
96 Boulton Notebook 10, coinage, AOLB.
97 F. N. Zagorskii, *L. F. Sabakin, a Russian Mechanic of the 18th Century, his Life and Work* (translated from Russian, Israel Program for Scientific Translations, Jerusalem, 1966). Zagorskii says: 'Where, and by whom Sabakin was trained in England is

impossible to establish' (p.7). Yet see p.16, where Sabakin is mentioned as having seen Boulton's steam engine at work at Soho.

[98] J. Duncan to M. Boulton, 28 December 1802, Russian Mint Box I, AOLB.
[99] Rev J. Smirnove [Ivan Smirnov] to M. Boulton, 19 September 1799, Russian Mint Box II, AOLB.
[100] M. Boulton to J. Smirnove [Ivan Smirnov], 29 September 1799, Russian Mint Box I, AOLB.
[101] Zagorskii, *op. cit.*, p. 16.
[102] J. Duncan to M. Boulton, 10 November 1802, OS, Russian Mint Box I, AOLB.
[103] M. Boulton to Rev J. Smirnove, 18 April 1802, *ibid.*
[104] Rev J. Smirnove to M. Boulton, 16 June 1799, *ibid.*
[105] M. Boulton to Rev J. Smirnove, 18 April 1800, *ibid.*
[106] Z. Walker to M. Boulton, 4 October 1804, OS, *ibid.*
[107] See A. A. Zvorikine, 'Inventions and scientific ideas in Russia', in G. S. Métraux and F. Crouzet, *The Nineteenth-century World* (UNESCO, 1963).
[108] Z. Walker to M. Boulton, 4 April 1805, OS, BRL.
[109] BM Add. MS 33,539, Samuel Bentham to Jeremy Bentham, 2 January 1782, OS.
[110] *Ibid.*, Samuel Bentham to Jeremy Bentham, 1784.
[111] Garbett asserted in a letter to Pitt, presumably of 1786, that British 'Coal and Pig Iron can be delivered in Russia at nearly the same Price if not cheaper than they are delivered in London', No. 20, S. Garbett correspondence, box 2, BRL.
[112] A. D. Chandler, jr., 'Anthracite coal and the beginnings of the industrial revolution in the United States', *Business History Review*, XLVI, 2, summer 1972, pp. 141–81.
[113] Zagorskii, *op. cit.*, ch. II, pp.13–25.
[114] J. Payen, *Capital et machine à vapeur au XVIIIe siècle: les frères Périer et l'introduction en France de la machine à vapeur de Watt* (Paris, 1969), pp.225–8.
[115] D. S. Landes, *The Unbound Prometheus* (Cambridge, 1970), ch. 3, 'Continental emulation', pp.124–47.
[116] P. Capper, jr., to M. Boulton, 24 November 1777, AOLB.
[117] I do not know what happened to cause this proposal to lapse.
[118] P. Capper, jr., to M. Boulton, 29 December 1777, AOLB; J. H. Magellan to James Watt, 28 August 1781, Dol., enclosing a cutting from the announcement made by the St Petersburg Academy of a prize for the best essay on steam engines, 1781.
[119] Z. Walker to Boulton Watt & Co., 4 April 1805, OS, BRL.
[120] For additional information on Charles Baird and steamboats see R. M. Haywood, *The Beginnings of Railway Development in Russia in the Reign of Nicholas I, 1835–1842* (Durham, N.C., 1969), pp.19–21, and especially p.20, note 71.

J. R. Harris

2

Saint-Gobain and Ravenhead[1]

I

The comparative study of the economies of Britain and France in their eras of industrialisation has been seen for some decades now as an important tool in the hands of the economic historian as he seeks to understand the nature of economic growth in the eighteenth and nineteenth centuries.[2] Within this general field of enquiry the methods of technological transfer between the two countries and the success of such transfusions must necessarily occupy much attention. In such studies the pioneering work of W. O. Henderson occupies an honoured place, and on his foundations we are happy to build.

It might seem in such exercises that to make a comparative analysis of a single French firm of the eighteenth century and its English parallel is to narrow unduly the historian's viewpoint. The intention is, however, to show that the two concerns to be treated here highlight many of the most interesting points of comparison between the industry of the two countries. In a sense, however, the present discussion can only be an interim one: in France an official history of Saint-Gobain is nearing completion at the hands of M. Pris and M. Thépot; in England Miss Pemberton has begun a full study of Ravenhead in its most significant period, and the one with which the present paper is concerned.[3]

Ravenhead and Saint-Gobain were manufacturing centres of great importance, and were concerned with one particular product, plate glass. Though at times in both works plate glass was made by the earlier method of blowing and cutting open a glass cylinder, their great significance was that they were the centres of the newer techniques of casting plate glass on a table, which enabled the production of larger plates but at the same time demanded very large buildings and expensive equipment.

The comparative interest, however, goes far beyond the comparison of two large units in the same industry but in two countries. To start with, the direction of technological transfer, or attempted transfer, between the two countries in the eighteenth century was heavily and increasingly from Britain to France. While it is possible to find numerous flows in the opposite direction, the balance is hardly in question, and the work in France of Englishmen like John Kay, John Holker and William Wilkinson is justly celebrated. But the case of cast plate glass is one of those on the opposite side of the balance: this was a great French success envied and coveted here. It illustrates the problems of techno-logical transference in the opposite, and less usual, direction.

The French enterprise, a large-scale business producing a luxury article of great prestige by techniques invented within the enterprise, was a natural recipient of the status of a *manufacture royale* and com-prehensive privileges, given the relations between State and industry in France in the late seventeenth and eighteenth centuries. The British Cast Plate Glass Company, however, which operated the Ravenhead works at St Helens, was also deliberately put into a privileged position. It was one of the few companies in the purely private sector—rather than in the realms of public utility—to be incorporated by Act of Parliament, and this virtually conferred limited liability.[4] The diffi-culties of raising the large capital involved without legal protection, in a high-risk, innovation-heavy industry, as well as the strong attempts made by the British company to keep its newly acquired technical secrets to itself may have helped the British firm to keep a virtual mono-poly of cast plate glass from 1773 to 1815.[5] The French firm had exclusive privileges renewed from the late seventeenth century to the revolution, but in fact the common inconsistencies of the apparently strong central direction of the French State in that period manifest themselves in this instance, and there were effective rivalries, not only from neighbouring countries, to which spies and defectors carried their process, but within France. At any rate the comparison is certainly not between a French manufacture under royal privilege and a British concern under a virtually free enterprise system. Indeed, though privileged in one sense, in another the British firm may have had much to complain of in terms of vexatious State interference by means of excessive and illogical taxation demands.

The industry could be pursued only on a large scale and with a great capital, and we would expect that in both countries the problems of organisation and control would be severe in eighteenth-century con-ditions. Good management was therefore at a premium. In France it was Lucas de Nehou who originally consolidated the concern in both technological and organisational terms, then, from the late 1750s, after a succession of unstable and sometimes short-lived managements, stability and efficiency once more returned under a devoted and skilful manager, Delaunay Deslandes. From its foundation in the 1770s the British company was beset by managerial and technological problems which were not really resolved until Robert Sherbourne, who had been with the company for some years, took over the direction at Ravenhead in 1792.

Both companies have interesting investors. The French company, despite the revocation of the Edict of Nantes, became a centre of Protestant capitalism, and its origin was the French-speaking business community of Geneva. The British company's investing group is now receiving detailed attention. It contains notable industrialists like the Mackworths and Mackays, but finance and banking capital played an unusually large role and there was a significant Scots and East India interest. Court influence was valuable if not essential to Saint-Gobain in the eighteenth century, as might be expected; its British rival was remarkably well connected, for a firm in a manufacturing industry, with the national Establishment.[6] The plant and buildings of both companies were on a great scale—the French Plate Glass Company, indeed, had a second large works, Tourlaville,[7] as well as Saint-Gobain,[8] though this was becoming less viable in the late eighteenth century. Saint-Gobain was a huge plant for the period, dominated by a series of great working halls; the great casting hall at Ravenhead, though its original dimensions were obscured by later alterations, was certainly one of the biggest industrial buildings in Britain.[9] Its enmured layout, its porticoed manager's house, even its stylish stable buildings and bell canopy were not utterly different from the appearance expected of a French *manufacture royale*, though it might lack the equivalent of the uniformed *suisses* at the gate, nor was it sited on and partly reconstructed out of an ancient castle, as was Saint-Gobain.[10] Both sites still retain buildings of the eighteenth century and are valuable specimens for the industrial archaeologist; indeed, an architectural survey of Ravenhead has just been completed.[11] Both concerns survive today as part of modern industrial complexes; both are fortunately managed by men with a sense of history, a pride in industrial tradition, and an interest in the preservation of archival and physical evidence.

For the eighteenth century the most interesting connection and comparison is technological. Here we had a key process pioneered by Frenchmen, the casting of large plates of glass, which they endeavoured to restrict to the pioneering firm and to France. The enticing or *débauchement* of managerial and operative personnel was not being done in England but in France, the problems of adjustment were not those of the settlement of British technicians in the alien social and religious atmosphere of France but of their French equivalents in England; British craftsmen had to try to make equipment to the specifications of French experts if the manufacture was to be set going. Again, there was a curious reversal of the roles in the technology of fuel. In most technological transference British technicians were endeavouring to teach processes perfected in a country which had long put its dependence on coal fuel to workmen whose experience was confined to wood fuel; now Frenchmen were endeavouring to take a French process, long based on wood, to England, at a time when, despite current experiments, the employment of coal had not been perfected in France. It is on this technological aspect that this paper will mainly concentrate.[12]

II

The French plate glass industry was not established without difficulty. Down to the 1660s France, like other countries, had been supplied from Venice with this high-quality flat glass, which used soda as its alkali, and was carefully ground and polished. To Colbert, seeking to stimulate French industry and save foreign exchange, and to Louis XIV, with his taste for palace building, the establishment of the manufacture in France had particular attractions. Venetian workmen were attracted to France, despite extreme penalties facing those who attempted to desert the Murano works, and in 1665 the king's letters patent set up the Royal Plate Glass Manufactory, which began production in Paris in 1666. At this point the method of manufacture was unchanged from that customary at Venice: a cylinder of glass was blown, trimmed of its ends, slit longitudinally, and then flattened, ground and polished.[13] Fuel and material costs being too high at Paris, the actual blowing of the glass was very soon moved to Tourlaville, near Cherbourg, where plate glass had been already made by one of the de Nehou family.[14] Grinding and polishing were continued at Paris, as these highly labour-intensive processes were extremely costly. The hazards of carriage were so considerable that it would not have paid to put costly work at Tourlaville into polishing glass of which a considerable percentage might have been shattered on arrival at Paris, the main market.

This first company was called the Dunoyer Company after the person in whose name the privilege was made out. Such persons were not necessarily the principal associates, or even associates at all, and later Royal Plate Glass Companies were operating under successive privileges given to successive 'men of straw'—the nominal heads of the concern being in fact clerks in the office.[15] Dunoyer, however, was at least a provincial tax collector, and there were a number of men of similar stamp among the associates, including his brother, who was Controller General and Paymaster of Rentes at the Hôtel de Ville of Paris. A second company was formed in 1684 in whose favour the privilege of exclusive manufacture of plate glass for mirrors was renewed, but it found itself confronted with a rival within four years. This was the company of Abraham Thévart, and this was as much the creation and protégé of Louvois as the first company had been of Colbert. The notion of having two privileged monopoly companies to produce plate glass seems absurd, but in fact the new company had a very real claim to State patronage by contemporary standards, for while the first company had merely introduced and domesticated in France an industrial process developed abroad, the Thévart company was formed to establish a new and adventurous technological process, destined to be the basis of the plate glass industry, wherever established, until well into the twentieth century. The idea was to cast glass by pouring it onto a perfectly flat metallic table—simple in concept, but extremely difficult of achievement. Who invented the process is not quite clear.[16] The man charged with the development of the new technique on a commercial basis was a Tourlaville glassworks official, Louis Lucas de Nehou, the only associate in the new company to have been similarly involved in the existing one, now known under the 1684 privilege as the Bagneux company.

After a brief period of manufacture in Paris the Thévart company, like the earlier foundation, moved its centre of glassmaking to an area where fuel and raw materials were more cheaply available and skilled labour fairly near at hand, and took over the crumbling Château de Saint-Gobain in Picardy in 1692, where operations were set up under de Nehou's technical management. Neither concern seems to have been particularly successful, the Bagneux company having to ingratiate itself with Louvois by setting up works in his under-utilised forests at Lézinnes (Yonne).[17] The Thévart company's main technological advantage was that it could cast much larger plates than could be produced under its rival's blowing process, and it was prohibited from making and selling plates under a fixed size. This meant that plates which were defective because of blemishes or poor annealing could not be cut down into less valuable but still commercially worthwhile smaller plates, but would have to be used as cullet or wasted. In 1695 the king amalgamated the two companies, and issued a new set of privileges in the name of François Plastrier. But this did not save the concerns, and by 1702 they were bankrupt, with an accumulated debt of over $1\frac{1}{2}$ million livres. The company was dissolved, but the prestige and interest of the Crown were too involved to allow the industry to perish, and a new, and fifth, company was established in 1702 with the name of Dagincourt.[18]

At the fifth attempt the corner was turned, and a viable and lasting concern founded. While it is not the intention of this paper to examine the investment aspect of the eighteenth-century plate glass industry, it is worthwhile to point out that an important new element was introduced by the entry of Swiss investors, mainly Genevan Protestants—a sufficient irony for a project which was so much the favoured *protégé* of the repealer of the Edict of Nantes—and these families jointly combined to exercise effective policy control during the eighteenth century, the Saladin and Buisson families being especially important. While the concern had its share of troubles and difficulties, and there were a number of unsatisfactory managers from time to time, there was until the revolution a considerable expansion of output, running, for instance, at about two million livres in annual value in the 1770s, and a physical output of upwards of 1,000 tons of glass per annum.

After the 1702 reorganisation manufacturing was cut down to the two main works at Tourlaville and Saint-Gobain, with finishing of the plates in Paris as before, less satisfactory sites being closed or converted to warehousing. For a time technical direction at Saint-Gobain was given to a group of three persons, one of whom adopted the name of M. Des Fourneaux,[19] but in 1710 de Nehou, who seems to have dropped out of the picture about the time of the 1695 merger, returned to direct the works for the final eighteen years of his life. For a long period there was no consistent policy of specialisation at the two different works. Blowing as well as casting had been introduced at Saint-Gobain under the merger regime, while under a notable director at Tourlaville, David Oury, casting was for a time established there.

The privileges of the 1702 company were prolonged under successive letters patent; it naturally endeavoured to retain its right of exclusive manufacture, and in 1713 gained a royal decree imposing severe penalties against workers who tried to defect from its service.[20] Nevertheless, the privileges did not altogether prevent the dispersal of workmen or their methods within France or beyond the frontiers. The company was able, early in the century, to have an infringer of its monopoly privileges put in the Bastille; much later it could have a senior technician who had defected to a rival concern imprisoned at Laon. But there were limits to its influence, especially in areas which were not fully incorporated in the French State, or where a provincial *parlement* gave some protection to a rival. From mid-century powerful administrators like Turgot were not happy about enforcing regulations inhibitive of free competition, and the company sometimes did not choose to ask the Crown to enforce its privileges to the letter.[21]

Like de Nehou, another permanent official of the Thévart company, De La Pommeraye, lost his connection with the enterprise at the merger of 1695 and went off to the independent principality of Dombes, which was under the Duc du Maine, and in 1698 built a factory at Beauregard. In 1700 the king forbade the enterprise to sell in France, but it was permitted to move glass across the country to foreign markets. This was apparently not a sufficient outlet for the product; the firm was detected in fraudulently smuggling glass into France, and it collapsed within a decade. A Lorraine glassworks endeavoured to make plate, as it claimed to be beyond the bounds of the privilege conferred by the

French royal *arrêt*, but lasted only a similar time. The Saint-Quirin works, founded about 1740, and destined to be the great rival of Saint-Gobain in the early nineteenth century (before the companies joined forces for certain purposes in 1830 and completely in 1858) also made plate glass. This seems to have been a white crystal using a potash alkali which was blown into a thick cylinder and then ground and polished like blown plate. The two firms were at law at one time: though the Compagnie des Glaces apparently had its rights upheld, the victory was perhaps a paper one.[22]

The imperfect implementation of the company's monopoly within the bounds of France is perhaps even better illustrated by the case of the plate works at Rouelles in Burgundy. These were founded in 1759 by Paul Bosc D'Antic[23] and two associates. D'Antic was a *savant*-industrialist who had been for two years at Saint-Gobain, but had left the company. He had then had a lawsuit with it over the remuneration of his services, which the company did not value highly. The states of Burgundy did much to back this enterprise, and the Company seems to have felt it prudent not to try to enforce its privilege against the new concern. D'Antic was dismissed after a couple of years, and another discarded Saint-Gobain technician was turned to, Besnard, who appears later in our story in an important but unflattering role. He in turn was succeeded by a former Saint-Gobain director, Delahaye, who was not able to pull the concern round. Finally the Compagnie des Glaces itself, after careful consideration, decided not to take over the collapsing firm, even though offered a subsidy by the states of Burgundy. Nevertheless, though often an ailing enterprise, Rouelles managed to infringe the supposed legal monopoly with virtual impunity for nearly two decades.

If it was so readily possible to steal techniques and workers within France, it can be imagined that there would be attempts to entice the industry abroad. There were such attempts, and successful ones—indeed, one of the interesting features is the self-righteous condemnation by French industrialists and administrators of that process of *débauchement* of workers which they had used so successfully on the Venetians in the previous century. The eventual theft of the casting process by the British makes a remarkable story, and it led to the establishment of a large and successful rival, but it was by no means the earliest instance. Spain had a plate glass works by about 1720, the De La Pommeraye who had set going the works in the principality of Dombes being the director; it was apparently a sort of royal manufacture and continued into the late eighteenth century.[24] The industry reached Germany at the very beginning of the same century. When in 1701 the combined French companies, about to fail, extinguished their furnaces, some of the workers were encouraged to remain at or near the works in the hope

of their being employed in a reconstituted company; some, like the
remaining Venetians, who had been troublesome, were merely dismissed. At this period a number of workmen emigrated and set up an
establishment which blew and cast plates in two separate halls in a
concern subsidised by the Archbishop of Mainz. Originally using soda,
as at Saint-Gobain, this works later turned to potash, which was cheaply
and locally available. This works was still making plate glass by both
techniques in the late eighteenth century, when its director corresponded with the director of Saint-Gobain, and it survived at least to
the end of the century, though it was then reported to have dropped the
casting process. Mirrors were made in the late eighteenth century at
about half a dozen places in Germany, but in many cases this was by
grinding and polishing some sort of blown white glass, usually much
thinner than true plate glass, and based on a potash and not a soda
alkali. These products could hardly be said to owe anything decisive
either to Venice or to France. There was, nevertheless, a substantial
export of French plate glass to Germany, as there was to Holland,
England and Russia.[25]

III

It would be expected that in England, where the progress of technology
was very marked at the end of the seventeenth century and the opening
of the eighteenth, there would be interest in—indeed, imitation of—the
French plate glass developments. During the life of the first French
company articles of agreement were signed in 1673 between two
Englishmen, George Ravenscroft—perhaps the same who later invented
flint glass—and John Burrough. Over a three-year period Ravenscroft
engaged to obtain crude French plate glass for mirror making on
Burrough's behalf to the value of £200 a year, in certain specified sizes
and of the quality which he was already importing. Moreover Ravenscroft bound himself not to bring plate glass over for general sale or sale
to anyone else except with Burrough's consent. The agreement was
countersigned by Dunoyer and three other members of the French
company, showing that this interesting sub-monopoly for the English
market was arranged with their approval.[26]

In 1691 an English patent was taken out for 'the Art of Casting Glass
and particularly looking Glass Plates' which would be larger than any
plates known hitherto. Later in the year the patentees were involved in a
petition to Parliament to incorporate a Company of Glassmakers with
powers to raise a joint stock; as Professor Barker has pointed out, this
constitutes strong evidence that an attempt was being made to raise
capital to cover the initially heavy outlay involved in the casting process.
Though no Act was gained, some glass entrepreneurs did associate to

sell plate glass and were putting it on the market in 1692. In 1701 a Vauxhall glasshouse was casting plates of exceptional size;[27] this firm continued to make plates, and was reported on by a French visitor in the 1760s. It was by then, presumably, only blowing, as in 1773 the proprietor said he had long destroyed his casting equipment. There are references in the mid-1740s to a Southwark glasshouse which was both blowing and casting plates, and in the third quarter of the century plates were being made at South Shields.[28]

All this did not mean, however, that a really successful British plate glass industry had been established. In fact by the early 1770s only smaller-sized plates were being produced by blowing, and all large plates were imported from France at a cost said to be between £60,000 and £100,000 a year.[29] As a result there was an attempt to introduce the French technology into Britain—indeed, it now appears there were two attempts, though their inception and background are by no means wholly clear, and there are some considerable problems of dating.

IV

There was, according to his own statement, an approach made by a group of English entrepreneurs to Delaunay Deslandes, the director of the Saint-Gobain works since 1758, and certainly one of the greatest technologists and most successful industrial managers in eighteenth-century France. However, as Deslandes put it, 'I always have had a French heart and I always held to the principle that while one must eat bread it did not have to be gall'—perhaps reflecting his feelings about English cooking. One of those who approached Deslandes was Lord Mansfield, and it was on a visit to Saint-Gobain by Mansfield and another English peer, whose name Deslandes most unfortunately seems to have forgotten, that Mansfield told Deslandes that, unable to secure his services, they had obtained those of Philip Besnard, formerly at Saint-Gobain. Deslandes says he told the Englishmen that he would have not been at all displeased at their having Besnard were it not that he and they as individuals—and their two countries—were on good terms. Deslandes had dismissed Besnard from Saint-Gobain,[30] whence he had gone to take charge of the Rouelles plate glass works in Burgundy, from which he had been dismissed in turn.[31]

From this point on we are faced with a jigsaw of facts with many missing pieces. The attempt to fit it together must necessarily partly fail until more pieces are found, and there can only be guesswork as to what is in the incomplete part of the picture. Besnard arrived in England in the autumn of 1771 and in the first months of 1772 was going through the preliminary stages of obtaining a patent for 'a new method of casting and making Plate Glass not only in a less expensive manner but in greater Perfection and of larger Dimensions than hath yet been done in the Country'.[32] The requests got as far as the Patent Office warrant book[33] with Besnard's statement 'that he is the only Person as he verily believes in this our Kingdom possessed of this method of making Plate Glass'. Curiously, however, this was as far as it got. We can only speculate whether (for instance) Besnard lacked the money to pay fees, whether the fact that casting had been done earlier in England presented a problem, or whether Besnard's patrons believed that secrecy was better than patenting.

We now know that there were two prospective companies, not one, in the 1770s. A French source of the early 1790s says that Besnard went to England to form a company in Lancashire—which must mean the Cast Plate Glass Company, the one actually incorporated by Parliament, whose works were at Ravenhead. However, he fell out with his partners and began to intrigue with another company near Newcastle and got a sum of money from them to quit his first backers.[34] Deslandes' account does not quite fit with this, though he certainly knew of the work we have just cited. Rather improbably he says it was the first company from which he fraudulently obtained 40,000 fr, and he talks of Besnard being pursued at law, hardly escaping the rope, and fleeing to Bayonne in disguise.[35] There is clearly something in this, because Deslaundes says that both he and Vergennes were separately informed from England of his return to France and corresponded about it. However, it is doubtful if Besnard had done anything here which was really criminal, because he turned up again in England in the 1780s and took out a patent in his own name—hardly the action of a wanted man.[36] Perhaps he was bribed to leave one group of projectors for the other and refused to return the payment when the second concern failed to get established. Members of either group might then feel vindictive and inform the French government of the return of a man who had broken the laws of his own country by defecting.

The second group of projectors was headed by the Duke of Northumberland, and it is said that it was on lands and mines owned by him near Newcastle that the proposed works were to be built. A solitary letter of February 1777[37] shows that the intermediary between Besnard and the duke was a M. Dutens and that Besnard had an associate, Pierre Theodore de Brûges, who was concerned with alkali manufacture and the making of saltpetre and of concentrates from potash and natural soda.[38] Louis Dutens, diplomat and writer, was a Huguenot who had lived much in England. He had taken orders and gone to Turin as chaplain to the British embassy, where he had been chargé d'affaires for a time, his services being rewarded with a State pension. From 1766 he had been attached to the duke's household, holding a living in his gift, and making the grand tour with one of his sons.[39] The letter of 1777 was written by de Brûges and exults in his favourable reception by the duke. After discussing the chemical venture the duke

> was delighted and offered me the protection of the Law and Parliament, adding that he would have no pleasure greater than to oblige me and my company. In truth, I was enchanted with his conversation, he is a nobleman of the greatest learning and well acquainted with chemistry. He offered me his Duchy of Northumberland together with all possible facilities in order that I might set up there plant to manufacture alkali, exterioration salt, and plate glass.

Attached to the letter, itself a copy, are a set of proposals for the formation of a plate glass company on lands of the Duke of Northumberland, described as 'the site in the whole of England which is most suitable to this enterprise'. This company would have a large soda- and saltpetre-producing section, supplying the plate glass works with alkali but also having a big outside sale, which was estimated as producing a profit of well over one million livres a year.

How Besnard came to part with the Cast Plate Glass Company, or exactly when, we do not know, though another Frenchman was well established as the technical expert at the Ravenhead works by the end of 1775; nor do we know why the negotiations so auspiciously opened with the Duke of Northumberland seem to have been without result. According to Deslandes, Besnard at one time offered his services to the Russian ambassador in London. The ambassador, however, was very circumspect, enquired why a man of his talents had wished to leave France, and asked for testimonials from intendants, deputies of commerce or similar persons of standing as to Besnard's merits. At some point Besnard approached Beaumarchais, who was in London on a mission for the French government. He boasted of his talents and complained of injustices at the hands of the Compagnie des Glaces, but Beaumarchais simply wrote to Vergennes, who in turn wrote to the company. Deslandes replied to the Minister on its behalf in a memoir in which he said 'avec beaucoup de sangfroid' what he thought about Besnard.[40] The dates of these negotiations are not clear, but it seems unlikely that Besnard could have met Beaumarchais in London until March 1774. In the late 1770s we lose sight of him until he appears in London between July and October 1782, when he successfully obtained a patent for a lamp. In the interval he could well have returned to France.

Two prospectuses survive for a plate glass works project in England about this time. One is undated; the other, dated 1777, is attached to the de Brûges letter of 1777 quoted above, and derives from de Brûges and Besnard. One is subtitled 'Tableau du Capital necessaire à l'éstablissment d'une manufacture de glaces coulées en Angleterre, à l'instar de celle de France établie à St Gobain en Picardie, et si bien connue [de?] tout le monde'. The other is in English: 'A Plan for establishing a Cast Plate Glass Manufactory in England similar to that of Saint-Gobain in the Province of Picardy in France and Estimate of the charge of establishing the same and of three months' work.[41] The two prospectuses are clearly linked, following much the same pattern and with phrases in the English version which are virtually identical to those of the French. Both recognise that labour will be dearer in England. The French version states that wages of English workers are generally a quarter more than those of their French counterparts; the English version puts it higher, at one-third more.[42] Both immediately, however, stress the opposite factor, in virtually the same terms: English coal means a saving of five-sixths in fuel costs as compared with France, 'besides the good quality thereof a very principal object'. If the output of the British and French factories were taken as equal, the advantage would still be with the former 'by the superior goodness of firing because it is a known fact that the ordinary glass made here is superior to the Ordinary Glass made in France only from the effect of the goodness of the coals'. The high demand for plate glass in London, coupled with the high duty on import, would at the same time mean that plate which was valued at £15 or £16 in France would sell for £70 in the London market.

In both documents there are costings on a similar basis. In each case a factory of five main buildings is envisaged, one, the casting hall, to be bigger than the others. A copper-topped casting table is a very expensive item, £2,500 in the English version, and fireclay had to be provided for building the smelting furnace and for making a stock of crucibles. Both prospectuses recognise the need to have working capital to finance three months' operations and pay for 1,000 tons of coal, 45,000 cwt of alkali, 25 tons of sand,[43] lime for flux, and wood, which, despite a main dependence on coal, was thought necessary for some fires. Fifty workmen would be wanted at wages of about 15s per week, and there would be management and clerical expenses. The English version seems to be estimated on a higher level of costs than the French, or on a higher conversion rate for the livre against the pound. Even on this basis, however, the estimate was made that, reckoning total building and equipment costs at £15,800 and the expense of three months' production at £2,360, to which was to be added £1,600 for grinding and polishing, the end of the first three months would see a break-even point reached, as the glass made would be worth just over £20,000 in a finished state.

The concern, according to the English version, would thus require £20,000 to be laid out within a period of eighteen months, the English investors being paid the customary 5 per cent interest on their money before any dividend was made. The profits, however, would be divided into two halves, one to be paid as dividends to the English subscribers, the other to go to the 'Artist ['L'Artiste entrepreneur' in the French version], as a Satisfaction for his Skill, attention, time and labour; and he, his Executors and Administrators to be forever entitled to the said share of the said clear profits, he and they conducting and carrying on the said work by him or themselves or he [*sic*] or their Sufficient Deputy . . .'. Moreover the investors were not all to have voting rights but were to be represented by four persons only. It was hardly to be expected that any men of property of this or any other period would have been prepared to reward technology to the extent of 50 per cent of profits, even when assured that those profits would prove to be 400 per cent per annum! No wonder Besnard failed to agree with two successive groups of British investors.[44]

V

The successful British company obtained its Act in 1773[45] and began to erect its works at St Helens in south Lancashire on the Ravenhead estates of John Mackay, close to the Sankey canal. The suitability of the site for glass manufacture had already been demonstrated, for a number of smaller concerns had come into existence in the district since the late seventeenth century. Two in the same township had been founded by Huguenot glassmakers. Mackay himself had become an investor in one of them, at Thatto Heath, only a few hundred yards from the site of the new plate glass works.[46] Mackay was a most enterprising industrialist: he came of a Scots merchant family, moved to London and later took an interest in the Cheshire salt industry. The fuel requirements of the saltfield brought him to south Lancashire, where he developed important coal mines at Thatto Heath and on his nearby Ravenhead estate. His most important contribution, however, was to go beyond the role of coalmaster and to attract fuel-voracious furnace industries to his coal mines; Mackay's predecessors had merely been concerned to sell coal to Liverpool and to the Cheshire saltfield, the coalfield's main external markets. His first major success was with the British Cast Plate Glass Company; but at least as important to contemporaries was the Parys Mine Company's great copper works, established at the other end of Mackay's estates in 1779. For the latter Mackay provided fire-clay and building clay, stone, limestone and other facilities at minimal cost, as well as a favourable long-term coal contract, and no doubt he did much the same for the new glass company; in this case, as one of the shareholders, he had even better cause.[47]

The network of relationship, acquaintance and contact essential to the assembling of the interesting (but not entirely identical) groups who petitioned for, and actually subscribed to, the British Cast Plate Glass

Company offers a fascinating subject of study.[48] We have no knowledge of the extent of the original shareholding of the first subscribers, though we know how it stood in 1794. Then Admiral Philip Affleck was one of the largest shareholders; later testimony suggests he had a very important part in the foundation of the company.[49] He was John Mackay's executor, and thus also controlled Mackay's shareholding, still a substantial one, though we know he had died much indebted. Other Scots were prominent in the early stages, and there was a strong East India influence which probably increased over time. Interesting, too, are a number of people whose names suggest at least a French ancestry—Samuel Chollet and James Bourdieu,[50] who, named in the petition but not in the Act of 1773, were in fact very large shareholders in the company, and Stephen Caesar Lemaistre. Eight of the proprietors of 1773 were MPs, seven practised, or had been trained in, the law. The Governor of the company was Sir Herbert Mackworth, of the well known family of south Wales industrialists, and the subscription list was headed by Bute's son, John Lord Mountstuart and by Major General Lord Fitzroy.[51]

Work on the Ravenhead factory was already well in progress in July 1774 when notice was given to those who had supplied materials about the settling of their accounts; production began from a pilot plant at the beginning of 1776.[52] Nevertheless, the early operation of the works was not very successful. One set of problems was technological and seems to have related mainly to the employment of coal in the furnaces. This in turn is clearly connected with the French technicians' relative lack of familiarity and facility with coal, a most interesting and complex issue, which we shall deal with later at some length. This led to a production problem of the greatest importance—the proportion of good glass made to the amount of waste created. Much of the enormous amount of waste may have been glass otherwise good but discoloured or spotted by the pollution of a coal furnace, though some probably came from errors in casting, annealing and cutting rather than from errors in furnace management. We know (if from witnesses who may have had an interest in exaggeration) that at certain periods Saint-Gobain made a great deal of cullet and that a high proportion of glasses cast there were broken or inferior.[53] Even at times of bad management, however, it is doubtful if they did as badly as Ravenhead, which, under its first French manager, De La Bruyère,[54] produced only 452 tons of saleable glass out of 1,385 tons of metal.

Jean-Baptiste François Graux—the De La Bruyère appears only after his defection to Britain—was the brother of François Graux, who had earlier defected from Saint-Gobain to a nearby French glasshouse and spent some time in prison at Laon when the Compagnie des Glaces urged the authorities to enforce the laws penalising those who left the firm without permission. Deslandes, the Saint-Gobain director, had a poor opinion of Jean-Baptiste, saying he was as much a 'mauvais sujet' as Besnard 'but absolutely without any kind of knowledge and talent'.[55]

Two men, Couturier and Poirier, accompanied Graux to Ravenhead. Though the works came into production only in 1776, they were already very unhappy the following year. Couturier was endeavouring both to find another place in England, where he wrote to the Cookson works at North Shields, and to obtain readmission to France. He told the North Shields manager that Poirier and he had quarelled with Graux because he did not give them proper wages, though they were able to 'blow and cast and make the metal with any man in England and France'. They thought little of Graux; should they leave, 'these Works here will entirely drop to the Ground for the person who manages the same knows nothing of the nature of working the Glass to Perfection'.[56] In the same year Couturier was in touch with the French ambassador and pleaded for a passport to return to France. Vergennes questioned whether he should be encouraged to return, and the Saint-Gobain company, having consulted its director, stated that Couturier was only a mediocre workman and that it would be a good thing to make him an example by refusing him a passport. Poirier had already offered his services to the company's rival at Rouelles, but apparently they both eventually crept back to Saint-Gobain.[57]

Graux, indeed, may have proved very much a failure, though he was persisted with until his death in 1787, and he certainly did not die in poverty.[58] Johnson's remark that 'in lapidary inscriptions a man is not upon oath' may be particularly true of the epitaph put upon Graux's tombstone by his English friends, local Catholic industrialists: 'He was the first / who brought to perfection / A work of very considerable magnitude / and importance / To the Commercial interest of the British nation / The Cast Plate Glass Manufactory'.[59] We do not know the sources from which Deslandes learned about what went on at Ravenhead, but he was probably nearer the mark when he wrote in 1784:

> the English, with workmen they have debauched from France, have not, despite all their efforts, achieved the perfection of the plates of this Kingdom. This arises firstly by the difficulty in succeeding in the art of casting; secondly, by the impossibility demonstrated and recognised by the English themselves of doing it with coal, in a manner to satisfy the customers.[60]

It was only with the embarkation on large-scale production that the wastage problem came into full perspective. A handful of letters newly available show that the main difficulty experienced at the end of 1775 was in obtaining a copper casting table which was true enough and smooth enough, despite the fact that Mackworth, the governor of the company, was an important figure in the copper industry. Though he had given the most careful specifications, De La Bruyère was seriously disappointed with the one delivered, but he went ahead with the lighting of a furnace in the hopes of producing plates by the end of January 1776. Six months later the defective table was still regarded as the sole technical snag, and another was apparently on order. It is evident that so far production had been deliberately on small scale, and in a pilot plant, but within these limitations things were going well. De La Bruyère's glass was a good colour, and he was proving a good manager and training English workmen so well that he could reject any suggestion of additional recruits from France. Full-scale plant was now needed, but crucible house, fritterie and salt house were yet to be completed and the necessary great hall and large furnace and grinding and polishing sheds were also not ready, perhaps not even begun, while dwelling houses had to be made available as the additional workmen needed were obtained. Affleck regretted that they had not built 'in grand' from the beginning.

De La Bruyère and Affleck may have agreed that no more Frenchmen were required, but clearly all the proprietors were not of their opinion, for in June 1776 a move was afoot to bring over Bosc D'Antic to Ravenhead. He had apparently lost influence after the fall of his patron, Turgot, but was trying to gain the favour of the Minister's successors, and for this purpose wanted to be elected a Fellow of the Royal Society. However, there was opposition to him among Fellows who believed 'he was an imposter who only wanted to be chosen a Fellow, in order to recommend himself to be employed in the Plate Glass'. If, as reported, Deslandes, 'the present chief and Head of the Saint-Gobain Manufactory, though an enemy of D'Antic . . . [had said he] . . . was certainly the first man in Europe for such a work', that astute Frenchman surely had his tongue in his cheek. In the event the Royal Society rejected D'Antic on this occasion by the narrowest of margins, and he was never brought over for the purposes of the Plate Glass Company, though a letter of Affleck's shows that it was touch and go in the late June of 1776. He was very optimistic about the state of Ravenhead, and believed that De La Bruyère was a 'good and faithful servant' and 'carries on his business with good order and good harmony'. On the contrary, he dreaded the introduction of 'such an untoward spirit as D['Antic]'s' at the works, where he was sure to 'depreciate and supplant' De La Bruyère, for 'his best friends represent him as a second, if not first Besnard'. D'Antic's arrival would have certainly caused dissension, and it doubtful whether it would have helped much technically; since he had left Saint-Gobain for Rouelles in the 1750s he probably knew little about the experiments with coal which had been made there. Equally, however, the early, optimistic opinions of De La

Bruyère's capabilities must have changed as huge amounts of unsaleable glass were produced at Ravenhead and financial difficulties increased.[61]

The problems caused by the creation of a very large quantity of waste at Ravenhead were soon remarkably exacerbated by a change in Customs and Excise regulations. Endeavouring to produce more revenue for the war, North in 1777 decided to increase considerably the excise duty placed on the materials entering into glass, while at the same time relieving the industry from customs duty on imported materials, and placing virtually prohibitory duties on the importation of glass. This arrangement, which he thought equitable,[62] was in fact a most damaging one for the British plate glass firm. Though it did not have to compete with imports, its costs of production were forced up sharply. Even when waste glass was used as cullet it would be taxed all over again, as it was the contents of each melting pot that were gauged for tax by the excise men. Some allowance was made by the Excise for wastage, but while this was reasonable for the makers of other types of glass, the amount of waste made at Ravenhead made it inadequate in their case. The company of course appealed to the Commissioners of Excise, who with some propriety replied that 'the inexperience and improper management of the workmen' was at fault, and pleas that extra waste was unavoidable in plate glass manufacture were disregarded.

The early 'eighties, Professor Barker has shown, were dismal ones for the British Plate Glass Company.[63] Its expenditure was greater than its sales, a quarter of the outgoings being in excise. One very serious miscalculation was the failure to grind and polish the glass: the price that unfinished glass could command was much lower. The reasons behind this are not clear; there may have been a parallel with the early days of Saint-Gobain, when the chances of breakage in transit meant that it was better to send the plates to the Paris warehouse unfinished, while a desire to placate the mirror manufacturers may have led to a belief that it was better to allow them the profits of finishing. Eventually the plates from Ravenhead reached the London warehouse at Blackfriars by canal, but before the London linkage was completed the route may have been to Liverpool via the Sankey canal and the Mersey and by coaster to the Thames.[64]

Under its accumulated difficulties the company nearly sank. For some years in the 'eighties casting was abandoned, and the great hall at Ravenhead saw only the blowing of plates, where the wastage allowance of the Excise was more favourable. By comparison with the Compagnie Royale des Glaces the production of the British Cast Plate Glass Company was trivial. A company with a different constitution might in fact have perished, but the effective limited liability given by the Act of incorporation meant that the creditors were less pressing than they might have been. The financial problem was most acute in the early 1790s; the term granted by the 1773 Act was due to expire in 1794, and not only the original subscription of £40,000 had been swallowed up but a loan debt of £60,000 as well. Clearly it was important that the Act should be renewed, but though a Bill passed the Commons in 1794 it went no further.[65] A specious 'State and Estimate of the Stock and Premises of the British Plate Glass Company' was published about this time, claiming that the company's writing down of its assets was overdone. Stocks of glasses had been written down by nearly half and the buildings by two-thirds, and this included new steam-powered plant which it was quite unjustifiable to mark down. Of course the marking down of the firm's property reflected pessimism as to whether the company could continue to make use of it, or had any hope of selling it. The anxiety of shareholders as to what would happen when the Act expired was great, and in the generally depressed conditions following the outbreak of war in 1793, with creditors pressing, the company was induced to put the concern up for sale, but only one—unacceptable —offer was received. The author of the 'State and Estimate' believed that if the prospective Act of 1794 was not obtained 'the Company would have been exposed to go to the hammer'. However, this fate was avoided.[66] Instead an ostensible sale was made to one Thomas Oakes.

The sale was confirmed on 30 September 1794; Oakes is described as being of Upper Wimpole Street. The company, with a total capital of £60,000 and additional debts of £67,530, was put up for sale under certain conditions at the end of August and again early in September. Oakes put in a bid of £105,600, which was accepted, with an immediate down payment of £70,000 in order to discharge the company's debts. But the document of sale shows that Oakes appointed as his attorneys to take possession at Ravenhead Robert Sherbourne and William Forster, the actual managers of the works for the existing company.[67] The reality emerged more clearly when, in 1796, Oakes, about to sail to the East Indies, reconveyed the property to John Grant, on behalf of the company, for ten shillings, and acknowledged that his name, 'both used in the said purchase and in the said written indenture', was in trust. Grant used Sherbourne and Forster as his attorneys in taking possession, and in turn acted as trustee for those who had 'shares and interests in the concern . . . in proportion to their several respective parts'. The British company, therefore, had in Thomas Oakes a man of straw—not unlike its French counterpart.[68] These trustee devices seem somehow to have bridged the gap between the expiry of the original Act in 1795 and the passing of a further Act in 1798 which incorporated a new company with a capital of £100,000, tenable in £100 shares rather than the £500 shares of the former concern. In part the subscribers consisted of some of the former proprietors of the original company, but there was also an increased banking element. Henry Hoare had been a subscriber to the first company, the second had the partners in the houses of Boyd, Benfield and Pybus, Call.[69] The East India element was, if anything, stronger: in 1812 a meeting of the committee was put off because so many members were attending an emergency meeting of the court of the East India Company on the same day.[70] The Mackay connection had disappeared at the formation of the new company.

The bridging period between the Acts was survived because in fact the outlook for the plate glass trade had improved and the technical difficulties which had so long dogged Ravenhead were surmounted. Just as the long favourable period at Saint-Gobain from the late 1750s to the revolution was largely due to Deslandes' management, so much of the improvement and affluence at Ravenhead was due to a new manager, Robert Sherbourne. It should not be overlooked, however, that external factors were also propitious. Competition with France, which had opened under the period of the Eden treaty, was now once again removed under wartime conditions: in any case Saint-Gobain had been hard hit by the dislocation of the revolution and the early stages of the war, and for some time production was at a standstill. The excise was altered in 1787 and for some years was exacted on a basis of square footage of glasses produced over a certain size.[71] When it reverted to a duty on the raw materials by weight in 1794 the effect was no longer so serious as it had been.[72]

VI

Advantageous as were these changes, it is clear that technological improvements, based on a profound alteration that had come over the operations at Ravenhead, had revolutionised the situation. Under De La Bruyère the 'Company, still in an infant state, had to militate under the want of experience' and sustained 'heavy losses . . . by dead expences, experiments and many fatalities well known to every member'.[73] In 1809 the second company pointed out that the works before 1792 had been in a bad state, 'as appears at great length in various complaints of the failure of expensive experiments, the misconduct of managers etc. with which the records of that period are filled'. They associated this change with the arrival at Ravenhead of Robert Sherbourne, who managed the works from 1792 till 1829. Though we can identify some important improvements which antedated 1792, there can be no doubt that his effect was immediate, for a minute of February 1793 records his proposal to double production, and mentions that an important feature was 'a temporary cuvette furnace'.[74]

The loss of the minutes of the company before 1807 means that we have to rely on retrospective eulogies to learn something about Sherbourne's improvements, and thus we unfortunately do not know the order in which they were introduced.

We know a little about his background. He was apparently a Dorsetshire man, but his acquaintance with the company went back to its earliest days. He was the illegitimate son of Admiral the Hon. Robert Digby,[75] one of the earliest shareholders. He had helped to lay the foundations of the Ravenhead works back in 1773, and was accountant there, working closely with De La Bruyère in 1776. Nevertheless, in the early years of the nineteenth century the committee talked of the 'introduction' of Sherbourne as manager in 1792. Possibly, though continuously in the employment of the company, he may have been away from Ravenhead for some years before 1792. From 1800 he may occasionally be glimpsed in the personal correspondence of his friend, Michael Hughes, the general manager of the copper factories of the Anglesey mines, who lived nearby. He was a water-colour artist of moderate talent.

The cuvette furnace trials were in 1792, and their success was such that the committee ordered extensions with a view to doubling production, though this took some years to achieve. Perhaps the most important development in securing the successful adaptation of the French cast plate process to the use of coal was the use of the caped pot. This had been long employed in England and was obligatory in flint glass production, and the French had found it impossible to produce that kind of glass without this essential bit of technology.[76] The use of these domed pots, with a shielded orifice to one side, prevented pollution of the glass in a coal furnace. There had been earlier attempts to employ them: 'The Caped or Covered Pots tho' they had been tried could never be brought to perfection until effected by Mr Sherbourne'. They preserved 'the glass from the great number of black drops which fall into the pots from the roof of the furnace', and this alone made a difference of 'some thousands per annum'.[77] Progress had already been made between De La Bruyère's death and Sherbourne's assumption of management, and wastage of metal reduced from 200 to 100 per cent. But Sherbourne's management reduced this to 25 per cent, so that in the end the company was prepared to encourage the Excise to revert to the measurement of materials once more, on the basis that the excise allowance given for wastage was now greater than the glass lost, so that effectively some duty was escaped. Eight thousand pounds was saved on 'cullet'. This was waste glass which had apparently been made so freely that it had not been possible to use it all up again in the batch, but which it later proved possible to incorporate into a new batch as Sherbourne reduced the wastage. Important, but lesser, sources of saving were in installing equipment to grind up emery for the finishing of the glasses instead of having to buy more expensive ground emery, and the use of local sand instead of that from East Anglia, though this in itself may not have been a qualitative improvement. In his first year Sherbourne raised the production of glass from £17,000 to £20,000 while improving quality, and by 1806 he was making £48,000 worth 'and that of such glasses as had never been made in England'.[78] In 1812–15, following a doubling of the excise in 1812, Sherbourne made another assault on the amount of wastage; it was believed that once this high wartime duty was removed, which so increased prices as to cause a cut-back in production, 'this great reduction in the rate of wastage . . . will probably afford results not less beneficial than what have been derived from all his former great improvements in the Manufactory'.[79]

We are here concerned primarily with the comparable technical changes in the plate glass industries of Britain and France, but it is worth pointing out of Sherbourne that he was spoken of in the same high terms in relation to his general management and to labour discipline in the factory as was the great French director of Saint-Gobain, Deslandes.[80] Though neither carried his technical ability to the point of significant invention, they both clearly possessed the skills of development in a high degree, combining this with organising ability which was quite outstanding. The praises of Sherbourne, and the generous increases of his unusually large salary, show that he was not regarded as an ordinary works manager: indeed, he was a substantial shareholder, which put him immediately on a different basis from a mere technician, however valuable.[81]

VII

The past presumption in accounts of the introduction of the plate glass industry to Britain has been that the great problem was the difficulties faced by a French technique when it was employed not with wood, the fuel customary in French glassmaking, but with the normal English fuel, coal. This view is not wrong, but it needs to be put with greater sophistication. For we are not talking of a French glass industry ignorant or disdainful of coal fuel, but one which, despite problems of coal supply, and without a broad national development of coal-fuel technology (similar to that of Britain) which could be drawn upon for technical support, had nevertheless made increasing use of coal. True, the main employment of coal in the French glass industry was in bottle glass manufacture,[82] where contamination of the glass by impurities in the fuel, the main problem, hardly arose because impurities in the sand employed were going to discolour the product to the point where the damage done by the coal was not significant. Furthermore, bottle glass of a tolerable standard—in a situation where demand was rising, supply inadequate and customers not too fussy—could be turned out without adopting the more refined features of coal-fuel technology with glass. The pots were not caped, the typical English cone was not employed to provide a powerful updraft and to eliminate smoke, and though the air supply came to the fuel largely through the *cave* and under the *grille* of the hearth, there was not the same development of air-access passages. The ability of French glassmakers to produce acceptable bottles without the full battery of English techniques may have been something of a handicap when it came to their attempts to make flint glass[83] or cast plate with coal, and have led at first to a failure to appreciate the greater complexity and sophistication of the process involved, and the necessity for refined and costly furnace equipment.

The use of coal in the French glass industry goes back to the very beginning of the eighteenth century, and an increasing number of bottle works using coal were built as the century went on. From 1723 new glassworks were supposed to require permission to start operations, in order to avoid problems of wood shortage. The entrepreneurs usually claimed in the case of wood-burning glasshouses that they were in an area of ample supply; if possible they claimed that there were local woodlands valueless to their owners unless some fuel-voracious industry could be established there. The bottle glasshouses employing only coal were able to make a strong case as being consistent with this rather laxly enforced policy.[84] In the 1780s, especially under the Calonne Ministry, it seems possible to discern a more positive emphasis on this fuel policy, involving the setting up of the furnace industry inspectorate (*des bouches à feu*) and the very interesting industrial fuel-use census of 1788–9.[85] In this period immediately before the revolution the attitude of the leading technologists was more complex than a mere fuel-saving policy; there seems to have been a recognition that the technological future lay with industrial processes in which, *à l'anglaise*, coal was an integral part.

However, the plate glass industry was not slow to take up the use of coal. According to an early history of the Manufacture Royale des Glaces, coal was being used at the Tourlaville works in 1737,[86] while a later work gives 1740.[87] Such use may perhaps have been in ancillary processes rather than in the furnaces themselves, for there survives a very careful report by Oury, the successful director of the Tourlaville works, written in 1747. The company had asked him to look into the possibility of using coal, and in order to do so he had visited and made a careful report on the *manufacture royale* at Sèvres, outside Paris, an important example of the employment of coal in bottle production. Oury's report is a cautious and factual one, very conscious of the important distinctions between the two products involved, bottle and plate, and the very significant qualitative differences between them. The Tourlaville works, however, were producing blown plate, which did not require as much heat as a cast plate furnace. The report is one of the most important technical documents we possess on the eighteenth-century glass industry and on the use of coal, given that there seems to be no other account of a coal-fired bottle plant in either Britain or France.[88]

Oury first pointed out to his superiors that there was a particular way of building a coal furnace, and that the hall in which one was erected would not be suitable for installing a wood furnace if that failed. He emphasised that the materials for the firebrick for furnace construction depended on particular clays and sands. He was very disturbed by the damage done in a short coal-fired campaign of five and a half months which had destroyed the sieges and burnt away other parts of the furnace interior at Sèvres.

The key element to Oury, however, was the art of stoking a coal-fired furnace, a skill one hears little of in contemporary British documents, because of the long earlier apprenticeship of British industry to the craft of managing coal fires. He describes the importance and the difficulty of acquiring of this knowledge.

> La manière de tiser en charbon a paru à Sr. Oury la partie la plus délicate de ce travail, il s'y est particulièrement attaché, et a travers les mensonges et l'ignorance des divers ouvriers et autres personnes qu'il a consulté et qu'il a interessé tant par le vin que par l'argent ainsi que par le spectacle des divers manoeuvres qu'il a eu la constance de soutenir (non sans peine) tant dans les halles que dans les caves . . . [so as to be assured by the evidence of his own eyes].

He observed the shifts the furnacemen worked, often enormously long, two stokers tending the furnace right through the refining period: [ils] sont bien entretenus et ont beaucoup de peine'. A single furnaceman, the *tiseur de jour*, operated throughout the period when the glass was worked—sixteen or eighteen hours. The long refining period for plate glass would, he thought, require a different working system at Tourlaville. 'Il est hors de doute que la tiserie est la fonction la plus forte et la plus pénible des verreries en charbon et c'est sans doute ce qui fait aussi que cette espèce d'ouvriers s'y trouve plus rare et y est plus recherchée et plus chère'. He goes into great detail, which we cannot follow here, as to how the fire should be maintained by the placing of many compressed layers of small coal on the *grille* during the period when the glass was being worked, when a mass of flame and smoke was to be avoided. He describes the special tools of iron required to deal with clinker, the air flow through the hearth, and the various operations of a coal furnace. He had grave doubts about the effects on the glass due to covering the *grille* with layers of small coal during the glassworking period, on account of 'une fumée très épaisse et noire et de laquelle il apréhende beaucoup de vice pour la verre des glaces'. The unavoidable heat would cause too much ebullition in the glass for a 'matière aussi douce et qui demande autant à estre travaillé dans le repos que la verre des glaces'. He seems to have envisaged a system by which the furnace would have been wood-fired during the glassworking period.

His final remarks conveyed his uncertainty at not having found methods of eliminating all the dangers from coal firing, or being prepared for all possible accidents and teething troubles despite the full application of 'ses lumières et son étude'. His new knowledge was more suited to set up a bottle works than a plate works: he would not himself want to commit the company to the new method, though he would do his best to make it work if he was ordered to try. There was, of course, the question of getting coal; he believed that the export of Newcastle coal was forbidden in England, but other coal from that country was not as good. The company should be certain that it could 'compte sur le charbon de neufchâtel' before it sanctioned the Tourlaville project. He gave the greatest attention to the question of the furnace hands. Their work was so hard and responsible that experts must be found for Tourlaville; the company must not expect to have 'tiseurs en charbon au même prix qu'elle paye ceux qui travaillent en bois'. Workers of the kind wanted at Tourlaville were 'libertins, coureurs et infiniment chers'; one of the two he had in mind from Sèvres was asking 600 livres a year, and it might be better to look elsewhere, 'surtout l'angelterre s'il étoit possible' or to the glassworks of Dombes, Dunkirk, Nantes, Flanders and other places. For furnace builder he recommended that Jean Mol, whom the company had already used, should be employed. Mol had not only built the halls and furnaces in France which worked with coal, but had also instructed the furnace hands of most of the works, including Sèvres; he should be secured by good pay and expenses and tax relief. Despite Oury's doubts his excellent report perhaps proved too good for his own peace of mind: within five days he was ordered to go ahead, authorised to employ foreign workmen if need be, 'in the hope that he will omit nothing that will perfect the carrying out of the project whose utility and necessity is perfectly known to him'.

The last sentence indicates that Tourlaville was already threatened with a wood shortage. Oury seems to have succeeded in converting the main melting furnaces to coal, but apparently Tourlaville never so converted all processes, and wood shortage continued to be a problem. In 1758 we hear of an Englishman, Egleton, at Tourlaville, who is said to have been teaching French workers to use coal, which may imply that success up to then had not been perfect. The works about this time was forbidden to use English coal and had to use the much nearer but more expensive source of Littry. However, the forest of Brix continued to decline, apparently through bad administration, and wood shortage seems to have been an important factor when Tourlaville stopped production at the end of the eighteenth century.[89]

Once coal was being used in the furnaces at Tourlaville it was inevitable that its use at Saint-Gobain should come under discussion. However, the supply of wood fuel for Saint-Gobain was much better, and the forest reserves were greater, so that it was only towards the end of the century that some reduction was forced on the company's Picardy works by the supply of wood fuel.[90] In fact wood remained the main fuel there till 1829 and was not finally dispensed with until 1850.[91] Pressure on the supply side was therefore much less acute at Saint-Gobain than at Tourlaville. In transferring the techniques of coal use from bottle to blown plate works, as between Sèvres and Tourlaville, there had been the problem of moving the technique from a part of the industry producing a low-quality glass to one using a higher, but in which blowing remained an essential technique. This was difficult enough, but in the transference between Tourlaville and Saint-Gobain there was the problem of providing a glass for casting instead—an utterly different method which required glass to be provided at the right moment for a process with a different working rhythm. A further factor inhibiting a rapid take-up of the new method at Saint-Gobain may have been the managerial crisis which the works passed through in the middle 'fifties, when much bad glass was being produced, before Deslandes was given full control in 1758.[92]

It was not long before Deslandes began moving in this direction, however. In 1762 the building of a fifth working hall was projected at Saint-Gobain, and Deslandes felt that this was the time to plan it in 'such a manner that it may work with either coal or wood'; the same size of hall would be needed in either case. To this end he had vaulting put under the furnace and the annealing ovens. 'Moreover this will serve to show those who buy up wood in the countryside that the company is ready to substitute the use of coal for that of wood'—in other words, it would give the wood dealers a fright and help to hold down wood prices. In part the company used cordwood from the *taillis* or copsewood with a twenty-five- or thirty-year cutting cycle; this was regularly replenished as it was cut. But another sort of wood provided a different sort of fuel. The *billettes* came from heavier trees or *futaie*, which were not being properly replenished with the hardwood needed for Saint-Gobain's purposes. 'The coal burnt at Tourlaville makes it evident that one could equally well burn coal at Saint-Gobain. I need hardly say that our establishment is handy for Flanders, where there is excellent coal'.[93]

In fact it seems to have been June 1768 before a campaign was actually

made with coal instead of wood, though it is clear that there were immediate problems in the method of fuelling the furnace; thick black smoke
poured out while it was being stoked, the soot fell back into the hall, the
floor of which became completely black, and the glass when it came out
of the cuvettes was also black. There was again the need to reduce the
activity of the furnace during the periods when cuvettes were to be filled
or removed for casting, and Deslandes was already developing special
fuelling techniques.[94] Thereafter we lose sight of coal firing for a time,
but it was certainly being used extensively in 1770 and 1771. The
furnace in the Belair hall burnt coal continuously from 15 June 1770 to
19 March 1771, and it was proposed to finish the campaign with the
remaining Valenciennes coal and that in transit from the Saint Quentin
depot. At this point, presumably, only one furnace was using coal, for
with its stoppage the remaining coal stock at Saint Quentin was to be
sold off. But at another period two halls were burning coal, the Grande
Halle also being employed, and Deslandes thought to be able to achieve
about four and a half meltings a week. At the time he claimed that,
when squared off, one glass in four was very good, one mediocre and
two bad.[95]

A later undated memorandum by Deslandes says that *for some years*
they had been firing one furnace at Saint-Gobain with Valenciennes
coal, at the rate of 3,000 muids of 920 livres' weight a year. The coal
from the best colliery, Longpré, cost 18 sous 9 deniers local measure at
the pit, but a minimum of 1 livre 10 sous to bring to Saint Quentin and
a further 15 sous to bring through to Saint Gobain. The coal from the
Longpré pit, however, must have been relatively cheap, for the average
price delivered at Saint-Gobain was 3*l* 8*s* 9*d* the measure. The outcome
was that, burning coal at the current rate, one melting would produce
nearly 10,000 livres' worth of small plates, or four meltings in a week
40,000 livres. A campaign in coal, therefore, would cost 20,250 livres
more than one in wood. Some afterthoughts allowed Deslandes to
decrease his calculation for coal consumption slightly, but the cost
factor was still very serious, though he felt that 'the method of burning
coal at Saint-Gobain is still very imperfect'; savings in coal had been
made and more could be hoped for.[96]

Certainly the use of coal did not stop at this point. In May 1773
Deslandes was writing to an important official that he was trying coal
from Forez instead of that of Valenciennes and finding that it burned
more clearly and gave a greater heat,[97] and in the same year he must
have felt confident of success in that his success with coal was made the
basis of an improvement, as we shall see, in his personal status. Nevertheless, by 1784 the use of coal had been abandoned at Saint-Gobain,
and this at a time when the company seems to have been under strong
pressure from the government to use coal. This pressure derived from a

campaign for wood economy and conversion to coal which was marked by the appointment of the inspectors *des bouches à feu*, the influence of technical experts like De Dietrich and Grignon, the concentration of large, State-promoted iron and glass works on the coal of Montcenis, and the fuel enquiry of 1788–9. Deslandes was questioned on the company's annual wood consumption, and the proprietors had to assure the Crown that his figures could be trusted. In a letter of January 1784 he agreed that all kinds of glass could be made with coal and that bottle and flint glass was made with coal as well as the blown plate of Tourlaville.

In order to anticipate the desires of the government the Compagnie des Glaces had spared neither care nor expense over ten years. 'I have put the effort into this that I have given to everything I have done. But we have not been able to succeed. The English have also wanted to try it, and have been even less happy, the technique [*manœuvre*] of casting plates, like the furnaces, being very different from that used in blowing.' The efforts of the local Maîtrise des Eaux et Fôrets to make Saint-Gobain use coal would, if successful, only stop production at the factory, from 'the impossibility recognised by the English themselves, of doing it with coal in a manner to satisfy the customers'.[98]

Deslandes' position over coal smelting is a little curious. He rated highly his achievement in using coal for melting glass at Saint-Gobain, and indeed this was the chief reason for his obtaining a letter of nobility in July 1773. After mentioning the high standing of his family and its services to Church and State, the patent pointed out Deslandes' ability in the sciences, especially mechanics and chemistry, and then emphasised his early work at Saint-Gobain on the mechanics of the casting process by which he made much larger glasses and increased output without increasing the labour force. By a better batch he achieved a 'plus grand netteté et une plus belle eau' in the glass. 'But these first successes were not sufficient for the zeal of the Sr. Deslandes.' His crowning achievement was the search for economy, gained by using coal. It is interesting that the letter states that Deslandes made the change because his plates sold so successfully that increased production, necessitating a greater consumption of wood, foreshadowed a position where the price of wood would increase. So he undertook to change the furnaces, developed an ingenious new plan, 'and by the preparation he learnt to give to coal, he prevented the shortage and dearness of wood, and obtained so large a reduction in the costs of the administration that it put the proprietors in a state where they could reduce the price of plates'.[99] Rather amusingly, the firm treated Deslandes' expenditure in receiving his letter of nobility, and in accepting his separate conferment of the Order of St Michel, as an expense account and reimbursed him! It is very interesting to see that this document of 1773 suggests that

Deslandes' coal experiments did not increase costs in the end, while in 1784 he put the poor quality of glass made with coal as the main problem, though also giving prominence to the greater cost.[100]

Fortunately, in his great 'Memoire' or 'Historique' Deslandes includes a long 'essay on the means of making glassworks coal-fired'.[101] Though this appears in a document which bears signs of having been written just after the turn of the nineteenth century, this section, like others, was put together from memoranda and jottings which Deslandes had preserved from a long working life. An important section is close to what Deslandes had written in a memoir on 'Four au charbon' about his use of coal in 1768; the whole may be largely based on a memoir he wrote in 1784 'to indicate to master glassmakers the means of applying the fire of coal to the melting of glass' to which he attached importance and intended to send to the Academy, of which he was a corresponding member.[102]

In this very important paper, which is unfortunately much too long to discuss in full here, Deslandes says his intention as a patriotic citizen is to help avoid the disastrous destruction of woodlands, though he agrees that it would be ridiculous for works situated in rich forests to convert to coal. Concentrating on the plate glass industry, he tells of his own use of coal and confesses, 'I have not been able to succeed except very imperfectly. The English have tried likewise, and they have spared no expense. They have devoted to it the genius which no one will deny them, and the persistence they give to all they undertake. They have succeeded even less well than I have'. Aware of the use of covered pots by the English in producing crystal and white glass, he seems to have doubted whether the very great heat needed for plate glass could be achieved with the less direct contact of the fire with the vitrifiable materials once they were placed in covered containers.

He begins his description of coal furnaces by making it clear that it is the part below ground which is essential and different. For these furnaces there have to be underground galleries by which the air can reach the furnace, which in the *cave* of the furnace emerge into a circular area or *rond point*. If more than one furnace is installed in a hall the galleries have to be diagonal to the walls, as they focus on each furnace. He goes into remarkable detail about the relationship of the vaults of these air tunnels to the prevailing winds, methods of stopping them up if need be so as to control the air supply, and the way in which their section narrowed as it neared the furnace so as to increase the rate of flow of the air. The vaulting of the *cave*, the position and dimensions of the *grille* of the hearth, and the height of the vault are given and explained. Given the important campaigns of 1771, it is almost certain that Deslandes' furnace building must have been completed and the furnaces alight before any Saint-Gobain worker left for Britain, so that the French defectors may have felt that they already had important information which would assist them to establish a coal-using works in Britain. Under the floor of the Ravenhead casting hall an interesting set of passages survives, and it might be an enlightening exercise for the future to see if these can be shown to be original and to correspond with the pattern of Deslandes. On the other hand we may perhaps find, as archaeological work proceeds on English glasshouses of the seventeenth and early eighteenth centuries, that he was only repeating English practice in other branches of the glass industry.

The essay continues with descriptions of the firebricks used in the hearth construction and the angled iron bars of the hearth, which would facilitate the passage and breaking up of clinker. When he comes to the sieges Deslandes suggests they should be higher above the hearth than in wood furnaces so as to reduce the bad effects of fragments of foreign matter in the coal which fly out and jump into the open pots.

Perhaps the most striking part of the essay is the long section, closely parallel to sections of the Oury document already cited, which deals with the question of how a coal furnace is to be fuelled, and which puts great emphasis on the importance of the skill and technique of the furnaceman, and the completely different method of working from that required with wood. The workmen would normally use coal by stoking vigorously at one end of the hearth and piling up the coal, then doing the same at the other end and waiting until it had burnt well down before refuelling. This was very damaging, however. Initially one got masses of heavy, black smoke from a choked hearth. 'When the pots are not covered the thick smoke passes over the surface of the glass and gives it a yellow and disagreeable colour.' Eventually the fire got going and burned so furiously as to damage pots and hearth, then died down considerably. 'This method, though general, is very bad, with a very heavy fuel consumption and a very uneven heat.' Deslandes then gives 'a method I worked out and which succeeded perfectly for the many years over which I made plate glass with coal'. It resembled normal practice with wood in that there was a rapid alternation between one end of the hearth and the other, a little fuel being added each time. The director had designed a special small shovel in sheet iron with raised edges (much like that used in putting the heated *fritte* in the pots) which would hold a proper quantity of coal. He then divided the *grille* area into sixteen separate sections and, with the aid of a plan (now lost), indicated how every shovelful should be placed on the hearth. 'One must accustom [the furnaceman] to regulate his speed in such a way that when he puts his sixteenth shovelful at point 16 his first shovelful at point 1 is entirely burnt away.' There follows other advice about how to clear clinker from the *grille* with special iron tools, and how to reduce the heat of the fire by beating down layers of coal over the hearth, sometimes adding clinker.

All this indicates that although coal had been used in certain parts of the French glass industry for some time the techniques of using it were still crude; the necessity to spell out the furnaceman's work in this way shows that the French were endeavouring to gain by rationally ordered system what had been a long, virtually unconscious acquisition of craft skill by the English workers over a couple of centuries, its unconscious and craft nature meaning that there is virtually no written evidence about the employment of what were technologically fundamental skills behind the British industrial revolution. In France, of course, there was a much smaller band of coal-using industries from which to gather spin-off, and I have argued elsewhere that the range of possibilities with coal may have helped induce a willingness to innovate and a freedom from unthinking routine in English workers.[103] 'In general,' says Deslandes of the French workmen, '[they] never think out what they have to do. The greater part only act mechanically so as to make a big fire, they have no other secret than to put on a lot of fuel. They obtain the opposite of what they anticipate; the furnace is choked and the flame can be seen emerging a yellowish black, that is to say still containing much combustible material which has not been burned.'

There is some element of ambiguity in the essay. On the one hand Deslandes is proudly exhibiting his own furnace method; on the other he is admitting his failure in terms of good cast plate production with coal. He indicates that his improved method has avoided the staining of the glass by fumes, though not completely. He admits that there is a further grave, unsolved problem, the small explosions of the burning coal which mean that fragments of coal or foreign matter in the coal jump into pots. Technically this may have been the critical unsolved element in Deslandes' long endeavours.[104] Ironically, he knew the answer. He was aware of the use of caped pots in glassworks producing white glass and crystal. Nevertheless the greater difficulty of melting and refining in these pots was an obstacle in plate glass, increased fuel was needed to help melting, which would weaken the glass, and he points out that success was often obtained where the glass contained much lead, as in flint glass. He in fact included a drawing of a covered crucible in the group of plans which accompanied his essay. As far as we are aware Deslandes did not know of the success with caped pots at Ravenhead.

Towards the end of the document there is some useful material on coal and its supply. He claimed to have burnt 'all the coals which are in France' as well as Scottish and English coal; 'unfortunately the last are infinitely superior to ours'. Over two years he had burnt about 12,000 measures of both Valenciennes and Forez coal in each year, together with over 11,000 measures of English coal, which gave a cleaner and clearer fire than either, and melted the glass more rapidly, giving a larger output of better glass. Deslandes' observations on his fuel were very careful: he related the weight of coals in the different coalfields to a standard measure and listed them in terms of their specific gravity.

VIII

While the English producers certainly succeeded with coal, they may have achieved a glass which was distinctly inferior to that produced with wood at Saint-Gobain,[105] just as the French, despite their success in acquiring flint glass production, conceded that theirs was not quite up to the English standard. However, the English achievement was not exhausted by the conversion of furnaces to coal. They brought into the glass industry the latest product of their advanced coal technology in order to mechanise the grinding and polishing of the glass. Ravenhead, in bringing these processes into the glass factory itself instead of leaving them to mirror makers outside, was in part, and probably unknowingly, paralleling Saint-Gobain. For Deslandes had decided to have some grinding and polishing done there rather than at Paris, one reason being that it was the only effective way in which those who produced the raw glass could know the quality of the final product and understand and appreciate the technological problems which their glass created at later stages of production.

Who first thought of the idea is not known, but in 1786 the English company, having begun to grind and polish its own glass instead of sending it out from the works unfinished, approached the firm of Boulton & Watt to do it by steam: they already used a steam engine for some purpose, as well as a windmill for grinding materials. On 28 April of that year Watt warned the governor, Sir Herbert Mackworth, in a beautifully characteristic letter, that an order for a double-acting engine would take longer. 'Your engine would have been in hand before now but I understood it was determined to be a double one, and I have not yet hit off a plan for that sort of engine that pleases me and I do not wish to do things imperfectly. Before an unexceptionable plan of that kind can be made it will require much meditation and contrivance.' A single engine could be put in their existing house, even with a 60 in. cylinder, but 'a double one will require a new house'. For the former everything could be prepared at once, 'but if you fix upon a double one I cannot be hurried, as I am not able to obviate all the faults of that construction till God enlarges my ideas upon it'. In September 1786 a letter makes it clear that it was thought that a very large engine was needed, and it was to grind glass.[106]

There matters seem to have rested until the late winter of 1788, when Boulton informed his partner that he had attended a committee of the company, 'but after all I found they knew not what they wanted', so that matters were to be left over for some months until Watt could accompany two of the committee to Ravenhead and look at the problem on the spot. However, they knew what they wanted to the extent that an engine was desired to do the work of 100 men by grinding and polishing glass, and by grinding up 200 tons of barilla a year and the same weight of clay.[107] After some delay Boulton & Watt were invited to meet Mackworth and Affleck at Ravenhead about the beginning of August.[108] Thereafter events moved quickly, and on 1 September a draft agreement was signed for an engine at an annual licence premium of £70.[109] The whole operation depended on Watt's ability to work out a mechanical polishing system, for which he appears to have made no charge whatever. Working notes of 7 August survive in Watt's hand, probably made on his return from Ravenhead, in which he calculated that a 14 h.p. engine would power ten grinding tables and their related polishers in two workrooms, one above the other.[110] A few weeks later he wrote, 'We had previously begun to plan the machinery for grinding and polishing but for want of a sufficient knowledge of the business are not proper judges of what may suit in point of convenience.' George Mackay and Mr Forster from the finishing department came over to Birmingham to lend their advice; nevertheless, it seems that it was Watt who did the 'contriving' while they gave the specifications. Watt found that 'to do the job completely and well turns out more difficult than appeared at first.' He was not sure whether the glasses in passing over each other should move in an ellipse or circle; he had to find out how to be able to stop each separate glass being ground without stopping all the others 'and to set it going again without shock which is a matter of great difficulty but I have some hopes'.

The problem was not quickly resolved. In June 1789 the engine parts were nearly ready but Watt had still not completed the design of the machinery it was to drive. He had found out that the glasses had to move circularly and not elliptically and proposed to use cranks from upright shafts, each of which would move a frame rotating four glasses. Watt, however, felt, 'we shall fall into errors if we attempt to settle the matter without the advice of professional men' and wanted Forster and the millwright who would build the machinery at Ravenhead to come to Birmingham. 'I am sorry to give you the trouble, but . . . the subject is foreign to our general business.' He wished Forster 'to be satisfied before he went and the sketches made so far that nothing may occur afterwards to render any part impracticable'.[111]

Apparently nothing did. The plant was put into operation later in the year, and in 1790 Watt was pleased to hear that the engine worked well and enquired about the polishing machinery, though the company's lack of comment on it was perhaps a sufficient, if ungracious, indication.[112] A few years later a careful observer described the grinding and polishing equipment as 'a very curious piece of mechanism, and not only saves a great deal of labour, but does the work with more exactness and expedition. The invention is said to perform as much work as would employ 160 men.'[113]

A member of the Saladin family, influential in the affairs of Saint-Gobain, visited Ravenhead soon after the end of the wars and inspected the steam-powered grinding and polishing ('here is the principal perfection of the manufacture and one may almost say the only one'), of which he proposed to have a model made for the French firm. The grinding benches, of which there were fourteen, were driven in pairs by the steam engine; the polishing shop, where very exact results were obtained, was largely operated by women. Saladin went on to admire and examine the engine itself, with its iron beam and its speed regulated by a governor. Saint-Gobain had some machinery for polishing at its Chauny works, but the complex movement of Watt's machinery was more sophisticated.

They take care to show in this workshop a French plate compared with the polish of an English plate, the first is dull, the other of a fine brilliance . . . The limited thickness of the small as well as the large plates struck me; I am tempted to think that it is this circumstance, joined to the more careful polishing, which gives their plates a more exact image of objects and a fine reflection.[114]

In 1827 the Saint-Quirin company, a rival of Saint-Gobain, though later to merge with it, was concerned that Saint-Gobain had obtained grinding and polishing machinery through Hall, a celebrated Dartford ironfounder whose firm still flourishes. In doubt whether to follow suit or to develop a new process by a technician already known to them, they sent a M. Desrousseaux to England, where he eventually obtained entry to the Thames Plate Glass Works but not to Ravenhead, though he conversed with Sherbourne. The outcome of his visit is not certain, but it is clear that one of the advantages which the British possessed was in their finishing machinery. Saint-Gobain, whose finishing machinery was not working too well, had paid an enormous amount for it. Hall had suborned foreman and workers from the Thames company in order to enable him to design the Saint-Gobain machinery, but the Saint-Quirin firm could get the same equipment from him for a fraction of the cost.[115]

Technological transference between France and England in the eighteenth and nineteenth centuries frequently depended on the facility with which industrial espionage could be conducted, the possibility of the enticing away or *débauchement* of workers, the effectiveness of security precautions on either side. The verdict must probably be that a deep enough purse and sufficient assiduity could always achieve its immediate object, the gaining of a specific piece of information or an individual workman or manager of the type desired. The repeated breaches of the privileges of the Compagnie des Glaces within France show that this was the case from an internal point of view; if the occasional imprisonment did not prevent desertions and leakages within the home country it would hardly, in the long run, prevent them within Europe. At one level the intellectual tendencies of the period made it seem that it was illiberal and unenlightened not to show persons of acknowledged social status or scientific pretensions round the more celebrated industrial enterprise in either country. At another, key workers and lesser managers were rarely well enough paid to be insusceptible to a heavy bribe, the promise of a wealthier or more privileged life in another country, or, in the case of minor pieces of information, generous treatment at a local public house or cabaret. War between England and France might sometimes make the transference of information or the movement of people difficult, but it did not make it impossible.

Deslandes, as we have seen, was himself approached and offered a position with one of the prospective British companies. In the case of Besnard we have a junior manager who had been perhaps harshly treated by Deslandes and eventually dismissed by him; such disaffected persons were always at risk to the temptations of desertion abroad. J.-B. Graux (self-styled De La Bruyère) belonged to a family which had already shown disloyalty to the Compagnie des Glaces and been punished and humiliated for it. The lesser skilled workmen, Couturier and Poirier, were able to get away to England. Quickly deciding that they disliked Ravenhead, they applied for alternative employment at South Shields and were able subsequently, despite opposition from Deslandes, to make their way back to France, and finally, apparently, to Saint-Gobain. The necessity to move technical men between countries in order to have successful technological transference was perhaps almost absolute at that time, when the manual and craft element was still large even in the most sophisticated and mechanised processes; it has not ceased to be a desideratum nowadays. However, the dissatisfied, the footloose and the disaffected were not necessarily the best employees to acquire, or the ones most likely to survive the difficult days of industrial innovation. They lacked the patience to face teething troubles, or to work alongside men trained in an alien industrial tradition. They were unlikely to stay the pace where, as in an industry with a metallurgical or chemical base, almost every raw material available and every building material employed had subtle differences in its properties and working characteristics, and was unlike those with which they were familiar.

In the case of the Compagnie des Glaces there were not merely the general regulations against defecting workers to fall back on, but specific regulations made by the government in the company's favour. An *arrêt de conseil* of 1701 forbade *gentilshommes verriers* and other workers to leave the manufacture, or glasshouse proprietors and other persons to receive them on pain of fines and damages. In 1713 workers were again forbidden, under penalty of corporal punishment, to leave the concern without a discharge note from the governing committee, which they had to ask for two years in advance! They were not to go more than a league from the factory without a chit from the director.[116] The company carefully filed amongst its papers the general *arrêt* and letters patent of 1749, which forbade the 'compagnons et ouvriers' of the kingdom to leave their employers without a written discharge, to depart without finishing the work on which they were engaged, or to combine against their masters. The archives similarly contain copies of letters of Vergennes and Calonne in the mid-1780s which are concerned with the enticement of French workers abroad together with their tools and secrets, and refer to the situation in the Cambrésis, where a liaison between the English and local workers was well established.[117]

Both the French and the British companies did their best to keep the industrial spy, and even the inconveniently nosey, out of their works. Of course, proprietors had to hasten down to Saint-Gobain to prepare a red-carpet treatment for the Controller General when he proposed to visit their main plant in 1774.[118] Nor was it possible (as we have seen) to prevent a tour by Lord Mansfield and another British peer about the same time, even though Mansfield was apparently interested in one of the British firms endeavouring to set up a plate glass company. They had been able to obtain letters of introduction from Mme Geoffrin; not merely did this prove their acceptability in terms of the inner circle of international intelligentsia to whom so many contemporary doors were so readily opened, but Mme Geoffrin was a major shareholder, to whose good opinion Deslandes believed his directorship was due.[119] Nevertheless, Deslandes was relieved that the works was not casting on that day. That this was not the normal degree of freedom can be seen from an incident at Tourlaville in 1777, where the unfortunate director, Dupuis, had peremptorily refused access to the Chevalier Grignon. The latter was being employed by the government on general industrial and technological enquiries, and it was he who subsequently persuaded the government to set up the inspectorate of furnace industries. Though 'M. Grignon insistat; menaçat même', he was denied entry. The company tactfully defended its manager: he had been acting under orders because of 'divers particuliers suspects, qui avaient cherché à s'introduire dans nos fabriques pour emporter les procédés dans les pays étrangers'. He could be admitted if it was clear he had 'quelque commission du Gouvernement analogue aux Arts'.[120]

The Ravenhead works was carefully guarded in its early days, but after a somewhat slacker period security became very tight. In 1790 an announcement was made in the public press about the works:

> The British Plate Glass Company, having experienced many inconveniences by the admission of strangers to view the Works at this place, they are much concerned to be under the necessity of enforcing the order on the gate of the Works, and that the public may not be offended at this apparent rigour, they are informed that the proprietors themselves are deprived of the pleasure of seeing the Works, without an order of admission from the Committee in London.[121]

Eighteen years later proprietors who wanted to visit the works, apart from the handful who conducted the annual official inspection, had to give ten days' notice.[122] That some visiting of a limited nature was, however, occasionally permitted can be seen from a minute of 1816, when a customer was allowed to visit Ravenhead by a letter 'authorising his seeing such parts of the Manufactory into which Strangers are admitted who go recommended by the Committee'.[123] Perhaps the perspicacious M. Saladin was allowed in under the same rule in that year. Such precautions, we have noted, did not prevent the acquiring of the Watt polishing and grinding machinery by other concerns; the suborning of workmen was probably easy enough. However, the great secret of all glassmen, the precise composition of their 'batch', remained so long a personal possession of Sherbourne that with his advancing years the company became terrified that it would die with him. The governor in visiting Ravenhead asked the manager to list

> the materials and the proportions thereof which he used for making his Glass, the Quality, Colour etc. being universally approved of; and it is proper [they delicately put it] in case of accident to Mr. Sherbourne that the Company should be possessed of the particulars of the ingredients he has employed in making it—Mr. Sherbourne has in consequence forwarded to him a list which is now sealed up (to be lodged in the Company's strong box) not to be opened but in the event of Mr. Sherbourne's death, or his resignation of his charge at Ravenhead.[124]

IX

Through the examination of two of the greatest industrial enterprises of the eighteenth century, one French and one English, each the sole national example of its branch of industry over long periods, we have attempted to illuminate some of the problems of industrial management in the eighteenth century, and particularly some technological ones. In this case the process of diffusion and of learning was a double one; Britain had to learn the technique of casting plate glass, in which she was about a century behind France; France had to learn the technique of using coal in glass furnaces. The achievements on either side were considerable. Benefiting from the earlier acquisition of English coal-using methods by the bottle glass branch of the industry, the Compagnie des Glaces was able to adopt these to making blown plate, though they never entirely freed the relevant works at Tourlaville from the use of wood. At Saint-Gobain it essayed the further step of changing the cast plate branch also to coal. Though the company built much more sophisticated furnaces, especially in terms of air supply, and further developed the level of skill of the furnacemen, in the end, after ten years' effort, success eluded it. The ten years' perseverance indicates how potentially important the transfer to coal was felt to be; the subsequent reduction in the furnaces employed shows that available forest resources put a ceiling on Saint-Gobain production. The price of coal—often enormously enhanced by transport costs—and its poor quality might eventually have proved factors too adverse to have been overcome. But they were not finally decisive in the sense that no new method of production will be persevered with indefinitely if it cannot be mastered technically, and in the end Deslandes had to admit technical failure. The failure was qualified in that Deslandes believed that his new coal-using methods would be of great use to other kinds of glassworks, but for cast plate glass they did not come up to scratch.

Nevertheless, when we come to examine the fairly successful transfer of French methods to Ravenhead, we have to recognise that the French technicians had not come from an industry totally ignorant of coal technology, and that, though we know little enough about the individuals concerned, it is highly probable that they knew a good deal about the preparations and trials that had been going on at Saint-Gobain since 1762 with a view to using coal. Even so, they were no more successful than Deslandes had been in producing good cast plate. The precise point of breakdown cannot be exactly pinned down, but it was very probably the covered crucible. Deslandes knew about this device, but perhaps not in time; in any case he doubted whether enough furnace heat could be produced to melt thoroughly glass which the flame was not able to reach directly. This suggests that Deslandes' furnaces might have been hotter if he had further improved his furnace draught by putting a chimney over the furnace, as at Ravenhead. He certainly felt that the French crucible production was capable of improvement; he made searches for clays with a *tarrière anglaise*, he proposed dedicating some of his retirement to nationally meritorious research into the where-abouts of good fireclays, and to experiments with them. At Ravenhead, then, the critical problem may have been how to use caped pots successfully, but this will have been in turn bound up with questions like the design of furnaces to achieve a range of temperatures only possible with coal and with the making of crucibles capable of standing such temperatures. Here, after French influence had disappeared, English technicians succeeded by incorporating methods already long established in other English coal-using glass furnaces.

Even so, there are other technical matters where we would wish to know more. Sherbourne seems to have refined his glass after the initial melting in a special furnace which contained the *cuvettes*, small cisterns filled from the main crucibles which were eventually swung by crane over the casting table, and from which the glass was poured out. Exactly how he prevented pollution from coal fuel at this stage is unclear. Again, but not initially, he pioneered the use of cast iron casting tables. These replaced the very expensive cast copper type with which Saint-Gobain persisted because of the poorer iron foundry expertise in France.

Finally, the case for technological comparison is perhaps rather clearer in the case of these large and celebrated French and English units because we are reasonably sure that general managerial incompetence did not finally stand in the way of technological implementation in either case. Deslandes and Sherbourne were at the top of the managerial profession in their respective countries. They both took over after periods of technical inefficiency and commercial difficulty and created an era of progress, confidence and stability in each company. Both took the broadest view of the economy and technology of the industry and were as concerned to cut raw material costs by good purchasing policy as they were to get the central furnace processes right or to invigilate the final preparation of the cast glass and its safe removal to distant warehouses. Both received admiring tributes for their handling of labour; both paid particular attention to housing their workers.[125] Deslandes and Sherbourne took some interest in science and were interested, as far as the scientific knowledge of their times enabled them to be, in the possibility of new chemical processes which might aid the glassmaker. But Sherbourne, while willing to pick Lord Dundonald's brains over alkali making, would not commit himself to his processes; Deslandes, while realising that it did his own reputation no harm to be thought to have scientific leanings, preserved a strong scepticism about the real contribution of science to glassmaking.[126] We must regret that Sherbourne's continuance in office to perhaps too advanced an age and his devotion to painting mean that we have no memoirs of his to set beside Deslandes' magnificent account of the Compagnie des Glaces and his role as director of Saint-Gobain. Even without it, it is to be hoped that this attempt at a technological comparison of the work of the two firms will have been interesting enough to prompt a further and fuller enquiry as work now proceeding in both countries provides new facts and insights, that the comparative industrial archaeology of Ravenhead and Saint-Gobain will be examined while eighteenth-century buildings still stand, and that similar comparative studies in other industries may be thought worthwhile.

NOTES

1 Strictly speaking we should talk of the Compagnie or Manufacture Royale des Glaces and of the British Cast Plate Glass Co. or the British Plate Glass Co. However, the French enterprise had as its most famous unit the Saint-Gobain works which gives its name to the present successor firm, the Compagnie de Saint-Gobain. Ravenhead was the sole manufacturing plant of the successive British companies and it is fittingly the site of the headquarters of Pilkington Brothers Ltd. today.

2 The outstanding recent study is François Crouzet, 'England and France in the eighteenth century: a comparative analysis of two economic growths'. The English version is in R. M. Hartwell, *The Causes of the Industrial Revolution in England* (1967), pp.139 ff., a French version is in *Annales*, 11, 2, (1966).

3 This paper has been possible only because of the assistance and co-operation of friends and colleagues in France and England. M. Dominic Perrin has facilitated my use of the rich archives of the Compagnie de Saint-Gobain and his encouragement and hospitality have been much appreciated. M. Pris and M. Thépot have discussed certain issues with me and M. Pris has set me right on several important points of eighteenth century documentation. I have had the opportunity of talking over certain issues with Professor Crouzet and owe to him some valuable introductions. Miss Pemberton has given me every help as Pilkington's archivist and as a researcher in the field. With Professor T. C. Barker and Dr D. W. Crossley I have been able to examine some of the difficulties of eighteenth century glass technology. Mr Leonard Schwarz has retrieved valuable information from obscure sources with flair and rapidity. Nevertheless, the source material is far from exhausted and this study can only be regarded as exploratory. The writer is grateful for a Social Science Research Council grant towards research into British and French technology and industry in the eighteenth century.

4 The original Bill of 1773 was 'strongly opposed' when before Parliament 'on the grounds of introducing a dangerous precedent, and on that of the governing principle on which the Bill was framed; namely, not being liable to pay more than a certain sum, and at the same time being at liberty to extend their credit as far as it might go'. *The History, Debates and Proceedings of Both Houses of Parliament*, VII, p.420.

5 T. C. Barker and J. R. Harris, *A Merseyside Town in the Industrial Revolution* (1954 and 1959), p.116.

6 Among early shareholders were Bute's son, Lord Mountstuart, Major General Fitzroy (later General and Baron Southampton), two members of the Affleck family, one later an Admiral and another a General, Thomas, later Lord Dundas, and the Hon. Robert (later Admiral) Digby.

7 Near Cherbourg.

8 In Picardy.

9 In a work published in 1807, when the dimensions were probably unaltered from the original, the casting hall was given as being 200 feet long and 78 feet wide. John Britton, *The Beauties of England and Wales*, IX, p.227.

10 A writer in 1795, trying to emphasise the value of the firm's assets at a time of financial difficulty wrote to the contrary. 'The Company's buildings are not to be compared with those whose owners build to gratify their vanity: with them all the value consists in the taste or elegance of the buildings: in the Company's every inch is of use; their object is *labour*, their effect is Profit . . .' While not comparable with (say) the Cristallerie de la Reine at Le Creusot (later converted into the family mansion of the Schneiders) Ravenhead was a cut above the average British glass-works in appearance. The manager's house and stabling (now offices) survive, and a section of the original casting hall stood until burnt down in 1974.

11 Commissioned by Pilkington Brothers Ltd.

[12] For a very general discussion of this question see J. R. Harris, *Industry and Technology in France and England* (University of Birmingham printed lecture, 1971).

[13] *Compagnie de Saint-Gobain 1665–1965* (Draeger Frères, Paris, 1965, published for the company). This tercentenary history is later cited as TCH.

[14] Archives Nationales (subsequently AN) F12 1490. A memoir of 1732 says that Lucas, Sieur de Nehou, a Norman gentleman, founded a works for fine white glass and also for *glaces à miroirs* at Tourlaville in the Generality of Caen. His nephews De Bonval and de Nehou succeeded him and the latter was the Lucas de Nehou who made a success of casting at Saint-Gobain.

[15] W. C. Scoville, *Capitalism and French Glassmaking 1640–1789* (California, 1950), p.34.

[16] The Bernard Perrot of Orléans who is sometimes credited with the development of cast plate was perhaps only responsible for inventing the casting of ornamental glass. His superb cast glass portrait of Louis XIV hangs in the Saint-Gobain offices Neuilly and is illustrated in their commemorative volume. But the fact that though specifically debarred from casting mirrors he was later paid a small pension by the Compagnie des Glaces may mean that he had contributed something. In the eighteenth century de Nehou was usually given the credit for the new process.

[17] Scoville, *op. cit.*, p.27.

[18] TCH, pp.20–6.

[19] Deslandes, 'Historique de la verrerie'. Two versions and at least three copies of this immensely important work exist, which must be among the most valuable documents for the history of industry in the eighteenth century, combining in different degrees and in different parts factual history, autobiography, industrial and technological analysis and proposals. I have used mainly the version in the Archives Nationales (26 AQ1) 'Essai historique sur la fabication des glaces'. This is a draft in the hand of Deslandes, the great manager of Saint-Gobain from the late 1750s to the Revolution, and is at times hard to read and contains many passages which have been crossed out. These are sometimes omitted in the copy I have used in the Saint-Gobain archives which however contains much additional material, and is over 450 pages long. Though I have compared my rough translation of the Archives Nationales copy with the relevant passages in one of the Saint-Gobain copies time has prohibited an exact collation of the texts. When quoting these papers I have referred to the Archives Nationales version as A and the Saint-Gobain one as B.

[20] Deslandes (A), 'List of letters patent'.

[21] Deslandes (A), 'Plate glass works set up in France without government authority'.

[22] *Ibid., loc. cit.*

[23] For Paul Bosc D'Antic see his *Œuvres* published in two volumes in 1780 and the articles in the *Dictionnaire universel* (1810), *Biographie universelle* (1854–65), *Dictionnaire de Biographie Française* (1854) and *Nouvelle biographie générale* (1862). The last perhaps takes him too much at his own valuation. A critical account of his contribution to the production of a better soda is in *Encyclopédie méthodique*, 'Arts et métiers méchaniques' (8 vols., 1781), III, *sub Glacerie*. A pamphlet warfare between D'Antic and the Compagnie des Glaces in the late 1750s survives relating to his dismissal and supposed financial claims on the Compagnie des Glaces. For his proposed recruitment for Ravenhead, see below, p.42.

[24] Deslandes (A), 'Spanish plate glass'.

[25] *Ibid.*, 'Manufacture of plate glass in Germany'.

[26] Archives, Compagnie de Saint-Gobain (subsequently ASG), articles of Agreement made between le Sieur George Ravenscroft and Jean Burrough, 20 October 1673.

[27] T. C. Barker, *Pilkington Brothers and the Glass Industry* (1960), pp.44–5. It is interesting that the Vauxhall glasses were being cast at the time that Tourlaville works was temporarily closed and some workers were coming to England.

[28] The visitor was Dr Roux, one of the *savants* in whom the Compagnie des Glaces put rather naive trust. He was engaged at a salary of 3,000 livres a year in 1765 to 'travailler à la perfection des glaces en tant ce qui concerne l'art de la chimie, et les sciences'. His London report was at first accepted and carefully studied with some approval, but not uncritically, by Deslandes, who later disparaged him. 'Le docteur Roux, comme tant d'autres, venu à St Gobain pour perfectionner la fabrique dont il n'avait aucune idée ... fit un voyage à Londres, et donna sur la

glacerie anglaise un détail très succinct et très resserré, qui montroit qu'il ne l'avait pas vue'. This view may be too severe. ASG, deliberations, 6 April 1765; Deslandes, 'Historique' (B). As Roux only appears in the Saint-Gobain records in the 1760s I presume his London visit was at this period.

29 *House of Commons Journal*, xxxiv, 24 February 1773, evidence of Mr James Christie, Auctioneer. In 1771, 'the desire to increase the sales of plate glass abroad' induced the Compagnie des Glaces to reduce, by 10 per cent, its charges on plates of over eighty inches (*pouces*) destined for England (ASG deliberations, 19 February 1771). There was a further 5 per cent reduction in the following year (*ibid.*, 17 July 1773)

30 Deslandes had apparently been tough with Besnard as a trainee. In 1762 it was said that he 'n'entend pas assez la partie de la Novice, il lui faudroit un peu plus de Douceur pour M. Morin et Besnard. Il [Deslandes] lui manque de la tête intelligent . . .' Besnard was learning the business well and might be the person to succeed Deslandes in the event of his death. But it was noted of Besnard 'Il a besoin d'être tenu de près. Il ne dit pas ce qu'il pense.' Such unfavourable judgements on Deslandes quickly died away, and indeed some documents of the late 1750s already praised him greatly, and later (see p.70, n.125) he was clearly held in high regard (ASG, C7, memorandum of September 1762).

31 Deslandes (A), 'English plate glass'.
32 PRO, SP/44/2664, p.467.
33 PRO, SP/44/380, pp.151–2.
34 P. Manuel, *La Police de Paris dévoilée* (An II), pp.247–8.
35 Deslandes (A), 'English Plate Glass'.
36 Patent No. 1332, 10 October 1782, alembic lamp or lantern.
37 Pilkington Brothers Ltd., group archives (subsequently PGA), PH 1.
38 Patent No. 1104, 26 February 1776.
39 Louis Dutens (1730–1812): see DNB and L. Dutens, *Mémoires d'un voyageur qui se repose* (2 vols., 1806), II, pp.22, 211. Neither source mentions the de Brûges and Besnard episode.
40 Deslandes (A), 'English plate glass'. For Beaumarchais' movements see Louis de Loménie, *Beaumarchais et son temps* (2 vols, 1873) I, pp.416, 434 ff.
41 PGA, PH1.
42 Deslandes thought that the higher wages of English workers would make English plate glass necessarily dearer. He told Lord Mansfield and his companion 'that given the manner in which the French and English lived . . . they could never make plate which could enter into competition with ours for the price. Our Frenchmen eat soup with a little butter and vegetables. They scarcely ever eat meat. They sometimes drink a little cider but more commonly water. Your Englishmen eat meat, and a great deal of it, and they drink beer continually in such a fashion that an Englishman spends three times more than a Frenchman.'
43 Thirty tons in one version.
44 The Besnard–de Brûges prospectus intended for the Duke of Northumberland refers to an arrangement by which 10,000 louis are subscribed by English shareholders and a similar amount by French. A marginal note, presumably not on the duke's copy, reads, 'It is preferred that the Company should be composed entirely of Frenchmen'. This was hardly a realistic attitude.
45 13 Geo. III, cap. 38.
46 J. R. Harris, 'The origins of the St Helens glass industry', *Northern History*, III, 1968, pp.105 ff.
47 For Mackay see Barker and Harris, *op. cit.*, pp.34–5 ff.
48 This subject, partly covered in *ibid*, pp.112 ff., is now being investigated in greater detail by Miss P. Pemberton.
49 General Sir James Affleck wrote in 1829 in a letter to the company about 'the concern itself having originated in my family', PGA, British Plate Glass Company minutes, 20 May 1829.
50 Bourdieu, in 1763, was a merchant in Lime Street, London, trading with France, Chollet at the same address traded with St Eustachia; in 1770 and 1774 the firm is given as Bourdieu and Chollet. The firm performed important services as financial agents and grain purchasers in London for the French government, especially under Necker (*Mortimer's Directory*, 1763; *London Directory*, 1770 and 1774; *Halden's*

Triennial Directory, 1803). Between the 1760s and 1790 the firm acted as unofficial agents to the French government. They were wheat exporters, and acted as Necker's agents in buying English grain on more than one occasion, and also assisted in obtaining silver for the purposes of the French East India Company on the London market. Bourdieu corresponded with Terray on Anglo–French colonial affairs. H. Lüthy, *La Banque protestante en France*, II (1961), pp.240, 382–7.

51 Lord Mansfield does not appear among the shareholders or petitioners, and his role remains an enigma. His meeting with Deslandes may have been in 1774 when he visited France on a secret mission; DNB; *Gentleman's Magazine*, 1774, p.440. On the other hand the reference may be to a person holding the title at a date subsequent to the events mentioned by Deslandes. Mansfield's nephew and heir, Lord Stormont, was ambassador to France from 1772–8, succeeding to the title in 1793.

52 *Gore's Liverpool Advertiser*, 19 August 1774; T. C. Barker, *op. cit.*, p.47.

53 Particularly D'Antic's lawsuit with the Compagnie des Glaces.

54 Barker, *op. cit.*

55 Deslandes (A), 'English plate glass works'. We do not know how or exactly when Graux was recruited by the last Plate Glass Company.

56 Northumberland Record Office, ZCK 8.

57 Deslandes, *loc. cit.*, E. Frémy, *Manufacture Royale des Glaces de France*, pp.349–51.

58 Lancashire Record Office, will, 17 April 1788.

59 From the tomb in St Helens Borough Cemetery; the grave was part of the old Catholic burial ground at Windleshaw Abbey, a ruined pre-Reformation chantry. Born at Saint Gobain, Graux died at Ravenhead on 5 December 1787, aged 47.

60 Deslandes (A), *loc. cit.* Also Deslandes to Marigny, 23 January 1784, AN O'1992A.

61 Neath Antiquarian Society, Mackworth papers. De La Bruyère to Mackworth, 21 December 1775; Philip Affleck to Mackworth, 2 June 1776; James Mowbray to Mackworth, 19 June 1776; Affleck to Mackworth, 23 June 1776; Mowbray to Mackworth, 27 June 1776; Hutton to Mackworth, June 1776.

62 See his speech in the Budget debate 1774.

63 T. C. Barker, *op. cit.*, pp.47–8.

64 Alternatively the glasses may have been sent by Sankey and then Trent and Mersey to the Trent and thence to the Humber and finally coastwise to London. This would have involved several transhipments.

65 Barker, *op. cit.*, pp.48–9.

66 PGA, BP 1, *A Correct State and Estimate of the Stock and Premises of the British Cast Plate Glass Company* (anon., n.d., *c.* 1794).

67 PGA, PB 147/31, indenture tripartite, 30 September 1794.

68 PGA, PB 147/31, indenture tripartite, 24 March 1796. Oakes, however, was a man of means, having risen from writer to senior merchant at Fort St George between 1770 and 1782. In 1804 he was senior member of the Board of Revenue.

69 38 Geo. III, cap. 90. The title of the company was now simply 'The British Plate Glass Company', omitting the word 'Cast'.

70 PGA, minutes of BPG Co., 26 March 1812.

71 Even so, this was not fully acceptable to the company because of vexatious definitions by the Excise of how the glass ought to be cut to meet the new regulations. (Customs 48/26: Plate Glass Company to Hawkesbury, 25 April 1809.)

72 S. Dowell, *History of Taxation and Taxes*, IV, pp.290–303.

73 PGA, *A Correct State and Estimate*, p.8.

74 PGA, minutes of BPG Co., 19 April 1809.

75 Digby died in 1815. The fact that Sherbourne's water colour drawings survive in Manchester Central Reference Library and that Derbyshire landscape was heavily represented formerly gave me the erroneous impression that his main associations were with that county. Sherbourne lived from 1756 to 1836 and married, as his first wife, a Bedfordshire heiress, Sophia Cator; his second wife was Margaret Dorothea Willis of the Lancashire mercantile and landed family of Halsnead. He was granted or adopted a coat of arms based on that of the Digby family: E. Axon, 'Sherborne's [*sic*] Derbyshire views', *Journal of the Derbyshire Archaeological Society*, XLIII, 1921, 19–21. See also Neath Antiquarian Society, Mackworth papers, Affleck to Mackworth, 2 June 1776.

76 AN, F.12, 1486.

77 PGA, minutes of BPG Co., 12 April 1815.
78 *Ibid., loc. cit.*
79 *Ibid.*, 1 March 1815.
80 See, p.70, n.125.
81 PGA, minutes of BPG Co., 19 April 1809. In the entry for that date the Governor minuted. 'Mr Sherborne [*sic*] being on a different footing from a common manager, not only from the services he has tendered, but as holding so many shares as a proprietor, that I wish it to be clearly understood that the salary and advantages which he enjoys is not to be considered as a precedent for any future manager, the business of the manufactory being brought to such a state of perfection that it goes on like clockwork.' Sherbourne's salary was successively raised from £500 to £700 and to £1,000 per annum and he retired on an annual pension of £500.
82 Scoville, *op. cit.*, pp.11–14.
83 AN, F. 12, 1486.
84 Scoville, *op. cit.*, p.60, and see pp.56 ff.
85 AN, F. 12, 680.
86 E. Frémy, *op. cit.*, p.253.
87 TCH, p.39.
88 What follows is taken from ASG, 'Observations faites à la Verrerie de Sèvres par le Sr. Oury directeur de la glacerie de Tourlaville'.
89 M. de Bouard (ed.), *Histoire de la Normandie* (1970), p.311.
90 Towards the end of the century wood supplies were only sufficient to keep two furnaces going indefinitely, though three had been maintained in the 1770s. SGA, 'Extrait de l'Histoire de la Glacerie Par M. Deslandes, directeur de la Glacerie de St Gobain'. This contains a long account of wood supplies and woodlands. See also deliberations, 25 May 1787.
91 TCH, p.85. Additional forests were purchased at Saint-Gobain in 1819.
92 Deslandes (A), 'Les directeurs de Saint-Gobain'.
93 ASG, Deslandes' memoir on a projected fifth hall, 1762.
94 ASG, H. de Coquereaumont, 'Fabrication de Glaces et Autres Produits dans les Glaceries de la Compagnie de Saint-Gobain, Depuis 1665 Jusqu'à 1914'. Typescript, p.54: Deslandes' memoir, 'Four au charbon'.
95 ASG, Deslandes: draft letter on number of *enfournaments*; memoir (n.d.) on 'Charbon de Terre'.
96 ASG, c. 24, p.245.
97 AN O'1991, Deslandes to Marigny, 29 May 1773.
98 *Ibid.*, letters from Deslandes, 23 January 1784 and from Saint-Gobain proprietors, 15 February 1784.
99 While the annual costs of using wood were lower than those of using coal, the output of glass for each type of fuel is not known. If it was higher with coal and, at the same time, the use of coal helped to lower or hold down the price of wood for those furnaces still using it, the diseconomy of using coal may not have been so huge as at first appears from the figures quoted above, and more weight may attach to the qualitative and technical deficiencies of the coal-made glass.
100 ASG, patent of nobility (copy), July 1773; deliberations, 4 June 1773; AN, O'1991, letter of 15 February 1784.
101 As this section of the memoirs is of such significance I have given some care to checking the Archives Nationales version in detail against that in the Archives of Saint-Gobain, so that subsequent statements in the text can be substantiated from either.
102 AN, O'1881: letter of Deslandes, 24 August 1784.
103 J. R. Harris, *Industry and Technology in the Eighteenth Century*, p.8.
104 ASG, H. De Coquereaumont, *op. cit.*, p.54, favours this view. See also Scoville, *op. cit.*, pp.42–3.
105 Ravenhead's production improved as time went on, poor glasses were removed from the Proprietors' London committee room itself and in 1808 Sherbourne was asked to select poor glasses from the warehouse there for cutting down 'such as he deems to be too imperfect to be offered for sales, disreputable to the Character the Company are desirous to establish of the perfection of the British manufacture and to vy [*sic*] in quality with the best French glasses; PGA, Plate Glass Company

minutes, 22 June 1809. Even so, towards the end of the war and in the early years of peace neither Ravenhead nor its new rivals at South Shields or London could compete with France in small plates; minutes, 18 October 1809.

[106] Boulton and Watt Collection, Birmingham City Library; Watt to Mackworth, 23 April, 1786; Watt to Boulton, 12 September 1786.

[107] Boulton to Watt, 20 February 1788.

[108] Alexander Black to Boulton & Watt, 23 July 1788.

[109] Agreement signed Watt, Boulton and Mackworth. It is interesting to note that in many of the working notes, engine drawings, etc. relating to this order, the Company is called the 'Royal Plate Glass Company'.

[110] Memorandum concerning Ravenhead glasshouse engine.

[111] Watt to George Mackay, 13 June 1789.

[112] Watt to Mackay, 12 February 1790.

[113] J. Aikin, Description of the Country . . . Round Manchester (1795), pp.312–13.

[114] ASG. This item is marked 'notes of my nephew Henry Saladin on the manufacture of plate glass in Lancashire'. Saladin's visit of course, is to be seen as one of the many visits by Continental observers at the end of the Napoleonic wars endeavouring to learn of British industrial progress during the war years. (See W. O. Henderson, Industrial Britain under the Regency (1968), passim.) From 1815 the continued attempts to employ coal and to improve melting and furnace techniques under brilliant directors like Tassaert and Clement Desormes at Saint-Gobain were certainly influenced by the English example, but it is interesting that the employment of coal from 1829 coincides with price reductions following the completion of the Saint-Quentin canal. M. Pris has made helpful suggestions on these points.

[115] ASG (Archives Saint-Quirin), 'Notice sur un voyage en Angleterre ayant pour objet de Comparer le mode de fabrication de douci et de poli des glaces de ce pays avec les procédés usites en france'. The Compagnie des Glaces had set up a water powered polisher at Chauny in 1803 called the Brancourt machine and a few years later a powered grinder at the same place. Presumably these had disadvantages or there would not have been an attempt to establish the English process at great expense in 1823; TCH, pp.62–3.

[116] ASG, Deslandes (A), 'List of letters patent of the company'.

[117] ASG, letters of Vergennes, 8 March 1785, and Calonne, 3 May 1785.

[118] ASG, deliberations, 19 August 1774.

[119] Deslandes, (A), 'English plate glass works'.

[120] AN, O'1992A.

[121] Mackworth papers, Affleck to Mackworth, 2 June 1776; Gore's Liverpool Advertiser, 29 April 1790.

[122] PGA, minutes of BPG Co., 13 July 1808.

[123] Ibid., 21 August 1816.

[124] Ibid., 11 November 1818.

[125] In 1771 it was said of Deslandes, 'The man who holds this place [the directorship of Saint-Gobain] today is so able and so useful that perhaps one could never replace him. We must at least do everything we can to keep him as long as possible and to take every care that he trains up under him some individual fit to succeed him.' The writer speaks of 'l'esprit d'honneur qui regne à Saint-Gobain, est un des plus grands services qui ait rendu Monsieur Deslandes'. In much the same way it was said of Sherbourne at Ravenhead that 'the moral order and regularity of the small community belonging to the works must be seen to enable the Committee to form a just estimate of their superintendent's merits in all his relations to the Company'. See Coquereaumont, op. cit., pp.40–1; PGA, Plate Glass Co. minutes, 12 April 1815.

[126] 'It is true that Chemistry has been pushed to a high point of perfection throughout Europe. But it must also be admitted that our Chemists have not acquired much knowledge in their little laboratories of the art of Glassmaking: it must also be said that they have not discovered a good and reliable method of identifying clays.' Deslandes (A).

A. E. Musson

3

Continental influences on the Industrial
Revolution in Great Britain

Great Britain is generally recognised as having been the birthplace of
the Industrial Revolution, that complex of technological invention and
capitalist enterprise which transformed first this country and then others
from rural, agricultural, handicraft society into urban, industrial,
mechanised society. The names of the great pioneering inventors and
captains of industry—Newcomen and Watt, Darby and Wilkinson,
Hargreaves and Arkwright, Trevithick and Stephenson—are almost
household words as the progenitors of this essentially British achievement. Here in Britain, it would seem, there occurred an extraordinary
concatenation of circumstances—geographical, commercial, industrial,
social and religious—which brought about that remarkable flowering of
mechanical genius and business enterprise which began this, the most
revolutionary transformation in the whole of human history. And now,
though we no longer lead the world, we can at least glory in the fact
that once we were supreme and taught all other nations. It all started
here! Greece and Rome may have their temples, but Britain has
monuments of industrial archaeology far more significant in human
development.

This view of the Industrial Revolution is undoubtedly based on an
extraordinary record of British achievement. It is not merely a salve to
national pride in an era of disintegrating empire and new super-powers.
Continental observers in the late eighteenth and early nineteenth
centuries were well aware of the revolutionary changes then taking
place in Britain, and the surviving diaries and descriptions of French,
German, Swedish and other travellers and industrial spies record their
wonder at the remarkable novelties they observed in Birmingham,
Manchester, Newcastle and elsewhere. At the same time, Continental
countries sought to attract British entrepreneurs and craftsmen, and to
acquire British technology. Despite British bans on the emigration of
artisans and export of machinery, the industrial revolution soon began to
spread to the Continent, and one of Dr W. O. Henderson's most important academic contributions has been to show, in his book *Britain
and Industrial Europe, 1770–1870*, how important was the migration of

British skill and capital in the economic development of France, Germany and other countries.

There are good grounds, then, for pride in British insular achievement. But the traffic across the Channel was not all one way. We are apt to exaggerate Britain's industrial leadership and to overlook the numerous Continental contributions to the industrial revolution. Whilst it is true that foreign observers showed astonished envy at British industrial innovations, British firms were at the same time seeking to acquire knowledge of various Continental techniques and to attract skilled artisans here from Europe. Although there developed a strong sense of British technical superiority, fears of foreign competition remained strong, even in the 'Manchester school' at the height of the free trade agitation.[1] Now, therefore, after Britain's recent entry into the Common Market, it seems appropriate to point out that, despite our island situation and former world-wide empire, we have, in fact, always been part of Europe.

The importance of Continental influences is strongly evident if we look at the 'preconditions' of the Industrial Revolution. Rostow, who has popularised this term, has argued nevertheless in favour of the view that the Industrial Revolution was a great historical discontinuity—a dramatic breakthrough in technology, business enterprise and investment which brought about industrial 'take-off' and 'self-sustained growth' in the late eighteenth century. The present writer, whilst agreeing that this period certainly did see a quickening of technological invention and economic growth—and that the century between 1760 and 1860 did witness an unprecedented industrial revolution—regards the origins and early stages of this phenomenon as deep-rooted and of gradual development, without any sudden, dramatic break with the past. Scholars both before and after Rostow, in fact, have long been reacting against the older Toynbee view of the Industrial Revolution, the origins of which they have been pushing back further into history, to the Renaissance and even earlier. Studies in the history of technology[2] show that even in the Middle Ages there had been important developments in the application of water and wind power (e.g. in grinding corn, working forge hammers, etc, and fulling cloth: Professor Carus-Wilson has even discerned 'an industrial revolution of the thirteenth century'[3]); there had been improvements in textiles (e.g. the introduction of the spinning wheel and development of the hand-loom); in the iron industry the blast furnace and cast iron had been introduced at the end of the Middle Ages; and that period also witnessed the invention of printing, potentially the most revolutionary development of all. Technological change continued in the sixteenth and seventeenth centuries: Professor Nef's 'industrial revolution' in that period may not have been as revolutionary as he at first suggested, but he was undoubtedly right to emphasise the importance of the growing British coal industry and of new coal- or coke-burning processes in the manufacture of glass, bricks, salt, sugar, etc.[4] Meanwhile the 'new draperies' were being introduced, together with further improvements in spinning and weaving; these, along with the invention of the stocking frame, ribbon loom, and gig mill (for raising the nap) foreshadowed the textile revolution of the eighteenth century. In the metallurgical industries, moreover, the use of coal or coke fuel in the smelting of copper and lead similarly preceded the better known discoveries of Darby, Cort and others in iron smelting and forging. Likewise, one can trace during this period important developments in clock- and instrument-making (with the use of drills, lathes and 'wheel-cutting' or gear-cutting 'engines' preparing the way for the later development of heavy mechanical engineering), and also in embryo chemical and allied manufactures producing alum, dye-stuffs, saltpetre, acids, potash, soda, soap, etc. Further developments also occurred in printing and paper-making. From a technological point of view, indeed, it may be said that the eighteenth century witnessed little that was really revolutionary, and that the early Industrial Revolution was, in fact, based largely on these previous advances; even the steam engine was a product of sixteenth- and seventeenth-century scientific theory and experiment, while in other fields older techniques, such as water-powered machinery, were developed and extended.

The majority of these technological developments from the late Middle Ages onwards appear to have been introduced into England from the Continent. Many of the early patents taken out in this country were not for new and original English inventions but for processes initially invented in France, Germany, the Low Countries, Italy and elsewhere and then brought over here. In fact at the beginning of this period England was, by comparison with the more progressive parts of Europe, a relatively 'underdeveloped' country, drawing heavily on the technological expertise and to some extent also on the capital of those areas. In the smelting and refining of metallic ores, for example, by the Mines Royal and the Mineral and Battery Works Companies in the sixteenth century, German skill and capital, applied by Höchstetter and others, were extremely important. Water-powered technology and mining operations were further developed here from Dutch and German experience. It was from the Continent, moreover, that the blast furnace and iron casting were introduced into England in the sixteenth century, followed by rolling and slitting mills for the products of the forge. Developments in the manufacture of clocks and instruments with metal-working tools, so important in the evolution of mechanical engineering, also owed a great deal to Continental craftsmen. From the Continent, too, in this period came other technological developments, such as the invention of printing, the paper mill, wire-drawing machines, the 'new draperies', the Saxony spinning wheel, and the Dutch swivel (or inkle or ribbon) loom. Foreign influences can also be traced in many other industries such as silk, pottery, glassmaking, sugar refining, tin-plate manufacture, brewing, etc. Alien craftsmen were attracted here in considerable numbers to develop these industrial processes, while others migrated to escape from religious intolerance on the Continent.[5] Flemish and Dutch engineers were also brought over to construct water mills, harbour works, and land drainage systems, making important contributions to the development of civil engineering in England.[6]

These Continental influences were not confined to the sixteenth and seventeenth centuries, but continued during the Industrial Revolution of the eighteenth and nineteenth centuries, although native British in-genuity and enterprise then became of greater importance and there was a reverse flow to the Continent. Even in textiles, even in the rising cotton industry, scene of the well known British achievements in the development of power-driven machinery and the factory system, there were some notable Continental contributions. The Lombe brothers, for example, acquired from Italy the plans for the silk-throwing machines installed in 1717–21 in their famous water-powered factory, a model for Arkwright's later cotton mills. Lewis Paul, inventor of roller spinning before Arkwright, was apparently of French Huguenot extraction. The introduction of the Dutch or 'engine loom' into the Manchester small-wares trade in the latter half of the seventeenth century, followed by that of the improved Dutch 'swivel loom' in the mid-eighteenth, was facilitated by the immigration of 'ingenious mechanics' from Holland, who were 'invited over to construct engines at great expence'.[7] These swivel looms were installed in what appears to have been the earliest attempt at a water-powered weaving mill in Lancashire, at Garratt Hall, Manchester, which was later converted into the first cotton-spinning mill in the town, using Arkwright's water frame.[8]

In the subsequent mechanisation of spinning and weaving, based on the inventions of Hargreaves, Arkwright, Crompton and Cartwright, and the improvements by Stones, Kennedy, Horrocks, Roberts and others, British inventors and entrepreneurs established a commanding predominance, but there were some notable Continental achievements too, such as Jacquard's loom, de Girard's improvements in flax spinning, Delaroche's shearing machine, and Heilmann's combing machine.[9] Moreover, in the contemporaneous developments in textile chemistry—in bleaching, dyeing and calico printing—Continental (especially French) contributions were of crucial importance.[10] The discovery of chlorine bleaching, for example, resulted from the re-searches of the Swedish chemist Scheele and the French chemist Berthollet, who communicated his discoveries to James Watt and others and thus brought about the development of the process in Britain in the late 1780s. Chemists from the bleaching firm set up on Merseyside by the Frenchman Bourboulon de Boneuil played a key role in diffusing and improving the new bleaching process in the British cotton-manufacturing districts, whilst the printed works of Berthollet and other French chemists provided the necessary chemical knowledge.[11]

In dyeing, similarly, French chemists such as Dufay, Hellot, Macquer, d'Apligny, Berthollet and Chaptal led the way in scientific–technical development, and their works were constantly referred to by those chemists and dyers in Britain who were interested in applying chemistry in this field. One can see this, for instance, in the researches, writings and industrial experiments of John Wilson, Thomas Henry, Charles Taylor, Thomas Cooper and others, who were the leading figures in the im-provement of dyeing and calico printing in the Manchester area,[12] and whose work, as Wadsworth and Mann pointed out, marks 'the beginning of the application of scientific method in the dyeing and finishing trades'.[13] Nor were French contributions limited to the production of scientific treatises. Just as the 'Javelle' method of chlorine bleaching was introduced and developed here by French industrial chemists such as Vallet and Foy, so too were French dyers in demand. In the 1780s we find Frenchmen such as Borelle, Papillon (or Cigale), Delaunay and others introducing new methods and establishing dyeworks, especially for 'Turkey red', in the Manchester and Glasgow textile areas.[14] Their methods were eagerly sought after by British dyers like Charles Taylor, who, in addition to developing Berthollet's chlorine bleaching process, also acquired knowledge of and developed Turkey-red dyeing, 'using the same method as was practised in Rouen', from which area a con-siderable number of dyers were attracted to this country.[15] Taylor, Cooper, Henry and others acquired chemical–technical information not only from French sources but also from German books, which were in similar demand here, either in the original or in translation, whilst some, such as Taylor and James Watt junior, also improved their knowledge by direct contact with Continental chemists and industrialists in the course of foreign travels, as did Charles Macintosh, who was similarly active at this time in the textile–chemical field in the Glasgow area.[16] It is also interesting to note that one of the leading figures in these developments in Manchester, in both bleaching and dyeing, was the German Theophilus L. Rupp, who established works there in the late eighteenth century.[17]

It is not, therefore, surprising that in other fields where industrial chemistry was becoming important French and German chemists played leading roles. Perhaps the most notable example is in the alkali trade, with the development of the famous Leblanc process. Whilst it is true that several British industrial chemists took out patents for the manufacture of synthetic soda in the 1780s, the French were even earlier in this development and it was the Leblanc process, discovered by this French chemist in 1790–1, which became the basis of the British alkali industry. This too, of course, was of great importance to the cotton industry (in the bleaching process), as well as in other soda-consuming manufactures such as glass and soap. Again, therefore, it is not surprising to find leading British entrepreneurs in these chemical–industrial fields, notably James Keir,[18] deriving many advantages from knowledge of Continental techniques and publications; so did James Watt, though his chemical interests in alkali, dyeing and pottery manufacture are much less well known.

In addition to providing Leblanc soda for soapmakers, French chemists also took the lead in chemical research into oils and fats and the saponification process, leading eventually to recovery of the by-product glycerine. Most outstanding were Chevreul's researches in the early nineteenth century, which 'gave, for the first time, a clear under-standing of the nature and reactions of the raw materials used by the soap industry and so made quantitative working possible'.[19] Though it is questionable whether these scientific researches had much immediate effect on practical soapmaking, there seems little doubt that British soapmakers did benefit from the general progress being made in industrial chemistry, stimulated mainly from France.[20]

In glassmaking, too, despite the British lead in the development of coal-fired furnaces, 'they still relied for the greater part on skilled, foreign craftsmen [mostly French] to work the molten glass', for making windows, bottles, etc, in the sixteenth and seventeenth centuries.[21] And when new methods of manufacture were later introduced they were usually of foreign origin. Thus the manufacture of cast plate glass by the British Cast Plate Glass Company at Ravenhead, St Helens, in the late eighteenth century was initially based on the methods used at Saint-Gobain, with management and key workers drawn from the famous French glassworks; and similarly in the 1830s the development in this country of the manufacture of sheet glass (called, significantly, 'German sheet glass') by an improved cylinder process also required techniques and workmen from France (the process having been deve-loped originally in Lorraine as well as in Germany). It is true that improvements were made here, as in the use of coal fuel, in grinding and polishing, and in the application of steam power, but the original processes and skills were mostly French.

Not only were French and German influences strong in these various industrial chemical areas, but so also was the Dutch, with the great medical school at Leyden attracting students and diffusing chemical knowledge. This influence may be illustrated very simply by mention of two Leyden graduates, John Roebuck, pioneer in the manufacture of vitriol by the lead chamber process, with later interests in the Carron ironworks, in Watt's steam engine and in soda manufacture, and also Bryan Higgins, outstanding in London for his chemical lecturing and various chemical–industrial interests, including the manufactures of soda, pottery, glass, cement, artificial mineral waters, and sugar, in all of which he carried out practical scientific research leading to industrial improvements.[22]

The Dutch were pre-eminent in the seventeenth century not only in trade and shipping, as well as in land drainage and hydraulic engineering, but also in various manufactures. In pottery, for example, 'Delft ware', imitating Chinese porcelain imported by the Dutch East India Company, was dominant throughout that century, before being supplanted in the eighteenth century by Meissen (near Dresden) and Sèvres, which became the most outstanding centres of European pottery manufacture before the rapid rise of Staffordshire in the later part of that century.[23] Indeed, British pottery before that period was crude by comparison with Italian, French and German as well as Dutch manufactures, and when improvements began to be introduced in the eighteenth century they were often in imitation of Continental techniques. Salt glazing, for example, appears to have been brought from Delft by the Elers brothers, two potters of Saxon stock who are reputed to have come over with William of Orange. 'To the Elers brothers are also due the first attempts to improve form and finish, and to establish new standards of excellence in Staffordshire . . . their technique brought about a complete revolution in potting methods in England.'[24] Similarly the Chelsea Porcelain Works, the principal centre of this manufacture in England until the 1770s, was managed by a French potter, Charles Gouyn, and at first frankly imitated Meissen, though later developing its own style.[25]

Continental leadership also continued to be demonstrated in printing and paper-making. In pioneering efforts at mechanical typefounding it appears that the French (e.g. Henri Didot) led the way;[26] the first steam-powered cylinder printing machine was produced by the German Friedrich Koenig;[27] the first paper-making machine was produced by the Frenchman, Louis Robert, and the Fourdrinier brothers;[28] and the earliest efforts at mechanical typesetting, by such men as Church, Delcambre and Rosenberg, were mostly foreign, while the names of Senefelder (lithography) and Kronheim (stereotyping) demonstrate Continental innovations in other branches of the printing trade.

In the primary processes of iron production (after the early innovations from the Continent), in the revolutionary development of coke-fired blast furnaces and puddling and rolling processes by the Darbys, the Cranages, Onions and Cort, there is little trace of Continental influence. One can refer to Darby's employment of Dutch moulders, to Réaumur's researches into iron and steel manufacture, and to Mushet's utilisation of Continental chemistry and mineralogy in his experiments in the iron industry, but these do not seriously modify the facts of British technological leadership in this field. In a wide range of small metal manufactures, however, such as those in the Birmingham area, using brass, copper and other metals and alloys to make buttons, buckles and a great variety of ornamental wares—many of which were not machine-produced for many years, but which were considerably improved by new handicraft skills, subdivision and specialisation of labour, and new chemical processes—it is clear that Continental techniques, tools and artisans were still being attracted here by industrialists such as Matthew Boulton at the same time as Birmingham artificers were being enticed abroad. There was, in fact, an 'international exchange of men and machines', and 'Continental craftsmen made quite a considerable contribution to the Birmingham hardware industry'.[29]

The coal industry, on the other hand, is generally regarded as one in which Britain's insular achievements were most strikingly pronounced and on which much of her industrial advance was based. Here, indeed, not only in the development of the coal industry itself but also in many other industrial processes, such as iron smelting and forging, the introduction of new types of furnaces in glassmaking, pottery manufacture, etc, and in the development of steam power, it was the exploitation of Britain's coal resources which was the key factor in the industrial revolution. This emphasises Nef's percipience and the truth of W. S. Jevons' much earlier observation[30] that 'Coal commands this age'. It was in this field particularly—largely owing to geographical and geological factors—that Britain's industrial supremacy over France was demonstrated. But as Ashton and Sykes emphasised,[31] there was not much really revolutionary technological development in the eighteenth-century coal industry itself, except in steam-powered mine drainage. Earlier developments, as we have noticed, owed a good deal to Continental mining techniques such as water-powered drainage engines of German or Dutch origin. Moreover, it is clear that the steam engine— at first used exclusively for pumping operations—was a product of scientific researches in the seventeenth century by Continental philosophers such as Torricelli, von Guericke and Huygens, as well as by Britons such as Boyle, and that experimental engines were built on the Continent by Salomon de Caus and Denys Papin as well as in England by David Ramsay, the Marquis of Worcester and Samuel Morland, before Savery and Newcomen built the first practically successful industrial engines; and it seems highly probable that Savery and Newcomen owed a good deal to the earlier experiments of the Frenchman Papin.[32]

James Watt, moreover, engineering genius though he undoubtedly was, has been revealed also as a man of wide and profound scientific interests, which were considerably enriched by Continental scientific publications.[33] Before he was fifteen he had read in translation Gravesande's *Mathematical Elements of Natural Philosophy*; later, when appointed instrument maker to Glasgow University, he started to learn German so that he could read Leupold's *Theatrum Machinarum*, and Italian for a similar purpose; and before his famous improvements of the steam engine he had read works by Continental engineers such as Belidor. He also continued in future years to take a profound interest in foreign publications and foreign developments in engineering, chemistry, etc (we have already noticed, his acquisition of the chlorine bleaching process from Berthollet), and, like Matthew Boulton, he was careful to provide Continental schooling and further education for his sons, with particular attention to applied science and to learning French and German.[34] These facts do not detract from his technological originality, but he certainly viewed himself as operating in a general environment of European culture, and had numerous contacts with Continental scientists and industrialists.

In the general field of engineering there is no doubt that Continental influences were considerable. As we have seen, the development of machine tools such as lathes, drills and gear-cutting engines evolved from clock- and instrument-making, to which Continental craftsmen and philosophers made important contributions. Early British mechanical engineers such as Bramah and Maudslay developed their heavy industrial machine tools from these earlier lighter 'engines', including the principle of the slide rest, often attributed to Maudslay but of much earlier Continental origin.[35] Foreign clock makers and instrument makers were attracted here, and some of the leading mechanical engineers came from the Continent, including the great Marc Isambard Brunel, a French refugee, and John Jacob Holtzappfel, a German who settled in London as a toolmaker in the late 1780s and had an annual turnover in lathes, etc, of £10,000 by 1811;[36] another remarkable foreign engineer, resident in Manchester, was the versatile Swiss, J. G. Bodmer, with mechanical inventions in many fields.[37]

In civil engineering, not then clearly differentiated from mechanical engineering, there is also abundant evidence of Continental influences.[38] In the work of river improvement and fen drainage, for example, including the construction of locks, etc, and leading to the building of canals, the main pioneering developments were made, from the Renaissance onwards, by the Italians, Dutch and French, whose techniques were adopted in this country. Foreign engineers were attracted here, from Peter Morris, the Dutch (or German) engineer who constructed pumping engines in the late sixteenth century, and

Cornelius Vermuyden, the famous fen drainage engineer, in the seven-teenth, to Charles Labelye, the Swiss-born engineer–architect who built the Westminster bridge in the early eighteenth. And British engineers visited the Continent to acquire experience, as did Robert Mylne in Italy, before building the Blackfriars bridge, and John Smeaton in Holland, where he was able to acquire knowledge of wind and water mills, harbour works, etc. Moreover, engineers such as Grundy, Mylne, Smeaton, Telford and Rennie, like Watt, eagerly read the works and studied the designs of foreign engineers, including those of Italian pioneers like Castelli and Guglielmini, and especially of French engineering scientists such as Belidor, Parent and others, whose con-structional ideas they applied in river improvements and the building of canals, bridges, etc. One must not, as Professor Hamilton and Pro-fessor Cardwell have warned, exaggerate the influence of Continental theory—British engineers, though often inferior in scientific theory (which, however, was sometimes defective), yet succeeded in great practical achievements—but it is now evident that they were not illiterate and innumerate empiricists, and that they learnt a great deal, both in theory and practice, from the Continent. In the building of roads and bridges, for instance, designs and practical examples could be studied in the works of the Ingénieurs des Ponts et Chaussées.

It is thus clearly evident that British manufacturers and technologists in many industries had much to learn from visits to Europe, from foreign publications, and by attracting foreign artificers to this country. In the same way, it may be added, British farming benefited from the imitation of Continental (especially Flemish or Dutch) crop rotation and other agricultural improvements—even Jethro Tull's famous seed drill was apparently of Continental origin. The importance of these Continental influences, moreover, is not a matter of recent historical observation but was clearly apparent to intelligent contemporaries. In the early eighteenth century Daniel Defoe 'was willing cheerfully to confess that the English were unoriginal and were best at exploiting other people's ideas'.[39]

> It is a kind of Proverb attending the Character of English Men, that they are *better to improve than to invent*, better to advance upon the Designs and Plans which other People have laid down than to form Schemes and Designs of their Own; and which is still more, the Thing seems to be really true in Fact, and the Observation very just . . .
>
> Even our Woollen Manufacture itself, with all the admirable Improvements made upon it by the *English* since it came into their hands is but a building upon other Foundations, and improving upon the Inventions of the *Flemings* . . .

In other industries, too, we had learnt from foreigners. Thus, Defoe pointed out, it was said that the English were able 'to learn the Art of building Ships from the *Genoese* and *French*'.

Defoe's remarks were echoed by J. Ryhiner, a Swiss calico printer, in a treatise on the trade in 1766.[40]

Everyone knows this nation whose industry and stubborn patience in over-coming every kind of obstacle are beyond all imagination. They cannot boast of many inventions, but only of having perfected the inventions of others; whence comes the proverb that for a thing to be perfect it must be invented in France and worked out in England.

These observations, of course, were made before the Industrial Revolution had really got under way, but later in the eighteenth century the letters of leading manufacturers such as Watt, Boulton, Keir, Wedgwood, Roebuck and others demonstrate their interest in Continental science and technology, and also their links with the Continent; so too do the growing number of books, periodicals, dictionaries and 'repertories of arts and manufactures' in this period, with their innumerable Continental references. The British did not have a monopoly of industrial inventiveness, as William Huskisson pointed out to a deputation from the Manchester Chamber of Commerce in 1826;[41] as John Farey, an eminent London engineering consultant, told the Select Committee on the Patent Laws in 1829,[42]

we have derived almost as many good inventions from foreigners, as we have originated among ourselves. The prevailing talent of the English and Scotch people is to apply new ideas to use, and to bring such applications to perfection, but they do not imagine so much as foreigners; clocks and watches, the coining press, the windmill for draining land, the diving bell, the cylinder paper machine, the stocking frame, figure weaving loom, silk throwsting mill, canal lock and turning bridge, the machine for dredging and deepening rivers, the manufacture of alum, glass, the art of dyeing, printing, and the earliest notions of the steam engine, were all of foreign origin; the modern paper-making machine, block machinery, printing machine, and steam boats, the same; there are a multitude of others . . .

Matthew Curtis, one of the leading Manchester machine makers, made a similar observation to the Select Committee on Exportation of Machinery in 1841:[43]

I should say that the greatest portion of new inventions lately introduced into this country have come from abroad; but I would have it to be understood that by that I mean not improvements in machines, but rather entirely new inventions. There are certainly more improvements carried out in this country; but I apprehend that the chief part, or a majority, at all events, of the really new inventions, that is, of new ideas altogether, in the carrying out of a certain process by new machinery, or in a new mode, have originated abroad, especially in America.

At the same time both Farey and Curtis remarked in their evidence how frequently foreigners had come to this country to develop or improve processes they had invented. Many immigrants, of course, were attracted here for non-economic reasons, coming as religious or political refugees but bringing their industrial skills with them. But there were also strong economic factors drawing them here to develop their inventions: the British patent system; greater availability of capital; greater freedom for private enterprise. Farey and Curtis both emphasised the greater opportunities in Britain for getting new inventions taken up, developed and brought into industrial use. Farey stated that foreigners came here 'because the means of executing and applying inventions abroad are so very inferior to ours'.[44] And Curtis attributed British superiority in this respect to the larger scale of industry, greater 'subdivision of labour' and specialisation, producing greater knowledge of particular processes and machines and of possible improvements; he also emphasised the importance of British machine tools in improving and cheapening machinery.[45] Whether consciously or not,[46] he was demonstrating the truth of Adam Smith's famous dictum that the scale, organisation and technical development of industry are determined by the size of the market—trade expansion resulting in increased division of labour and improvements in skills, technology and productivity—which would tend to support the view that the industrial revolution in Britain was a result largely of growing markets at home and overseas.

These various factors certainly help to explain why the industrial revolution occurred first in Britain rather than on the Continent; why so many inventions, like Papin's steam engine, or Berthollet's chlorine bleaching, or Leblanc's synthetic soda, or Jacquard's loom, were taken up and developed more rapidly here than in their country of origin; and why Britain, in many fields inferior in scientific–technological terms, nevertheless surpassed her European rivals in industrial achievements. Science and technology were not confined within national boundaries, and so, despite French leadership in many branches of industrial science, the British were able to adopt French advances fairly quickly, as well as making many of their own, and forged ahead in industrial development. Practical scientific knowledge seems to have been more widely and deeply diffused in Britain than in France. Britain also had substantial economic advantages in natural resources (especially coal) and wider overseas trade and empire, as well as institutional advantages such as freedom from tolls and fewer government restrictions, together with social advantages such as a more developed and enterprising middle class and greater social mobility.[47]

The Industrial Revolution in Britain, therefore, does not reflect national or ethnic superiority. Britain had drawn, and continued to draw, heavily on Continental industrial techniques, which were able to

lourish in the economic and social environment created by this
:ountry's very favourable geographical position, natural resources,
:ommercial expansion and socio-political development. Britain, in her
urn, was to make immense contributions to the industrial development
of Europe and the rest of the world.

NOTES

[1] A. E. Musson, 'The "Manchester school" and exportation of machinery', *Business
History*, XIV, 1 January 1972.

[2] See, for example, A. P. Usher, *A History of Mechanical Inventions* (1929; revised
edition, 1956); C. Singer *et al.* (ed.), *A History of Technology* (6 vols, 1954–8), con-
densed by T. K. Derry and T. I. Williams, *A Short History of Technology* (Oxford,
1960); W. H. Chaloner and A. E. Musson, *Industry and Technology* (1963); M.
Kranzberg and C. W. Pursell, jr. (ed.), *Technology and Western Civilization*, vol. 1
(1967); A. E. Musson and E. Robinson, *Science and Technology in the Industrial
Revolution* (Manchester, 1969).

[3] E. M. Carus-Wilson, 'An industrial revolution of the thirteenth century', *Economic
History Review*, XI, 1941.

[4] J. U. Nef, *The Rise of the British Coal Industry* (2 vols, 1932) and 'The progress of
technology and the growth of large-scale industry in Great Britain, 1540–1640',
Economic History Review, V, 1934. For a review of studies in this field, centring on the
third volume of the *History of Technology*, see D. C. Coleman, 'Technology and
economic history, 1500–1700', *Economic History Review*, new series, XI, 1959. Nef's
views have recently received support from W. Rees, *Industry before the Industrial
Revolution* (2 vols, 1968), mainly concerned with Welsh coal and metallurgical
developments.

[5] See, for example, E. Taube, 'German craftsmen in England during the Tudor
period', *Economic History*, February 1939; W. C. Scoville, 'Minority migrations and
the diffusion of technology', *Journal of Economic History*, II, 1951, and 'The Huguenots
and the diffusion of technology', *Journal of Political Economy*, LX, 1952.

[6] Samuel Smiles was well aware of Britain's early dependence on foreign technology:
see *Lives of the Engineers*, I, 1874, pp.iv–viii; also L. E. Harris, *Vermuyden and the Fens*
(1952).

[7] [J. Ogden], *A Description of Manchester* (Manchester, 1783), p.82; A. P. Wadsworth
and J. de L. Mann, *The Cotton Trade and Industrial Lancashire 1600–1780* (Manchester,
1931), pp.103 and 284–8.

[8] Musson and Robinson, *op. cit.*, pp.400 and 431.

[9] For these, see Miss J. de L. Mann's chapter on 'The textile industry: machinery for
cotton, flax, wool, 1760–1850', in the *History of Technology*, vol. IV.

[10] A. and N. L. Clow, *The Chemical Revolution* (1952), and Musson and Robinson,
op. cit., chs. III, VII, VIII and IX.

[11] Musson and Robinson, *op. cit.*, ch. VIII.

[12] *Ibid.*, ch. IX.

[13] Wadsworth and Mann, *op. cit.*, p.182.

[14] Musson and Robinson, *op. cit.*, p.344.

[15] *Ibid.*, pp.344–5.

[16] There are numerous references to these continental links in the works by Clow and
by Musson and Robinson previously cited.

[17] Musson and Robinson, *op. cit.*, pp.82–3, 243, 317–19, 349.

[18] In addition to numerous references to Keir in the previously cited works by Clow
and by Musson and Robinson, see B. M. D. Smith and J. L. Moilliet, 'James Keir
of the Lunar Society', *Notes and Records of the Royal Society of London*, XXII, 1 and 2,
1967.

[19] A. and N. L. Clow, in the *History of Technology*, IV, p.253.

[20] See A. E. Musson, *Enterprise in Soap and Chemicals* (Manchester, 1965), *passim*.

[21] T. C. Barker, *Pilkington Brothers and the Glass Industry* (1960), chs. 2 and 5. See also
W. C. Scoville, *Capitalism and French Glassmaking 1640–1789* (California, 1950), and

the chapter 'Glass' by L. M. Angus-Butterworth in the *History of Technology*, vol. IV, ch. 12.

22 For Roebuck's industrial–chemical interests, see references in Clow and in Musson and Robinson, *op. cit.* For Higgins, see F. W. Gibbs, 'Bryan Higgins and his circle', *Chemistry in Britain*, vol. I (1965), reprinted in A. E. Musson (ed.), *Science, Technology and Economic Growth in the Eighteenth Century* (1972). There are numerous references to Leyden's influence in Clow, *op. cit.*

23 See A. and N. L. Clow, 'Ceramics from the fifteenth century to the rise of the Staffordshire potteries', *History of Technology*, vol. IV, ch. XI.

24 *Ibid.*, p.345.

25 *Ibid.*, p.342.

26 A. E. Musson, 'The London Society of Master Letter-Founders, 1793–1820', *The Library* (Bibliographical Society), June 1955, p.97.

27 A. E. Musson 'Newspaper printing in the industrial revolution', *Economic History Review*, new series, x, 3, 1958. See also A. E. Musson, *The Typographical Association* (1954), ch. II.

28 D. C. Coleman, *The British Paper Industry, 1495–1860* (1958), ch. VII.

29 E. Robinson, 'The international exchange of men and machines 1750–1800', *Business History*, I, 1, December 1958, reprinted in Musson and Robinson, *op. cit.*, ch. VI.

30 In *The Coal Question* (1865).

31 T. S. Ashton and J. Sykes, *The Coal Industry of the Eighteenth Century* (Manchester, 1929).

32 A. E. Musson, introduction to the new edition of H. W. Dickinson, *Short History of the Steam Engine* (1963); C. Cabanes, *Denys Papin* (Paris, n.d., c. 1936).

33 Musson and Robinson, *op. cit.*, *passim*, and E. Robinson and A. E. Musson, *James Watt and the Steam Revolution* (1969).

34 Musson and Robinson, *op. cit.*, ch. V.

35 *Ibid.*, pp.23–4, 49–51, and *passim*; *History of Technology*, vol. IV, chs. 13 and 14, by M. Daumas and K. R. Gilbert respectively; J. W. Roe, *English and American Tool Builders* (1916); W. Steeds, *A History of Machine Tools, 1700–1910* (Oxford, 1969); and the various monographs by Professor R. S. Woodbury.

36 Musson and Robinson, *op. cit.*, p.63.

37 Roe, *op. cit.*, pp.75–80; D. Brownlie, 'John George Bodmer, his life and work', *Newcomen Society Transactions*, VI (1925–6).

38 S. B. Hamilton, 'Continental influences on British civil engineering to 1800', *Archives Internationales d'Histoire des Sciences*, XI, 1958; Musson and Robinson, *op. cit.*, chs. I, II, and III, *passim*; D. S. L. Cardwell, 'Power technologies and the advance of science, 1700–1825', *Technology and Culture*, VI, 2, spring 1965, and 'Some factors in the early development of the concepts of power, work and energy', *British Journal for the History of Science*, III (1966–7).

39 D. S. L. Cardwell, *Technology, Science and History* (1972), pp.56–7. The following quotation is from Defoe, *A Plan of the English Commerce* (1728), part III, ch. I, to which Cardwell's attention was drawn by Wadsworth and Man, *op. cit.*, p.413. Cardwell points out, however, that 'a society that is passing through, or has just passed through, an imitative phase may well be on the point of becoming a technologically original and creative society' (*op. cit.*, p.58), and he makes a comparison with modern Japanese development (*ibid.*, pp.5–6).

40 Quoted in D. Dollfus-Ausset, *Matériaux pour la coloration des étoffes* (1865), II, p.5, and referred to by Wadsworth and Mann, *op. cit.*, p.413.

41 *Proceedings of the Manchester Chamber of Commerce*, 13 December 1826; A. E. Musson, 'The "Manchester school" and exportation of machinery', *Business History*, XIV, 1 January 1972, p.35.

42 Select Committee on Patent Laws, *Parl. Papers*, 1829, III, p.153; Musson and Robinson, *op. cit.*, pp. 63–4.

43 Select Committee on Exportation of Machinery, *Parl. Papers*, 1841, VII, First Report, Q. 1544; Musson and Robinson, *op. cit.*, p.64. Curtis was referring particularly to fairly recent mechanical inventions in textiles.

44 *Loc. cit.*, p.153.

45 *Loc. cit.*, Qs. 1556, 1600, 1608.

[46] He was, in fact, a staunch free-trader, advocating removal of controls on exports of machinery, with the aim of expanding foreign markets.
[47] See F. Crouzet, 'Angleterre et France au XVIIIe siècle. Essai d'analyse comparée de deux croissances économiques', *Annales*, 1966, trans. in R. M. Hartwell (ed.), *The Causes of the Industrial Revolution in England* (1967).

Paul Leuilliot

4

Frédéric Zuber's visits to England, 1834-41

A great deal has been written on Anglo–French relations.[1] The author of *Britain and Industrial Europe, 1750–1850* has charted industrial relations with considerable scholarship.[2] However, the list of travellers' accounts and correspondence which still lie dormant in private archives is far from complete.[3]

We are therefore publishing Frédéric Zuber's letters. To throw light on these we might indicate the background of the Zuber family, wall-paper manufacturers in Rixheim, near Mulhouse in the Upper Rhine, and give a brief account of the rise of their factory, established in 1802 and held in high repute in its line of business.[4] This correspondence also helps bring to light the 'Anglo-Alsatian society' of the years 1834-41.

The father, who seems to have been a self-made man, was Jean Zuber[5] or Zuber-Spoerlin, after the maiden name of his wife, who was the daughter of a minister, sister to a minister and granddaughter of Samuel Koechlin, one of the three founders of the first calico-printing factory in Mulhouse in 1746. The son of an unsuccessful Mulhouse draper,[6] he was apprenticed to a commercial firm, 'where he used to sweep out the office every morning as was the custom at the time'! When he was seventeen (i.e. in 1790) he began to travel in Italy, armed with a wallpaper sample book, for Nicholas Dollfus: 'it was this that decided his career. From being a commercial traveller the young Zuber secured a financial interest in the firm, subsequently becoming a partner and finally the boss.' In 1797 he bought the Commandery of the Teutonic Order at Rixheim (which had been sold as a *bien national*). The following year Mulhouse was reunited with France, and Zuber, in order to manu-facture his own paper, bought a paper mill at Roppentzwiller (1804). From 1802 (and until 1890) the firm's name was Jean Zuber & Co. and was a partnership before it became a limited company. The paper mill at Roppentzwiller was transferred to the Ile Napoléon, where a new factory was built between 1840 and 1842 to plans drawn up by Amédée Rieder, whom we shall meet again.

Jean Zuber was also the founder of a chamber of commerce in

Mulhouse, a company for mutal fire insurance in the department in 1818, and a company to search for coal deposits in the Upper Rhine. He was president of the Bible Society and member of the Society for Christian Ethics, 'always publicly professing his religion and showing the greatest zeal for it ... Family celebrations always began with prayer.'[7] He was a liberal mayor of Rixheim during the Restoration who, though he was later removed from office, set up a school on the monitorial system.[8] A philhellene and president of the Mulhouse 'Greek Committee' (his wife presided over the 'ladies for the Greeks') he edited the 'Vue des plages de la Grèce représentant le brulôt de l'immortel Canaris incendiant le vaisseau amiral turc'.

When he retired to Mulhouse in 1835 his two sons became joint partners in the business: Jean Zuber fils (1799–1853), who survived his father only briefly, and Frédéric Zuber (1803–91), our visitor to England.[9] Frédéric Zuber had been employed in his father's factory since the age of fifteen, before which he had spent six years at the boarding school run by a Colmar pastor whose son, Amédée Rieder, was his childhood companion and later became engaged to his sister who died aged twenty-five in 1832.

It might be said that he had been brought up in daily contact with the Bible, which, as a convinced Christian, he continued to read every day throughout his long life of eighty-eight years.[10] His elder brother studied chemistry in Paris and then entered into partnership with his father in 1822. He was secretary of the Mulhouse Industrial Society from its foundation in 1826 and its president from 1829 to 1834. From 1835 to 1840 reasons of health forced him to live in the south of France and in Italy. Already in 1825 he had visited England in search of new markets, 'despite an enormous duty of a shilling a square yard!' In fact in 1827 sales of Rixheim wallpaper in England reached 30,000 francs (out of a total, it is true, of 315,000 francs).[11]

However, it was not so much markets as methods of production that interested the Zubers and particularly Amédée Rieder (1807–81).[12] A native of Colmar, Rieder was employed at the Rixheim factory from 1828 and had a particular interest in the Roppentzwiller paper works. He had an inventive mind, together with a rare manual dexterity, and made a number of technical inventions 'at a time when the paper industry was changing from hand- to machine production'. Until 1827 indeed, the only paper available came in sheets, and this had to be glued end to end to make up the rolls.[13] It was only between 1829 and 1830 that the Roppentzwiller paper works succeeded in manufacturing the first rolls of paper in one piece. In 1829 Zuber & Co. acquired a new paper-making machine invented by the German Leistenschneider, and Rieder was given the job of supervising its assembly: 'to make it work properly it had to be reconstructed piece by piece. After many unsuccessful attempts Rieder modified it and thus managed to manufacture the first wallpaper in continuous rolls, and this was an important breakthrough.'[14] Afterwards Rieder spent nearly a year in England (1830–31), where he sold the patent for a continuous drying process to John Hall & Sons, millwrights and engineers, at Dartford in Kent.[15]

Amédée Rieder was to accompany Frédéric Zuber on his visit of 1834, and the latter mentioned him in his letters to his wife (Amélie Franger, whom he had married in 1829). Artistic, something of a dreamer if not a romantic, Zuber had, as we shall see, a talent for observation, a passion for botany, a love of flowers and an appreciation of music—hence his purchase of pianos. He attended to the artistic as well as to the commercial side of his business. Wallpaper manufacture required both a laboratory with chemists for the colours, which for a time Rixheim manufactured for its own needs, and a design studio employing well-known artists.[16] And the high reputation of the firm owed as much to the talent of the painters as to the constant search for technical improvements pursued most vigorously by Amédée Rieder, the factory's mechanical engineer. 'Between 1834 and 1845 mechanical drying and even the drying by cast iron cylinder invented by Mr Donkin replaced the continuous drying process invented by M. Rieder . . .' In 1849 Rieder was to install at Rixheim the first English cylinder printing machine on the Continent. Around 1850 Jean Zuber *fils* was to introduce another English machine which printed in five or six colours by means of embossed rollers. In a report read to the Mulhouse Industrial Society he compared Alsace with England and concluded: 'in Manchester, where fifteen colours can be printed at the same time, the Potter Brothers' firm alone, with its paper mill with eight printing machines, produces between 8,000 and 10,000 rolls a day, which is more than all the London factories put together . . . In the last six months this mechanical process has been introduced here.'[17] Again, after 1850 Zuber was to be one of the first in France fully to mechanise production by the use of steam engines. The construction of the new paper mill at the Ile Napoléon was directed by Rieder, and 'thanks to him nearly everything that can be done for the well-being and intellectual advance of the worker was introduced at the factory'.

In the context of this paternalism we may note another of Jean Zuber's imports from across the Channel—his 'note on workers' dwellings', read at the Mulhouse Industrial Society in 1852, where he gives a description of the model house that Prince Albert had built close to the Crystal Palace which was intended to house four working-class households, as well as informing members of the work of the Metropolitan Association for Improving the Dwellings of the Industrious Classes (specifications and plans of a number of buildings to house the working class that had been recently erected in London). He then proposed holding a competition for the best design for workers' dwellings in Mulhouse.[18] The consequence of this initiative was the setting up in the following year of the Mulhouse Society for Working-class Housing (Société mulhousienne des Cités ouvrières). Jean Zuber once said that 'industry is not merely a machine—a spinning mill, for instance, where the worker is himself *almost* a machine'.

Official recognition accompanied industrial and commercial success. Jean Zuber *père* was awarded the gold medal at the French exhibition of 1834, while the Légion d'Honneur was conferred on Jean Zuber *fils*, who also won a prize medal at the Great Exhibition in 1851.

In the 'Anglo-Alsatian society' of 1834–41 a special place has to be accorded to Frédéric Steiner.[19] He was an Alsatian from Ribeauvillé in the Upper Rhine, who, 'seeing business in Alsace depressed after the Restoration, decided to emigrate to England, where he set up the firm of Steiner & Co. [at Church] near Accrington (Lancashire) which for long was considered the leading dye- and printing-works for Turkey reds . . .'[20] In his letter of 28 October 1834 Frédéric Zuber also mentions James Thomson, who seems to have had close ties with the Mulhouse circle, to judge from the obituary notice that was read to the Industrial Society.[21] The society 'decides that this notice will, as a departure from precedent, be inserted in its Bulletin 'to honour the memory of a distinguished correspondent abroad'. We think the notice worth mentioning in this introduction to Frédéric Zuber's letters: 'Few men have contributed as much to the advance of his industry as this capable manufacturer by his services as a talented businessman and as a distinguished chemist.' Daniel Koechlin-Schouch, the author of the notice, recalled his 'close links with the Peels, James and Gregory Watt, Humphry Davy, Wollaston and other famous Englishmen'. He also recalled his studies at Glasgow Academy, his joining the firm of Jos. Peel & Co. at the age of fifteen, where he worked six years, and his employment at Church, near Accrington, where for nine years he worked in cloth printing. Finally, 'in 1811 he set up a factory on his own account at Primrose, near Clitheroe (Thomson, Chippendale & Co., which later became James Thomson, the name under which the firm became so well known)'. The notice praised 'his commercial ability and his great knowledge of chemistry' and recalled in particular that he had been 'the first to introduce Turkey red cottons to England' and that by an agreement of 1815 he had granted Nicolas Koechlin & Frères the right 'alone as inventor's to sell these cottons throughout the British empire. D. Koechlin-Schouch also pointed out that James Thomson had been the founder in 1838 of the Manchester School of Art, 'modelled on the one in Mulhouse'. Finally and most important, he praised

Thomson's 'attractive personality' and 'the generous hospitality he accorded foreigners, which several Alsace manufacturers still have pleasant memories of'! Thus the far-off days of industrial espionage which had earned F. C. L. Albert five years' imprisonment in Lancaster castle[22] were long past.

I

Londres 21 octobre 1834[23]

... C'est un spectacle magnifique que l'entrée dans la Tamise peuplée de milliers de vaisseaux, à voile et à vapeur; ce n'est pas sans peine et rarement sans accidents qu'on traverse cette foule merveilleuse ... Enfin nous fûmes à l'ancre devant la douane et je vis arriver Amédée[24] dans une barque; nous fîmes encore une grande promenade nocturne parmi les principales rues de la Cité ...

Nous avons commencé aujourd'hui nos courses et je n'ai pas été peu frappé de la beauté des rues de Londres et de ses magasins qui effacent ceux de Paris ... Nous avons vu l'église de Westminster en détail et les plus belles rues du quartier ... Demain nous entamerons un peu les affaires. Je pense que dans quelques jours nous nous remettrons en route pour faire un séjour plus long ici à notre retour.

Manchester mardi 28 octobre. Enfin nous sommes débarassés de nos visites qui se régalaient de port wine plus longtemps que nous ne voullions et je ne puis te raconter de nos exploits de ces derniers jours. Nous quittames *Londres* ... et après une froide nuit, traversant au galop dans une diligence vraiment anglaise ces fertiles comtés. Nous arrivames dans cette ville de fumée et de cheminées samedi soir et je me suis fait depuis à voir ces merveilles de l'industrie et à voir ces établissements gigantesques que l'on ne peut voir qu'ici et dont on ne peut se faire une idée si on ne les a vus; aussi loin qu'on peut voir et plusieurs lieues à l'entour on ne voit que des cheminées immenses qui vomissent la fumée de houille, et des bâtiments d'une immense étendue, le brouillard qui règne toujours ici se confond avec la fumée et donne au pays un caractère tout particulier; Manchester a près de 300 mille habitants et quelques rues fort belles, mais beaucoup de bien sales à cause du mouvement continuel qui y règne; mais les manufacturiers ont tous des campagnes charmantes aux environs où ils trouvent tous les conforts imaginables ...

Nous fumes d'accord de passer le dimanche à Church chez M. Steiner ..., ils demeurent à huit lieues d'ici, il a fait un temps superbe et notre voyage était fort agréable, car les environs de Manchester sont très pitoresques; nous reçumes toutes les honetetés imaginables chez M. Steiner qui se pique de bien recevoir ses compatriotes; comme nous devions voir l'établissement de M. Thompson à trois lieues de là, nous nous décidames de coucher là et hier M. Steiner nous conduisit lui même à Primrose, moitiè à cheval moitié en gig, toujours par un pays charmant et des routes unies comme le plancher—la fabrique de M. Thompson est une des plus grandes et m'interssa beaucoup; obligés d'attendre une diligence pour ce matin qui nous ramenait ici, nous couchames une seconde fois à Church chez M. Steiner, après avoir fait de la musique et vecu avec une profusion alsacienne et la ponctualité anglaise ... Enfin je dormais profondément dans un lit de sept pieds carrés ...

Aujourd'hui seulement nous avons commencé nos affaires . . . Je vois que pour en faire, il nous faudra plus de temps que je ne pensais, car il faut d'abord faire connaissance avec ces Anglais et puis les faire boire et alors tenter seulement une affaire; l'ami Adam, qui est toujours le même bon vivant farceur, mais prêt à rendre tous les services, a couru avec moi dans cent boutiques pour y chercher des échantillons de toiles peintes, il m'a fait voir les magasins, les eglises et les railways . . . Voilà bientôt trois semaines que je t'ai quittée et à peine nous commençons à voir le pays et il nous reste beaucoup à voir et à faire, nous ne pourrons guère quitter *Manchester* avant dimanche, par contre Liverpool ne prendra que quelques jours et Dublin cinq ou six jours,[25] alors nous reviendrons promptement à *Londres* où il faudra laisser bien des choses pour une autre fois. Avant de quitter [Londres] nous avons été voir encore le Tunel sous la Tamise et la Tower où il y a un arsenal de toute beauté . . . Nous sommes partis ce matin avant le jour de Church et j'ai couru toute la journée—cela est si different de notre vie tranquille de Rixheim que nous en sommes plutôt fatigués . . . Bonsoir donc . . .

II

Manchester 31 octobre 1834

Nous voilà déjà fatigués de cette grande cité que nous parcourons depuis cinq jours . . . Nous irons demain sur le *chemin de fer* à Liverpool où nous devons trouver des lettres. Hier soir, nous avons fait la promenade à Mid[d]leton chez l'ami farceur;[26] il faisait nuit lorsque nous y arrivâmes et ce n'est qu'à force de demander le chemin que nous sommes parvenus à découvrir sa fabrique; il nous régala d'un excellent thé et de jambon de renne. Nous voulions retourner à Manchester, mais il a fait si noir qu'il n'a pas voulu nous laisser partir à pied et il a fallu coucher chez lui. Il a un fort joli ménage de garçon tout anglais, un grand potager près de sa fabrique et s'y trouve si bien que s. d. [sans doute] il ne quittera jamais son Mid[d]leton. De retour ce matin, nous avons pris une chaise de poste pour courir les environs, nous pensions qu'en arrivant en gentlemen on nous accuellerait mieux dans les papeteries, mais c'était une cruelle erreur et qui nous coute encore fort cher; pleins d'appétit et de dépit, nous avons mangé notre bifsteck et notre chester et puis avons fait un tour dans les rues pour voir de nuit les filatures aux mille croisées illuminées, ce qui a manqué couter un oeil à Amédée qui, pendant qu'il regardait en l'air, a été heurté par une caisse que portait un individu. Au surplus, il n'est pas rare que dans ces étroites rues du faubourg on soit battu et volé, ce qui est arrivé il y a peu de jours encore. La dessus tu sais maintenant que nous sommes sains et saufs à l'Hotel Royal . . .

III

Liverpool 1er novembre 1834

Nous voici arrivés . . . En une heure et demie nous sommes venus de Manchester ici voir ces merveilleux railways. Amédée a eu l'idée de nous placer outside sans songer au vent contraire, en sorte que nous avons eu la fumée dans es yeux jusqu'à ce que nous ayions pu rentrer dans la diligence de 100 places. La vitesse est effrayante lorsqu'on se croise avec une autre suite de voitures, ou que l'on passe sous un pont. Cependant j'avais tant vu et entendu de ces voitures à vapeur que je n'ai pas été étonné et que cela me semblait tout naturel et simple. On y voyage avec tant de sécurité que les belles dames en toilette ne craignent pas de venir faire le trajet et de s'en retourner souvent le même jour. Liverpool est une charmante ville, les rues, les magasins, les maisons sont superbes. Manchester est comme un ouvrier noir de fumée et Liverpool une princesse en costume et bijoux. Nous avons été voir le marché St Jean, un immense bâtiment de 600 pieds de long éclairé au gaz. On y vend des légumes, des poissons et mille denrées de cuisine. L'ensemble est magnifique de nuit, nous avons regretté seulement de ne pouvoir vous envoyer un turbot grand comme un homme pour votre dîner de dimanche.

Il ne faut pas envoyer de billet dans les lettres pour ce pays ci, sinon on paie double ou triple port . . .

IV

Liverpool 3 novembre 1834

. . . Nous avons été reçu ici fort amicalement par l'ami de Jean M. Clow qui nous traite en vrais amis, nous déjeunons et soupons chez lui et il ne nous quitte presque pas dans nos courses. Hier nous avons eu la visite d'Adam avec quatre autres Messieurs de *Manchester* dont nous avions fait la connaissance, en sorte que nous avons passé le dimanche fort agréablement à voir les environs de Liverpool, les bassins superbes où mille vaisseaux débarquent et embarquent leurs cargaisons, nous avons visité un pakbot américain qui est meublé si richement comme le plus bel appartement de seigneur, en sorte que ce doit être un délice d'y avoir le mal de mer. Nous avons été dîner sur l'autre rive de la Mersey d'où l'on a une vue des plus ravissantes vers la ville et le port rempli de vaisseaux; après avoir vu repartir nos visites dans les voitures à vapeur mais sans chevaux ni vapeur, puisque le chemin de fer, en sortant de Liverpool, se trouve sur un plan incliné, nous avons été passer deux heures avec M. Clow à l'*église anglicane* du soir; le service a lieu dans un beau salon éclairé au gaz, un espèce de chant qui ressemble à la messe catholique alterne avec d'autres chants fort beaux executés par des aveugles et tout se termine par un sermon auquel nous n'avons guère compris que le sens; au surplus je comprends et m'explique déjà mieux qu'à mon arrivée, puisque l'usage seul peut rendre familière une multitude d'expressions qu'on ne peut apprendre que dans le pays même.

Aujourd'hui nous avons vu le cimetière et le *Jardin Zoologique*, deux choses fort interessantes . . .

V

Londres, le 8 novembre [1834]

. . . Nous voici bien reposés et en train de terminer nos exploits à Londres que nous espérons quitter à la fin de la semaine . . . Nous avons vu des choses fort interessantes à *Liverpool* et puis à *Birmingham* où nous sommes restés un jour, ce qui est peu pour une si grande et belle ville; nous y arrivâmes dans la nuit du 5 au 6 et tu ne saurais croire quelles impressions nous fît le spectacle dont on jouit à plusieurs lieues avant d'y arriver; aussi loin qu'on peut voir tout est parsemé de hauts fourneaux dont sortent de larges flammes en sorte qu'on croit se trouver au milieu d'un immense incendie. A Liverpool et à Birmingham il y a des rues et des magasins aussi beaux que ceux de Londres, preuve qu'il y a dans ce pays une richesse et une industrie dont nous sommes encore loin en France. En voyant tous ces établissements j'ai souvent pensé comment il est possible d'avoir quelques sous en poche et ne pas venir faire un tour en *Angleterre* et je me félicite d'avoir pris le parti de m'y envoyer moi-même puisque personne d'autre m'y a plutot envoyé; de reste pour aller vite comme nous et pour voir quelque chose il faut dépenser terriblement de guinées, c'est le côté sombre du pays.

J'ai reçu à *Liverpool* la lettre de Jean[27] . . . Tu peux lui dire que sa commission est soignée et nos pianos payés, j'en ai vu chez un fabricant d'un ton délicieux et j'espère trouver le nôtre de même . . . Je t'écrirai avant de quitter Londres . . . Il faudrait rester un mois pour faire des affaires, on perd ici encore plus de temps qu'à Paris, les distances sont plus grandes, de même que les distractions, car à chaque pas on est tenté de s'arrêter devant les magasins; demain dimanche il faudrait forcement se promener car tout est fermé sauf les églises . . .

Dimanche matin

Amédée vient de partir pour Dartford pour profiter du dimanche, moi je resterai ici pour mettre ordre à mes affaires, et mes mille petites choses, racomoder les poches et les boutons, et faire quelques croquis, si la pluie m'empêche de sortir . . .

VI

Londres 25 août [18]41

Arrivé ici cet après midi . . . Ce matin la blanche ligne de la cote d'Angleterre était déjà en vue, mais il faut six à sept heures pour remonter la Tamise qui est encore presque pleine mer, un soleil d'été éclairait le beau spectacle des centaines de navires à voiles et à vapeur qui se croisent et dont le nombre augmente à mesure qu'on approche . . . Comme il y a sept ans, j'étais comme effrayé et étourdi lorsque nous fumes arrivés dans le port à travers la forêt de plusieurs mille navires qui, à mesure qu'ils arrivent, s'alignent en ordre comme des pelottons de soldats . . .

L'ennui du débarquement à la douane, de la visite du bureau de passeports, des pourboires infinis passé, un cabriolet me transporte au London Coffee House, c'est une maison sans apparence quoiqu'un des premiers hotels, après une course inutile pour trouver mon M. Shik j'ai cherché à m'orienter dans mon quartier de la *Cité*, le seul dont je me ressouvienne un peu; j'ai vu des magasins de papiers et d'étoffes; les premiers me font plaisir puisqu'il n'y a rien de bon goût, les seconds puisqu'ils sont magnifiques; il y en a de plus riches que ce que j'avais vu précédemment . . . au pis aller ces quelques jours à passer ici me laissent toujours une impression utile quoique sans résultat immédiat; il est bien difficile de faire quelque chose ici en peu de temps et de jours lorsqu'il faut commencer par faire des connaissances; il faudra que je me ramasse bien pour ne pas me distraire de mon but, les distractions sont par trop engageantes, même si je ne voulais voir que ce qui m'a échappé la dernière fois . . .

mardi 26

Je suis en courses . . . Le temps est superbe. Douze heures de sommeil d'un seul trait et un déjeuner d'huîtres m'ont considérablement remonté. Demain je dîne chez le banquier Schnitzler, ce qui m'arrange peu avec mon air provincial, mais la curiosité m'a fait accepter. Je te quitte pour aller au *Strand*, ce beau quartier . . .

VII

Londres 27 août minuit [1841]

Depuis deux jours je cours les rues pour voir les magasins de papier et je commence à connaître ce qui se fait à *Londres*; ces courses sont longues et fatiguantes et je ne suis pas trop à mon aise quelquefois lorsque je suis reçu avec hauteur ou avec un air de compassion méprisante, j'ai infiniment de peine à m'expliquer, mais du moins je prononce mieux que mon intrepide Shik qui détache hardiment son mauvais anglais.

Ce matin, après une course de plus d'une lieue, nous avons [*illisible*] d'un des premiers constructeurs qui a des centaines de palais en construction, il a été fort aimable . . . il m'a fait voir le modèle d'une statue colossale de Lord *Wellington* à cheval qui aura vingt-sept pieds de haut, puis j'ai examiné quelques appartements dans un quartier neuf trois fois grand comme Mulhouse près du Hyde Park; en revenant dans la Cité, j'ai eu à peine le temps pour me faire aussi beau que possible croyant assister à un grand dîner, aussi n'ai-je pas été peu étonné de ne trouver que mon couvert à côté de celui de M. Schnitzler qui est vieux garçon . . .; cela n'empêche qu'on nous a servi brillamment et cérémonieusement du poisson, du gigot avec trois ou quatre légumes, du pud[d]ing, du dessert et du vin du Rhin et enfin du caviar de Russie qu'on mange sur une tartine de pain grillé et qu'il m'a fallu malgré moi dire excellent vu que c'est un mets recherché dont je me serais bien passé, après cela mon banquier m'a conduit au spectacle français pour voir jouer . . . le *Misanthrope* et un morceau de Scribe dont j'ai été assez satisfait; en résumé ce M. Schnitzler est un bon homme, mais trop grand sire pour moi et, ma foi, je ne changerai pas avec lui. Demain je me dirigerai d'un autre côté . . . Je pense quitter ici aux premiers jours de la semaine . . .

du 28

. . . Les beaux équipages et les belles femmes du *Strand* m'ont donné le vertige et la bière m'a dérangé le ventre . . . Ils se croient bien heureux ces gens à deux valets dorés derrière leur voiture et un cocher à perruque! et ils sont plus esclaves que le moindre cultivateur.[28] Ce superbe *London* doit devenir insuportable à ceux qui n'y sont pas pour s'amuser, qui ne veulent ou ne peuvent faire des folies, et à ceux qui ont leurs enfans à 200 lieues . . . Je suis vraiment contrarié de n'avoir aucune occasion de barragouiner mon anglais avec quelque jolie anglaise de la Cité, pourtant l'occasion serait facile à se procurer. Once more goodnight.

Le vendredi 29

Je reviens de *Greenwich*, j'y suis allé à pied en prenant le Tunnel qui n'est pas achevé comme on le fait à croire et j'en suis revenu en chemin de fer, un chemin qui est tout entier bâti en arcades de maçonnerie. J'avais voulu voir l'hopital de Greenwich, un palais vraiment royal et près les docks ou entrepôts où chargent les navires . . . ainsi au galop ; j'en suis abîmé et soupire après le tranquille mouvement du Steamer qui me ramènera sur terre ferme. Le jardin doit être bien beau. Si les arbres sont en fleurs comme ici, c'est admirable et je me réjouis de revoir le pays, j'ai déjà besoin de sortir de ce pays-ci . . . lundi je tâcherai d'en finir ici avec mes courses . . .

NOTES

[1] Mention may be made of Ethel Jones, *Les Voyageurs français en Angleterre de 1815 à 1830* (Paris, 1930), and Sylvaine Marandon, *L'image de la France dans la conscience anglaise dans l'Angleterre victorienne (1848–1900)* (Paris, 1967).

[2] See the bibliography of the third edition, Leicester University Press, 1972.

[3] We are most grateful to M. Paul-René Zuber for communicating the letters published here. Family genealogist and historian, he has published a number of 'Cahiers Zuber' (cyclostyled and privately circulated). Our thanks also go to W. H. Chaloner and D. A. Farnie for biographical details on Steiner, Potter and Thomson.

[4] Besides the *Histoire documentaire de l'industrie de Mulhouse au XIXe siècle* (vol. II, Mulhouse, 1902), pp.559–66 and 570–2, see also our study *L'Alsace au début du XIXe siècle*, vol. II ('Les Transformations économiques') (Paris 1959), pp.469–73 and 476–7.

[5] 1773–1852. Obituary notice in the *Bulletin de la Société industrielle de Mulhouse* (1852), pp.269–81 (the *Bulletin* will be cited hereafter as *BSIM*) and Cahiers Zuber, XIV, 1954. The *Reminiscences et Souvenirs de Jean Zuber père* were published in Mulhouse in 1895.

[6] 'Threatened with prosecution, he abandoned wife and child. We see the unfortunate boy and his sickly mother turned out of the father's house, taken in by an aunt, sleeping in a gloomy back room and owing his schooling to the generosity of a few other relations . . . ; between classes he nursed his mother, bringing water and wood, and earning a few pennies tying up bundles of washing for laundries.' (BSIM, 1852, p.271).

[7] Elisabeth Spoerlin always kept Lavater's *Chants Spirituels* from her father's library on her bedside table. See Cahiers Zuber, IX ('Centenaire des noces d'or Zuber-Spoerlin', 1846), 1946.

[8] This system whereby pupils were taught through monitors had the especial advantage of cheapness and had been devised by the Anglican Dr Alexander Bell of Madras and the Quaker Joseph Lancaster. For its introduction in France, see Paul Leuilliot, *op. cit.*, vol. III (1960), pp.303–11.

[9] 'Notice sur Jean Zuber fils', *BSIM*, 1853, pp.111–29 and Cahiers Zuber, XIX, 1972 ; 'Notice sur Frédéric Zuber', *BSIM*, 1892, pp.78–81 and Cahiers Zuber, XIII, 1954.

[10] He once told of a most thrilling crossing when returning from Denmark in 1825, when the sailing ship he was on lost its rudder and was crippled by a storm and was tossed about for six days. The danger of sudden death made such an impression on him that his religious convictions were strengthened for life.

[11] The firm also sold 93,000 francs' worth in northern and central Europe, 73,000 in France (including 27,000 in Paris), 45,000 in Switzerland, 19,000 in Italy and 42,000 in the United States (a warehouse had just been set up in New York, which in 1832 became a sales office and in 1835 was changed into a limited partnership).

12 'Notice', *BSIM*, 1881, pp.273–80.
13 For an indication of the lead England enjoyed, see D. C. Coleman, *The British Paper Industry* (Oxford, 1848). According to Coleman (p.211, n. 4), the first paper machine in France dated from 1811, and there were only four in 1827. Not until after 1830 did they become at all widespread and even then they were still manufactured in England.
14 We have drawn attention to one of Zuber's patents in *L'Alsace au début du XIXe siècle*, II, p.471, n. 5. This was 'moyen de substituer au mode actuel d'impression des papiers à la main celui d'impression au rouleau en creux et en relief' (*Bulletin de la Société d'encouragement pour l'industrie nationale*, XXV, 1826). The early date may be noted, though we should point out that the process was already in use in calico printing.
15 For John Hall, see Everard Hesketh, *J. & E. Hall Ltd., 1785–1935* (Glasgow, 1935) and Coleman, *op. cit.*; Léger Didot had introduced mechanised paper production at Dartford in the early nineteenth century. According to Coleman, it is very difficult to distinguish the respective roles of Robert, the Fourdriniers, Gamble and the engineer Donkin (p.182). There is a reference to Dartford at the end of the fifth of Zuber's letters.
16 On the artistic aspects of production, see *Trois siècles de papiers peints* (Exposition du Musée parisien des Arts décoratifs, Paris, 1967), pp.95–7.
17 *BSIM*, 1851, p.350. This report, which followed the Great Exhibition of 1851, constitutes a history of wallpaper. For C. E. and J. G. Potter of Darwen, see Coleman, *op. cit.*, p.340. The paper-staining firm of C. & J. G. Potter was founded in 1841, originated in calico-printing and gave Darwen a new industry which survived after the extinction of the local calico-printing industry in 1878; J. E. Shaw, *History and Traditions of Darwen and its People* (Blackburn, 1889), pp.157–61.
18 *BSIM*, 1852, pp.127–9.
19 R. S. Crossley, *Accrington Captains of Industry* (Accrington, 1930), pp.80–3: 'Frederick Steiner (born 30 March 1787; died 29 November 1869)'. Steiner became a naturalised British subject when he established his own firm in 1836 and bought Hyndburn House from the Peels *c*. 1849. He also invited to England the Alsatian Frederick Albert Gatty (1819–88), who founded a Turkey red dyeing firm in Accrington in 1843. Gatty improved the dyeing of Turkey red with garancine, for the manufacture of which Steiner took out a patent on 8 August 1843. He made 'Gatty red' famous in Eastern markets. Finally, he discovered the mineral khaki dye which he produced by using oxides of chromium and iron and which he patented on 20 August 1884. See Crossley, pp.199–201.
20 'Turkey red cottons of the Steiner factory, which were so much to the Eastern taste, spread throughout India and Persia and sold in far greater quantities than similar products from Switzerland ... Old England with a marked preference for bright red things, as the jackets of her soldiers and her huntsmen prove, consumed very large amounts of fine printed calicoes, dyes with red madder, from the Steiner factory. Another article produced by this firm that is popular in England is the red eiderdown, each of which is the equivalent of three of the finest woollen blankets. The founder of this important factory died in 1870'. Fr Edouard Sitzman, *Dictionnaire de biographie des hommes célèbres de l'Alsace*, vol. II (Rixheim, 1910). This notice with its advertising style unfortunately has no bibliographical references. The entry that follows it concerns Frédéric's nephew, Charles Steiner (1814–66): 'called to England by his uncle in 1834 he became his collaborator in dyeing Turkey red cottons and in setting up the works at Church, one of the largest in Lancashire, which he managed until 1839 ... After eight years' residence in England he gave up an excellent post to return to Ribeauvillé where with limited resources he set up a red dye-works to which he added printing-works shortly after. The low price and high quality of his products quickly ensured the rapid expansion of the new establishment ...'
21 See the first letter and *BSIM*, 1851, pp.182–5. J. Thomson, 'of the Royal Society of London, corresponding member of the Mulhouse Industrial Society' was born in Blackburn in 1779 and died on 17 September 1850. A brief obituary may be found in the *Manchester Guardian*, 21 September 1850, 7i, alluding to the close family connection between the Thomsons and the Peels. There is no obituary in the

Proceedings of the Royal Society. Thomson patented in England on 3 March 1813 and 4 February 1815 the process patented in France in 1811 by Daniel Koechlin for the acid and bleaching-powder discharge upon Turkey red. He also invented the process for the discharge of indigo blue by the application of potassium bicarbonate which came into general use. He also secured the first reliable microscopical investigation of the form of the cotton fibre by Bauer. 'His scientific knowledge and highly cultivated taste, combined with the great energy and enterprise of his character, placed him in the very foremost rank amongst the philosophical manufacturers of his time', *Manchester Guardian*, 21 September 1850, 7i. The Primrose Works, which were opened in 1801 and closed in 1854, specialised in the manufacture of high quality prints. Thomson Bros. & Co. ranked as the sixth largest calico-printers in 1839 in the number of pieces printed but as the fourth in the number of its printing tables and as the second in the number of its employees, being thus a far more important firm than that of Steiner. See G. Turnbull, *A History of the Calico Printing Industry of Great Britain* (Altrincham, 1951), p.424 and James Thomson, *A Letter to the Right Honourable Sir Robert Peel, Bart. on Copyright in Original Designs and Patterns for Printing* (Clitheroe, Whalley, 1840, 60 pp.), 36. Thomson's other publications included *A Letter to the Vice-President of the Board of Trade, on Protection to Original Designs and Patterns, Printed upon Woven Fabrics* (Clitheroe, Whalley, 1840, 28 pp., 15 plates) and *Notes on the Present State of Calico Printing in Belgium, with Prefatory Observations on the Competition and Tariff of Different Countries* (Clitheroe, Whalley, 1841, 75 pp.). These works helped to secure the extension in 1842 of the period of copyright in printed designs from three months to nine months.

[22] Paul Leuilliot, *La 'Biographie industrielle' de F. C. L. Albert (1764–1831), Contribution à l'histoire de l'introduction du machinisme en France* (offprint from the *Annales historiques de la Révolution française*, 1952).

[23] All the letters are addressed to his wife in Rixheim.

[24] Amédée Rieder.

[25] The trip to Ireland was never made.

[26] This was probably Thomas Dickin or Dickins, a silk printer, who had a works and private house side by side at Spring Vale, Middleton in the early 1840s. (Information kindly supplied by Mr W. John Smith of Middleton.)

[27] Jean Zuber, Frédéric's brother.

[28] In 1838 Frédéric Zuber wrote that 'l'état normal de l'homme est celui de cultivateur'.

B. L. Anderson

5

Law, finance and economic growth in England: some long-term influences

This paper attempts to explore some of the relations between the law, its profession, and the development of financial institutions in England during the eighteenth and nineteenth centuries.[1] It takes a long view, and so a fairly generalised one, of just some of those neglected influences in economic development that help to determine how far, and in what ways, the savings potential of the community is capable of being translated into productive investment. While the impact of such factors on the pace and character of economic growth has usually been indirect, difficult to specify and assess, it may be that closer consideration of them can provide an important aid in the interpretation of much of the recent literature relating to the role of financial change in English economic growth. Hopefully, it may also draw attention to the functional significance of the legal–institutional framework within which economic growth necessarily takes place.[2] The discussion begins by tracing a few of the more formative influences emanating from certain technical devices that originated in the English land law; then it examines the ways in which the law attempted to mould these to existing financial needs. Finally, an attempt is made to show how the particular contribution of the legal profession as financial intermediary forms part of a more general rationale that can be used for explaining the particular form in which financial institutions emerged during industrialisation, and how they were related to that process.

I

Anyone seeking to unravel the land law must approach it with considerable trepidation, for, as the author of a treatise on estates of 1820 observed, 'The difficulty of comprehending the reason and the scope of the rules of property, will occasion to every person, at the commencement of his studies, some difficulties, and lay him under some embarrassments'.[3] The difficulty arises, of course, because the English land law has never undergone a root-and-branch reform, as in Ireland or on the Continent, partly because of the peculiar sanctity with which the

English have always endowed property rights, but also because it never became, even during the age of reform, a burning political issue as elsewhere.[4] If there is any single key to understanding the links between the land law and economic development it is the doctrine of 'estates in land'. This was grafted on to the English conception of tenure as early as the twelfth century, and henceforth men were regarded not as owning land *per se* but as owning *interests* in land, these being classified according to their quality and duration, viz. fee simple, fee tail, etc. Continuity has been so much a feature of the land law that one can safely return to the treatise of 1820 for a short definition of these interests which does not differ essentially from what the medieval lawyers had in mind. 'The material difference between fees-simple and other fees is, that the former estate *will*, the latter estate *may*, continue for ever.'[5] In other words, there were two types of landowner in England—one for whom land was a marketable commodity, which could be used and improved, or sold during life, or bequeathed at death; another for whom land was a 'family estate', a holding (to call it a trust would be premature) which was to be preserved for posterity.

Another medieval concept, the 'equitable use', had the effect of complicating the land law even further by creating a second distinction, between the legal and the equitable estate in land. It was for long used to deny the Crown its feudal revenues, and an attempt was made to abolish it by the Statute of Uses of 1535. But it was a tenacious creature, and seventeenth-century lawyers and conveyancers, of whom Sir Orlando Bridgeman is best known, redeveloped the use in the form of the 'strict settlement'. In this device, by which a landowner carved up his fee simple into a life estate for himself, a life estate for his eldest son, and an estate tail for his eldest son's eldest son, we see the archetype of the eighteenth-century trust. There are two important characteristics of this legal–financial technique that should be noted. First, the trust has deep-rooted origins going back a very long way in the land law, where its apprenticeship was served and the mark of which it never really lost. Second, it is distinctively English (and later American); indeed, legal historians have been unable to find any true parallel in Continental systems of law, and attribute its emergence in the English tradition to the fact that only here was a system of equity developed to run alongside the common law.[6] Between the late seventeenth and the early nineteenth centuries, from Lord Nottingham to Lord Eldon, in the progress of equity and the growth of trusts the one owed much to the existence of the other. Successive chancellors transformed them from a 'benevolent, but incalculable, control of legal rights, into a body of settled rules and principles'.[7] Equity was the main vehicle by which the jurisdiction of the Court of Chancery was extended, while the trust became a highly effective precautionary method of shielding the ownership of property, not just real estate, against almost every conceivable incident which an owner might regard as inimical to his well laid plans.

Some adverse effects did, of course, flow from the creation and growth of trust estates after the Restoration. Innumerable obstacles were placed in the way of simple conveyancing, and all attempts to introduce a land registry in England—and there were many over the next two hundred years—were doomed to failure.[8] It certainly meant, too, that much land was artificially held off the land market for long periods; that is, in so far as one can speak of a market in land and property at all beyond the local level, and akin to the money market, say, or the markets in commodities.[9] On the other hand its influence on the process of consolidation and accumulation in agriculture, particularly when it facilitated improvement through the landlord–tenant relationship, could be of considerable, if indirect, importance.[10] By the eighteenth century we know that there were formidable obstacles in the way of family estates ever going out of settlement. Directly the eldest son came of age the options were put to him

> do your duty to the family by surrendering your future estate tail, receiving instead a future life estate and a present handsome allowance, or remain during your father's lifetime without funds. Whether through family pride, or the knowledge that he could scarcely raise a mortgage himself on such terms, the son yields. Father and son then disentail the property, and then resettle it, restoring the father's life estate, giving a life estate to the son on the father's death, and an estate in tail male to *his* sons successively. When he marries and *his* eldest son comes of age, the same ingenious process is repeated, each heir being induced, like some latter-day Esau, to sell his birthright for a financial mess of pottage.[11]

It is believed that by the middle of the eighteenth century something approaching one half the land of England was held in this way. The owner of such an estate for the time being, since he could not alienate it and was only entitled to the income for life, had a vested interest, when making financial provision for his dependants, in raising lump sums by mortgage rather than by the creation of rent charges which would have reduced his disposable income.

Several important socio-economic effects followed from this greater reliance of English landowners on strict settlements and mortgages. The younger sons of landed families now stood a better chance of obtaining a more secure patrimony and were now more independent of the eldest son than previously: this must have given a boost to that age-old process of cross-fertilisation between land and trade which, in the eighteenth century, enabled landed offspring to exploit widening avenues of opportunity in commerce and the professions from a firmer base position. The same set of circumstances also influenced the working of the marriage market, by altering the relationship between the size of the portion or dowry which the wife initially brought from her father, and the size of the jointure, the annual income which her husband settled on her to provide for her needs in the likely event she survived him. Over the period there appears to have been a progressive increase in the size of the portion necessary to yield a given jointure.[12] Leaving aside a number of secondary reasons for this, of which a falling rate of interest is only the most obvious, the evidence suggests that the bait of larger portions to secure good marriage was primarily symptomatic of a more vigorous approach to the extension of landed wealth; by allowing the most substantial jointure to command the largest portion, though (presumably) not always the most desirable bride, the marriage market was being more closely integrated with, not to say subordinated to, the accumulative process.

Side by side with its growing enforcement of these trusts for terms of years which had been left untouched by the Statute of Uses, the Court of Chancery was also extending its jurisdiction over mortgages, establishing a general right of redemption and separating the debt itself from the underlying security.[13] This joint development had been obscured during the Civil War and Commonwealth periods, but with the abolition of the chief feudal tenures at the Restoration the last restraint on Chancery, the loss to the king's revenue occasioned by an extension of trusts, was removed. Under Lord Chancellor Nottingham, the 'father of equity', the volume of trusts and their attendant mortgages rose very quickly, and the principles relating to them were considerably refined. The Statute of Frauds of 1677, which formalised procedure for the creation of trusts, also established guidelines for the execution of wills; this too is important because it highlights the peculiar role of the testamentary executor and trustee in England as compared with elsewhere in Europe. Without pausing to discover the origins of this divergence in the differing impact of the ancient Roman and Germanic laws relating to property and succession, suffice it to say that the lack of a persistent Roman influence in English legal development had the effect of vesting considerable powers in the executor, who virtually came to assume the position of an heir, particularly as regards personal estate.[14] In a testamentary trust the beneficiary, especially if he is not competent, is relieved of the task of handling investment by a fit person who handles them directly as if they were his own. By the late seventeenth century the executor as trustee was answerable to the courts of equity, where he could seek advice and must ultimately account for his actions.[15] He could intermingle the trust fund with his own estate and was allowed wide discretion as long as the trust fund was beyond risk. If bankruptcy of the trustee occurred, then a new one was appointed; the trustee was also liable not only in respect of what he had received from the testator but also in respect of any failure to get in property which he ought to have received. In a largely non-institutionalised capital market such as that of the eighteenth century was, those responsible for safeguarding and disposing of personal wealth have a special significance; to find the English law investing them with such powers and responsibility is surely indicative of a legal framework closely aligned to private accumulation. By way of comparison it is interesting to notice, for example, that the French civil code of 1804 provides an executor with little real power; he is no longer the representative of the deceased and his rights do not materially limit the rights of the heirs. In Germany also, Roman influence on the common law appears to have had the effect of narrowing down his functions.[16]

II

Eighteenth-century England saw a marvellous proliferation of trusts out of the context of landed property. The process seems to have begun when Lord Nottingham first enunciated the principle that a trust was to be protected against the creditors of the trustee in 1673. By the 1750s Lord Mansfield could conclude:

> In my opinion, trusts were not on a true foundation till Lord Nottingham held the great seal. By steadily pursuing, from plain principles, trusts in all their consequences, and by some assistance from the legislature, a noble, rational, and uniform system of law has been since raised. Trusts are made to answer the exigencies of families, and all purposes, without producing one inconvenience, fraud, or private mischief, which the statute of Henry VIII meant to avoid.[17]

Without a viable trust device the whole range of charitable endowments in England would have been impossible, as would the economic well-being of barely tolerated minority groups; each of these was an important focus of private accumulation. Trusts of money became as usual as trusts of land, as the device passed from an over-developed land law and fanned out amongst the growing commercial interests. Unincorporate bodies of all types were able to grow behind 'a hedge of trustees'; indeed, as probate records show, almost everyone of any substance was a trustee for somebody else. It enabled married women to have property that was all their own, long before there was any legislation to that effect, but then the financially independent woman was no stranger to the eighteenth century. Similarly with the social and political club; the eighteenth century has been called 'the most clubbable of all centuries' and it too flourished on the basis of contract and trust. This form of association was preferred to corporateness because it was relatively free of the petrifying action of juristic theory; those ancient institutions the Inns of Court, for example, could have dissolved themselves at any time and divided the property that was held for them by trustees among their members.[18] It does seem as ironic that these societies of lawyers had themselves no juristic personality, no corporate face, as it is of economic significance that the judges who communicated the law of corporations to eighteenth-century businessmen were to a man members of these same bodies. If these rich and influential lawyers had not found their own want of a legal persona a misfortune— and no doubt they could have obtained incorporation had they wanted it—why should it be thought that the majority of entrepreneurs would wish to ignore what the lawyers themselves found satisfactory and long for a legal privilege of association that most would have found to be of dubious value?

It is never fully appreciated how far the English law of association departed from the European norm at this period.[19] In general, on the Continent the only legal relation arising out of agreement between persons, i.e. voluntary association, was a contract. The position of unincorporated societies was thereby made highly unsatisfactory, which doubtless accounts for the early use of the corporate principle and the greater enthusiasm for extending it. The great advantage of English law, on the other hand, possessing the trust as well as the contractual obligation, was not only that it allowed associations to form and maintain themselves without being legally incorporated, but that by going beyond the confines of contract it enabled the trust to plug the gaps in corporation law at the time of greatest State hostility towards corporations. As is well known, it could do this by vesting the property of the group, firm, society or whatever in trustees who applied it for the benefit of the members, and who appeared in any legal actions concerning the property, thereby circumventing the rule that only a corporate body could sue or be sued directly.[20] A further advantage, not unimportant when bankruptcy was so commonplace, was that the trust property was kept safe from the creditors of individual partners: in fact a debtor was better placed to defeat his creditors if he was a member of an unincorporated association than if he was a shareholder in a corporation; the shares of a corporate debtor could simply be transferred to the creditor, whereas no single member's stake in an unincorporated body could be claimed by creditors until dissolution by the consent, not of a majority, but of all the members.[21] It is not surprising that eighteenth-century Jews, Catholics and Nonconformists found in the trust an ideal financial vehicle and used it to promote their economic activities without having to face external litigation as a group personality like a corporation. In the same way entrepreneurs, so often the same people, largely rejected incorporation in favour of the trust, if only because the first implied privilege and favour, and attracted official scrutiny, whereas the other was quite adequate to the task of making the basic partnership form expand to the requirements of larger enterprise.[22]

The typical entrepreneur of the period rarely felt the need for the conferment of what amounted to a quasi-public status, and certainly would have wished to avoid the considerable expense involved at a time when the legal profession drafted its documents in circumlocutory fashion and then charged per folio for them. But even the larger financial institutions of the eighteenth century, with good expectations of a long life, also utilised the trust form and continued with it long after alternative forms of association had become readily available. The London stock exchange, which drew up its deed of settlement as late as 1802, actually refused the privilege of incorporation recommended by Royal Commission in 1878 and contented itself with the possession of a simple trust deed.[23] Similarly, the 'Committee for regulating the affairs of Lloyd's Coffee House' did not execute a trust deed until 1811 and became incorporated only in 1871. When it came to competing with the Royal Exchange and London Assurance companies in the marine insurance market after 1720, such a loosely held organisation certainly did not work to Lloyd's disadvantage.[24] It is also worth recalling that most of the basic economic functions of English local government and administration over much of the period of the Industrial Revolution were performed by unincorporated bodies of trustees, some of them administering substantial corporate estates and the more successful providing considerable impetus to local public endeavour for a century or more before the Municipal Corporations Act.[25]

There is no question, of course, that the Bubble Act hindered the formation of *some* joint-stock companies, though it also seems clear that long before its repeal in 1825 there was ample scope for lawyers to draw its teeth where, and when, it was necessary. The question of its impact, in detail, on English industrial organisation during the following century is still open; but whatever its effects it is worth remembering that the absence of conditions for easy incorporation had a positive effect in stimulating the law into providing a better framework for enterprise along existing lines—by group and partnership. Eighteenth-century common lawyers, especially Mansfield, built up the obligations of partners to each other and to third parties in their case law; while the Court of Chancery quickly mapped out a new area of development for itself by treating the unincorporate business association as a trust. In the eighteenth-century trust deed of settlement we see the forerunner of the articles of association required by nineteenth-century company law; and limitations on liability going further than ever before could be inserted into it, which opened the way for Lord Hardwicke to model the director's responsibilities on those of the trustee.[26] As A. B. Dubois remarked, 'Such an organisation as the Birmingham Metal Company was perhaps more influential in the evolution of the business corporation of the nineteenth century than was the chartered Bank of England.'[27] It could be added that, in comparison with the experience of other countries, the need for legislative intervention to hasten that evolution was, in the case of England, also reduced in view of the large area of comparative freedom for business association that remained after the passage of the Bubble Act. In fact, in retrospect, incorporation in the English context takes on the appearance of a quite unwieldy device by comparison with the subtle flexibility of the well tried partnership extended via the trust form.[28] For this reason, in part at least, the existing law of partnership continued to be regarded as broadly appropriate to English business conditions until well into the nineteenth century, and even after the advent of modern company legislation. Or, as Pollock wrote, 'the convenience of mankind and the actual usages of men of business have, on the whole, prevailed in the formation of our modern commercial law, so that the great bulk of it only wants putting into shape to be accepted as satisfactory. This is eminently the case with the law of partnership.[29]

III

The influence of legal factors on the working of the land market appears to have had a stabilising effect for considerable periods, not only during the half-century after 1680 but at times during the nineteenth century as well.[30] This condition, which was characterised by a stable to falling level of direct sales and a not unconnected longer-term trend towards larger holdings of land, also had some impact on the role of that professional group most closely associated with it, the attorneys. They were already gaining ground at the expense of the Bar, particularly in the provinces, by the late seventeenth century.[31] This was to some degree a reflection of the growing demand for the attorney's administrative services vis-à-vis the traditional barrister's counselling; but there seems little doubt that any status changes within the legal profession resulting from improved prospects for attorneys cannot be separated from, and were probably hastened by, the increase in trust and mortgage business which added the function of financial intermediary to that of simple conveyancer.[32] In the eighteenth century, perhaps more clearly than at any other period, this professional group held the middle ground between land and trade; at a time when his professional mould had not yet become fixed the attorney's experience gave him access to knowledge and influence in both of these areas of economic life. There is much evidence to show that the growing wealth of the merchant community at this time was constantly liable to setback, even ruin, by virtue of the high risks of trade, which made profits and merchant fortunes inherently unstable.[33] The simultaneous growth in numbers and social position of attorneys, in addition to representing one of the classical channels along which landed and trading wealth met and mingled, may also at times have provided a counterbalancing area of more stable employment for unsuccessful merchants as well as contributing its own brand of entrepreneurial talent.[34]

A comprehensive assessment of the attorney's functions at many points in the development of the capital market during industrialisation cannot be undertaken here. But at the local level, and via institutional changes, it was a very considerable contribution and raises the question whether, even on *prima facie* grounds, the law has been accorded adequate recognition as the key profession to study in the period of English economic growth.[35] It alone had the necessary Janus face to familiarise itself with, and frequently exploit to advantage, the two great sources of wealth—land and trade. It had always been important in a society dominated by property-based oligarchies of gentry and magnates; but increasingly during the eighteenth century it also came to serve the commercial classes as well, most notably by helping to incorporate the law merchant into the common law.[36] As in the case of banking, the law produced some of the very greatest families, like the Finches and the Norths; there was also considerable geographical as well as social mobility, with a national network of legal relations linking provincial attorneys to the London Inns, and sometimes overlapping with other eighteenth-century financial connections like the agency arrangements amongst bankers. We know that the legal profession was a significant source of recruits for banking, and indeed their activities can be regarded as adjacent within the broad field of financial mediation. The place of London as the natural focus of much of this activity is very important because so many of these interpersonal links in banking and the law have common origins in the remittance, by estate stewards, land agents and revenue farmers, of gentry incomes and taxes from the provinces to the capital.[37] Yet having said this it remains true that the attorney's continuing role in the capital market was essentially localised —urban and rural mortgage finance, turnpike trust and canal investment, even the marketing of railway shares—and can be likened to the way in which the lower echelons of the profession fed upon urban growth by inserting themselves at all the strategic points of local administration from an early stage.[38]

In view of this background it was natural that when professional demarcations began to harden somewhat among the urban middle classes during the course of the nineteenth century the type of investment advice and the extent of investment horizons amongst local solicitors reflected to a high degree the earlier economic activities in which they had been engaged, either for clients or for themselves.[39] Socially, of course, their sphere was always a broad one; hence their usefulness in the nineteenth-century financial world, which continued to be conducted in largely personal terms. But as to their investments' range, it was quite provincial: property and mortgages, followed by local transport and public utility securities of all kinds, remained, as they had always been, the common currency of their financial advice. It was an area of investment which solicitors had made their own since the late seventeenth century, with Chancery's controlling influence at their back, and which by the nineteenth century they had come to know well, and had reared generations of investor clients to know it too. In short, risk investment, much less speculation, probably held small attraction for the nineteenth-century solicitor; and to judge from his continuing dominance of trustee and executor work, the bulk of the risk-avoiding investment public appear to have agreed his caution.

The growth of trusts probably reinforced and helped perpetuate this tradition in the investment of funds, if only because a trustee acting not for himself but for the advantage of beneficiaries had to adopt a safety-first approach. The obligation to operate neutrally as between one client and another reduced the scope for an active investment policy on the part of trustees, and, of course, their behaviour was in any event largely conditioned by the range of secure investment options open to them. For much of the eighteenth century mortgages and government fixed-interest securities virtually exhausted that range, which helps to explain why the supply side of the mortgage market appears so buoyant and, indeed, why the development of government long-term borrowing met with so few obstacles.[40] In fact Walpole's conversion of 1717 and Pelham's of 1752, when the national debt acquired a new permanence, can be properly interpreted only against a background of falling interest rates and relatively plentiful funds; at the same time joint and multiple holdings on the part of executors and trustees were common in most of the public funds, especially in South Sea annuities, and they were tending to increase. It may be significant here that although there was a substantial provincial stake in the earliest of all the public loans—the Tontine of 1693—suggesting an early availability of provincial funds for such purposes, this interest was not maintained, and by mid-century domestic investment in the national debt was closely based on London.[41] Without pursuing the point one can think of a number of localised outlets for provincial long-term money, even at this stage, much of it in local mortgages and property.[42]

During the course of the eighteenth century turnpikes, docks and inland waterways extended the range of safe investments to some extent, though leaving their localised character unchanged: the attorney continued to be prominent in directing funds to these outlets. But there was one factor at work continually pushing trust funds in the direction of the national debt: following the impoverishment of many beneficiaries as a result of the speculative use of some trust funds in the Bubble period, the Chancery judges adopted a stricter attitude and became much more inclined to call trustees to account if they had invested outside mortgages and the public debt.[43] There must always have been some pressure from trustees for broadening the range further —quite how much is difficult to decide early on—and there is no doubt that the reorganisation of local government after the Municipal Corporations Act of 1835 set up fresh demands for extending the field. But whether through professional caution or, remembering the case of the savings banks, the convenience to governments of knowing that any new flotation of debt would be fully and easily taken up, there was no radical change. A clear line was consistently drawn between government stocks, together with those of certain public utilities subject to statutory regulation, and industrial and commercial investments, right down to the Trustee Act of 1925. The Trustees' Relief Act of 1859 permitted trust investment in Bank of England, Irish and East India stock for the first time; and when the interest on consols, for so long regarded as the standard trustee investment, was reduced from 3 to $2\frac{1}{2}$ per cent following the National Debt Reduction Act of 1886, there was again demand for greater freedom. It was only after 1889, with the Trust Investment Act, that trustees were officially allowed to invest in railway debentures and preference shares, provided the company had paid an ordinary share dividend of 3 per cent over the previous two years. By the next Trustee Act in 1893 the law, finding it had taken two steps forward, now came back one, and needed to be sure that the railway in question had paid an ordinary dividend over the previous ten years; though at the same time it did extend the range of public utility and local authority investments. In fact not until the last year of the century, with the Colonial Stock Act, was any overseas investment officially permitted, and then only in the empire under Treasury-prescribed conditions.[44]

It is difficult to decide how much importance should be placed on the fact that this record of legislation on trustee investment in the nineteenth century clearly lagged far behind the underlying pattern of investment activity. But it seems reasonable to suggest that it was one channel along which 'rentier' savings were being directed away from industry and trade.[45] It is even more difficult, given the paucity of solicitors' records available, to know what changes were occurring in their role as financial intermediaries. Allowing for the fact that much of the trust legislation must have been anticipated or contravened in practice, and that solicitors at least handled non-trust funds as well, it does seem that they were more inclined to follow than to lead where financial innovation was concerned. The importance of private sources of funds for business investment outside the formal institutions of the capital market has received frequent emphasis for the nineteenth century,[46] but little attention has been given to the nature and extent of the legal profession's part in the private investment scene generally. What evidence there is suggests a broad continuity of association with traditional fields of interest, such as the local mortgage and property markets, where personal knowledge and close attention were all-important. At the same time the prominence of solicitors in the early building society movement, their connection with the promotion of railway companies in the 1840s and, more generally, with the often highly speculative joint-stock companies of the 1860s, perhaps signifies that any professional hardening of the arteries was limited.[47] But the really important feature of all these activities lies in their regional, even local scope. In Scotland solicitors appear to have turned their long-established investment function towards overseas lending earlier in the century; after 1870 their contribution was especially significant in American cattle and land companies, and in the Australian pastoral industry.[48] It is not possible to assess the extent of this contrast with English experience, or its timing; but it seems clear that in both cases legal influence on the flow of funds worked away from, rather than towards, risk investment in domestic industry. This trend would appear to be in line with existing evidence that after the rapid accumulation of railway capital English investors from the 1850s, and Scottish from the 1870s, were increasingly searching out new investment opportunities, largely overseas.[49]

By the later nineteenth century this legal influence on the management of savings was especially strong in Scotland; there the legal profession displayed the same talent for fund-raising among numerous small savers as its English counterpart had shown earlier in the marketing of railway shares at home.[50] In particular the Scots lawyer was one of the prime movers in the invention and propagation of investment trusts, perhaps the most distinctive contribution of the law and legal expertise in late nineteenth-century financial development. A number of Scottish investment trusts originally centred on the offices of local solicitors and accountants, not just in Edinburgh but in Glasgow, Aberdeen and Dundee to a lesser extent.[51] This contrasts remarkably with the situation in England, where these institutions largely by-passed the major provincial centres and instead concentrated in London. It is possible that these different patterns of development reflect a more generally divergent experience in the two countries. The evidence is only suggestive, but in view of the emphasis usually laid on the high degree of specialisation in financial services by the second half of the nineteenth century, largely centred on the City, it is interesting to discover that the Scottish savings movement preferred to place its investment department funds in local municipal utilities and mortgages rather than in the national debt long after the purchase of consols by them was permitted.[52]

Returning to the influence of the trust device, it is also significant that a number of early investment trusts actually used this device for a time, when, following the crisis of 1866, widespread mistrust of limited companies made it a useful substitute for that form; at the same time, among those responsible for trustee investment at the local level who exerted most pressure to broaden the range of acceptable securities, Scottish savings bankers were well to the fore.[53] In institutional forms such as these there was a culmination by the late nineteenth century, in Britain at least, of long-run traditional practices in which the functions of executorship and trust had been linked to numerous individual financial tributaries. Here it is arguable whether these practices were better preserved in Scotland than in England at this stage. But if they were, then it may be partly attributable to the fact that Scots property and contract law helped in keeping alive the function of the attorney as a general 'man of affairs'. Being more open to Franco–Roman legal influence, conveyancing had become simpler and more direct than in England, where a division of labour between solicitor and estate agent had already grown up; not only was the Scots solicitor's purview wider, but he was more likely to be well versed in financial matters, and this, combined with the fact that he faced a property market even more highly localised than in England, enabled him to retain a more dominant position in property transactions.[54] To the extent that this was the case the solicitor's position became virtually that of a local monopolist in the supply of fixed-interest funds.

IV

The significance of these interrelations between the law and finance can perhaps be seen more clearly in the context of long-run developments in the formal institutions of the capital market in England. One problem here—perhaps the most important still outstanding in discussions of how industrialisation was financed—is that not enough is known about the precise nature of the relationship between London and the manufacturing districts of the country. The question is normally discussed solely in terms of the role of the banks in liquidating the surpluses of the agricultural and older industrial centres and distributing them in response to the financial requirements of the new industrial areas of the North and Midlands by means of the agency system of the London bankers.[55] And there are certainly a number of instances where such links released local resources for financing elsewhere. The difficulty arises when it is argued that this provision was characteristic and amounted, in effect, to straightforward risk lending. Instances of industrial lending might have been important in cases where banking business was carried on in tandem with other commercial interests; but then it is the merchant or industrialist concerned who should take the accolade rather than the banker.[56] However, with this kind of argument it takes a great many swallows ever to make a summer; instead it is probably a better guide, when deciding the banker's main contribution, to ask how he earned the bulk of his profits.

For the typical country banker the answer lies in his note-issuing activities; this was how he supplied liquidity, and it was a function that was more characteristic than any financing role. In England, with few exceptions even in more recent times, the relatively small reserves of bankers, carrying on a business using other people's capital rather than their own, and with liabilities subject to immediate repayment, meant that they were just not equipped for industrial financing. Instead they were well fitted to the task of providing a growing economy with currency and remittance arrangements, lack of which would have been a far more important drawback on growth. In helping to ameliorate those local payments imbalances and seasonal fluctuations in credit requirements which made the industrial revolution such a fitful experience the banker was providing that most basic of all financial services, money itself.[57] It is here that the essential function of English banking is to be found, and its subsequent development shows an unwavering conformity to this self-liquidating principle. Thus by the late nineteenth century the note issues of the small eighteenth-century country banks had become the cheques of the great deposit banks, connected through a nation-wide clearing system pioneered by the London bankers in their clearing house from the 1770s.[58] Similarly, the bill of exchange, forged by law and mercantile custom in the imperfect money market of the eighteenth century, became the dominant clearing instrument for the finance of world trade in the form of the 'bill on London'.

These so far comprised the standard fare of the English banker that as late as 1917 H. S. Foxwell was still emphasising the distinctive function of discounting among the English banks, in contrast with the belief, widely held elsewhere, that the proper business of a banking system was the finance of industry and trade. At the time the German banks seemed to many to be strongest in just those areas where the British seemed the weakest, yet Foxwell's view was typical in maintaining the essential distinction between banking and the rest of the financial structure.[59] If the developed capital market of late nineteenth-century London knew so little of British industries, then a degree of scepticism concerning its importance to them even earlier seems justified. It is certainly true that the unitary banking system of the eighteenth and early nineteenth centuries aided the cash-hungry industrial areas by means of its rediscounting of bills in the discount market, thereby transferring liquidity from largely agricultural areas where the supply of money was high relative to demand. The traditional interpretation of the decline of the inland bill, which set in after mid-century, was to consider it as having been superseded by the growth of more advanced deposit banks, with branches which enabled the rapid transference of funds to take place without need of bills.[60] More recently attention has been drawn to the discrepancy in timing between the emergence of truly nation-wide branching, which came only with the bank amalgamations of the 1890s, and the inland bill's decline, which had set in by the early 1870s, at latest, when the National Provincial was the only bank with a network that was in any real sense national. Furthermore, banks in Lancashire and Yorkshire, whence most bills were sent to London, remained relatively aloof from the amalgamation movement. Instead it has now been established that the decline was attributable to two quite different factors: first, to the communications revolution after 1870, when the steamship and telegraph at last began to remove the slowness and uncertainty in payments and supplies, together with the necessity for relatively large inventory investment, that had made the merchant–middleman such a key figure in the industrial revolution from the very start;[61] second, to the more rapid spread of banking habits in the industrial areas after 1870, enabling larger and longer-term deposits to be built up, with the result that more local lending took the form of overdrafts and less through the creation of bills.[62] In short, the inland bill of exchange declined only when a larger and more efficient supply of money for currency and short credits from a more effective banking system made it increasingly redundant. It is this long-drawn-out process by which bank liabilities, mainly deposits, became the more or less exclusive instrument of private expenditure, which is the contribution of banking to economic growth in England; 'to attribute more than this before 1914 is to ascribe too much'.[63]

A similar continuity in terms of increasing specialisation can be seen in the development of the securities market. The canals of the late eighteenth century, and the docks, insurance companies and public utilities of the early decades of the nineteenth, while they brought the use of shares and debentures as finance instruments to fruition, did not materially alter the formal organisation of the capital market or its regional basis. The companies boom of 1824–5 showed a speculative and temporary interest in these securities, but relatively few were to survive the end of the boom. It is, of course, railway shares and debentures which have come to be regarded as the main instruments in the creation of a national market in company securities for the first time. Following Clapham's assessment, subsequent research has shown how

far railway capital extended the range of investments during the 1830s
and 1840s, and how much railway shares were responsible for altering
the traditional orientation of the London stock exchange, to the extent
that by the mid-forties they accounted for about one-third of the joint-
stock company capital quoted there.[64] In the provinces, too, it was
railway finance which hastened the appearance of specialist share
brokers as a distinct professional group working in a series of organised
markets; and it was the railway share boom which led to the foundation
of stock exchanges at Liverpool and Manchester in the mid-thirties,
thereby enabling Lancashire investors to finance railway development
in the south, Scotland and Ireland. In the 1840s, when most of the
other provincial exchanges were founded, the stimulus again came from
the railway mania.[65] Indeed, not only have the close links between
railways and the development of the capital market been reasserted but,
more generally, it has tended to be viewed as a new, vital, force which,
in the depressed conditions of the later 1830s and early 1840s, came to
the rescue of an industrialising economy about to face the prospect of an
exhaustion of new investment opportunities.

On the other hand the effect of detailed studies of the impact of the
railway on the economy generally has been to reduce somewhat its
appeal as a portmanteau explanation of continuing growth. In particular, the usual assumption that its influence sustained output and
employment in related sectors is now more open to question.[66] Similarly
in the case of its relationship to the capital market, where related
institutional changes do not appear to have greatly affected the underlying continuity of the regional, even local, limits of finance before the
mid-thirties (this applies to railway share trading in London as well as
in the provinces). It is also clear that, however interconnected the
national capital market became in response to the direct impact of
railway finance, it was not a permanent realignment; the very expansion and amalgamation of the railway itself, together with the spread of
the electric telegraph, brought about the growing concentration of such
business on the London exchange after the 1840s. During the second
half of the nineteenth century the provincial exchanges, having steadily
lost much of the business which had originally brought them into
existence, eventually came to find a more permanent role as segments of
local capital markets dealing increasingly in local private and public
stocks. The willingness of brokers in London to share their brokerage
fees with banks and solicitors in the provinces forestalled any further
specialisation of function between jobbers and brokers there.[67] On a
longer view, then, the ultimate effects of railway financing on the
evolution of the capital market appear to have worked towards re-
establishing the traditional lines of development in English financial
history. By enlarging the dealing scope of the London stock exchange,

financial concentration in the City was still further increased; and by ushering in company securities at a time when the volume of British government debt was declining, a new form of financial asset was provided for the wary investor, who was still, as yet, distrustful of foreign investment.

The evidence on the composition of the investing groups for whom these financial institutions were making a market also appears to confirm earlier interpretation. The bulk of railway finance came from local investors, mostly merchants and manufacturers, at first with a direct interest in improving communications: the 'mania' element was contributed by 'first in' speculators (usually from London), who made an active market in a share during the initial stages of its life when the amount of capital involved was comparatively small. There is little here to disturb the conventional view that it was the longer-term, risk-shunning holder of fully paid shares who was the real mainstay of railway finance. On the other hand the notion that the demand for railway capital was the decisive step towards the advent of limited liability now seems unconvincing. Not only did the well entrenched hostility towards that principle continue long after the 1840s, but opposition to it was still evident when trading in railway securities on the provincial stock exchanges was no longer important. It is noticeable that the revival of stock exchange trading in the regions came about only with the rise of municipal debts; and this occurred during the aftermath of disenchantment which followed on the crisis of 1866, when the deficiencies of the recent companies legislation were beginning to be better understood. In this way, again, the traditional patterns of inter-personal financing, only rarely transcending the regional level and industry grouping, proved to be a powerful influence on institutional change in the capital market. Between 1850 and 1914 the long-run trend appears to become even more clearly defined, for this period saw a virtual doubling in the proportion of the total nominal value of British investments attributed to overseas securities, from about a quarter to almost half. If the degree of external commitment of resources of the late Victorian capital market seems clear, explanation of the phenomenon would appear to depend to some extent on which capital market is being looked at.

If the London market is considered, then the fact that the financial structure of the metropolis had proved capable of accommodating large government loans and other issues of a public nature since the end of the seventeenth century suggests that it was well adapted to the provision of this type of financial service. Not only had there been considerable specialisation of function within the City's financial community over two centuries or more, but it possessed well tried sources of finance within its own region. As has recently been shown, the 'foreign

bias' of the London capital market was in large measure the consequence
of its specialisation on the larger, more profitable and frequently less
risky area of the loan market, and by the late nineteenth century the
demand was increasingly coming from overseas.[68] At the same time
the provincial capital markets presented a quite different picture; for the
most part any question of foreign bias there would be misapplied, since
for long after the advent of limited liability the vast majority of companies floated in the provinces, where the bulk of British industry was
to be found, managed on the basis of local resources. The financial
expertise of the City remained largely inappropriate to the relatively
modest capital needs of most concerns, and the supply of local professional services—solicitors, bankers, stockbrokers, etc—plus numerous
personal contacts amongst the investing public, was adequate.[69] Since
the type of security marketed in provincial centres before the late 'thirties
consisted mainly of local public utility, canal and mining shares, the
possibility of a truly national market in securities which the railway
heralded, however this is defined, could not have been expected to have
gained much further momentum from second- and third-generation
industry and commerce. The latter continued to rely very largely on its
own internal devices and private contacts. Of course, provincial
brokers were pushing their securities on the London market, but before
the last quarter of the nineteenth century government and foreign
stocks hardly appear to have received a quotation outside London. This
inability to fill the gap left by the large trading volume in railway
securities, whether it is attributable to the prevailing structure of
industrial organisation in Britain or to a lack of need for external
finance, or to both, does suggest some powerful long-run consistencies in
the financial development of the English economy which neither the
railways nor the companies legislation managed to upset.

V

Evidence of the type surveyed above has been used to lend support to
the fairly frequent assertion of a developing financial constraint which,
along with other factors making for retardation, impeded the competitive organisation of British industry in the late nineteenth century.
It has been argued, for instance, that the relatively late arrival of
incorporation with limited liability may have contributed towards
inhibiting the ability of much of British industry to continue to hold its
own under changing competitive conditions. Thus as late as 1885
limited companies accounted for only between 5 and 10 per cent of the
total of even the larger business organisations, and only in shipping,
iron and steel, and cotton was their role very important.[70] And even
later the scale of merger activity in Britain was hardly comparable with

he American trust movement at the same period. But then, as has been
rgued here, the great age of English trustification had already
ccurred more than a century earlier, in a different form and in
esponse to different conditions. On the other hand, there is no doubt
hat when it came incorporation with limited liability was remarkably
omplete in England: the Act of 1862 placed it within easy reach of *any*
even or more persons associated together for *any* lawful purpose; it is
oteworthy that it did at the same time prohibit the formation of large
nincorporated companies consisting of more than twenty persons.
There are, nonetheless, a number of difficulties in the way of regarding
he Companies Acts as enabling legislation for financing the growth of
arger business units. One is that much of the pressure for reform came
rom investors, the legal profession, and even from middle-class philan-
hropists wanting to create co-operative working men's associations. It
vas very much part of a general response to the expansionist climate of
he 1850s rather than a deliberate effort to accommodate any genuine
nvestment needs in industry.[71] Another problem is that the most
notable consequence of this legislation was the growth of 'one-man
companies', though it had formed no part of the official intention to
extend limited liability to sole traders and small partnerships.[72] Indeed,
he alacrity with which private business adopted the device sub-
equently, often in order to strengthen control over its own small-scale
concerns, could be taken as evidence that, in the event, Britain's late
capitulation to general limited liability may have amounted to an over-
compensation for earlier delay. By way of comparison, there is also the
ather perverse fact that in the United States, where large-scale
ndustry and financial concentration frequently coincided, some of the
nost striking examples of large aggregations of capital took the form of
rusts. In fact what has been described as 'the Trust's last exploit' can be
egarded as an eminently logical response in a country where opposition
o big business was so vehement.[73]

The point is that the shared Anglo–American legal tradition relating
o corporateness and association was probably as capable of abetting the
growth of financially powerful business units as it was of hindering their
development, depending on conditions. In Britain, too, a number of
nstances of trust management occur in complex and relatively heavily
capitalised enterprises. The Bridgewater estates, for example, which at
he duke's death had become one of the great coal–canal complexes of
he Industrial Revolution, were subsequently managed by trustees: it
vas a mixed performance, which included the running down of the
canal in the face of railway competition as well as the prospering condition of the Worsley mines after the 1850s.[74] The early links between
Birmingham's metal and mining firms and the unincorporated company
form are also of some relevance here, in view of the fact that by the

mid-nineteenth century the Birmingham trades were already exhibiting
many of the future weaknesses of Britain's industrial structure as
whole to a high degree.[75] Similarly with the agricultural estates of th
Marquess of Ailesbury, where trust management enabled a large b
heavily encumbered agricultural investment to be handed on intact.[7]
Examples such as these indicate that whatever the form of industria
organisation, in Britain at least, it tended to follow well entrenche
precedents and was less capable of positive reaction to the challenges o
organisational change than elsewhere by the late nineteenth century.

It is easy to push this argument too far, however, and to attribute an
alleged deficiency in the scale and integration of British industry, b
comparison with America and Germany, to any overall lack of financ
in some sense. On the contrary, the long-run continuity of developmen
in English financial institutions, characterised by degrees of specia
isation of function unparalleled among later industrial experiences
seems to indicate that if there was any financial constraint in Britain'
case, then it was not of sufficient weight to merit the creation of quit
new financial devices or for existing institutions to change their way
radically.[77] To this extent the situation was not at all comparable wit
American experience, where the success of entrepreneurs like Carnegi
and Morgan can be attributed to their expertise in acquiring larg
blocks of finance for internal growth as much as to the production scal
at which they operated. For this reason the trust form found its tru
focus in investment banking in America, simply because it afforded th
industrial financier opportunity to extend his activities well beyon
those usually associated with an industrial firm or a financial institutio
separately, and facilitated growth at the expense of less well place
competitors.[78] It was a different situation also from Germany, wher
the industrial banks used their strength in the financial arena to encour
age large-scale industry by merger and consolidation. Because Germa
industrial growth, at least in its early phase, coincided with the comin
of the railways, rather than preceding them as in Britain, the partner
ship and family firm proved inadequate for the task of financing such
steep rise in the level of accumulation from their own resources. As
result German banking early departed from orthodox practice an
accustomed itself to undertaking direct long-term investment an
promotional services for industry. At the same time the Prussian Stat
saw in the note-issuing function of the banks a more obvious candidat
for central control than was the case in Britain, thereby relieving man
bankers of the necessity of providing currency for the community.[79]

Thus whereas in America and Germany the conditions of industrial
isation exerted a strong stimulus towards an institutional linkage be
tween the financial and industrial sectors of the economy, in Britain, or
the other hand, comparatively few concerns were capable of making a

unique impact on the scale and structure of their industries, and so rarely required more than a limited access to institutional finance. The fact that in the British context growth had been largely financed out of resources generated within industry itself can be taken as a caution against attributing shortcomings in industrial performance to supposed imperfections in the capital market or in the nature of its institutions. For industrialisation in Britain depended far less on the existence of a formalised capital market than on facilities and practices that were easily internalised in the highly flexible extended partnership, or were otherwise available through the mesh of interpersonal connections in which the individual entrepreneur operated. Financial activity was consequently able to spread itself over a large number and variety of specialist areas—foreign exchange, bill discounting, foreign trade services and issuing business, for example. Against the background of late nineteenth-century economic performance it became only too easy to argue that such a degree of specialisation was excessive and had been pursued to a fault; by then those who questioned the appropriateness of the economy's financial structure for promoting its growth tended to see the problem in terms of the degree of financial specialisation achieved under the conditions of previous growth versus the degree of financial concentration necessary to maintain an internationally competitive position. In practice, however, the relationship between financial institutions and industrial growth was almost certainly much less simple, and the explanation for any deterioration in relative economic performance, where it is not to be found within industry itself, seems likely to have been much more complex. What does seem clear is that it was the very adequacy and wide diffusion of sources of loanable funds from the eighteenth century on, and that involving the legal profession was only one of many, plus the small-scale nature of so much of industrial and commercial growth over a comparatively long time span, that posed so few bottlenecks in financing further development.

NOTES

1 I am indebted to the Trustees of the Houblon-Norman Fund for a grant in aid of research, of which this essay forms a part; and also to Professor L. S. Pressnell and Mr W. A. Thomas for helpful comments.
2 Although the interrelations of law and economics occupy an important place in the tradition of Anglo-American legal history, the subject has been neglected by economic historians. This despite an early warning from a legal historian that the 'connection is so very close that I do not think that either the legal or the economic historian can do justice to his subject without extensive borrowings from the other's learnings'; W. S. Holdsworth, 'A neglected aspect of the relations between economic and legal history', *Economic History Review*, 1 (1927–8). Explicit acknowledgements or denials of its significance are few, but see D. S. Landes, *The Unbound Prometheus. Technological change and industrial development in Western Europe from 1750 to the present* (Cambridge, 1969), p.199, and P. Mathias, *The First Industrial Nation. An Economic History of Britain 1700–1914* (1969), pp.33 ff. But see also the interesting

questions raised by A. Alchian and H. Demsetz, 'The property rights paradigm, *Journal of Economic History*, XXXIII, 1973.

[3] R. Preston, *An Elementary Treatise on Estates . . .* (London, 1820), I, p.2.

[4] F. M. L. Thompson, 'Land and politics in England in the nineteenth century', *Transactions of the Royal Historical Society*, XV, 1965.

[5] Preston, *op. cit.*, p.429.

[6] A useful discussion of this point is in H. D. Hazeltine, G. Lapsley and P. H. Winfield (eds.), *Maitland: Selected Essays* (Cambridge, 1936), III and IV. For the growth of equity jurisdiction see H. Potter, *An Introduction to the History of Equity and its Courts* (1931).

[7] G. W. Keeton and D. Lloyd (eds.), *The British Commonwealth, The Development of its Laws and Constitutions* (1955), I, pp.138–50.

[8] Real Property Commission, *Parl. Papers*, 1829. Evidence of H. Tyrrel, appendix, p.525.

[9] H. J. Habakkuk, 'The land market in the eighteenth century', in J. S. Bromley and E. H. Kossman (eds.), *Britain and the Netherlands* (1960).

[10] F. M. L. Thompson, 'The social distribution of landed property in England since the sixteenth century', *Economic History Review*, XIX, 1966.

[11] A. Underhill, 'Changes in the English law of real property during the nineteenth century', *Select Essays in Anglo-American Legal History* (Boston, 1909), III, pp. 673–719, and Sir W. S. Holdsworth, *Essays in Law and History* (London, 1946), pp. 100–27.

[12] H. J. Habakkuk, 'Marriage settlements in the eighteenth century', *Transactions of the Royal Historical Society*, XXXII, 1950.

[13] R. W. Turner, *The Equity of Redemption* (London, 1931), pp.23–44. Beginning with Nottingham, the 'father of equity' (1673–82), the most important figures in the process of systematising equity were Hardwicke (1737–56) and Eldon (1801–27), by which time the delays, abuses and expense involved had become intolerable.

[14] For an extensive discussion of this neglected area see R. J. R. Goffin, *The Testamentary Executor in England and Elsewhere* (London, 1901).

[15] From this time on it is no coincidence that another of equity's exploits, the recognition that non-physical property, e.g. personal debts, was assignable, also began to gain ground.

[16] For this see O. W. Holmes, 'Executors in earlier English law', and R. Caillemer, 'The executor in England and on the Continent', in *Select Essays in Anglo-American Legal History* (Boston, 1909), vol. III. Very little is known of the activities of such people, but they appear to have figured prominently in the management of local sources of credit, such as charity endowments, even after the provision of banking facilities became widespread; and before the growth of practical alternatives to personal debt and mortgages had become significant outside of traditional financial circles. See F. G. James, 'Charity endowments as sources of local credit in seventeenth and eighteenth century England', *Journal of Economic History*, VIII, 1948.

[17] Quoted in R. W. Turner, *loc. cit.*

[18] F. W. Maitland, *op. cit.*, pp.189–91.

[19] D. Lloyd, *The Law relating to Unincorporated Corporations* (London, 1938), p.19.

[20] A. B. Dubois, *The English Business Company after the Bubble Act* (New York, 1938), p.226.

[21] *Ibid.*, p. 252, and Maitland, *op. cit.*, III, p.196. This appears to have been the case in the absence of anything to the contrary appearing in the trust deed. Of course these were advantages from the standpoint of minimising risks rather than allocating resources efficiently.

[22] See for example S. Williston, 'History of the law of business corporations before 1800', *Harvard Law Review*, II, 1888. That the notion of a corporation was inseparable from that of a public agency can be seen from the title of the first English work on the subject, William Shepheard's *Law of Corporations, Fraternities, and Guilds . .* (1659). The idea that exclusive control, though not yet limited liability, might be necessary in cases where public management was indistinguishable from the private profit-seeking of the membership was a dominant theme in subsequent writing, e.g. in an anonymous work of 1702 entitled *The Law of Corporations*, and in the better-known treatise on the subject by Stewart Kyd published in 1793

Colonial American practice also followed English precedent by widely utilising the unincorporated association, without limited liability; see S. Livermore, 'Unlimited liability in early American corporations', *Journal of Political Economy*, XLIII, 1935.

23 E. V. Morgan and W. A. Thomas, *The Stock Exchange: its History and Functions* (1962), p.74.

24 H. E. Raynes, *A History of British Insurance* (1948), pp.156–83 and B. E. Supple, *The Royal Exchange Assurance: a History of British Insurance, 1720–1970* (Cambridge, 1970), pp.187–91, 194–9 and 203.

25 The compulsory legislation and central control associated with, say, the Poor Law administration was largely exceptional and local government relied heavily on local initiative and resources throughout the nineteenth century. See for example E. P. Hennock, 'Finance and politics in urban local government in England, 1835–1900', *The Historical Journal*, VI, 2, 1963.

26 C. A. Cooke, *Corporation, Trust and Company* (Manchester, 1950), pp.80–94.

27 A. B. Dubois, *op. cit.*, p.437.

28 W. S. Holdsworth, *A History of English Law* (1938), VIII, pp.220–1.

29 F. Pollock, *Essays in Jurisprudence and Ethics* (1882), pp.95–6.

30 H. J. Habakkuk, 'The land market in the eighteenth century', *loc. cit.* and F. M. L. Thompson, 'The land market in the nineteenth century', *Oxford Economic Papers*, IX, 1957.

31 W. S. Holdsworth, *op. cit.*, pp.51–75 and R. Robson, *The Attorney in the Eighteenth Century* (1959), pp.3–5.

32 For example see B. L. Anderson, 'The attorney and the early capital market in Lancashire' in F. Crouzet (ed.), *Capital Formation in the Industrial Revolution* (London, 1972).

33 For example see R. Grassby, 'English merchant capitalism in the late seventeenth century', 'The composition of business fortunes', *Past and Present*, 46, 1970; and B. L. Anderson, 'Money and the structure of credit', *Business History*, XII, 1970.

34 As early as 1683 the author of *The Compleat Solicitor* noted that 'every idle fellow whose prodigality and ill-husbandry hath forced him out of his trade or employment, takes upon himself to be a solicitor'.

35 On this question see the remarks of R. M. Hartwell, *The Industrial Revolution and Economic Growth* (1971), II, pp.244–61. The law had always provided a useful vehicle of social mobility as well as the knowledge necessary to consolidate such gains; see A. Simpson, *The Wealth of the Gentry 1540–1660* (Cambridge, 1961), II, pp.22–114.

36 L. S. Sutherland, 'The law merchant in England in the seventeenth and eighteenth centuries', *Transactions of the Royal Historical Society*, XVI, 1934.

37 See for example, Margaret G. Davies, 'Country gentry and payments to London, 1650–1714', *Economic History Review*, XXIV, 1971. In this connection it is interesting that from their first years of publication the Law Lists included not only the details of barristers and attorneys resident in London, but also those of bankers. See, for example, Browne's Law List of 1777, pp.176–7. I am grateful to Mr Stephen Simmons of the Library of the Institute of Advanced Legal Studies for information on this point.

38 R. Robson, *op. cit.*, p.109; at the central level, of course, this process had begun much earlier; see W. S. Holdsworth, *op. cit.*, XII, pp.10 f. The fact that the attorney had for some time been taking over functions formerly associated with the scrivener meant that he brought financial expertise to this work.

39 The consistency of the attorney's professional involvements over long periods does appear to have been remarkable, especially in country towns. See, for example, Margaret Blatcher, *History of the Firm of Thompson, Snell and Passmore, Solicitors, of Tonbridge, Kent, 1570–1970* (1970), where extensive intermarriage with other local law firms enabled this firm to play an important part in local financial administration at every stage.

40 P. G. M. Dickson, *The Financial Revolution: a Study in the Development of Public Credit* (London, 1967), pp.244–5.

41 *Ibid.*, p.256.

42 See for example, B. L. Anderson, 'Provincial aspects of the financial revolution of the eighteenth century', *Business History*, XI, 1969.

[43] This trend had become well-entrenched by the 1830s at latest. See for example Thomas Lewin, *A Practical Treatise on The Law of Trusts and Trustees* (London, 1837) pp.305–15, where it is clear that by this time the laying out of a trust fund on well secured real estates was even being frowned upon. 'In the absence of any express power', says Lewin, 'the only unobjectionable investment is in one of the *Government* or *Bank Annuities*; for here, as the directors have nothing to do with the principal but merely superintend the payment of the dividends and interest till such time as the government may pay off the capital, it is not in their power, by mismanagement or speculation, to hazard the property of the shareholder. And of the Government or Bank Annuities, the one which the Court has thought proper to adopt is the Three per cent. Consolidated Bank Annuities, the fund, from its low rate of interest the least likely to be determined by redemption.' Significantly, chancery funds appear as a separate item in Pebrer's estimate of the national capital of 1833, presumably a reflection of their importance as a source of finance; see R. Giffen, *The Growth of Capital* (1889), p.164. The accountant-General of Chancery's office had been in existence since 1726; it was the largest corporate owner of securities by the mid-eighteenth century, and already an important stabilising influence in the market; see Dickson, *op. cit.*, pp.283, 293 and 434.

[44] On the development of trust law see G. W. Keeton, *The Law of Trusts* (London, 9th edition, 1968), II and *The Investment and Taxation of Trust Funds* (London, 1964) part I. The legislation was firmly in line with established precedent to the effect that trust moneys should not be invested in trading companies because of the great loss to which capital was thereby exposed. The classic case in the eighteenth century was *Trafford v. Boehm* (1746), 3 Atk 447.

[45] Such preferences were clearly quite rational for investors, especially those acting as trustees, who were primarily concerned with income rather than capital growth, and for whom frequent instances of company failures and foreign loan defaults must have been a discouragement. Contemporary explanations of cyclical behaviour took some account of this type of investment attitude. See, for example, Sir Robert Giffen, *Economic Inquiries and Studies* (1904), x, pp.101–3.

[46] A. K. Cairncross, *Home and Foreign Investment 1870–1913* (Cambridge, 1953), pp. 84–102, and earlier by F. Lavington, *The English Capital Market* (1921), pp.204 ff

[47] A barrister writing at mid-century estimated that three-quarters at least of a solicitor's work was taken up with handling accounts. He admonished solicitors for allowing accountants to take the more difficult cases away from them; nevertheless his precept for the profession was clear. 'Eschew speculation. Who would knowingly intrust his property to a speculating attorney or solicitor, any more than to a speculating banker?' S. Warren, *The Moral, Social and Professional Duties of Attornies and Solicitors* (1848), pp.73–6 and 368.

[48] J. D. Bailey, 'Australian borrowing in Scotland in the nineteenth century', *Economic History Review*, XII (1959–60), and W. Turrentine Jackson, *The Enterprising Scot: Investors in the American West after 1873* (Edinburgh, 1968), p.13.

[49] A. K. Cairncross, *op. cit.*, pp.187–208.

[50] H. Pollins, 'The marketing of railway shares in the first half of the nineteenth century', *Economic History Review*, VII, 1954.

[51] J. C. Gilbert, *A History of Investment Trusts in Dundee, 1873–1938* (1939), p.10.

[52] On this see P. L. Payne, 'The savings bank of Glasgow, 1836–1914', in P. L. Payne (ed.), *Studies in Scottish Business History* (1967), p.177.

[53] *The Economist*, 28 March 1868. For details of lawyer participation in investment trusts, see H. Burton and D. C. Corner, *Investment and Unit Trusts in Britain and America* (1968), pp.91–114 and appendix A5.

[54] See, for example, J. H. Romanes, *The Economic Studies of a Lawyer* (Edinburgh, 1930), I, and *passim*.

[55] A contemporary account is contained in J. Taylor, *A Letter to William Leatham: Money, a Servant of the People* . . . (1842). For a recent assessment of the role of the English banks in these terms see R. Cameron, *Banking in the Early Stages of Industrialisation* (1967), II, pp.15–59. The essentially unit basis of English banking development meant that any transition from bill finance to the provision of venture capital as a regular feature of its activities would have been impossible to sustain.

[56] In fact an early criticism of country banking was precisely that the typical firm

'... consists of four persons; the acting partner honest and industrious, but with inconsiderable property; the tradesman with a fair capital, principally engaged in his particular business; the manufacturer, of extensive concerns, and with money, but very much employed in his works; and a neighbouring country gentleman of landed estate; or more frequently the attorney of the place: the firm so constituted, is undoubted in security, and of great respectability. This description of partnership, or others nearly similar, established in every large town, and many smaller ones, it is, that now supplies the currency in the country.' (M. D. Magens, *An Inquiry into the Real Difference between actual money . . . and paper money* (1804), p.36.) See also P. Mathias, 'The entrepreneur in brewing, 1700–1830', *Explorations in Entrepreneurial History*, x, 1957, reprinted in H. G. J. Aitken (ed.), *Explorations in Enterprise* (Cambridge, Mass., 1965), pp.309–26.

57 On this point see L. S. Pressnell, 'Banks and their predecessors in the economy of eighteenth-century England', paper presented to the fourth Settimana di Studio, Prato, April 1972, in which emphasis is placed upon the role of banks and other early financial intermediaries in smoothing seasonal and inter-regional imbalances in the demand for an availability of credit.

58 P. W. Matthews, *The Bankers Clearing House* (1921). The importance of the emergence of such institutions, accompanied by the legal enforceability of contracts, has been underestimated. Satisfactory contract law and a reasonably effective clearing system are necessary for minimising transactions costs, so enabling private debt instruments to be used for the settlement of transactions and as financial assets. See, for example, P. Davidson, 'Money and the real world', *Economic Journal*, LXXXII, 1972. Liquidity transfers by the banks were, of course, also facilitated by eighteenth-century improvements in road transport, as were tax remittances to the government.

59 'I am convinced that the radical fault of our system lies in the fact that our financial, as distinguished from our banking, institutions are out of touch with our industries, with the natural consequence that these industries, or the majority of them, are defective in their organisation and equipment.' H. S. Foxwell, 'The finance of industry and trade', *Economic Journal*, XXVII, 1917.

60 W. T. C. King, *The History of the London Discount Market* (1936).

61 R. B. Westerfield, *Middlemen in English Business, 1660–1760* (New Haven, Conn., 1915). They played a similar role in the early American economy also. See for example H. C. Livesay and G. Porter, 'The financial role of merchants in the development of U.S. manufacturing, 1815–60', *Explorations in Economic History*, IX (1971–2), where it is argued that merchant involvement in manufacturing finance had the effect of delaying the entry of formal financial institutions in this area, in much the same way as in Britain.

62 S. Nishimura, *The Decline of Inland Bills of Exchange in the London Money Market, 1855–1913* (Cambridge, 1971), pp.55–64.

63 D. K. Sheppard, *The Growth and Role of UK Financial Institutions, 1880–1962* (1971), p.108.

64 M. C. Reed, 'Railways and the growth of the capital market', in M. C. Reed (ed.), *Railways in the Victorian Economy* (1969), pp.162–83, and S. Broadbridge, *Studies in Railway Expansion and the Capital Market in England, 1825–73* (1970).

65 J. R. Killick and W. A. Thomas, 'The provincial stock exchanges, 1830–70', *Economic History Review*, XXIII, 1970.

66 G. R. Hawke, *Railways and Economic Growth in England and Wales, 1840–70* (1970); also B. R. Mitchell, 'The coming of the railway and United Kingdom economic growth' and W. Vamplew, 'The railways and the iron industry: a study of their relationship in Scotland', both in M. C. Reed, *op. cit.*

67 For the changing nature of country share business see W. A. Thomas, *The Provincial Stock Exchanges*, forthcoming publication (1974). Local specialist share markets were, of course, also important, e.g. textiles in Manchester and Oldham, iron and steel in Sheffield and Newcastle, mining in Cardiff and Newcastle, metal manufactures in Birmingham, and insurance in Liverpool and Manchester.

68 M. Edelstein, 'Rigidity and bias in the British capital market, 1870–1913', in D. N. McCloskey (ed.), *Essays on a Mature Economy: Britain after 1840* (1971). In view of the lack of evidence, capital market imperfections are not a convincing explanation

of the growth of investment abroad. For a discussion of the point see D. N. McCloskey, 'Did Victorian Britain fail?' *Economic History Review*, xxiii, 1970.

[69] F. Lavington, *op. cit.*, p.208. Company promoters of the type of H. Osborne
O'Hagan and David Chadwick fall into this group as well, but they appear to have
been less important in Britain than in America where such expertise in the procure-
ment of industrial finance brought richer rewards; see the comparison of O'Hagan
with J. P. Morgan in L. Davis, 'The capital markets and industrial concentration:
the US and UK, a comparative study', *Economic History Review*, xix, 1966.

[70] P. L. Payne, 'The emergence of the large-scale company in Great Britain, 1870–
1914', *Economic History Review*, xx, 1967. This does, of course, beg the question
whether the fact that limited companies were the dominant firms in their industries
may not have meant that they alone were capable of effectively utilising this legal
form towards attaining a more competitive position internationally.

[71] J. Saville, 'Sleeping partnership and limited liability, 1850–6', *Economic History
Review*, viii, 1956. A comparative assessment is in D. S. Landes, 'The structure of
enterprise in the nineteenth century: the cases of Britain and Germany', in Comite
International des Sciences Historiques, *XI Congres International des Sciences Historiques*
(Stockholm, 1960), *Rapports*, v, pp.107–28.

[72] In joining the privacy of the traditional partnership to the permanent character of
the corporate form 'the private company is not so much a natural offshoot from the
original stock of our company system as a graft upon it'; E. Manson, 'The evolution
of the private company', *Law Quarterly Review*, xxvi, 1910.

[73] H. D. Hazeltine *et al.*, *op. cit.*, p.142. As used by Rockefeller the trust form of
combination meant control of competing companies in order to influence prices,
market allocation and finance, rather than economies of scale: 'There is probably
no aspect of big business growth that suggests concentration of economic power as
dramatically as the increase in the financial resources of the large industrials . . .
The large corporations are the very firms that require the pooling of investments
because they operate in industries requiring heavy capital investment. 'A. D. H.
Kaplan, *Big Enterprise in a Competitive System* (Washington, D.C., 1954), pp.7–9 and
238.

[74] F. C. Mather, 'The Duke of Bridgewater's trustees and the coming of the railways',
Transactions of the Royal Historical Society, xiv, 1964.

[75] A. B. Dubois, *op. cit.*, p.435, and N. Rosenberg (ed.), *The American System of
Manufactures* (Edinburgh, 1969), pp.78–9.

[76] F. M. L. Thompson, 'English landownership: the Ailesbury trust, 1832–56',
Economic History Review, xi, 1958. Given the popular conception that nineteenth-
century settlements were inordinately restrictive, it is worth mentioning that the
rigour of their conditions always varied considerably. Despite the fact that many
life-tenants found it necessary to obtain greater management powers through
private Acts of Parliament, in practice landowners usually retained much more
room for manœuvre than is commonly thought. For evidence from the Fitzwilliam,
Percy and Lampton estates see Eileen Spring, 'The settlement of land in nineteenth
century England', *American Journal of Legal History*, viii, 1964. Only after the
passage of the Settled Land Act of 1882 can the landed trust be said to have gone
into decline; see generally J. E. R. de Villiers, *The History of Legislation concerning
Real and Personal Property in England during the Reign of Queen Victoria* (1901).

[77] In this connection it is important to note that where such constraints reflect capital
immobility, this need not necessarily imply any capital market imperfections. Nor
can these be said to have been removed once inter-regional differences in interest
rates cease to be significant. See, for example, L. Davis, 'The investment market,
1870–1914: the evolution of a national market', *Journal of Economic History*, xxv,
1963, and the useful discussion of this point in G. J. Stigler, 'Imperfections in the
capital market', *Journal of Political Economy*, lxxv, 1967.

[78] For a statement of this argument as part of a general discussion of factors inhibiting
industrial concentration in Britain see H. J. Habakkuk, 'Industrial organisation
since the industrial revolution', *Fifteenth Fawley Foundation Lecture*, University of
Southampton, 1968.

[79] R. Tilly, *Financial Institutions and Industrialization in the Rhineland, 1815–70* (Madison,
Wis., 1966), pp.94–110.

Barrie M. Ratcliffe

6

The origins of the Anglo-French commercial treaty of 1860: a reassessment

For a fleeting aberrant moment in the third quarter of the nineteenth century it seemed that Western Europe would emulate Britain's example in reducing tariff barriers. This moment has been termed the 'low-tariff era', and was the nearest Europe came to free trade until after World War II. It was inaugurated in two stages: by Britain's unilateral adoption of free trade from the 1840s onwards, and by the Anglo-French commercial treaty of 1860, which was the first of a series of tariff agreements between European States, each of which contained the 'most favoured nation' clause that ensured that tariff reductions would be generalised.

A number of optimistic explanations have been put forward to explain the existence of this low-tariff era. In 1919 Joseph Schumpeter could describe nineteenth-century moves to reduce tariffs as the consequence of the advance of rational, pacific capitalism and Britain's early espousal of free trade as the result of her position as the most advanced and capitalistic of European nations.[1] With rather more justification others have pointed out that lower tariffs at this time were an instance of the coincidence of periods of economic growth and business confidence and periods of liberalisation of international exchange and a part of the general process in Western Europe of clearing away the legal hindrances to nascent industrial capitalism. Certainly, tariff reductions coincided with the greater confidence generated by the re-establishment of stable regimes, accelerating economic growth, rising prices and freedom from major wars in Western Europe in the 1850s and 1860s. This confidence and increasing trade bred some international co-operation, to reduce charges on major waterways and to fix parities between different currencies. There is, however, a considerable difference between an agreement to abolish dues and tolls on, say, the Rhine and to compensate those who lost their privileges and an agreement to lower customs duties, which might mean not only the possibility of a loss of government revenue but the danger of the competition of cheaper foreign goods on home markets. Besides, the low-tariff era was not begun in the bonanza years of the 1850s but only from 1860 onwards, when international conditions were somewhat less favourable.

It has often been assumed, too, that the tariff agreements of the 1860s were the result of an acceptance, by pressure groups, politicians and civil servants, of the free trade theory of classical political economy. Yet we know surprisingly little about many aspects of this. It is clear, for example, that civil servants played a disproportionately large role in influencing commercial policy not merely in Britain but in Prussia and the Zollverein and in France. We know much about the civil servants at the British Board of Trade but less about their Continental counter- parts. It has been claimed that Prussian civil servants, trained in Smithian economics in the German universities, were free-traders,[2] but more research needs to be done to substantiate this. There are, in any case, reasons for questioning the importance of free trade theory in policy making, even though the theory that was propagated by popular journals like the *Economist*, the *Economiste belge* and the *Journal des Economistes* was usually only a simplified and optimistic interpreta- tion of the subtle, sober and even pessimistic writings of early nineteenth-century English classical economists. Remarkably little reference to economic theory was made in the political debates on tariff policy in Britain or elsewhere. Nassau Senior boasted in the 1850s that Britain's prosperity was 'the triumph of theory. We are governed by philosophers and political economists.'[3] In fact, English economists had been restrained in their advocacy of free trade, had advised caution, made exceptions. Thus John Stuart Mill admitted that there might be a case for protecting infant industries,[4] and Alfred Marshall was later to point out that had British free trade propagandists given more recogni- tion to this, reaction in Europe to British tariff policy from the 1840s onwards might have been less hostile. There were also limits to the cosmopolitanism of the classicals. They discussed foreign trade in terms of the advantages nations would derive from it[5] and many of them felt that, though international exchange was generally beneficial, an industrial nation like Britain would gain more than any other. John Stuart Mill, for example, thought that a country with varied exports and with exports whose value was high in relation to their bulk would be in a better position to expand its foreign trade than its trading partners.

Not only did classical political economy undergo some modification in its transfer to the Continent but it did not hold the field unchallenged even at the mid-century. The refurbishing of protectionist theories was very nearly coeval with the emergence of the theory of *laisser-faire*. The challenge to the underlying philosophical principles of Smithian economics came early, with Adam Müller and the German Romantic school, for instance. If protectionist writings in the nineteenth century on the whole lacked the rigour of classical theory, they compensated for it with arguments of *Realpolitik*, resuscitating national power as a policy aim. The debate that resulted anticipated twentieth-century discussions of the relationship between rich and poor nations, of 'economic imperialism'. Friedrich List, a leading German protectionist, emphasised that economic life is carried on within the framework not of an ideal world order but of competing nation States. He was the declared spokesman of a less developed Europe faced with British economic predominance and, stressing that industrialisation is desirable for a variety of reasons, offered a blueprint for industrialisation in such a world. He willingly conceded that free trade is eminently suitable for a world where all the major economies have acquired a solid industrial base but argued that, since only Britain had such a base, Europe still needed protection. British commercial policy, then, was, as Oastler later declared, 'that great idol, free trade, moulded in Manchester and electroplated in Birmingham', and British policy makers were only following the advice of Lord John Russell, who had once urged his colleagues, 'Let us be Englishmen first and economists second.'[6]

Many free-traders in the debates of the 1830s and 1840s in Britain believed that it was desirable that their government should institute unilateral tariff reductions, and that it would be advantageous, even if the British example were not followed elsewhere. But many also believed that free trade doctrines were scientifically exact and would create greater prosperity and that Britain's new commercial policies would therefore be emulated abroad and thus inaugurate an era of free trade, peace and prosperity. Richard Cobden told his countrymen that if the corn laws were abolished and free trade adopted, 'there will not be a tariff in Europe that will not be changed in less than five years to follow your example'.[7] Though they recognised that producer interest on the Continent was far from free trading, they felt that the example of British prosperity plus consumer interest in each country would push governments towards free trade. Many in Britain also claimed that using tariffs in Europe had in part been retaliation against protectionist policies at home. John Bowring, Board of Trade official and free trader, claimed that the corn laws were responsible for the increasing Zollverein tariffs which were keeping British goods out of a large and growing market because they hindered the export of East Elbian food grains.[8] Even in his tariff reforms of 1841–6 Peel retained the duties on wines and spirits, partly in the hope of reducing them in reciprocity treaties with other governments, and particularly with France. Once free trade had become British policy the government sent representatives and memoranda to foreign governments to publicise the joys of freedom of commerce.[9]

Continental emulation of British tariff reductions was, however, no easy process, for Britain's new policy was a leap in the dark and hopes that others would follow suit in the 1840s at best optimistic. At least one economist, Robert Torrens, had warned against unilateral tariff disarmament and argued instead for reciprocity agreements.[10] Indeed, Britain adopted free trade in the face of repeated failure to reach commercial agreements with other European governments, since her diplomatic onslaught on Western Europe since the 1820s had met with scant success. The Anglo-Austrian treaty of 1838 was an exception because special diplomatic considerations worked in favour of the accord.[11] In contrast, the British had on three different occasions in the 1830s and 1840s undertaken protracted but abortive negotiations with France. French reluctance to reach agreement resulted not merely from political considerations, from fear of the competition of more efficiently produced British goods, but also, paradoxically, from fear of creating in France the kind of economy and society that rapid industrialistaion had generated in Britain, with the attendant social problems, the severity and frequency of industrial depressions and the dependence on foreign trade and its vagaries. Certainly Britain's new policy in the 1840s was an example for free-traders and moderates in Europe, but if many could regard it as the shining beacon that would guide Europe away from protection and prohibitions, many more in Europe could regard British commercial policy as less a beacon than a siren beckoning a less developed Europe to destruction. They could also argue that Britain could safely adopt free trade because not only was her industry technically more advanced than her rivals' but she also possessed a large empire and a well established extra-European commerce. Adolphe Thiers described free trade as a weapon the British hoped to use to increase their domination of world markets, saying that 'si la liberté politique est la protection des faibles, la liberté des échanges est le droit du plus fort'.

It was only to be expected, therefore, that, following the conversion to free trade, British representatives to Western European governments met with but little response. Immediately after the repeal of the corn laws Cobden undertook a fourteen-month tour of Europe, proclaiming on his departure that he would be 'an ambassador from the free-traders of England to the governments of the great nations of the Continent'.[12] But the only leader of any import who expressed himself favourable to free trade was the Pope, who told Cobden that he would do all in his power to help promote it, 'adding modestly that it was but *little*'.[13] Sir Louis Mallet, who was an official at the Board of Trade from 1847 to 1872, complained in 1877 that he had 'spent some of my best years in writing admirable papers of argument and facts addressed by Lord Clarendon to foreign governments, none of which produced the smallest result'.[14] This helps explain why, when he was setting out for Paris in October 1859 with the intention of discussing the possibility of a commercial treaty between France and Britain, Cobden wrote to Bright:

> Governments seem as a rule to be standing conspiracies to rob and bamboozle people, and why should that of Louis Napoleon be an exception? The more I see of the rulers of the world, the less of wisdom or greatness do I find necessary for the government of mankind.[15]

Yet the discussions he initiated led to the Anglo-French commercial treaty of 1860, and it was this treaty, more than Britain's earlier adoption of free trade, that was the trigger which began the series of tariff reductions by the major European powers that constituted the low-tariff Era.

II

Perhaps the most difficult problem concerning the 1860 treaty is why Napoleon III agreed to its signature when he realised that such a treaty would raise vociferous opposition from the majority of French manufacturers, hitherto strong supporters of the regime, and why such a treaty was not concluded earlier, as the constitutional provision that enabled him to do so, the Sénatus-Consulte, dated back to 1852. It is difficult, firstly, because tariffs are the delicate products of compromise, and tariff changes involve not merely economic but also strategic and political considerations. Customs and excise, moreover, provided a substantial proportion of government revenue. Previous regimes in France had been unable and unwilling to alter policy in the face of opposition from manufacturing and agricultural interests, and while the imperial constitution enabled Napoleon to reduce tariffs through reciprocity, this did not mean that he could act without running the danger of losing important support. In part, therefore, an interpretation of the 1860 treaty must be based on an understanding of the political system of the Second Empire, the nature of its ruling elite (were the *grande bourgeoisie* in power?[16]) and the strength of Bonapartism. Such an understanding is made more difficult because the regime changed: in 1852 Napoleon was the absolute ruler of France; by 1870 he was a constitutional monarch divested of most of his power.[17] The commercial treaty was signed in the year that saw the first steps—the political reforms of 24 November—that were to change the Second Empire from an authoritarian to a liberal regime.

A second difficulty stems from the power and the personality of Napoleon III himself. The treaty was his decision, for there can be no doubt that at this time he was still at the height of his powers. Rouher told Cobden that there was 'but one man in the Government, the Emperor, and but one will, that of the Emperor'.[18] Yet, given his taciturn nature, his manner of conducting the business of government, he remained a mystery even to his intimates. Bismarck called him a sphinx, though he sardonically added that this was a sphinx without a riddle. He has remained as much an enigma for historians as he was for his contemporaries. In an age when statesmen were compulsive writers of letters, memoranda and memoirs Napoleon III left very few written records—he was a man who spoke little, and wrote less.

The manner in which the treaty was concluded enhances the difficulty. It was not signed in response to a campaign in favour of lower tariffs, because the relatively weak pressure group, set up in 1846 to campaign for moderate tariffs and led by journalists and academics rather than business groups, had collapsed in 1850 and had not been revived.[19] It was not even inaugurated by Napoleon and his Council of Ministers but by Napoleon in consultation with individual Ministers and advisers, without the knowledge of the rest, and it was negotiated in absolute secrecy in Paris. The first intimation the legislative body and the public had was the publication of Napoleon's letter on economic and social policy to his Minister, Achille Fould, in the *Moniteur* a few days before the announcement of the signature of the accord. As Gladstone later wrote, it was 'brought into the world without so much as a blue or a yellow book to describe its ante-natal stages, or even to register its birth'.[20]

Historical interpretation of the 1860 treaty has followed two lines. The first has been an attempt at the very difficult task of evaluating the impact of the treaty on the French economy. The major work has been that of A. L. Dunham,[21] a believer in economic liberalism, who, writing in the late 1920s, was intent on showing that the treaty was to the advantage of the French economy. His conclusions have been ratified by Marcel Rist, who agreed that no major change resulted in the structure of France's foreign trade and that industry successfully met foreign competition.[22] But the issue has been joined by J. Coussy, who points out that the French growth rate was already slowing down in the late 1850s and that this deceleration continued in the next decade.[23] The second line has been to explain why the treaty was signed. In the absence of Napoleon's papers and official sources, the most common approach has been to emphasise the role of different individuals in persuading Napoleon and British Ministers to begin talks and in bringing the negotiations to a successful conclusion. The original thesis, based on English sources, was that the treaty was essentially the work of Richard Cobden, who thereby added a new dimension to his earlier role in the campaign for free trade in Britain.[24] The antithesis was Dunham's work, which, as he admitted,[25] was partly written to counteract the myth that the treaty was Cobden's single-handed achievement. Using English and French sources, Dunham insisted instead that it was essentially the result of the endeavours of Michel Chevalier. A new synthesis has subsequently emerged, as a result of studies of the papers of men who were Napoleon's Ministers at the time. The historian Jean Maurain, using papers at the Bibliothèque Thiers, has emphasised the part played by Jules Baroche.[26] Robert Schnerb has shown that Eugène Rouher was an economic liberal who played an important part in the events leading up to the treaty.[27] The role of the Duc de Persigny, who at the time was ambassador in London, has also been emphasised.[28] It will be our contention that the financier Emile Pereire played a more important part in bringing about the treaty than has previously been realised.

Historians have also made some effort to put the treaty in the context of the economic philosophy and policy of Napoleon III, for it was one of the weaknesses of Dunham's work that little attempt was made to put the treaty into the context of either foreign or economic policy. Though important work has been done on some aspects of economic policy, such as that of Louis Girard on public works,[29] there remain lacunae, and much still needs to be done on the relationship between the regime and industry and finance. What can be said, however, is that there has been a tendency to exaggerate the originality, consistency and importance of Second Empire economic policies. The coincidence of the *coup d'état* of 2 December with the return of prosperity and the rapid economic growth in the upswing of the trade cycle between 1851 and 1857 has frequently led to the linking of the two and an exaggeration of the importance of government policies. Félix Ponteil has claimed that with Napoleon III 'l'économique a la priorité sur le politique'.[30] whatever that means, and Professor Girard talks about a 'coup d'état industriel' between 1849 and 1851 and refers to the 'économie politique du 2 décembre'. Even the much vaunted public works programme of the Second Empire, however, appears less original and less important when viewed against the outlay of the July monarchy in the 1840s and against the background of government intervention elsewhere at this time.

In contrast to French industrialists, who at this time combined a rigorous belief in the desirability of *laisser-faire* with a belief in the necessity of protection,[31] Napoleon III—in the eyes of his admirers, at least—combined a belief in greater government intervention in the economy with a belief in the advantages of lower tariffs and perhaps even of free trade, both of these beliefs showing in imperial policies from the beginning. Dunham, for instance, declared that though he had found no direct evidence to prove it, it was his opinion, 'after many years of investigation', that Napoleon was genuinely in favour of moderate duties by 1860, and he tried to explain away the protectionist sentiments that Napoleon had expressed in his 1842 pamphlet *Analyse de la question des sucres* as an appeal for popular sympathy rather than a statement of his true beliefs.[32] The origins of Napoleon's belief in moderate tariffs have been variously attributed to his visits to England and attendance at Anti-Corn Law League meetings in the 1840s,[33] and to the influence of private individuals and Ministers in the 1850s. There is, however, little evidence that the emperor had any strong desire for a general reduction of French tariff levels before the end of 1859. Indeed, Dunham cites Chevalier's lament of 1852 that he had often discussed lowering tariffs with the emperor but that the latter still inclined towards protection, and when Cobden discussed tariffs with Napoleon late in 1859 he found him very ill informed on the subject. All that can be said with certainty is that some of the men in close contact with Napoleon had strong free trade tendencies—Michel Chevalier, the Duc de Morny, Prince Napoleon, Persigny and Rouher.

With the benefit of hindsight some scholars have seen the treaty as but the last step in a series of moves in the 1850s all pointing in the direction of moderate tariffs. During this time the government was moving towards general reform through legislative means but was finally thwarted by protectionist agitation in the legislative body and in the country. The experience of the 1850s, however, gives little credence to this view. To many contemporaries in favour of lower tariffs the policy of the government appeared vacillatory rather than reforming, dependent for its tariff policies on the changing personalities at the Ministry of Commerce. The changes proposed and made were for specific objects rather than for general reform—suspension of the sliding scale for grainstuffs in a year of poor harvests, reduction of duties on iron products to facilitate railway building.[34] As such they were in the tradition of the kinds of change that had earlier been introduced, such as those on iron goods in 1836, again to help early railway construction, brought in by Thiers, who was later to become the most eloquent of protectionists. It is true that in June 1856 the government did put before the legislative body a plan of wider reform, but the changes proposed were still limited and the government must have realised that a protectionist outcry would ensue.

It has frequently been asserted that Napoleon III owed his economic policies in general and his moderate tariff policy in particular to the Saint-Simonians. Louis Girard calls him 'a Saint-Simonian Caesar', just as at the time Sainte-Beuve had seen him as 'Saint-Simon on horseback', and writes of a 'coup d'état industriel' on his accession, just as the Saint-Simonians had themselves proposed a 'coup d'état pacifique' in 1832. Similarly, Félix Ponteil asserts that 'la pensée saint-simonienne anime la politique économique du Second Empire',[35] while for Marcel Blanchard their ideas were so widely diffused that he finds the question of Saint-Simonian influence an irrelevant one.[36] Not only has it been claimed that the main lines of policy derived from Saint-Simonism but particular aspects as well. Thus the historian of public works in Paris, David H. Pinkney, considers it possible that Napoleon III picked up the plan for remodelling the capital from articles published in the Saint-Simonian journal *le Globe* in 1832.[37] The commercial policy inaugurated in 1860 has also been seen to be the work of Saint-Simonians. First there was the influence of particular Saint-Simonians, Michel Chevalier, the Pereire brothers, and perhaps Arlès-Dufour, the Lyons industrialist, and second there was the influence of Saint-Simonian ideas. J. Coussy has written that

> Le principe d'une libéralisation des échanges françaises fut, sinon introduit, du moins essentiellement diffusé par des saint-simoniens ou d'anciens saint-simoniens. Leurs enseignements au milieu du XIXe siècle se proposaient bien essentiellement une modification des structures de production et d'échanges, modification qui ne serait atteinte que par un abandon de la politique commerciale francaise traditionnelle.[38]

The source of these supposed Saint-Simonian policies has been variously ascribed to the young Napoleon's tutor, Vieillard, who had briefly been a member of the sect in 1832, and to the influence of ex-Saint-Simonians around him when he came to power who were, we are told, 'à peu près le seul groupement intellectuel dont Napoléon III pût disposer après son accaparement du pouvoir'.[39] Such policies are one aspect of a theme that recurs in Saint-Simonian historiography from the major works of Weill and Charléty[40] onwards: the role Saint-Simonians are reputed to have played in the French economy, as engineers, entrepreneurs, financiers, theorists. In large part this role is mythical.

There are a number of reasons, other than the truth of the assertion, as to why it should have gained such wide currency. In their own time the Saint-Simonians' role was emphasised and criticised by journalists and commentators and thus kept in the forefront of public opinion. Saint-Simonians in business, for example, were the target of a number of critics of the speculation of the so-called 'new feudalism' of the railway mania of the 1840s. Fourier and his disciples made a number of anti-semitic attacks on what they called 'Jewish Saint-Simonians', and the best known of these was Alphonse Toussenel's *Les Juifs rois de l'époque* (1845), which was the most effective anti-semitic diatribe before Drumont's in the 1880s. The vituperation against Saint-Simonians increased during the Second Empire when, in the 1850s, Capefigue, among others, condemned what he regarded as the nefarious influence of Jews and Saint-Simonians.[41] And since the Pereires and Michel Chevalier, who had once been involved in the sect, were for a time in close contact with Napoleon III and involved in the 1860 treaty, Saint-Simonians were attacked both in the general condemnation of the Second Empire and in the criticisms of protectionists. In the legislative body in 1867 Pouyer-Quertier, an industrialist and a leading protectionist, denounced what he called 'l'influence néfaste de la secte saint-simonienne sur les destinées industrielles et financières du pays'.

Whatever the accuracy of this picture, there is no doubt that it is a picture drawn by pamphleteers and publicists using their view of Saint-Simonism as a weapon to condemn opponents. There is another aspect to the assertion: in the twentieth century the view of its widespread influence has been refurbished, above all, by a group of American historians, like David S. Landes, John E. Sawyer and Bert. F. Hoselitz, who, using the entrepreneurial approach to economic growth, have seen the Saint-Simonians as a group of innovators who were a powerful influence in the dynamic orientation of French capitalism at the mid-nineteenth century. Another distinguished American scholar, Alexander Gerschenkron, using a different approach, sees Saint-Simonism as providing France with an ideology for expansive capitalism and as an example of an ideology of delayed industrialisation.[42]

The validity of this widespread thesis depends on one or two things: that Saint-Simonian theories, either singly or collectively, had some originality and/or that those who had been involved in the sect before its dissolution in 1832 still constituted a group during the Second Empire. The originality and cohesion of Saint-Simonian economic theories can be questioned. Admittedly, they were enthusiastic believers in an industrial future and they showed a number of insights into the manner in which the economy was to develop, especially during the Second Empire. They believed in the need for some kind of central direction of the economy. Already in 1825 they were questioning the viability of unbridled competition and, though they never completely abandoned a belief in the interplay of market forces, they moved more and more towards a review of the government distributing the means of production to the most able entrepreneurs and to the growth sectors of the economy. The chief instrument by which some kind of order and planning could be imparted to the economy was a centralised banking system. This would have a dual function: it would be an anti-cyclical instrument and it would be a means by which the powers of capitalists would be reduced. The Saint-Simonians also emphasised the importance of communications not merely for the French economy but for linking Europe and the Arab world. Whilst the credit system was to be the nerve centre, ensuring the co-ordination of factors of production, communications—and especially railways, whose significance they early realised—were to be the arteries of expanding industry.

There are, however, important limitations to the originality of the Saint-Simonians. Sociologists have long pointed out that every economic doctrine, however 'scientific', contains some element of ideology. It might be said that in the case of Saint-Simonism it was rather the reverse: it was an ideology with an element of economic thought. The economic *aperçus* of the Saint-Simonians cannot really be raised to the status of a system. If the Saint-Simonians carried anything over into their later careers it was no blueprint of economic development. It was not even a detailed plan for a banking system[43] or a railway network.[44] Their discussions were not generally concerned with technical details or theory, and their economic ideas were always just one part of their response to what they regarded as an existential crisis. Thus many of their criticisms and proposals were never fully developed, and one searches in vain, for example, for a real development of their theory of industrial crises or their view of the market mechanism. Many of their ideas, moreover, were not original but were being put forward by others of their contemporaries. It is even difficult to prove that the Saint-Simonians believed in free trade. They attacked the corn laws as well as protectionist arguments like the balance of trade, and they praised J.-B. Say's theories, but commercial policy was never a central theme of their writings. In fact, while some later became ardent advocates of lower tariffs, others became protectionists. Paulin Talabot, who had been involved in the sect for a time, became a leading protectionist during the Second Empire, while Enfantin, one-time leader of the sect, was never a thoroughgoing free-trader, though he did welcome the 1860 treaty. Even Michel Chevalier, who played a vital role in the treaty, was only converted to free trade in the mid-1840s by Frédéric Bastiat.[45]

It is not true, either, that, following the dissolution of the sect, Saint-Simonians continued to constitute a group with shared memories and a common outlook. The leaders of the sect had quarrelled before the dissolution in 1832 and continued to disagree thereafter. If some Saint-Simonians turned towards successful business careers, rising to prominence during the Second Empire, these were a tiny handful, and others turned in a contrary direction, towards Comtism and Fourierism, to hostility towards the capitalist economy and economic and social developments from the 1840s onwards. It is for these reasons that it is hard to believe that Saint-Simonianism played any major role in the French economy in the nineteenth century or in the formulation of the economic policies of Napoleon III or the moderate tariff policy from 1860 onwards.

Whether or no their free trade beliefs can be traced back to their earlier involvement with the sect, a number of ex-Saint-Simonians applauded the 1860 treaty and played some part in bringing it about.

As is well known, Michel Chevalier played a major role in suggesting the treaty and in the subsequent negotiations. Arlès-Dufour, friend of both Cobden and Chevalier, played some part in preparing the ground for a commercial treaty, may well have been in on the secret of the negotiations at the end of 1859 and wrote a congratulatory letter to the emperor, offering his services in the implementation of the new policy.[46] Enfantin was enthusiastic about the treaty and for a moment hoped that its signature heralded the arrival in power of a new group led by Chevalier.[47] However, what needs emphasising is the role played by Emile Pereire, the financier who had founded the Crédit mobilier in 1852 and had subsequently become a multi-millionaire and a leading figure in the economic life of the Second Empire. In October 1859 Pereire drew up a memorandum in favour of lower tariffs which he submitted to the emperor and which was discussed by the Council of Ministers. The existence of this memorandum was forgotten until Jean Maurain discovered a copy in the Baroche papers.[48] Maurain felt that Pereire had drawn the memorandum up without the knowledge of Chevalier, who was away in London, and considered that it was of some significance, pointing out that it was only a few days after the Ministers' examination of it that Cobden began his clandestine negotiations in Paris and that there was a similarity between several points in the memorandum and several in the emperor's January letter to Fould. Though the importance of the memorandum has since been questioned by Gordon Wright, who emphasised that it appeared only in October, which was, he felt, late, and that it suggested only unilateral tariff changes rather than the bilateral treaty that was actually signed,[49] other evidence indicates that Emile Pereire played a noteworthy part in the decision to change tariff policy in 1859–60.

The concern of both Emile Pereire and his brother, Isaac, for lowering tariff barriers antedated Chevalier's, for they had begun agitating for tariff reform during their first career as journalists, which lasted from 1828 to 1835. Along with friends like Adolphe Blanqui and Léon Faucher they participated in the first movement for freer trade which coincided with the prosperous years of the 1830s and with the tariff inquiry of 1834–5 initiated by Duchâtel, the Minister of Commerce.[50] They interpreted the French tariff system at this time as the child of vested interests who had a powerful voice in the press and dominated the chambers—the vested interests of the large landowners and a few privileged manufacturers. Protection and prohibitions had thus been introduced and were maintained in the interests of a small section of French society, and were contrary to the interests of commerce and industry and consumers in general. Emile Pereire castigated, above all, the duties and prohibitions on iron and coal, for these helped to hold back the greater use of these two vital sinews of nineteenth-century industrialisation and were maintained at the behest not of the French iron industry as a whole but of a few proprietors of woodlands and the shareholders of the three largest coal-mining companies,[51] and those of the Anzin company in particular, which Pereire singled out for attack.[52]

The problem was how and when this situation was to be remedied. In common with most of his fellow reformers in the 1830s and later, Pereire adopted a moderate stance: he rejected as untenable the advocacy of complete free trade, which he claimed in 1834 was as absurd as the advocacy of prohibitions,[53] and proposed instead that tariffs be lowered gradually over a period,[54] suggesting that indemnities be given to those industries formed behind prohibitive barriers and likely to be injured by the adoption of more moderate duties.[55] He set as a priority the abolition of duties on raw material imports and advocated that such exotic products as coffee and sugar be freed from the system of colonial preference. Recognising Britain's lead in manufacturing, however, he recommended 'une grande réserve' in the reduction of duties on manufactured goods,[56] but was in favour of reciprocity and supported English moves for a commercial treaty, putting the question in the wider context of an Anglo-French alliance, claiming that no lasting accord could be concluded by diplomatic manoeuvring because only a trade treaty could cement a durable alliance.[57] These moderate reforms were essentially those that Emile Pereire was to advocate in his 1859 memorandum.

It should be noted that the Pereires always viewed tariffs in the wider context of indirect taxation and government revenue. They attacked indirect taxes throughout their writings because they regarded them as injurious to production, iniquitous to the lower classes and costly to raise. As early as 1832 Emile Pereire was proposing reforms intended to ensure that funds to cover government expenditure were raised in such a way as to interfere as little as possible with the productive process, that taxes fell principally on unearned income and that these taxes were raised in as inexpensive a manner as possible.[58] They were lifelong advocates of government loans, and during their more radical early years even advocated that loans replace taxation altogether. One of the aims of their Crédit mobilier, indeed, was the floatation of government loans and the breaking of the *haute banque* stranglehold on floatations. The Pereires claimed that the Mobilier played a major role in guaranteeing the Bineau loan of 1854, a major innovation in that the government appealed directly to the public rather than using the costly mediation of merchant banks. In the 1859 memorandum Emile Pereire proposed to raise the funds to cover the probable budget deficit resulting from his suggested tariff reductions by a loan floatation. The memorandum also made frequent references to the success of the British example of lowering indirect duties and tariffs. In the 1830s the Pereires were already impressed by Sir Henry Parnell's *Financial Reform*, published in French translation in 1832, and by moves to lower the level of indirect duties by British administrations, which had served to increase the tax yield.[59]

The concern for lower customs duties the Pereires had shown in the early 1830s was enhanced during their later careers as financiers and entrepreneurs, when they were frequently faced with the problems created by high and prohibitive tariff levels. Whilst building the Paris–Saint-Germain railway they played a part in the first breach in the tariff wall when, in 1836, Thiers agreed to discriminatory reductions in iron tariffs to facilitate railway construction. In the 1840s they unsuccessfully appealed for tariff exemption for special equipment needed for the atmospheric railway they were building. In November 1854, when the French iron and steel industry was swamped by railway orders, the government allowed their Midi company to import a quantity of iron rails at a specially reduced rate. In October 1855 they requested and received government permission for their Compagnie générale maritime to purchase, duty-free, a sailing ship and six steam vessels in Britain. And though they did not participate in the tariff reform movement during the upswing of the trade cycle of the 1840s, the Pereires continued to make their views known. Thus in his 1856 report to the Crédit mobilier shareholders Isaac Pereire advocated a European low-tariff policy as a necessary accompaniment to an envisaged network of Mobilier institutions, guiding investment and opening up under-developed agricultural regions across the continent.[60]

In view of their writings and experience it is not surprising, then, that the Pereires should have approved a move to reduce customs duties such as the 1860 commercial treaty. There are, moreover, a number of obvious indications that Emile Pereire played some part in bringing it about. His likeness appeared on the composite photo portrait made to commemorate the signing of the treaty. He was present, along with some fifty other partisans of lower tariffs, at Steiner's celebration dinner,[61] and he gave a splendid dinner for the negotiators at his Faubourg Saint-Honoré home.[62] The Pereires were themselves later to claim to have contributed to bringing the treaty about.[63] The clearest evidence of the Pereire role is the October memorandum. This, however, has two rivals, earlier advice to reduce tariffs. In July and August 1859 Persigny had written two important letters from London, advocating a commercial treaty with Britain and a four-point programme for economic development, every point of which appeared in the emperor's January 1860 letter to Fould. The emperor thought enough of these proposals to call Persigny to Paris.[64] Secondly, A. L. Dunham discovered an undated and unsigned memorandum, apparently written by Chevalier at about the same time as the Persigny letters, also advocating a commercial treaty with Britain.[65] The difficulty with this last memorandum is that there is no evidence that the emperor or anyone else ever saw this plan and only circumstantial evidence as to its authorship. Its strength is that, like the Persigny letters, it has a number of points in common with Napoleon's open letter to Fould in January 1860.

The case that Emile Pereire played a significant part in bringing about the change in policy can be based not merely on the October 1859 memorandum and the strength of its arguments but also on Pereire's previous discussions with the emperor. The 1850s, the golden years of the empire, marked the apogée of Pereire success and influence. From 1849 onwards Napoleon regularly consulted Emile Pereire on economic and financial affairs. According to Pereire, protocol demanded that only the emperor could initiate discussion of a topic but thereafter frankness was encouraged and contradiction countenanced. As for the principal topics of conversation,

> les voies de communications, le crédit public, le système des banques, les encouragements à l'industrie, le commerce des grains, la suppression de l'échelle mobile, les caisses d'épargne et de retraites, les pensions civiles, les associations ouvrières, les associations coopératives, les asyles, la réforme des impôts, des octrois, des douanes etc, ont été les principaux sujets que, dans une période de vingt années il m'a été donné de traiter avec celui qui pouvait les réaliser . . . La liberté de commerce a été le sujet des plus grandes préoccupations, reprise vingt fois, successivement ajournée, ces longues hésitations qui m'étaient témoignées et qui devaient se produire avec d'autres dans les sortes d'enquêtes individuelles dont l'Empereur fait précéder les réformes qu'il veut introduire prouvaient à la fois l'importance qu'il attachait à la solution de cette grave question et les précautions dont il voulait l'entourer.[66]

On three separate occasions, moreover, Emile Pereire had in the autumn of 1859 discussed the state of economy and the need for tariff revision with the emperor. In September and October he made three journeys with Napoleon, from Bordeaux to Tarbes, Tarbes to Bayonne and Bayonne to Paris. During these there took place *tête-à-tête* discussions dealing exclusively with the tariff question, each lasting three to four hours. In the interval between them Pereire was called upon to provide statistics to support his case, which necessitated his making two special trips to Paris. These documents, indeed, formed the basis of the unsigned memorandum that Pereire handed to Mocquard, the emperor's secretary, on 18 October[67] and which Napoleon submitted to his Council of Ministers on 19 October. This memorandum was discussed at two successive ministerial meetings.[68]

The memorandum itself bears such a resemblance, both in suggested tariff cuts and in the method of meeting any budget deficits, to the one discovered by Dunham and ascribed to Chevalier that it is clear that there had been some collaboration in its preparation between Chevalier and Pereire. Chevalier had certainly been consulted on the arguments and statistics to be used in the Pereire proposals.[69] The arguments used in the memorandum were of a kind that would have some impact on Napoleon's thinking. It was argued, first, that the economic situation in France demanded a new set of government policies such as had helped launch the very rapid growth rates of the 1850s—a new *coup d'état industriel* like that which was to be announced in the *Moniteur* letter of 5 January 1860 and which was intended to be the equivalent of the Bordeaux speech of 1851. Pereire had his own reasons for desiring this because, though the economic recession from 1857 had not been as severe in France as elsewhere, it had helped bring about the Pereires' first important failure, the collapse of the Grand Central railway, and 1859 had been a difficult year for their railway companies, as it was for all French railway companies.

The most important policy change Pereire suggested to improve the economic situation was the lowering of tariffs. France had the natural resources and geographical situation to enable her to become an industrial leader. Besides,

> Il ne faut pas qu'on dise d'elle qu'elle est la première nation quand il s'agit de faire la guerre et qu'elle n'est qu'en second rang quand il s'agit de faire de l'industrie, de l'agriculture et du commerce.[70]

As did other reformers, they compared the fortune of British commerce under free trade with that of France under high protection. Not only had British exports almost tripled in value between 1845 and 1857 but this, the world's leading industrial nation, had manufactured imports twenty times the value of France's. France could begin to follow the British example for another reason: government revenue was less dependent on customs duties than the British had been and still was. Changes could therefore be made without seriously imbalancing the budget.

The tariff changes proposed in the memorandum were modest— more modest than those previously put forward in the Chevalier proposals and more modest than those that were to be agreed in the 1860 treaty. It was suggested, first of all, that the tariff system could be simplified without affecting either the French economy or government revenue. Besides, if in the arithmetic of customs one and one make not two but very often nothing, the British example had shown that the lowering of duties might mean an increase in revenue rather than a reduction. Following the lead of the highly influential report of the 1840 Select Committee on Import Duties in Britain, Pereire pointed out that there were 1,430 dutiable articles and only thirty produced 163 million francs, while the remaining 1,400 yielded a mere 19 millions. Of these thirty articles, five—sugar, coffee, cotton, coal and wool— produced 138 millions. The vast majority of these duties could be abolished, thus reducing administrative costs and smuggling, without any loss to the revenue. The memorandum recommended, secondly, specific changes: the suppression of all duties on raw materials for industry, except for those on iron and coal which, in the first instance, were to be retained; the abolition of duties on tea and cocoa; the reduction of coffee duties by 75 per cent and of those on sugar by 50 per cent. These changes would not mean a corresponding loss of revenue, since increasing trade and prosperity would bring in revenue in other ways and since consumption of these goods would undoubtedly increase. Thus sugar consumption would certainly double in the near future, given the low level of consumption in France as compared with Great Britain, and given the 66 per cent increase in consumption that had taken place in France in 1851–8. The annual loss consequent upon all these reductions Pereire calculated at a maximum of 50 million francs in the years immediately following, and suggested that, in view of the 2,000 millions the government had raised in loans for the Crimean and Italian wars, the government could float a loan to make up the budget deficit. The result of these proposed reforms would be that in a short period French commerce would be doubled, the merchant marine would similarly increase, and new outlets for French industry and agriculture would be found. They would mean that the poorer classes, in town and country, would be able to enjoy the sugar, coffee and tea that were already within the reach of their counterparts in Britain. Pereire concluded: 'c'est faire de la vraie économie sociale et de la bonne finance, c'est continuer la grande politique qui a inauguré le règne de l'Empereur'.[71]

It may be that the Pereire memorandum was used by Napoleon only to sound out his Ministers' reactions to proposals for lowering tariffs and that their reaction was not encouraging, and it must be admitted that there is no suggestion in it of a commercial treaty with Britain. Yet the arguments put forward in the plan, together with the evidence of the emperor's earlier discussions with Pereire, help to explain, in part, why Napoleon was receptive to proposals from Cobden and Chevalier that France negotiate a treaty, proposals they began to make from 22 October onwards. Cobden's notes and correspondence, along with Chevalier's own letters, indicate that the emperor required little persuasion to agree to their suggestion.[72] When Chevalier had his audience with Napoleon on 27 October he found him still preoccupied with the Pereire project and discussing it with an enthusiastic Haussmann.[73] Chevalier was later to claim that Rouher early gave his approval to plans for a commercial treaty chiefly because he knew the emperor would agree to it rather than because he was for once a hardy innovator.[74] Already, then, by the time Cobden and Chevalier arrived in Paris the Pereires had played a significant role in persuading the emperor that a new set of economic policies, and especially lower tariffs, were needed.

There is another dimension to the explanation of why Napoleon III agreed to a commercial treaty: the political one. A further reason why he was so receptive to the proposal, and why some British Ministers also gave their support, was that both sides felt that some political benefit would result. It might be argued that on both sides the vital ingredient in the success of proposals for a commercial treaty was political.

III

Economic relations between States are never determined solely by economic considerations but are influenced by history, and by political and strategic considerations. Yet the political dimension of international economics has not received sufficient attention from scholars partly because, though the concept of economic man has been revealed as a fiction, the parallel concept of the economic State has lived on and, as a result, much less is known about predominant motivations in foreign economic policy making than about, say, defence and strategic policy making.[75] Not enough work has been done, then, to break down disciplinary barriers in the study of such multi-faceted phenomena as imperialism,[76] and more work needs to be done on political aspects of capital flows, aid, so-called multi-national corporations, international trade and the settlement of accounts.[77] Politicians and diplomats, on the other hand, have usually attached some political importance to tariff agreements and disagreements, to customs unions and tariff wars, and it might be postulated, with some justification, that political considerations have always been a necessary ingredient in tariff agreements.

Customs unions have traditionally been regarded as having more than economic significance because they have been thought to pave the way towards political union. Some of the founders of the Zollverein, like Friedrich von Motz as early as 1818, saw it as a means to political co-operation, while some have claimed that this customs union played a part in ushering in German unification.[78] The belief that it did so lived on to influence those, like Joseph Chamberlain, who advocated a British imperial Zollverein to serve more than economic ends. Those Europeans who, during World War II, began to work in earnest for a European economic community set themselves partly political goals: to counteract the dwarfing of Europe by the two super-powers, to solve the German problem by absorbing Germany into a customs union that would, it was hoped, ultimately lead to a politically united Europe. On the other hand, some proposed customs unions and agreements have failed precisely because of fears that they would have political repercussions. Plans for a Franco-Belgian customs union in the 1830s and 1840s were complicated by Belgian fears that the expected economic advantages for Belgian industry would be offset by an erosion of the country's sovereignty, and negotiations finally failed in the face of opposition from the British, who believed that a customs union would be the first stage in a French absorption of neutral Belgium.[79] Similarly, suggestions for an Austro-German customs union in 1931–2—like Bruck's proposals in the middle of the nineteenth century—were partly if not chiefly motivated by political considerations, and they too were blocked by opposition from the French, the British and members of the Little Entente, all of whom feared its political implications.[80] There have also been political elements in tariff wars, such as those between Italy and France, 1888–98, Germany and Russia, 1890–4, and Austro-Hungary and Serbia, 1906–9.

The low-tariff era had a significant political dimension. Thus throughout the nineteenth century European powers signed commercial treaties with non-European governments by which European goods, capital and enterprise were to be admitted with little or no restraint, and these agreements were in part the consequence of disparities of political power, frequently a *quid pro quo* for diplomatic recognition or alliance, more rarely, as in the case of China, the result of war and the threat of war. In 1824 Canning wrote of the commercial possibilities offered by Latin America: 'Spanish America is free; and if we do not mismanage our affairs sadly, she is English'. In 1862 Prussia signed a commercial treaty with France partly to thwart Austro-Hungary's attempt to join the Zollverein and to exercise a greater influence on German affairs. The fact that Europe had been at peace since 1815 and that even the Crimean war had been a limited war, with two of the major European powers remaining neutral, may have influenced tariff reductions. Peace and prosperity may have generated a greater confidence in the international system and temporarily weakened politicians' belief in the desirability of a country exporting more than it imported and their fear of foreign competition, just as later in the century rising tariffs owed something to the more rigid division of the powers into blocs and alliances, and economic writings—especially those of journalists and politicians—adopted aggressive postures similar to those of political nationalists and there was talk of struggle rather than competition for markets, of tariff wars and reprisals. Jules Ferry, looking back in 1891, described free trade in 1860 as 'le fruit hâtif de trente-cinq années de paix, une page détachée de l'idylle des Etats-Unis d'Europe'. Many of the leading free-traders of the day,

men like Richard Cobden and Frédéric Bastiat, were primarily
moralists and pacifists who regarded free trade as serving more than
economic ends. Free trade would be an anodyne in international
relations because it would generate a mutual dependence and a prosperity that war would endanger, since war brought strife, waste of
resources, higher taxes and industrial crises. Such sentiments were
certainly given wide publicity, though there is little evidence that free
trade or low tariffs have ever helped maintain peaceful relations and
little likelihood that the diplomats and politicians in Britain and
France fully shared this optimism when they negotiated the 1860
treaty. What is more certain is that both sides in the negotiations felt
that some immediate political gain would result from a treaty of
commerce.[81] Many critics of the treaty quickly saw it as a political
move. The *Times* found the treaty contrary to the principles laid down
by Peel in 1846 and doubted whether France would gain greater
economic advantages from it but saw it as 'a surer guarantee of
amicable relations with England, and of a pacific feeling in Europe,
than if half the army of France were disembodied, and sent to their
homes, or half the fleet disarmed'.[82] When Napoleon announced his
intentions towards Nice and Savoy it was said in the House of Commons
that the treaty would appear to be a bribe to Britain to allow France to
extend her frontiers,[83] and in France the protectionist deputy,
Estancelin, claimed that 'le prix de Nice et de la Savoie a été le marché
industriel français livré à l'Angleterre'.[84]

Both sides had reason to want to stop the deterioration in Anglo-
French relations that had been taking place since the last months of the
Crimean war. Though differences had been patched up during
Napoleon's state visit to England in August 1857, relations became
ever more strained by English fears of the French naval challenge,
especially with the launching of ironclads at Brest and Toulon, and of
the strength of the French army. Orsini's bombs, manufactured in
Birmingham, French intervention in Rumania and *rapprochement* with
Russia also helped the estrangement, while the Italian war of 1859 had
witnessed invasion scares, the volunteer movement and anti-French
outbursts in the press and Parliament in Britain. The major problem
that remained unsolved at the end of 1859, creating considerable
diplomatic uncertainty in Europe, was the Italian question. For the
British the war had demonstrated French military strength and
renewed fears that Napoleon III's regime was, after all, as expansionist
as his uncle's had been, or at least that European problems would be
settled without reference to Britain. For Napoleon III the Villafranca
and Zürich agreements had not gone far enough towards a settlement
and another war was a likelihood. At the same time Prussian mobilisa-
tion along the Rhine during the hostilities had impressed on him the

need to ensure the friendship or at least the neutrality of Prussia and Britain, Russian neutrality having already been secured by the secret agreement of March 1859.

A number of British politicians and diplomats held the view that to increase trade between nations was to increase friendship and the chances of peace. Thus when in 1858 Lord Malmesbury became Foreign Secretary he sent a memorandum to British diplomats which stressed that the best guarantee of peace was the increase of international trade, for which the British government was always willing to negotiate.[85] In 1843, during fruitless negotiations for a commercial treaty with France, Peel had claimed that increased trade would give 'an additional security for peace'. In the preliminaries to the 1860 treaty it was the pacifist Cobden who most loudly proclaimed that such a treaty would be the best way to cement Anglo-French relations. Both before and after 1860 Cobden was preoccupied with improving relations between the two countries, with trying to prove to his fellow countrymen that Napoleon had no aggressive intentions towards England, and with combating the arms race. As early as January 1852 he was writing to the editor of the *Times* to deny that there were any grounds for fearing a French invasion,[86] and as early as 1853 his friend Bright was writing that it would be a glorious revolution for England and France 'when we can scan our mutual imports and exports, instead of counting up the number of our ships of war.'[87] After the signature of the treaty and throughout 1861 Cobden remained preoccupied in his correspondence with the arms race and tension between the two nations, and early in 1862 published his pamphlet *The Three Panics*, where he argued against armaments and again denied there was a danger of war with France. In November 1859, when he was negotiating the treaty, he told Gladstone that he would not have crossed the street merely to secure material gain but would have walked barefoot to Paris to improve the 'moral and political relations of France and England by bringing them into greater intercourse and increased commercial dependence',[88] and he described free trade to Chevalier as 'la méthode de Dieu lui-même pour produire une entente cordiale, et tout autre système ne vaut pas un liard'.[89]

The difficulty, of course, is to what extent Cobden's long-held views were shared by the less sanguine members of Palmerston's government: whether they, too, believed that a commercial treaty would have any great political or diplomatic significance. What can be said is that Cobden's unofficial negotiations in Paris coincided with moves by a minority in the Cabinet, including Palmerston, Gladstone and Russell, to bring Britain into closer alliance with France and Sardinia in order both to settle the Italian question without recourse to war and, more deviously, to prevent further increases in French power or territory.

As early as September Palmerston had agreed with Persigny that an alliance between Britain and France would be desirable,[90] and early in January 1860 he put his plan for an alliance with France and Sardinia before the Cabinet.[91] Though such a policy was supported neither by the majority in the Cabinet nor by the Queen,[92] most regarded a relaxing of the tension of the previous months as desirable. Gladstone, for one, who responded the earliest and most enthusiastically to the suggestion of a treaty, seems to have believed that a commercial treaty would improve political relations. At the time he described it as a 'sedative'[93] and in 1887 wrote that the treaty had averted a war which had been a real possibility at the end of 1859.[94] The official British attitude to the negotiations set out in the letter from Russell, the Foreign Secretary, appointing Lord Cowley and Cobden as plenipotentiaries was that the government attached 'a high social and political value to the conclusion of a commercial treaty'[95] and that, given the prevailing uncertainty, such a treaty would demonstrate Anglo-French amity. Russell may well have hoped that the treaty would help prevent the threatened war over Italy.[96] It may also be that Palmerston, informed as early as August 1859 of the proposed cession of Nice and Savoy to France and realising the adverse effect this would have on British public opinion, felt that a commercial treaty might act as a counterweight.[97]

Napoleon III, for his part, had perhaps stronger reasons to want to improve political relations between the two countries after the Italian war and in the light of the deal he had made with Cavour for France to acquire Nice and Savoy. Cowley, the British ambassador in Paris, reported after a private dinner with Napoleon on 6 August 1859, 'I defy anyone to listen to the Emperor when he is speaking of the English alliance without the conviction that the preservation of it is that which he has most at heart.'[98] Towards the end of the year the international situation worsened when Austro-Hungary withdrew its support for a proposed congress of the major powers to settle the Italian question following the publication in December of the pamphlet *Le Pape et le Congrès*, strongly rumoured to have been written or inspired by Napoleon III. In this situation the emperor felt that some understanding with Britain over Italy was vital, since British support would keep Austria isolated and might even obviate the need for hostilities altogether. On more than one occasion late in 1859 he sent out feelers to ascertain what the British attitude would be in the event of a second war between France and Austria, and in January 1860 even proposed an alliance between France, Sardinia and Britain, just after a similar suggestion had been made by Palmerston and the Italophiles. It has been suggested that it was when this proposal was rejected in Britain that Napoleon finally decided to sign the treaty of

commerce and run the gauntlet of protectionist opposition,[99] for, as
Rouher later put it, 'il y avait là un thème politique périlleux pour la
popularité du gouvernement'.[100]

The importance of political considerations can be gauged from the
testimony of those who were involved in the discussions that led up to
the 1860 treaty. Chevalier categorically denied that political factors
were paramount,[101] as has A. L. Dunham. But Cobden, who had
several important interviews with Napoleon, argued in his diary and
in correspondence with Ministers and friends that the political situation was the most important consideration for the emperor. It is clear
that the chief preoccupation of Cobden's discussions with Napoleon
was less the economic consequences of a trade treaty than the possible
political repercussions. Cobden set out to convince the emperor that
such a treaty was the only way to improve relations between the
countries, while the emperor expressed greatest interest in just this
problem, and the first hour of their first interview in October 1859 was
devoted to the anti-French feeling in Britain and the need to improve
Anglo-French understanding. Cobden later confided to Charles
Sumner that he felt Napoleon's motives for signing the treaty were
nine-tenths political, with the aim of cementing the alliance with
Britain,[102] while Arlès-Dufour, ardent free-trader and friend and
confidant of Cobden, wrote of the emperor's motives:

> Cobden . . . croit, comme moi, qu'il a fallu des raisons majeurs pour l'amener
> à signer le traité qui refoule toute velléité de guerre avec l'Angleterre si elle a
> existé. Il croit que la question italienne, romaine et celle d'orient y sont pour
> beaucoup, mais les armements monstres de l'Angleterre ont dominé . . .[103]

A number of French Ministers were also concerned about Anglo-
French relations. When Cobden had discussions with Achille Fould on
2 November he found him preoccupied with the uneasy and hostile
state of public opinion across the Channel.[104] But it was Persigny,
French ambassador to the Court of St James's, who was the staunchest
supporter of a commercial treaty with Britain for political reasons.
Throughout the 1850s, except for an aberrant bellicose outburst
following the Orsini plot in January 1858, he had stressed the need to
maintain good relations with the British. Moreover, as early as 1852 he
was stating his belief that the best way to ensure good relations was to
encourage Anglo-French trade. He was under the erroneous impression
that the 1832 Reform Act had transferred political power to the middle
classes, and claimed that the best appeal for their friendship was to
facilitate commerce between the two countries.[105] In July 1859 he had
an interview with Russell and suggested that France might sign a
commercial treaty as an earnest of her pacific intentions, and he
followed this up by immediately making the same suggestion to

Napoleon. Persigny was speedily called to Paris to elucidate his proposals before the Council of Ministers. Though nothing came of this at the time, he played a part in the negotiations at the end of the year, for when, in December, the emperor seemed to be hesitating over the proposed treaty Persigny arrived from Paris to warn of persistent Francophobia, the danger of war and the need for closer ties between the two powers.[106]

There are indications, therefore, that political considerations were important in the signing of the 1860 treaty. They helped determine the timing of the treaty, and had the political situation not been as taut neither side would have been so anxious to conclude a commercial treaty. For the Italophile minority in the British Cabinet and for Napoleon III such a treaty was as near to an *entente* as could be reached. In the event both sides expected too much of its political repercussions, because between January 1860 and the final conventions of the following October differences and hostility remained,[107] and in March Napoleon gave Cowley a public dressing-down in Paris.[108] However, Napoleon had other reasons for signing the treaty because the need for a new set of economic policies to relaunch growth and the possibility of lowering tariffs without gravely injuring government finance had already been impressed on him by the time Cobden and Chevalier arrived in Paris with their suggestion for a treaty of commerce. In this Emile Pereire played an important part. It is not, however, possible to measure the relative weight of political and economic considerations in Napoleon's decision to sign the agreement.

NOTES

[1] J. A. Schumpeter, *Imperialism and Social Classes*, ed. Paul M. Sweezy (Oxford, 1951), pp.120–2.
[2] W. O. Henderson, *The Zollverein* (London, 1939), p.37; Wilhelm Treue, *Wirtschaftszustände und Wirtschaftspolitik in Preussen, 1815–25* (Stuttgart, 1937), ch. II.
[3] *Conversations with M. Thiers, M. Guizot, and Other Distinguished Persons during the Second Empire* (London, 1878), I, p.169.
[4] *Principles of Political Economy* (London, 1871), pp.593–4.
[5] Lord Robbins, *The Theory of Economic Policy in English Classical Political Economy* (London, 1961), p.9.
[6] Cited by S. E. Finer, *The Life and Times of Edwin Chadwick* (London, 1952), p.96.
[7] *Richard Cobden: Speeches on Questions of Public Policy*, ed. John Bright and J. E. Thorold Rogers, 2 vols. (London, 1870), I, p.360.
[8] John Bowring, *Report on the Prussian Commercial Union* (1840). It should be said that Bowring misunderstood the reasons for rising Zollverein tariffs and exaggerated the possibilities of the German market.
[9] D. C. M. Platt, *Finance, Trade and Politics in British Foreign Policy, 1815–1914* (Oxford, 1968), pp.143–4.
[10] Robert Torrens, *The Budget. On Commercial and Colonial Policy* (London, 1844).
[11] For the negotiations of the 1840s see Lucy Brown, *The Board of Trade and the Free Trade Movement, 1830–42* (Oxford, 1958), ch. VII; and F. E. Hyde, *Mr Gladstone at the Board of Trade* (London, 1934), pp.125–6.
[12] J. A. Hobson, *Richard Cobden, the International Man* (London, 1918), pp.41–2.

13 Richard Cobden to Mrs Schwabe, *Reminiscences of Richard Cobden*, compiled by Mrs Salis Schwabe (London, 1895), p.57.
14 Bernard Mallet, *Sir Louis Mallet: a Record of Public Service and Political Ideals* (London, 1905), pp.58–9.
15 John Morley, *The Life of Richard Cobden* (London), 1903 edition, p.705.
16 As has been claimed by Jean Lhomme in his *La Grande Bourgeoisie au pouvoir (1830–80)* (Paris, 1960).
17 Theodore Zeldin, *The Political System of Napoleon III* (London, 1958).
18 Cited by John Morley, *op. cit.*, p.718.
19 Though Charles P. Kindleberger claims that there were pressure groups at work at this time. See his *Economic Growth in France and Britain* (London, 1964), p.283.
20 W. E. Gladstone, 'Greville's latest journals', *English Historical Review*, 1887, pp.281–302.
21 A. L. Dunham, *The Anglo-French Treaty of Commerce of 1860 and the Progress of the Industrial Revolution in France* (Ann Arbor, Mich., 1930).
22 Marcel Rist, 'Une Expérience française de libération des échanges au XIXᵉ siècle: le Traité de 1860', *Revue d'economie politique*, 1956, pp.908–62.
23 J. Coussy, 'La Politique commerciale du Second Empire et la continuité de l'évolution structurelle française', *Cahiers de l'Institut de science économique appliquée*, 1961, pp.1–47.
24 The biographies of Cobden by John Morley and John A. Hobson.
25 A. L. Dunham, *op. cit.*, p.377.
26 Jean Maurain, *Un Bourgeois français au XIXᵉ siècle: Baroche ministre de Napoléon III, d'après ses papiers inédits* (Paris, 1936), especially pp.184–92.
27 Robert Schnerb, *Rouher et le Second Empire* (Paris, 1949), especially pp.89–117.
28 Gordon Wright, 'The origins of Napoleon III's free trade', *Economic History Review*, 1937, pp.64–8.
29 Louis Girard, *La Politique des travaux publics du Second Empire* (Paris, 1951).
30 Félix Ponteil, *Les Classes bourgeoises et l'avènement de la démocratie, 1815–1914* (Paris, 1968), p.269.
31 As has been shown by Claude Fohlen, 'Bourgeoisie française, liberté économique et intervention de l'État', *Revue économique*, 1956, pp.414–28.
32 A. L. Dunham, *op. cit.*, pp.62–3.
33 On Napoleon and England see F. C. Palm, *England and Napoleon III* (Duke University Press, 1944).
34 For the decrees of 1853 and 1855 as well as the 1855 government investigation of tariffs see Archives nationales, F. 12.6200, Ministère du Commerce.
35 Félix Ponteil, *op. cit.*, p.269.
36 Marcel Blanchard, *Le Second Empire* (Paris, 1957 edition), p.60. On Saint-Simonians during the Second Empire, see George Weill, 'Les Saint-Simoniens sous Napoléon III', *Revue des Études napoléoniennes*, 1913, pp.391–406.
37 David H. Pinkney, *Napoleon III and the Rebuilding of Paris* (Princeton, 1958), p.30.
38 J. Coussy, *loc. cit.*
39 H.-N. Boon, *Rêve et réalité dans l'œuvre économique et sociale de Napoléon III* (Paris, 1936), p.103.
40 Georges Weill, *L'École Saint-Simonienne: son histoire, son influence jusqu'à nos jours* (Paris, 1896); Sébastien Charléty, *Histoire du Saint-Simonisme, 1825–64* (Paris, 1896), especially book IV.
41 J. B. H. R. Capefigue, *Histoire des grandes opérations financières* (Paris, 1860), v, pp.132–3.
42 Alexander Gerschenkron, *Economic Backwardness in Historical Perspective: a Book of Essays* (Harvard, 1962), p.24.
43 I have questioned the originality of Saint-Simonian banking ideas in 'Some banking ideas in France in the 1830s: the example of the Pereires, 1830–5', *Revue internationale d'histoire de la banque* 1973, pp.23–47.
44 Cf. Maurice Wallon, 'Les Saint-Simoniens et les chemins de fer' (Paris, thesis, 1908)
45 J.-B. Duroselle, 'Michel Chevalier et le libre-échange avant 1860', *Bulletin de la Société d'histoire moderne*, 1956, pp.2–5; Marlis Steinert, 'Michel Chevalier: l'évolution de sa pensée économique, sociale et politique, 1830–1852' (Saarbrüken, unpublished thesis, 1956), pp.131–42.

46 Letters from Arlès-Dufour to Enfantin, January ?, 16, 26, February 1, 2, 10, 20 and March 8, Fonds Enfantin, 7687, fos. 2, 5, 6, 7, 9, 11, 12, 14, Bibliothèque de l'Arsenal. Arlès-Dufour's devotion to the cause of free trade has been described by Michel Chevalier, 'Deux défenseurs de la liberté commerciale: MM. Arlès-Dufour et Combes', *Journal des Economistes*, 1872, pp.447–57, and by the anonymous biography, *Arlès-Dufour* (Paris, 1874), a copy of which is to be found at the Bibliothèque de l'Arsenal.

47 Letters from Enfantin to Arlès-Dufour, 26 and 30 January 1860, *Œuvres de Saint-Simon et d'Enfantin*, XIII, pp.51–4.

48 Papiers Baroche, 1184, Bibliothèque Thiers; Jean Maurain, *op. cit.*, pp.184–7. There is also a draft of the Pereire memorandum in the Pereire papers: Archives de la famille Pereire, dossier VII.

49 Gordon Wright, *loc. cit.*

50 Ministère du Commerce: *Enquête relative à diverses prohibitions établies à l'entrée des produits étrangers, commencée le 8 octobre 1834, sous la présidence de M. Duchâtel*, 3 vols. (Paris, 1835).

51 'Projet de loi sur les douanes', *le National*, 12 February 1834.

52 'Du tarif sur les charbons étrangers et du salaire des ouvriers d'Anzin', *ibid.*, 30 May 1833; 'De la non-intervention du pouvoir en matière d'industrie, à propos des mineurs d'Anzin', *ibid.*, 6 June 1833.

53 'Conditions de notre navigation marchande', *ibid.*, 11 July 1834.

54 'De l'Assiette de l'impôt', *la Revue encyclopédique*, 8 April 1832.

55 'Moyen d'accélérer la réforme commerciale', *le National*, 14 December 1833.

56 'De la réforme commerciale', *ibid.*, 12 June 1834.

57 'Du Rapport de MM. Bowring et Villiers sur les relations commerciales de la France et de l'Angleterre', *ibid.*, 26 May 1834.

58 'De l'Assiette de l'impôt', *la Revue encyclopédique*, 8 April 1832.

59 'Le Rendement des impôts indirects', *le National*, 16 July 1835.

60 Assemblée générale du Crédit mobilier, Archives de la famille Pereire, dossier XV.

61 William Nassau Senior, *Conversations with Distinguished Persons, 1860–63*, II, p.314.

62 J. Grosstête, 'Les idées des frères Pereire sur la monnaie et le crédit' (unpublished thesis, Paris, 1950), p.11.

63 As did Isaac Pereire in 1877: *Politique industrielle et commerciale. Budget des réformes* (Paris 1877), p.17.

64 Gordon Wright, *loc. cit.*

65 A. L. Dunham, *op. cit.*, appendix, pp.369–71, and 'Chevalier's plan of 1859: the basis of the new commercial policy of Napoleon III', *American Historical Review*, 1934, pp.72–5.

66 Pencilled, undated manuscript in the hand of Emile Pereire, Archives de la famille Pereire, dossier VII.

67 Emile Pereire to Jean Mocquard, 18 October 1859, *ibid.*, dossier VII.

68 Jean Mocquard to Emile Pereire, 19 October 1859, *ibid.*

69 Michel Chevalier to Emile Pereire, 27 October 1859, Correspondance Chevalier, *ibid.*, dossier IV.

70 Pereire memorandum, p.15, *ibid.*, dossier VII.

71 Pereire memorandum, p.19, *ibid.*

72 *Inter alia*, A. L. Dunham, *op. cit.*, p.61 and the letter from Chevalier to Price in Bonamy Price, *The Principles of Currency; Six Lectures Delivered at Oxford* (London, 1869), appendix II, pp.228–40.

73 Michel Chevalier to Emile Pereire, 27 October 1859, Correspondance Chevalier, Archives de la famille Pereire, dossier IV.

74 In a letter to Emile Pereire, on 2 June 1864, Chevalier wrote that Haussmann had said of Rouher: 'Vous le croyez un homme à principes, vous avez tort. Il a été novateur et hardi dans l'affaire de la liberté du commerce parce que l'Empereur voulait la liberté du commerce; mais hors de là il sera comme les autres.' Correspondance Chevalier, *loc. cit.*

75 Susan Strange, 'International economic relations, 1: the need for an interdisciplinary approach', in *The Study of International Affairs*, ed. Roger Morgan (London, 1972), pp.63–85 (p.65).

76 Notable exceptions to this are D. C. M. Platt, *op. cit.* and H.-U. Wehler, *Bismarck und der Imperialismus* (Cologne, 1969).
77 Charles P. Kindleberger has made a beginning with his textbook, *Power and Money: the Economics of International Politics and the Politics of International Economics* (London, 1970).
78 See, for example, W. O. Henderson, *The Zollverein*, pp.336–44.
79 Alfred de Ridder, *Les Projets d'union douanière franco-belge et les puissances européennes, 1836–1843* (Brussels, 1932), *passim*.
80 Jan Krulis-Randa, *Das Deutsch-österreichische Zollunionsprojekt von 1931* (Zurich, 1955), *passim*.
81 That the 1860 treaty was largely political in its objectives has recently been argued, from English sources, by A. A. Iliasu, 'The Cobden–Chevalier commercial treaty of 1860', *Historical Journal*, 1971, pp.67–98. The groundwork still needs to be done on the diplomatic aspects of the 1860 treaty from the French point of view.
82 *The Times*, 17 and 23 January 1860.
83 *Hansard*, third series, vol. CLVI, cls.22 28–2264; K. B. Clayton, 'Anglo-French Commercial Relations 1860–1882' (University of Manchester, unpublished M.A. thesis, 1954), p.26.
84 Cited by Robert Schnerb, *op. cit.*, p.105.
85 W. G. Beasley, 'Lord Malmesbury's Foreign Office circular of 8 March 1858', *Bulletin of the Institute of Historical Research*, 1950, pp.225–8.
86 *Reminiscences of Richard Cobden*, pp.179–83.
87 Bright to George Wilson, cited by Herman Ausubel, *John Bright: Victorian Reformer* (London, 1966), p.59.
88 Cited by Donald Read, *Cobden and Bright, a Victorian Political Partnership* (London, 1967), p.140.
89 Cobden to Chevalier, 14 September 1859, cited by J. A. Hobson, *op. cit.*, pp.244–5.
90 Derek Beales, *England and Italy, 1859–60* (London, 1961), pp.107 ff.
91 E. Ashley, *The Life of Henry John Temple, Viscount Palmerston, 1846–65* (London, 1876), vol. II, pp.174–80; A. A. Iliasu, *loc. cit.*
92 H. Hearder, 'Queen Victoria and foreign policy. Royal intervention in the Italian question, 1859–60', *Studies in International History*, ed. K. Bourne and D. C. Watt (London, 1967), pp.172–88.
93 Gladstone to Graham, cited by Derek Beales, *op. cit.*, p.132.
94 John Morley, *The Life of William Ewart Gladstone* (London, 1903), II, p.23; W. E. Gladstone, *loc. cit.*
95 Cmd. 2605, letter number 2.
96 This is argued by A. A. Iliasu, *loc. cit.*, pp.86–7.
97 Kenneth Bourne, *The Foreign Policy of Victorian England 1860–1902* (Oxford, 1970), pp.102–3.
98 *The Paris Embassy during the Second Empire: from the Papers of Earl Cowley*, ed. Col. the Hon. F. Wellesley (London, 1928), pp.187–9.
99 A. A. Iliasu, *loc. cit.*, pp.85–7.
100 Robert Schnerb, *op. cit.*, p.104.
101 Chevalier also claimed, erroneously, that the emperor had not thought of a commercial treaty until it was suggested to him by Cobden and himself in October: W. Nassau senior, *op. cit.*, II, pp.314–15.
102 Cobden to Charles Sumner, 3 December 1861, cited by J. A. Hobson *op. cit.*, p.348.
103 Arlès-Dufour to Enfantin, 10 February 1860, Fonds Enfantin, 7687, fo. 11, Bibliothèque de l'Arsenal.
104 John Morley, *The Life of Richard Cobden*, p.715.
105 *Mémoires du duc de Persigny*, publiés avec des documents inédits, un avant-propos et un épiloque par M. H. de Laire Comte d'Espagny (Paris, 1896), pp.199–217.
106 Cobden's Diary, cited by John Morley, *op. cit.*, pp.719–20.
107 G. Pagès, 'The annexation of Savoy and the crisis in Anglo-French relations, January to April 1860', in A. Coville and Harold Temperley (eds.), *Studies in Anglo-French History* (Cambridge, 1935).
108 *The Paris Embassy during the Second Empire*, p.201.

D. A. Farnie

7

The Cotton Famine in Great Britain

> The Cotton Famine is an event that has burnt itself into the history of
> Lancashire.
>
> *London Quarterly Review*, January 1865, p.313

Dr Henderson's history of the Cotton Famine was the first monograph
to survey the history of the cotton industry during the nineteenth century as distinct from the period of the Industrial Revolution. The
author's pioneer venture into that field was inspired by H. L. Beales,
who had been invited to write the successor volume to Arthur Redford's
The Economic History of England, 1760–1860 (1931). The subject was a
relatively unknown episode in history, although it had earlier been
considered from various aspects as an illustration of the social role of
public works,[1] as a phase in the history of poor relief,[2] as an example of
a commercial crisis within a capitalist economy[3] and as an occasion for
an inspiring display of Anglo-American solidarity.[4] Dr Henderson
was, however, the first scholar to consider the subject as a whole and
to approach it with a refreshing freedom from insular prejudices. He
brought to bear upon his chosen field of investigation the full range
of Continental scholarship[5] as well as the traditions of Continental
political economy. His bibliography alone was a monument of erudition
and provided a comprehensive guide to the literature of the whole
history of the cotton industry. The work won immediate acceptance
as a full and definitive survey of its subject, ranking with the great work
by Ernst von Halle.[6] It was especially esteemed as an indispensable
source of reference in America, where historians remained until 1968
understandably hypnotised by the fascination of the internal rather
than the external repercussions of the Civil War. Nor were its conclusions challenged by the younger generation of iconoclastic econo-
metric historians. When the subject became again one for research the
wide perspective of Dr Henderson's analysis was indeed abandoned
in favour of a stultifying concern with the subject of cotton supply,
so that the Cotton Famine was studied merely as an episode in the
history of British relations with India or with Egypt in the newly

fashionable terms of economic imperialism or of economic development. Such an approach needs to be balanced by reference to Dr
Henderson's well documented demonstration that the Cotton Famine
was much more than a crisis in the supply of raw material. The following
essay will therefore consider the contemporary crisis in the industry's
markets in an attempt to ascertain whether the Cotton Famine marks
the true end of an era in the history of the industry.

THE COTTON INDUSTRY IN 1860

'The greatest manufacturing industry which ever has been established'[7]
dominated the foreign trade of Britain between 1831 and 1873.
Cotton manufactures provided the most valuable single export from
1803 until 1938, while raw cotton formed the main import from 1825
until 1873 as well as the chief re-export from 1831 until 1873. During
the 1850s the industry had enjoyed a great wave of expansion which
increased its consumption of cotton by 66 per cent and raised the value
of its home trade for the first time above that of the woollen trade.
That boom culminated in the unprecedented imports and exports of
1858–61, in a vast extension of productive capacity and in the industry's
first joint-stock company boom in 1860–1. In the climactic year of
1860 raw cotton supplied 17 per cent of the total value of imports and
18·9 per cent of the total value of re-exports, while cotton manufactures accounted for 38·3 per cent of the total value of exports, and
the value added by the industry amounted to 7·5 per cent of the gross
national income.

The industry had become increasingly dependent upon foreign
sources of supply and foreign markets, and appeared more than ever an
exotic industry as its export trade expanded even faster than its home
trade. The USA had been the main source of raw cotton since 1803
and had defeated successive attempts by Britain to raise up rival
producers, driving all competitors out of the world market by its
overwhelming ability to export the best and the cheapest cotton. It
supplied 77·5 per cent of the total quantity of cotton imported into
Britain during the decade 1851–60 and 80 per cent in the exceptional
year 1860, when it produced two-thirds of the world's cotton and
supplied more than three-quarters of all the cotton entering into world
trade.[8] The cotton industry was far less dependent upon a single market
but nevertheless exported 64·5 per cent of the total value of its products.
Between 1850 and 1860 its exports of piece goods doubled in value and
its exports of yarn increased by 50 per cent. Increasingly those exports
flowed to Asia, and especially to India, which in defiance of all
expectation had become in 1843 the industry's most valuable single
overseas market. In the boom which followed the suppression of the

Indian Mutiny India and China raised the value of their imports in 1858–60 to double the level of 1855–7. In 1860 43 per cent of the value of the industry's exports was taken by four markets, 20·7 per cent by India, 8·7 per cent by the USA, 6·8 per cent by Turkey and 6·5 per cent by China. In that year a crisis of over-production began to afflict the industry in both Britain and Europe.

THE CRISIS OF OVERPRODUCTION, 1860–1

The unprecedented prosperity of the four years 1858–61 brought about an inevitable reaction, since productive capacity had grown by one-fifth since 1856 and had surpassed the absorptive capacity of the industry's markets, arousing grave concern among informed observers.[9] The home trade in fancy goods and muslins was 'almost annihilated' during 1860 by a cold summer and a deficient harvest.[10] Exports to India also shrank in 1860, and to the Levant as well as to the USA in 1861. The export of piece goods to India declined from their peak level of 1859 by 18·5 per cent in quantity and by 15·25 per cent in value during 1860, sharply reducing that market's share in the total volume exported from 34·6 to 24·9 per cent: the average time of turnover of consignments rose sharply, and prices in Calcutta began in March 1860 to recede towards their level of 1856. During the summer India houses began to fail as their expected returns failed to materialise, under the depressing influence of the doubling in 1859 of the import duties on cotton goods, of the 'enormous enhancement' in the customs valuations in 1860[11] and of the diversion of expenditure from clothing to food after the failure of the monsoon rains. From September the first of a series of six bad harvests attracted the capital of merchants in India from the textile trade into the grain trade, in quest of the profits from the famine which was expected to occur during 1861. That succession of bad crops destroyed the prosperity of Lancashire's largest foreign market at a time when the close association between the Indian harvest and the consumption of Manchester goods was not understood. The price of such characteristic export products as T cloths reached a low point during February 1861, at a level 7½ per cent below that of twelve months earlier, while shirtings reached their nadir between February and June at a price level 15 per cent lower than that of a year earlier.

During 1861 the decline in the export of piece goods to Madras was offset by the expansion of exports to the much larger markets of Bombay and Calcutta. Exports of cotton manufactures to the industry's fourth largest foreign market, Turkey, declined, however, by 22 per cent in quantity and by 32 per cent in value after the Levant crisis of 1860, a loss which was only half offset by the expansion of exports to

Naples and Sicily which followed in the wake of the expedition of the Thousand. The export of cotton manufactures to the USA sank by 64·5 per cent in quantity and by 67 per cent in value after the outbreak of war, representing 30 per cent of the total loss in exports by the industry during 1861. Little compensation was provided for the loss of the industry's second largest foreign market in the expansion of its exports to France by £336,000, which amounted to only one-ninth of the decline in exports to the USA. The crisis of overproduction was indeed accentuated by the optimistic expectations entertained of the potential capacity of the French market, which was opened only from 1 October 1861 after the expiry of twenty-one months' grace from the signature of the Anglo-French treaty of commerce. Similar delusive hopes were entertained of 'that huge market of four hundred millions'[12] opened by treaty in 1860 in China, exports to which in fact declined during 1861 by 2 per cent from their 1860 peak before plunging by a further 55 per cent during 1862. The reduction in the value of the exports of cotton manufactures by £6,140,000 accounted for 57 per cent of the total reduction in British exports during 1861.

The saturation of the markets for cotton goods led to a decline in the number of orders placed with the industry and to an increase in manufacture for stock. Such stocks had built up rapidly towards the end of 1860, when their value amounted to over £20 millions, the equivalent of 23·5 per cent of the industry's annual product. During 1861 their volume increased by a further 21·4 per cent from 242 million to 293 million lb of goods[13] worth over £25 millions, the equivalent of 33·6 per cent of the industry's annual product. That progressive accumulation of stocks reflected a growing excess of supply over demand and the sheer incapacity of supply to create its own demand, so ushering the industry from a phase of prosperity into one of depression. Mill margins, the most sensitive index of profitability, had averaged 68 per cent upon the price of raw cotton during the decade 1850–9 and had reached 81 per cent in 1860 but were halved in 1861 to a meagre 40 per cent. That shrinkage in margins exerted a growing pressure upon costs as producers began reluctantly to reconcile themselves to a future of lower prices. Efforts made during February 1861 to reduce wages by 5 per cent proved successful, and strikes in opposition failed in Bolton, Ashton under Lyne and Blackburn, since employers could afford to work short time in a falling market. In May the weavers of Colne finally capitulated after a strike of fifty weeks, so shattering the power of the first Weavers' Amalgamation, which had been established in 1858. In April, May and June many Manchester shippers were compelled to suspend payment,[14] while others were brought to the verge of bankruptcy, since they could not dispose of their shipments except at a ruinous sacrifice of 40–50 per cent of their value.

The influence of the Civil War nevertheless served to avert the impending threat of ruin: it brought a shower of riches in place of the anticipated hard times and opened up a prospect of unparalleled rewards to the fortunate holders of stocks.

THE INFLUENCE OF THE CIVIL WAR

The war of 1861–5 not only reduced the export of cotton manufactures to the USA but also imperilled the security of the supply of raw cotton to the mills of Lancashire. The cotton industry had, however, accumulated very large stocks of raw material and had already begun to suffer from a market crisis, so that no shortage of cotton existed even when distress became most acute during 1862. The cotton harvest of 1859 had been the largest in the history of the USA, being twice as abundant as that of 1850 and reducing the price of the raw material to its lowest level of $5\frac{7}{8}d$ per lb in July 1860. The good harvest of 1860 and its accelerated shipment in anticipation of the eventuality of war, especially after the election of Lincoln, permitted the heaping up of stocks in England. End-of-year stocks had declined from their peak level of 1845, sufficing in 1850–4 for twenty-one weeks' supply and in 1855–9 for thirteen weeks' supply, but rose to sixteen weeks' supply at the close of 1860. Thus the price of cotton remained low for six months after the bombardment of Fort Sumter on 12 April. The belief in a war of ninety days' duration checked the advance in price which alone could have called forth increased supplies from outside the USA: that belief was not dispelled until the Confederacy secured its first military victory at Bull Run on 21 July.

The declaration on 19 April of a blockade of the Southern ports by the North remained a symbolic act, since effective enforcement for long proved impossible. That act nevertheless raised freight rates, insurance premiums and cotton prices:[15] it encouraged from July a recourse to short-time working, a transfer from coarse to fine spinning and a renewal of efforts to replace the USA by India as a source of supply. The invincible faith of the *Economist* in the commanding power of a market economy to call forth the necessary supplies remained, however, unshaken. 'We share to a considerable extent the instinctive conviction of the Lancashire merchants and manufacturers, that an article grown by an eager seller and consumed by an eager buyer will find its way from the one to the other, in spite of all hostile barriers and prohibitions.'[16] The initial rise in prices attracted a swarm of speculative buyers into the Liverpool market during July, in search of profit from gambling on the continued absence of American stocks from the markets of Europe. Even American buyers were attracted into that market at the end of August by the prospect of buying cotton for speculation or for reshipment to New York. During August margins began to shrink as yarn and cloth prices failed to respond to the rise in price of raw cotton. During September cotton prices first surpassed the famine level reached four years earlier. From October mills resorted increasingly to short-time or to half-time working or even closed down, especially in the coarse spinning trade, which used much more raw cotton than the fine trade and was most affected by the saturation of its markets.

The influence of the market crisis was both compounded and concealed by the influence of the war. Supplies of American cotton were raised in price by the risks of blockade running but continued to flow across the Atlantic and furnished in 1861 71 per cent of the cotton imported by Europe and 65 per cent of that imported by Britain. Imports into England remained at a very high level throughout the year and proved to be only 12 per cent below the level of 1860, since India increased its contribution by a massive 75 per cent. By the end of the year aggregate stocks had risen to a peak quantity of 789,300 bales,[17] or to the equivalent of seventeen weeks' supply, the highest level since 1854. Those stocks were nevertheless less useful to Lancashire than they appeared to be, since half comprised short-stapled Surat, which was no substitute for the medium-stapled American most favoured for wefts. Speculators had moreover raised their purchases to an all-time peak level, buying 5 per cent more than the total volume of imports and securing control of all the stocks held in the ports. Those stocks must be clearly distinguished from those held at the mills because of the immense socio-economic distance between Liverpool and Lancashire, which was increased by the growing diversion of enterprise from industry into commerce and especially into speculative commerce. Stocks at the mills had declined during 1861 by 55 per cent from four weeks' supply to two weeks' supply, while those held in the ports had increased by 17·6 per cent from twelve weeks' supply to fifteen weeks' supply.

Any further ruinous depression of prices was checked by the outbreak of war and by the locking up of the 1861 crop by the blockade. It also became possible to represent the crisis as one of supply rather than of demand and to blame the war for the industrial depression, since short-time working began only after the start of hostilities. Such an interpretation harmonised with the fashionable political economy in its concern with scarcity rather than with abundance as the central problem of economic life. The cotton industry had always hitherto been far more concerned with the supply of raw cotton than with the markets for its finished goods and had been repeatedly fearful of a cotton dearth in 1846, in 1850 and again in 1857, when the Cotton Supply Association had been founded. Its spokesmen inevitably preferred to accept and to diffuse an explanation of the depression which conformed to their own world outlook. Their interpretation served an important social function, since it effectively concealed the congested nature of the industry's markets and the notable imperfections of a market-oriented system of production, so encouraging the spread of a stupefying mis-conception in both Lancashire and England. In their view Lancashire had fallen victim to an act of God, and the operatives were therefore called upon to display heroic fortitude under suffering which was no fault of their own or of their employers.

Du Fay & Co., the authors of the most authoritative cotton circular of the day, first revealed to the public the disturbing truth of the industry's overstocked markets in Asia[18] and were roundly rebuked by Samuel Mendel in the assured tones of the pander–publicist presenting as accepted fact the most debatable of propositions. 'However tedious and wearisome may be the reiteration of the fact, still it must be admitted that the course of our market is more seriously influenced by the war in America than by any other cause or causes.'[19] Mendel was the leading shipper from Manchester to Asia and, having raised his declared profits to £250,000–£300,000 per annum in the post-Mutiny boom, knew better than any other merchant in Manchester the truth of Du Fay's assertions. He nevertheless deliberately misrepresented the influence of the war and so misled all who accepted his asseverations at their face value instead of treating them as controversial contributions made to a debate by an interested party.

The oppressive influence of overstocked markets was forgotten after the 1860s and was submerged for two generations thereafter beneath the general consensus of later opinion, which attributed the great economic crisis of the decade to a shortage of cotton which had not in fact existed. Thus the free trade interpretation was diffused amongst an uncritical posterity without either rebuttal or demurrer, even from socialists such as Hyndman. It was first undermined by Owsley in 1931 and by Henderson in 1932,[20] a generation before it was finally demolished by Fohlen in 1956 and by Brady in 1963.[21] Brady undertook a drastic revision of the conventional interpretation of the crisis. He showed convincingly that the Civil War was not responsible for the industrial depression in Lancashire, did not seriously deplete the stocks of raw cotton held in Britain and was important only in so far as it induced expectations of a future shortage of supplies. He blamed the depression almost wholly upon the preceding period of production which had expanded far in excess of any existing demand. His thesis has not yet been challenged: even less has it been refuted in its inter-pretation of the crucial years 1861 and 1862, since it explains so much that would otherwise remain inexplicable. Thus the saturated markets of the cotton industry remained largely unresponsive for eighteen

months after the close of 1860 until the autumn of 1862. In such a
situation producers remained more concerned with their markets than
with their supply of raw material. Lancashire therefore launched a
campaign against the Indian import duty, under whose apparent
protection the number of cotton mills in Bombay had risen from seven
in 1860 to fifteen in 1861. The campaign succeeded in securing in three
successive stages between November 1860 and April 1862 a revision
of the customs valuations and a halving of the obnoxious duty,[22] so
setting a precedent for the similar campaigns of 1874-9 and 1894-5.
The immediate effects were to facilitate the sale of existing stocks rather
than to reduce the incidence of unemployment, since margins remained
unprofitable. Cotton spinners therefore showed little or no interest in
the efforts of the Cotton Supply Association to develop alternative
sources of supply.

THE CRISIS OF 1862

Consumption and employment had been reduced by one-third by
December 1861 when news of the *Trent* affair provoked an outburst of
war fever in England, especially in Liverpool. The new hope that the
Royal Navy might break the blockade reduced the price of cotton by
17 per cent in a precautionary anticipation of the advent of the
American crop. That hope vanished by the end of December, when
prices resumed their rise and wholly eliminated the margin of spinners
during January 1862, the price of raw cotton even exceeding that of
coarse yarn. By May consumption had been reduced by half and
employment in only slightly less degree. Then cotton prices doubled
during the next three months, rising by an astounding 50 per cent in
the three weeks after 15 August in the greatest single fluctuation of the
war, precipitated by the series of reverses suffered by the North.

The Union navy completed its blockade of the main cotton ports by
the capture of New Orleans on 29 April, but the Union army was
repelled in its first bid to capture Richmond at the second battle of
Bull Run on 29-30 August in Lee's most brilliant campaign. Thereafter
the great military aristocracy of the planter states threatened to en-
throne itself in permanence upon the American continent from the
Potomac to Panama. All hopes of a speedy end to the war receded and
expectations of future cotton supply were fundamentally transformed
in harmony with the interlinked assumptions of a continuation of
hostilities, the exclusion of American cotton from the world market and
the consequent perpetuation of rising prices. Stocks in Liverpool were
markedly depleted by the consequent sudden increase in demand.
They had been thought sufficient in July for six months' consumption
but were deemed adequate in September for only three weeks' con-

sumption,[23] as the demand for export raised prices sharply and excluded Lancashire spinners from the market in favour of speculators. The average number of days of work available per operative had sunk from the customary six to four in December 1861 and to three and a half in April 1862, but shrank to two and a third in November 1862. Unemployment reached its peak in December, when cotton was at thrice its pre-war price and one-fifth of the total population of Lancashire was drawing relief.

During 1862 the volume of the imports of cotton plummeted by 58 per cent. The USA furnished a smaller quantity than in any year since 1813 and supplied only 3·2 per cent of the total volume. Egypt became an additional source of supply, especially of long-stapled cotton, and increased the volume of its exports to England by 50 per cent. India increased the volume of her exports to England by only 8·6 per cent after their great upward leap during 1861 but provided more cotton than the USA for the first time since 1819 and furnished 74 per cent of the total imports. In that worst of years for production and employment the consumption of cotton fell, however, by 55 per cent to the lowest level since 1849 and to 42 per cent of the peak consumption of the exceptionally prosperous year 1860. In the year of scantiest supply the expanded spindleage of the industry was thus restricted to half its peak pre-war consumption. Stocks held at the mills declined by 80 per cent during the year, or much more rapidly than in 1861, and were sufficient at its close for only two and a third weeks at the current level of reduced consumption. Stocks held in the ports, however, declined only half as much, by 38 per cent, and represented the equivalent of over twenty weeks' supply.

Mill margins reached their lowest point during 1862, averaging only 18 per cent upon the price of raw cotton. The gross value of the industry's product sank by 42·5 per cent. The quantity of goods consumed in the home market declined by 41 per cent and the quantity exported by 39 per cent, shipments of piece goods to China falling by 67 per cent and those to India by 31·6 per cent. Exports of yarn declined much more than exports of cloth, sinking in volume by 48 per cent while exports of piece goods fell by 34·4 per cent in the biggest slump in the whole history of the industry. The increase in prices half offset the decline in the volume of trade, exports of yarn and piece goods shrinking in volume by 37·8 per cent but in value by only 21·6 per cent. The decline in shipments to India and China represented 38·6 per cent of the total loss in value of exports. Cotton manufactures nevertheless retained their primacy in the export trade, reducing their share from 38·3 per cent in 1860 to 29·6 per cent in 1862. The terms of trade were unfavourably affected as the price of imports rose more than that of exports. The doubling of cotton prices raised import prices in general by 12·5 per cent during 1862 in one of the steepest increases in British economic history. In that year the gross barter terms of trade sank by one-third below their level of 1859. The balance of payments was not plunged into deficit, but the surplus on current account declined in 1861 and 1862 to half the average annual level of 1856–60.[24]

THE BOOM IN THE RE-EXPORT OF RAW COTTON

During 1862 Liverpool's shipping tonnage declined by only 7 per cent and the receipts of the Mersey Docks and Harbour Board shrank by only 12 per cent, despite the reduction in the volume of cotton imports by nearly three-fifths. The port found compensation in the transfer of American vessels to Liverpool registry, in the organisation of blockade-running ventures, in the expansion of the jute and grain trades and in the development of trade with India and with the Mediterranean. Above all, cotton broking enjoyed a golden age, despite the reduced volume of imports. The number of brokers nearly doubled under the influence of the rise in prices, the increase in the number of trans-actions and the boom in re-exports. The Cotton Brokers' Association projected in 1862 the construction of a new Exchange, which was completed in 1867; it also found it necessary for the first time to establish its own rules and committee in 1863 and to issue its own circular in 1864.

The port had been in 1861 the main centre of opposition to the blockade but developed from 1862 a vested interest in its maintenance as rising prices brought in their wake an influx of unearned wealth to the holders of stocks and re-exports expanded from 22 per cent of total imports in 1861 to the all-time peak proportion of 41 per cent in 1862. It established its full autonomy in the service of the world market and became the main repository of stocks, which outweighed those held at the mills threefold at the close of 1860 but ninefold at the close of 1862. Those stocks, together with its contraband trade, gave Liverpool an overwhelming advantage in the entrepôt trade over Glasgow and Le Havre and enabled it to reap monopoly profits as prices rose. Sales to speculators for the rise required the investment of large capitals and rose from 15 per cent of total sales in 1860 to the peak proportion of 46 per cent in 1862,[25] effectively excluding Lancashire spinners from the market.

The average annual exports of raw cotton almost doubled, from 131,670,000 lb in 1850–9 to 256,150,000 lb in 1860–5, and increased their proportion of total imports from 14·3 per cent to 29 per cent. If those exports had not doubled, then the consumption of cotton by the mills of Lancashire could have been maintained in 1862–5 at an average level of 683,680,000 lb, or only one-seventh less than in 1850–9. Thus Liverpool exalted the interests of the re-export trade over those of secondary industry and divorced its function from that of its manufacturing hinterland, even attracting cotton back from the mills to its market and re-exporting it to New York. Such re-exports helped, together with the expansion in the carrying trade for foreigners, to pay for the vast increase in the price of cotton imports. The stocks of raw cotton in the port were, however, increasingly composed of Surat and were not in demand in Lancashire to the extent that they were on the Continent. France was much more dependent even than England on American cotton but adapted the machinery of its spinning mills to the consumption of Surat more extensively than did England. Thus it replaced Russia as the main foreign customer of Liverpool from 1862 until 1866 and made Britain the main source of its supply in place of the USA, since it could secure the substitute Indian cotton in no other market. That increase in the demand for exports maintained domestic prices at a high level and prevented them from declining as imports increased after 1862.

THE QUESTION OF COTTON SUPPLY

The severity of the shortage of cotton has undoubtedly been exaggerated by the habitual representation of the exceptional consumption of 1860 as typical. The average annual consumption had been 796,240,000 lb in the decade 1850–9, rising by 31·3 per cent in 1860–1 to 1,045,500,000 lb, the largest consumption thitherto ever attained. It sank in 1862–5 to 559,200,000 lb, which was 55·5 per cent of the level reached in the years 1860–1 but only 22·7 per cent below the average level of 1850–9. To describe such a reduction in consumption as a dearth would be sheer hyperbole unless the phrase were intended to divert attention from the real cause of economic distress. 'If a man surfeited himself with food daily, and circumstances should arise that restricted him to half supplies, we would not say that individual was suffering from famine. This was precisely the case as to manufactures.'[26]

There was no real shortage of cotton in Lancashire even during 1862, when distress was most acute, though the stocks were located in Liverpool rather than at the mills. As the war continued stocks began to be depleted and the essential inelasticity of cotton supply was strikingly revealed. Lancashire had developed what was essentially 'a forced exotic trade',[27] ineluctably dependent upon the Cotton Kingdom of the South for its supply of medium-stapled cotton. No potential competitor could respond in less than a year to the stimulus of high prices, and most required five years in order to reach their maximum productive capacity. No other country would, however, try to fill the void left by the USA for fear of the immense stocks locked up in the South by the blockade and of the threat of overpowering competition from America in the future. The most effective guarantee to other producers would have been a differential import duty on slave-grown cotton, which could not, however, be imposed because of the deep entrenchment of the policy of free trade in England and the massive inertia of the vast commercial complex focused on the USA. Thus Brazil continued to exploit its comparative advantages for the production of coffee, west Africa remained devoted to the production of palm oil, Natal and Queensland developed the cultivation of sugar rather than of cotton, while Burma expanded its cultivation of rice at the expense of cotton. No substantial or sustained material support was given in Lancashire, least of all in Liverpool, to the propaganda of the Cotton Supply Association or to the covey of cotton companies which sought to supplement its activities.

India had become in 1861 the main focus of the aspirations of all who hoped to end Britain's slavish dependence upon the USA. She ranked second to the USA as a grower of cotton in 1860 but produced only 18 per cent of the world's total supply, in contrast to the 66 per cent produced by the USA, and supplied only 15 per cent of Britain's imports. In 1862–5 she furnished, on average, 55 per cent of those imports. She would nevertheless have needed to increase her production threefold and her exports ninefold in order fully to replace the USA as a source of supply and to shift back from west to east the centre of gravity of the cotton trade. Thus she revealed for the first time the limited size of her cotton crop and so dispelled the dream of an Anglo-Indian economic symbiosis based upon the exchange of cotton for calico. The increase in her exports to England was achieved by diverting cotton from the China market as well as from home consumption, by planting cotton in preference to cereals and finally by extending the area under cultivation.[28] Indian cotton was short in staple, weak and coarse in fibre and defective in colour: it could not compete in price or quality with American and could not overcome the persistent partiality of Lancashire for Middling Orleans. Thus it became a great staple of the re-export trade of Liverpool rather than a staple of consumption in the mills of Lancashire. The increase in the import of Indian cotton raised the volume of intra-imperial trade to new heights but precipitated a great drain of bullion from 1863, when the value of cotton imports first exceeded the value of the exports of cotton manufactures and so paved the way for the financial crisis of 1864. Fortunately the exporters of raw cotton increased their imports of piece goods, which expanded notably to Colombia, Egypt and Bombay during 1863 and to Brazil during 1864 and so prevented any further deterioration in Britain's terms of trade.

The shortage of American cotton compelled employers to re-equip their mills in order to spin Surat, and especially to improve their preparatory processes, so exerting a similar influence to the cotton dearth of 1857. Spinners speedily discovered to their astonishment the real capacity of Surat and raised by 1862 the highest counts spun from pure Surat from 24s to 50s but did not succeed in permanently reducing their deep-rooted distaste for Indian cotton. The process of opening the tightly packed raw material became wholly automatic through the use of the Crighton opener, invented in 1861, as did the subsequent process of scutching through the application of the ingenious piano-feed regulator developed in 1862. The rollers of the drawing frame were readjusted to handle the short-stapled Surat. In the process of weaving heavy sizing became customary on warps of Surat and waste yarn in order to give them the tenacity of twist essential for good weaving and to permit the increased use of China clay or 'Lancashire cotton' as the most economical substitute for cotton yarn, carrying further a trend which was to reach its height during the 1870s. Steam jets were also used from 1862 to humidify weaving sheds using Surat yarn so as to reduce the number of breakages of warp and weft. Both techniques of over-sizing and of steaming were accepted as necessities in the 1860s but became the object of hostile agitation by the operative weavers in the 1870s and 1880s. The reorganisation of the preparatory processes entailed such an extensive investment of capital that it amounted almost to the creation of a new industry. Those processes were so greatly improved that the self-acting mule could be used in place of the hand mule in the spinning of coarse and medium counts up to 60s where the previous limit had been 50s. The labour-saving effects of such innovations were counterbalanced by the need for increased labour in the manufacture of Surat, so that the employment of labour did not decline to the same extent as the consumption of cotton. Those innovations gave a great stimulus to the textile engineering industry and consolidated the technical supremacy of the Lancashire cotton industry in the world.

THE ORGANISATION OF THE FIRM AND THE INDUSTRY

In the field of business organisation the crisis benefited private employers at the expense of companies, large firms at the expense of small ones, spinners at the expense of manufacturers and merchants at the expense of producers. The surviving hand-loom weavers were adversely affected by the reduction in the supply of yarn, by the cutting off of the sole surviving demand for hand-woven muslins—that from the western USA and Canada—by the increase in the competitive capacity of the power loom in the fancy trade and by its application in

1864 to the weaving of woollens, which closed off a large field of alternative employment. The depression also abruptly ended the first era of company formation in the cotton industry. The new co-operative manufacturing companies were wholly unprepared for such an eventuality, and their prospects for profit sharing were blighted before they had made any profits to divide. The use of loan capital proved a fair-weather technique of industrial finance, since the increased burden of interest payments devoured the capital of shareholders. Working men found that their shares had lost all market value but had to be mortgaged as an essential precondition to drawing relief. Forty-seven of the ninety-two companies registered in the industry in 1860–1 survived for less than ten years, their mills reverting to the possession of private employers and often into the hands of those who had been the original vendors. The surviving companies tended to become less co-operative in spirit and more considerate of the rights of capital, so conforming to the dominant ethos of the trade. The aspirations of the working class to economic independence were not, however, extinguished but diverted into the sphere of consumers' co-operation, where the CWS was successfully established in 1863.

Specialised manufacturers of cloth had expanded more than any other group of employers during the 1850s and had trebled in number but occupied the lowliest position in the industry's hierarchy of status, operating with a low proportion of floating capital and working virtually from hand to mouth. Such small masters could not exploit the opportunities open to wealthier employers. They carried no stocks on which to make a profit, since they did not unite the business of spinner or of exporter to that of manufacturer. They had no funds for speculation, and found that much more capital was necessary than formerly in order merely to carry on their business in a time of rapidly rising prices. Their profit margins were reduced to the minimum during 1863 as those of spinners expanded from their low point of 1862. Their ranks provided the bulk of the casualties after prices began to decline in 1864.

The depression encouraged the withdrawal from the cotton industry of its leading employers, led by Thomas Bazley (1797–1885),[29] and reinforced the geographical concentration of the British cotton industry within the Lancashire region, where society displayed the greatest resilience under pressure. Country mills on the fringes of the shire were adversely affected and closed down from Flintshire to Lonsdale and Carlisle. In Lancaster the cotton mills completed the process of adaptation to the manufacture of table baize, while the new mills established in Warwickshire in 1860 after the Cobden–Chevalier treaty were converted to the manufacture of worsted. The industry became stabilised in Derbyshire as well as in Cheshire and underwent further expansion after the 1860s only in the West Riding, particularly in the

Pennine valleys linking it to Lancashire. The textile industry of Ulster underwent a large-scale conversion from the use of cotton to the use of flax and that of Scotland from the manufacture of muslin to that of sewing thread,[30] using the automatic spooling machine invented in 1858 and the highly productive ring doubling frame from 1867. The production of thread, being undertaken for a world market, proved far less susceptible to cyclical depression than muslin manufacture as well as the most profitable branch of the whole cotton trade.

The crisis ended the great age of the small firm in cotton spinning, since such concerns lacked the necessary capital to maintain their purchases of cotton and to adapt their machinery to handle Surat. Its other effects within the field of business organisation are more debatable. It may have encouraged the rise of separate spinning and weaving firms but did not deprive the combined spinning and weaving firm of its dominant position within the industry, since vertical integration served to cushion the impact of depression, and the combined firms continued to increase their spindleage until 1870 and their loomage until 1880. Nor did it precipitate the decline of the spinning industry in north-east Lancashire, since that industry expanded to a peak in the 1870s. The weaving trade became the main sphere in which new small firms were established, control of the industry as a whole being thereafter concentrated in the hands of the large firms.

THE CONDITION OF THE COTTON OPERATIVES

The cotton operatives of Lancashire were far more numerous and far more concentrated than any comparable group on the Continent and were much more dependent upon the export market. They had enjoyed a luxurious standard of living since the 1830s and had become the best-paid workers in the world during the 1850s, being praised as 'the industrial defence of the country and conquerors of the world—the true army and navy, the source of our wealth, the payers of our taxes, and the maintainers of our glory'.[31] Their invincible immobility and excessive specialisation had, however, made them 'mere animate machines, with one function and no more'[32] and compelled them to bear an increasing burden of unemployment.

The extent of the distress in Lancashire seems, however, to have been exaggerated by outside observers in order either to make political capital in the Conservative interest or to facilitate the raising of relief funds. The cotton industry was less important than in 1830, when it had supplied 51 per cent of the country's total exports and had been less concentrated in its location. It was not the sole industry of Lancashire and had never dominated the life of the shire to the extent that cotton cultivation had dominated the Cotton States. The operatives had never made the mill a centre of their life and preserved intact their friendly societies, co-operative societies, trade unions and family structures. They remained the proudest people in the proudest of English counties[33] and had ample reserves of psychic strength in addition to their accumulated savings.

The health of the operatives does not seem to have suffered, although the evidence for a balanced judgement is difficult to secure because of the general lack of information about the condition of the labouring classes, the prompt publication of patent apologias,[34] the undeveloped nature of public health administration and the traditional technique of the organs of public opinion of minimising the significance of national disasters. No shortage of food or harvest crisis coincided with the industrial crisis. No general rise in the death rate occurred comparable to the fall in the marriage rate and birth rate. The reduction in the employment of women strengthened family structures and improved the health of their children, as the reduction in the consumption of drink improved the health of adults.

> It is incredible how little harm has been done by the cotton famine. Even the public houses go on as usual. The truth is the operatives living on two-thirds of their former wages are better off than the average English labourers; and what cotton has lost, wool and flax have gained. Still even these explanations do not account for the facts. All one can say is the facts are so.[35]

The unemployed bore their affliction with the phlegm of the Saxon and the stoicism of the peasant: they remained in imaginative bondage to the most popular of American novels in *Uncle Tom's Cabin* and they therefore endured their ordeal in the belief, held rightly or wrongly, that it served the realisation of the noblest of causes.[36] They suffered far less in physical health than in the loss of their treasured independence, finding that the soup they supped lacked savour and the bread they broke was bitter:

> To thrust to sum'dy else for bread,
> An' by th' relief keep torin' on,
> Maks honest folk to hang their yead,
> An' crushes th' heart o' th' preawdest mon.
> We know'n it's not eawr bread we ate,
> We know'n they're not eawr clooas we wear,
> We want agen eawr former state,
> Eawr former dhrudgin' life o' care.[37]

The poor law authorities were forced during the summer of 1862 to replace the humiliating labour test by sewing classes and adult schools. Those schools helped to bridge the gulf between the middle class and the working class: they first educated the womenfolk of the cotton towns in their domestic duties and the menfolk in their letters, extending the market for thread as well as for printed literature. The tardy acceptance of public works on the French model produced a permanent improvement in the public health of those communities.

Unemployment was least in those towns with a diversified economy and greatest in those most dependent on the cotton industry, on the supply of American cotton and on the spinning of coarse counts and the weaving of plain cloth. The demand for relief was nevertheless not directly related to the intensity of distress: it was apparently greatest where the Irish were most numerous, where public houses flourished most, where co-operation was weakest and where wealthy residents were fewest. Many towns successfully adapted their industry to the changed conditions of trade. Blackburn had profited more than any other town by the expansion of the Eastern trade during the 1850s and had become more dependent than any other upon the cotton industry, which together with engineering provided subsistence for 89 per cent of its population.[38] Thus it was the worst afflicted by the Indian famines, by the shrinkage in margins, and by the reduction in the supply of American cotton. In response its employers introduced in 1862-3 the manufacture of bordered dhotis, using the Blackburn dobby, developed in 1858. They increased their spindleage by a massive 50 per cent and their loomage by 33 per cent,[39] raising their share of the power looms in the British cotton industry from one-sixth to a quarter. The Blackburn Exchange was built between 1863 and 1865 as the centre for a weekly yarn market serving all of east Lancashire and as a potential rival to the Manchester Exchange.

Oldham depended wholly upon American cotton but carried on a coarse trade wherein Surat could effectively replace the customary staple. The local textile engineers Hibbert & Platt successfully adapted their machines to the spinning of Surat and so gave their district a great competitive advantage over other towns. They transformed the self-acting mule for medium counts into a machine unequalled elsewhere in its productive capacity and so enabled whole mills to be built thenceforward on a self-actor basis. Local spinners made large profits by speculating in cotton, which was held in the large stocks necessary to their coarse trade. Between 1860 and 1863 they profited by the low prices for machinery, undertook the construction of new mills and extended their spindleage by one-fifth at a time when other towns were suffering deep distress. Finding that Surat could be used to spin far finer counts than had thitherto been thought possible, they greatly reduced their production of very coarse yarns and increasingly left that trade to Rossendale. Their large new mills contained longer mules and more spindles than those of any other town in the district and served as models for the limited mills launched in 1874-5. They spun Oldham counts of 32s which required little twist and could therefore be spun at progressively faster speeds, to the benefit of the operative spinners earning piece rates. Hibbert & Platt doubled the number of their hands, from 3,500 in 1859 to 7,000 in 1871, became the largest firm in the whole engineering industry and supplied the borough with both of its MPs in 1865, their expansion being one of the major by-products of the Cotton Famine. Oldham also became a main centre of the trade in cotton waste, which experienced an unprecedented boom as the demand for waste grew faster than the supply. The proportion of waste in spinning rose sharply from 10·5 per cent in 1860 to 17 per cent in 1862, while the demand for waste, as an economical substitute for cotton, increased vastly. Oldham opened its Exchange for that trade in 1864, five years before Manchester followed its example.[40] The expansion in the number of waste dealers provided a large reservoir of commercial ability and capital for investment in the joint-stock companies of 1873–5.

During the decade of 1861–71 Oldham increased its population by 20 per cent, Bolton by 32 per cent, Burnley by 42 per cent and Rochdale by 66 per cent. Rochdale benefited by the boom in the woollen industry, and its flannel manufacturers accumulated capital which was to be reinvested in the Rochdale limiteds of the 1880s. Burnley developed the manufacture of light printing cloths in the place of T cloths, installed new narrow and fast-running looms and experienced as great an expansion as Oldham, which increasingly supplied it with yarn. Bolton suffered least of all the cotton towns, being one of the last to establish a relief committee and earning no mention by Arnold in his *History of the Cotton Famine* (1864). The local ironworks and bleachworks were largely independent of the cotton industry. As a centre of medium fine spinning Bolton consumed far less cotton than Blackburn and did not depend so much upon American cotton. Its trade benefited by the increased supply of Egyptian long-stapled cotton and by the new French demand for fine yarns and mixed fabrics. Its operative spinners were successfully unionised from 1861 and set the example followed by its weavers in 1865.

Manchester benefited as much as Bolton by the Anglo-French treaty of commerce and at the peak of distress in December 1862 had fewer recipients of relief than Ashton. That great market of the industry possessed a multiplicity of trades and had a smaller proportion of factory operatives in its population than the mill towns of Lancashire. It also profited by the growth of the home trade in textiles other than cotton and expanded its commerce at the expense of its industry, increasing the number of its merchants by half during the 1860s. Residences in its central township were replaced by commercial offices, while house building continued unchecked in the other townships. Mancunian influence was further extended within the cotton district as market prices became increasingly important to producers. Manchester banks established branches in the cotton towns from 1862, as stocks of cloth were sold off at much higher prices than had been expected. The Royal Exchange was rebuilt from 1867 for the third time since its foundation in 1809. 'Cottonborough' was also fortunate in having many wealthy residents, many local relief committees and a poor law administered with humanity rather than with the rigour characteristic of Salford.

THE TURNING POINT OF 1864

The rise in prices continued for eighteen months after unemployment had begun to decline from its peak in December 1862. Margins remained low, however, for only twelve months from July 1862 to June 1863. During 1863 the total value of exports rose by 26 per cent, and shipments to the East, especially to Bombay and Madras, cleared away the stocks accumulated since 1860. Fears of a speedy settlement of the war receded after the invading forces of the North were repulsed, at Chancellorsville on 2–4 May 1863, for the fifth time in twenty-one months. In August–October an immense demand for goods for all foreign markets sprang up in Manchester, and the price of cotton rose by 31 per cent as stocks were finally exhausted and sank to their lowest level since 1839. During 1863 the average weekly consumption of cotton rose by one-sixth above the level of 1862 and its average price, which in 1860 had been one-third that of wool, first exceeded that of its old rival. The threat of a true cotton famine emerged for the first time into the realm of possibilities and led to a marked increase in the number of speculative transactions in cotton 'to arrive' (i.e. in maritime sales), especially in Indian and Egyptian cotton. The inflation of prices raised the share of imported cotton in the total value of imports from 17 per cent in 1860 to the all-time peak of 28·5 per cent in 1864: it also doubled the share of re-exports of cotton in the total value of re-exports so that it formed 40 per cent thereof in 1864.

A self-perpetuating cycle of expectations had been generated since 1862, based upon the assumption of a continuation of the war and its associated rising prices. Those prices reached their peak in Liverpool in the week ending 23 July 1864, when Fair Uplands touched $32\frac{1}{4}d$ per lb, or fourfold its price in 1860 and almost as much as the peak price of 1814, so measuring the true dependence of Lancashire upon the medium-stapled cotton of America. As the tide of war turned finally and decisively against the South a long-term decline in prices inevitably followed. That decline preceded by a decade the onset of the 'great depression' in the economy as a whole and took place in four cyclical slumps, interrupted by four booms, reaching its nadir in

1898. It reduced the wealth of all merchants holding large stocks but benefited mill owners holding small stocks. It permitted the progressive recapture of the industry's export markets and opened up new opportunities to such firms as those of Rylands, Tootal, Haworth and Armitage. Such entrepreneurs with strong capital backing and a secure basis in the home trade could acquire or build mills cheaply and install machinery at a much lower cost as well as in a more durable manner than they could in seasons of busy trade. Their example was imitated by merchants in Manchester and by engineers in Bolton and Blackburn. Those firms rapidly expanded their operations and supplied the industry with a new generation of leaders. Rylands & Sons in particular became during the 1860s 'the recognised and undisputed head and leader of the cotton trade', 'the monarchs of the cotton industry of England'.[41]

The deflation of prices took place in a series of embarrassing fluctuations and agonised spasms.[42] That decline was bitterly resented by businessmen, in the absence of any system of 'hedging' capable of reducing the impact of such unforeseen fluctuations, and produced successive waves of business failures which inspired Marx's meditations on the mutability of capital. In September–October 1864 the price of cotton sank by 30 per cent, its average weekly consumption shrank by 67 per cent 120–130 manufacturers were reduced to bankruptcy as margins reached their lowest point. Between January and March 1865 the price of cotton plunged by 43·5 per cent as the Confederacy finally disintegrated, and another hundred manufacturers became insolvent. The revival of trade thereafter restored full employment to the industry, with cotton selling at virtually the same price as in the season of deepest distress in November 1862, i.e. an inflated level treble that of 1860. The financial crisis of October 1865 then reduced cotton prices by 20 per cent and caused a third wave of failures among manufacturers.

The crisis of 1866 ushered in three years of depression which proved gloomier than the years of the 'cotton famine' itself and served as a harbinger of the 'great depression' of 1873–96 in so far as they saw a depression of prices rather than of production. The re-entry of the USA into the cotton market during 1866 was reflected in the record volume of imports of cotton, which first exceeded those of the *annus mirabilis* 1860. The massive expansion in the export to the USA of cotton manufactures, the value of which doubled in 1865 and 1866, also helped to re-establish Anglo-American commerce on its pre-war basis. During 1867 the imports of cotton from the USA exceeded those from India for the first time since 1861, the exports of cotton goods first exceeded the record level of 1860 as abundant harvests in India stimulated the import of piece goods, and the value of the exports of otton manufactures exceeded the value of the imports of raw cotton for he first time since 1862. The expansion of production and of exports vas nevertheless accompanied by a drastic shrinkage in margins to a ow point in 1869 as the price of cloth fell even more rapidly than that f cotton. Between 1867 and 1869 two-thirds of the manufacturers in ast Lancashire failed to meet their financial engagements, compounded vith their creditors or retired from the trade, while the property of urviving firms was reduced in value by as much as 60 per cent. 'rophecies of ruin abounded on the Manchester Exchange in 1869, as hey had in 1826 and 1842, and only disappeared on the revival of trade n 1870–3.

The traumatic experiences of the 1860s had important repercussions n the development of economic thought, especially in relation to ommercial fluctuations. The basic pattern of the trade cycle was lucidated by the Manchester banker John Mills.[43] The foundations of lemand theory were laid by Hoyle in relation to the home trade[44] and y Ollerenshaw in relation to the export trade.[45] Hoyle located the asic cause of the industrial depression in the increased expenditure on lrink by an intemperate population. 'Here is the great secret of our resent bad trade; people cannot pour the money down their throats nd put it on their backs at the same time; and so long as we spend eventeen times as much on drink as we do on cotton goods, we can ever, long together, have anything but stagnation in trade.'[46])llerenshaw revealed the close dependence of the export trade upon he fortunes of the Indian harvest. 'In proportion that grain is cheap nd plentiful or scarce and dear in India, will our trade in Lancashire e flourishing or depressed.'[47] Thus he paved the way for the formula- ion in 1875 of Jevons's sun-spot theory of the trade cycle. A decade arlier Jevons had assumed the material basis of British power to lie in oal and iron rather than in textiles, thus formally depriving the cotton ndustry of its primacy within the British economy. Applying Malthus's rinciple of population to the supply of coal, he gloomily foretold an ventual coal famine on the model of the cotton famine and a tragic nd to the brief span of British greatness.[48] For his part Marx was argely unconcerned with the crisis of overproduction but deduced in 865 from the convulsive expansion and contraction in the sources of otton supply that the capitalist system of industry was fundamentally rreconcilable with rational patterns of production in agriculture.[49] 'roude concluded from the boom in imperial commerce that 'trade ollows the flag'.[50] Thus both industry and empire were revalued in omprehensible materialist terms in place of the idealistic interpreta- ion characteristic of the 1850s, when 'civilisation and commerce' had eemed to march hand in hand.

The effects of the crisis continued to be felt throughout the 1860s

and 1870s. The imports of Indian cotton increased sharply once more
in 1869 in response to the rise in prices during 1868 and 1869, and
consumption thereof exceeded that of American cotton. They were
surpassed by the imports of cotton from the USA in 1870, despite the
opening of the Suez Canal, but rose again in 1872, though for re-export
rather than for consumption by the mills of Lancashire. Not until 1872
was the Cotton Supply Association dissolved and not until 1873 did the
government of India reluctantly recognise Indian incapacity to compete
in the world market with American cotton. Thus Lancashire increased
its dependence upon the supply of American cotton and upon the
markets of Asia for piece goods, so reverting to the pre-war pattern of
its trade. The consumption of raw cotton in England, the production
of yarn and the profits of cotton spinning regained the level of 1860 in
1871, but the price of cotton did not return to the average level of 1860
until 1876, when the USA decisively re-established its supremacy as the
world's leading producer and exporter.

THE ECLIPSE OF THE MANCHESTER SCHOOL

The true significance of the 'cotton famine' has been obscured by the
conventional interpretation of history in the evolutionary perspective
favoured by the Victorian and Edwardian age. The crisis of the 1860s
was no transient episode: it had political as well as economic repercussions, making it a fundamental turning point in the history of
Lancashire, as it was not in that of Scotland or of the Continent.[5]
Its influence undermined the predominance of the Manchester school
in national affairs, dethroned cotton from its pride of place in the
national economy and shattered its hypnotic hold on the national
imagination. Paradoxically that displacement occurred at the very
time that the Manchester school appeared at its noblest in the defence
of the cause of non-intervention against the prevailing current of
pro-Southern sentiment[52] and at the same time that the cotton
industry was liberated from its guilt-laden association with the Slave
Power in America. Furthermore, the distribution of relief vindicated
the principle of individualism, since it was effected without any recourse to intervention by the State and without the benefit of a
grant from the Exchequer, a national rate-in-aid or even parochial
loans.

   The 'Cotton Famine' inflicted a spectacular humiliation upon the
great industry of Lancashire but did not create any distress outside that
one region. Indeed, it served to divert capital from the cotton trade
into banking and finance, encouraged the reinvestment of cotton
profits in the iron industry and thereby fostered the spirit of speculation
characteristic of the boom which culminated in the crises of 1864 and

866. The decline of 8 per cent in the total value of British exports during 1861 reflected the dependence of the economy upon the cotton industry: the decline of only 2 per cent therein during the black year of 1862 measured the country's ability to reduce that dependence. England as a whole was not plunged into a depression and even enjoyed extraordinary prosperity. Government revenues persistently exceeded expenditure, and the deficits of 1860–1 and 1861–2 did not recur until 1868–9. 'An industry which we conceived to be essential to our commercial greatness has been utterly prostrated, without affecting that greatness in any perceptible degree.'[53]

The cotton lords became the object of a new attack by the Conservative press of the metropolis and were reproved for their 'brutal indifference', their 'monstrous stinginess and ingratitude' and their shameful neglect of 'their enormous obligations to Cotton labour'.[54] 'They sit as still as their own machinery, and as cold as their own boilers; or they are gone off nobody knows where . . . The great Cotton Lords have disappeared with their own cotton.'[55] Secure in the support of a sycophantic local press, the cotton magnates remained unmoved by the public reproaches of the Prime Minister,[56] Charles Kingsley,[57] Dr Bridges[58] and the *Times*[59] but thereby widened the gulf of incomprehension between the two worlds of 'North and South'. National charity filled the gap left by the inadequacy of local subscriptions for the relief of distress and enabled Lancashire to survive with its staple industry working at only half capacity. The cotton trade was reduced in status from a national to a regional interest and never regained the image of a world-regenerating power which it had proudly borne during the 1850s. It became more specialised and therefore more fragmented: it lacked any national spokesman of the stature of Bazley until the advent of Macara in the 1890s, since John Rylands remained the most unassuming of captains of industry.

The History of the Cotton Famine (1864) by the radical Arthur Arnold dilated at length upon the limited contributions made by the cotton lords to the relief funds[60] and ungenerously revealed the extent of their profits during the crisis.[61] That work was bitterly resented in Manchester as 'a so-called history' written 'before events were completed or facts made clear',[62] so that the author was forced to withdraw in the second edition the original dedication to the members of the Central Relief Committee. Dr Watts dismissed Arnold's book as 'a hurried compilation, got up to hit the humour of the passing hour'[63] and deliberately gave his own history the polemical title of *The Facts of the Cotton Famine* in order to rebuke Arnold and to vindicate the political economy of free trade, a task which he performed with all the fervour of a convert from the faith of Owenite socialism. His work duly earned its meed of local praise[64] but remained powerless to stem the growing

revulsion within Lancashire from the philosophy of economic an
political liberalism.

Within the most central sphere of life the cotton operatives estab
lished their moral independence of their masters in a powerful Cor
servative reaction which manifested itself in the organisation c
Conservative Working Men's Associations, in an extensive revival c
the Anglican Church, in an increase in popular hostility towards th
Irish and in the birth of an agitation in favour of reciprocity an
against free trade.[65] The cotton lords paid a heavy price for their socia
abdication during the crisis of the 1860s. Firstly they were forced t
increase wages by one-fifth between 1865 and 1868 in a labour mark
tightened by emigration. Then they suffered in the general election c
1868 the catastrophic loss of their political pre-eminence in so far a
that was identified with the Liberal Party. Derby's grant of the vote t
the artisans paid a well deserved tribute to the stoical bearing unde
privation of the cotton operatives of his home county and was justifie
by the sweeping Conservative victories in Lancashire in 1868[66] and i
England in 1874, when Grant Duff's prophecy proved true: 'Wha
Lancashire thinks today, England thinks tomorrow.'[67]

NOTES

[1] R. A. Arnold, *The History of the Cotton Famine* (London, 1864, 1865, 1966).
[2] J. Watts, *The Facts of the Cotton Famine* (London, 1866, 1968).
[3] M. von Tugan-Baranowsky, *Studien zur Theorie und Geschichte der Handelskrisen England* (Jena, 1901), pp.353–81, 'Der Baumwollhunger'.
[4] C. F. Adams, *Trans-Atlantic Historical Solidarity. Lectures Delivered before the Universi of Oxford in Easter and Trinity Terms 1913* (Oxford, 1913).
[5] W. O. Henderson, *The Lancashire Cotton Famine 1861–1865* (Manchester, 193 1969). The second edition includes the chapters dealing with the Continent an with Scotland which were excised by the publisher from the first edition.
[6] E. von Halle, *Baumwollproduktion und Pflanzungwirtschaft in den Nordamerikanisch Südstaaten. Zweiter Teil, Sezessionskrieg und Rekonstruktion. Grundzüge einer Wirtschaft geschichte der Baumwollstaaten von 1861–80* (Leipzig, 1906).
[7] T. Bazley, 'The difficulties and dangers of the cotton trade', *The Exchange*, Januar 1863, p.201.
[8] G. McHenry, *The Cotton Trade: its Bearing upon the Prosperity of Great Britain a Commerce of the American Republics* (London, 1863), pp.59–61.
[9] A. Redgrave, 'On the progress of textile manufactures in Great Britain', *Journal the Society of Arts*, 8 March 1861, p.259, T. Bazley.
[10] *Manchester Examiner*, 1 January 1861, p.7iii.
[11] *Ibid.*
[12] S. Osborn, *The Past and Future of British Relations in China* (Edinburgh, 1860), pp.1 132.
[13] W. B. Forwood, 'On the influence of price upon the cultivation and consumptic of cotton during the past ten years', *Journal of the Statistical Society*, September 187 p.382.
[14] McHenry, *op. cit.*, p.54.
[15] *The Economist*, 13 July 1861, pp.758–60, 'Threatened famine of cotton'.
[16] *The Economist*, 10 August 1861, p.870, 'Cotton and the Civil War'.
[17] John Pender & Co., *Statistics of the Trade of the United Kingdom with Foreign Countri from 1840* (London, 1869), pp.6, 9.

18 *Manchester Guardian*, 3 August 1861, p.4ii.
19 *Ibid.*, 4 September 1861, p.2ii.
20 F. L. Owsley, *King Cotton Diplomacy. Foreign Relations of the Confederate States of America* (Chicago, 1931, 1959), pp.549–50.
   W. O. Henderson, 'The Cotton Famine in Lancashire', *Transactions of the Historic Society of Lancashire and Cheshire*, 3 March 1932, pp.38–9.
21 C. Fohlen, *L'Industrie textile au temps du Second Empire* (Paris, 1956), pp.253–4, 285, 314.
   E. A. Brady, 'A reconsideration of the Lancashire "Cotton Famine" ', *Agricultural History*, July 1963, pp.156–62.
22 P. Harnetty, 'The imperialism of free trade: Lancashire and the Indian cotton duties, 1859–62', *Economic History Review*, August 1965, pp.177–86. *Idem*, *Imperialism and Free Trade: Lancashire and India in the Mid-Nineteenth Century* (Vancouver and Manchester, 1972), pp. 7–30.
23 *The Economist*, 5 July 1862, p.730, 'The cotton market'; 6 September 1862, p.981, 'The state of the cotton market'.
24 A. H. Imlah, *Economic Elements in the Pax Britannica: Studies in British Foreign Trade in the Nineteenth Century* (Harvard, 1958), pp.72, 96.
25 W. O. Henderson, *The Lancashire Cotton Famine 1861–5* (1934, 1969), p.15.
26 M. J. McHaffie, *'Was It A Cotton Famine?' Being Twelve Letters from The 'Times' Money Article* (London, 1865, 24pp.), p.iii.
27 W. B. Adams, 'The political economy of the cotton manufactures', *The Spectator*, 27 December 1862, pp.1433–4, 1444–5.
28 P. Harnetty, *Imperialism and Free Trade: Lancashire and India in the Mid-Nineteenth Century* (1972), pp.132–3, which lists the eight articles published by the author between 1962 and 1971. F. A. Logan, 'India—Britain's substitute for American cotton, 1861–5', *Journal of Southern History*, November 1958, pp.472–80; *idem*, 'India's loss of the British cotton market after 1865', *Journal of Southern History*, February 1965, pp.40–50; A. W. Silver, *Manchester Men and Indian Cotton 1847–72* (Manchester, 1966). D. Tripathi, 'Opportunism of free trade: Lancashire Cotton Famine and Indian cotton cultivation', *Indian Economic and Social History Review*, September 1967, pp.255–63.
29 *Great Industries of Great Britain* (London, 1879), 1, p.8, R. Smiles, 'Sir Thomas Bazley, Bart., M.P.'; *Manchester Faces and Places*, III, 10 December 1891, pp.43–5.
30 A. J. Robertson, 'The decline of the Scottish cotton industry 1860–1914', *Business History*, July 1970, pp.116–28.
31 *The Times*, 25 August 1862, p.8iii.
32 *Ibid.*, 14 August 1862, p.8iv–v.
33 T. Ellison, 'Distress in Lancashire', *The Exchange*, June 1862, pp.153–4.
34 D. Noble, 'Fluctuations in the death rate', *Transactions of the Manchester Statistical Society*, 26 October 1863, pp.1–18; J. Whitehead, *Notes on the Rate of Mortality in Manchester* (Manchester, 1863, 38 pp.).
35 W.D. Jones, 'British Conservatives and the American Civil War', *American Historical Review*, April 1953, p.540, quoting Lord Stanley to Disraeli, 31 October 1863.
36 In a radically revisionist study, *Support for Secession. Lancashire and the American Civil War* (Chicago, 1972), Dr Mary Ellison has forcefully argued that support for the cause of the South, though not for slavery, was general in the factory towns. This pioneer reinterpretation supplies a welcome corrective to the conventional view embodied in Stanley Broadbridge, 'The Lancashire Cotton Famine, 1861–5', *Our History*, winter 1961, reprinted in Lionel M. Munby (ed.), *The Luddites and Other Essays* (London, 1971), pp.143–60.
37 Joseph Ramsbottom, *Phases of Distress: Lancashire Rhymes* (Manchester, 1864), p.88, 'Gooin' t' Schoo' '.
38 W. Gourlay, *History of the Distress in Blackburn, 1861–5* (Blackburn, 1865), pp.15–16.
39 *Ibid.*, p.177.
40 *Manchester Guardian*, 30 January 1864, p.5v; 21 April 1869, p.5i.
41 *Manchester of Today* (London, 1888), p.79; *Bulletin of the John Rylands Library of the University of Manchester*, Autumn 1973, pp.93–129, 'John Rylands of Manchester'.
42 J. Kelly, 'The end of the famine: the Manchester cotton trade, 1864–67—a merchant's eye view', in N. B. Harte and K. G. Ponting (eds.), *Textile History and*

Economic History: Essays in Honour of Miss Julia de Lacy Mann (Manchester, 1973), pp.354–86.

[43] J. Mills, 'On credit cycles, and the origin of commercial panics', *Transactions of the Manchester Statistical Society*, 11 December 1867, pp.5–40; *idem*, 'On the post-panic period 1866–70', *ibid.*, 8 March 1871, pp.81–104.

[44] W. Hoyle, *An Inquiry into the Causes of the Present Long-Continued Depression in the Cotton Trade with Suggestions for its Improvement, By a Cotton Manufacturer* (London, 1869, 17 pp.).

[45] J. E. Ollerenshaw, 'Our export trade in cotton goods to India', *Transactions of the Manchester Statistical Society*, 13 April 1870, pp.109–24.

[46] Hoyle, *op. cit.*, p.11.

[47] Ollerenshaw, *op. cit.*, p.114.

[48] W. S. Jevons, *The Coal Question; an Inquiry Concerning the Progress of the Nation, and the Probable Exhaustion of our Coal-Mines* (London, 1865).

[49] K. Marx, *Capital* (Chicago, 1909), III, pp.141–4, 152–62.

[50] J. A. Froude, 'England and her colonies', *Fraser's Magazine*, January 1870, p.4.

[51] H. Galle, *La 'Famine du Coton' 1861–5. Effets de la guerre de sécession sur l'industrie cotonnière gantoise* (Université Libre de Bruxelles, 1967), pp.138–9.

[52] *The Spectator*, 15 February 1862, p.179, 'The Manchester school at its best'.

[53] *The Times*, 7 January 1864, p.8vi.

[54] *The Times*, 27 August 1862, p.10iii; 12 November 1862, p.8v–vi.

[55] *Ibid.*, 2 September 1862, p.8iii.

[56] Hansard, *Commons Debates*, 30 July 1862, p.1027, Palmerston.

[57] *The Times*, 18 November 1862, p.4i; 22 November, p.5ii, C. Kingsley, *North and South*, criticised by *The Economist*, 22 November 1862, pp.1289–90 and 29 November, pp.1319–20.

[58] *The Times*, 14 March 1863, p.14ii–iii; 20 March, p.5v–vi; 4 April, p.5vi; S. Liveing, *A Nineteenth Century Teacher. John Henry Bridges, MB, FRCP* (London, 1926), pp.96–103.

[59] *The Times*, 11 August 1862, p.8iv; 27 August, p.8iv–v; 3 September, p.6iv; 6 September, p.6vi; 9 September, p.6ii–iv, criticised by *The Spectator*, 30 August 1862, pp.963–4; 6 September, pp.988–9; 22 November, pp.1292–3; 29 November, pp.1321–2.

[60] R. A. Arnold, *The History of the Cotton Famine* (1864), pp. 196–243.

[61] *Ibid.*, pp.77, 83.

[62] *Manchester Guardian*, 23 January 1866, p.3iv.

[63] J. Watts, *The Facts of the Cotton Famine* (1866), p.iii.

[64] *Manchester Guardian*, 23 January 1866, p.3iv–vi.

[65] *Ibid.*, 20 September 1869, p.3iii; 7 December 1869, p.5iii.

[66] W. A. Abram, 'Social condition and political prospects of the Lancashire workmen', *Fortnightly Review*, 1 October 1868, pp.426–41. R. S. S. [Sowler], *The General Election in the Great Centres of Population* (London, 1869), pp.8–24. H. J. Hanham, 'A Lancashire election: 1868', in *Elections and Party Management. Politics in the Time of Disraeli and Gladstone* (London, 1959), pp.284–322. J. R. Vincent, 'The effect of the second Reform Act in Lancashire', *Historical Journal*, 1968, pp.84–94.

[67] M. E. Grant Duff, *Manchester Guardian*, 10 August 1868, p.3iii.

W. H. Chaloner

8

Currency problems of the British empire, 1814–1914

Only rarely do economic historians pay much attention to the numismatic side of their subject, and conversely, writers on numismatics frequently either ignore completely the social and economic background of the coin series with which they are dealing or present a few scraps of history with such naivety and inaccuracy that economic historians become suspicious of their competence even in the numismatic field. Philip Grierson's plea, made in 1948, for the 'more perfect marriage of numismatics and history'[1] seems to have been largely ignored.[2] This contribution is an attempt to show how the two disciplines may be combined, particularly as the use of coinage was one of the most effective ways in which the people were brought into everyday contact with the State and educated in the practicalities of economic and financial life. Indeed, it is safe to say that the educative power of money has been greater than that of all the popular textbooks on economics ever written.[3]

It has often been pointed out that the so-called 'British empire,' a convenient phrase which had no legal meaning, covered a diversity of territories even in 1814, territories which contained peoples with widely differing cultures and standards of living. Between 1814 and 1914 the collection of imperial territories became even more heterogeneous, ranging from the headhunters of Borneo and Sarawak to representatives of such ancient civilisations as the Chinese of Hong Kong and Wei-hai-wei and the subtle Greeks of Cyprus.

THE ORIGINS OF THE GOLD SOVEREIGN STANDARD

In 1814 no uniform system of currency existed in the empire, but from 1816 to 1821 two powerful unifying forces existed: first, a newly equipped Royal Mint on Tower Hill in London and, secondly, the British gold standard and its monetary expression, the British gold sovereign or 20s piece (£1 sterling). The spread of the sovereign as an international unit naturally aided the growth of the economic power of the City of London in the century of the *Pax Britannica*. Other countries showed their faith in the gold standard by allowing British sovereigns to circulate freely instead of striking their own gold coins in sufficient quantity, e.g. Chalmers stated in 1893, '. . . the gold currency of Portugal consists mainly of British sovereigns'.[4] As late as 1920 it could be said of the land-locked republic of Bolivia, high in the Andes: 'British sovereigns and Peruvian gold are the only coins accepted to an un-limited extent at a fixed value of B[oliviano]s 12·50.'[5]

The adoption by the second Lord Liverpool's government of a gold standard between 1816 and 1821 was not, as has sometimes been sug-gested in the textbooks, a far-seeing move, but rather a measure to restore Sir Isaac Newton's eighteenth-century gold standard system, which had been rudely interfered with by the liquidity crisis of 1797 and the consequent suspension of cash payments. After 1797 Britain man-aged with a paper currency and gold guineas circulated at a varying premium in terms of paper pounds.[6]

Under the terms of Lord Liverpool's[7] Coinage Act of 1816 (56 Geo. III, c. 68) the new gold unit or sovereign (20s) was to replace the old guinea (21s), last struck in 1813. These sovereigns weighed 'five penny-weights, three grains 2740/10,000 troy weight of *standard* gold', i.e. they were to be 22 carat (fine or pure gold is 24 carat), and were to be legal tender to any amount.[8] Private persons could have their gold bullion freely coined into sovereigns at the mint at the rate of £3 17s 10½d per standard ounce (or £4 4s 11d per fine ounce).

Sovereigns and half-sovereigns were accordingly put into circulation in 1817. Under the terms of the Act provision was also made for a badly needed coinage of sixpences, shillings, half-crowns (2s 6d) and crowns (5s) at the rate of 66s sterling silver, i.e. 92·5 per cent fine, to the pound troy (12 oz). These remained the standards of weight and fineness of the British silver coinage until 1920. By the end of 1817 £2·5 millions' worth of the new silver coins had been minted and put into circulation, but they were not legal tender for debts of more than 40s. The Act also provided that after a date to be proclaimed it should be lawful for any person to bring any quantity of silver bullion to the mint and have it coined at the rate of 62s to the pound troy; the remaining 4s out of the pound troy was to be taken by the mint for its trouble. It was clearly the intention of the framers of the Act that there should be a free coinage of gold side-by-side with an almost free coinage of silver. The proclama-tion was, in fact, never issued, and the country was thereby saved from the confusions of a so-called bimetallic standard.

The successful restoration of a gold standard and the maintenance of the new silver currency in circulation depended on the price of silver remaining below 5s 6d per standard or sterling ounce (i.e. 66s per lb troy). Above this price there would be a temptation to melt down or export the new silver currency. In fact in 1815 the price of silver had fluctuated between 5s 9d (low) and 6s 9½d (high) per standard ounce, but had then fallen rapidly in 1816 to between 4s 11½d and 5s 4½d per ounce. Only in 1818 did silver reach 5s 6d for a short period, and until 1872 it fluctuated within very narrow limits around 5s per ounce, so that although the new British silver currency of the nineteenth century became a subsidiary token currency, it contained very nearly its face value in silver until the great fall in the value of silver began after 1872.

It should be borne in mind that until the 1870s a gold standard of the British type was regarded as unusual. Only one major financial power, the Netherlands, followed Great Britain's example after the Napoleonic wars, and so strong was the belief in the stability of silver that even the Dutch switched from what was practically gold monometallism to silver monometallism in 1847, because her statesmen believed

> it had proved disastrous to the commercial and industrial interests of Holland to have a monetary system identical with that of England, whose financial revulsions, after the adoption of the gold standard, had been more frequent and severe than in any other country.[9]

Even in Britain all statesmen did not regard the question of the standard as a settled issue. In 1826, after the liquidity crisis of 1825, Huskisson actually proposed that the government should issue silver certificates which would be full legal tender. In 1828 the banker Alexander Baring gave it as his opinion that the gold standard, far from being the cause of Britain's commercial prosperity, was a hindrance to it, as it tended to isolate her from those countries which were on a silver basis, i.e. most of the rest of the world.[10] Even as late as 1844 Peel introduced a clause into the Bank Charter Act allowing the Bank of England to hold up to a quarter of its metallic reserves, against which notes could be issued, in the form of silver bullion.[11]

Most of the sovereigns—possibly as many as two-thirds—struck at the Royal Mint between 1816 and 1914 were exported. For example, in the ten years 1852–61, busy years for the London mint, 58,495,000 sovereigns were struck, but no fewer than 37,505,000 were exported. During the seven years ending 31 December 1910, another busy period for the mint, 104 million sovereigns were struck, but during the same period 86 millions were exported or withdrawn for remelting as being too light. It is estimated that of the 460 million sovereigns issued since the accession of Victoria in 1837 only 120 million were still in circulation in Great Britain and Ireland in 1914.[12]

THE EMPIRE OF THE RUPEE

While Great Britain struggled to maintain a gold standard with some difficulty the East India Company, on the other side of the world, was moving inexorably towards a silver standard. Like any other benevolent despotism of the eighteenth century the court of directors had begun to reform, to concentrate and to simplify the administrative arrangements and, among them the currency systems, of the diverse territories under its control. The basic currency unit of the Mughal empire had been the silver rupee, which, considering the political anarchy of eighteenth-century India, differed remarkably little in weight and silver content from mint to mint. The company had minted currencies under licence from the Mughal emperors and lesser native rulers since the 1670s, and by 1800 controlled a considerable number of mints in its three presidencies of Bombay, Calcutta and Madras.[13] The guidelines of reform were laid down by the court of directors of the company in a despatch dated 25 April 1806 which expounded theory and then fixed a new rupee of account:

> It is an opinion supported by the best authorities, and proved by experience, that coins of gold and silver cannot circulate as legal tenders of payment at fixed relative values . . . without loss; this loss is occasioned by the fluctuating value of the metals of which the coins are formed. A proportion between the gold and silver coin is fixed by law, according to the value of the metals, and it may be on the justest principles, but owing to the change of circumstances gold may become of greater value in relation to silver than at the time the proportion was fixed, it therefore becomes profitable to exchange silver for gold, so the coin of that metal is withdrawn from circulation; and if silver should increase in its value in relation to gold, the same circumstances would tend to reduce the quantity of silver coin in circulation. As it is impossible to prevent the fluctuation in the value of the metals, so it is also equally impracticable to prevent the consequences thereof on the coins made from these metals . . . To adjust the relative values of gold and silver coin according to the fluctuations in the values of the metals would create continual difficulties, and the establishment of such a principle would of itself tend to perpetuate inconvenience and loss.

The court then laid it down that 'silver should be the universal money of account [in India], and that all . . . accounts should be kept in the same denominations of rupees, annas and pice . . .'[14] The new rupee was to be of the gross weight of 180 grains troy, of which 15 grains were to be base metal alloy, so that the company's new rupee would contain 165 grains troy of fine silver and be eleven-twelfths fine.

The court of directors wished not merely to rationalise the currency of its Indian possessions but also to facilitate the transfer of money or 'supply' between the three presidencies, for although each presidency had its own fiscal system and mints, yet they depended upon one another for the finance of their deficits, and the money coined at the mints of one presidency was not legal tender in the territories of the other two; e.g. on 9 April 1824 the Bombay government had been forced to issue a proclamation declaring rupees of 1819 minted at Farrukhabad in Bengal as legal tender within its territories in order to facilitate the transfer of money from Bengal to Bombay.

But things moved slowly in the East, and not until 1835 could it be said that the directors' orders of 1806 had been carried out in their entirety. In 1818 the Madras presidency superseded its old Arcot rupee and proclaimed the new one of 180 grains troy, eleven-twelfths fine, as the standard. Bombay presidency followed suit in 1824, but in the Bengal presidency the situation was complicated by the existence of mints at Benares, Farrukhabad, Murshidabad and Sagar as well as that at Calcutta. The Benares mint was closed down in 1819, the Farruk-habad mint in 1825 and the Sagar mint in 1835, but the Bengal presidency was reluctant to abandon its 'heavy' *sicca* rupee (192 grains troy, eleven-twelfths fine, i.e. containing 176 grains of fine silver) and wished, like Bombay and Madras, to continue coining gold mohurs (fifteen-rupee pieces) at a fixed ratio to the silver rupee:

> At the end of 1833, therefore, the position was that the Court desired to have a uniform currency with a single standard of silver, while the authorities [i.e. the governments of the three presidencies] in India wished for a common currency with a bimetallic standard.[15]

The India Act of 1833 setting up a unitary Government of India was followed by the passing of a Currency Act (xvii of 1835) overruling the wishes of the presidencies, and finally fixing the silver rupee weighing 180 grains troy, and containing 165 grains troy of fine silver, as the common currency and sole legal tender throughout the Indian terri-tories of the East India Company. Dies for the Indian mints at Bombay, Calcutta and Madras now came from the London mint, and the new standard rupees of 1835, although struck in the name of the East India Company as agent for the imperial government, bore for the first time the head of a British monarch, William IV. The Government of India's Act xix of 1861 set up a Department of Paper Currency, modelled on the British Bank Charter Act of 1844, to issue State paper money, but the average note circulation for 1882–91 was only 15·74 million rupees, i.e. around £1 million.[16]

The need for safeguarding the overland route to India via Egypt, the extension of British power in India itself and later the emigration of Indian merchants and labourers led to a rapid expansion of the 'Empire of the Rupee' after 1835. Ceylon, which had become a British Crown colony after 1801, continued for a time on the old Dutch colonial standard, in which the rix-dollar (*rijks-daalder*) valued at 1s 6d British, was divided into 192 doits or 48 stuivers. In 1825 the British sterling system was introduced for government accounts, and at various dates between 1828 and 1842 the London mint coined, first, copper half farthings and then quarter farthings for circulation in Ceylon. Silver $1\frac{1}{2}d$ pieces were also struck between 1834 and 1862. These minute coins were designed to replace the old Madras silver fanams, twelve of which passed for 1s 6d or one rix-dollar.

In spite of all this the pull of the rupee area to the north prevailed. Rupees imported from Madras formed so large a proportion of the local monetary circulation that the governor of Ceylon issued a proclamation in 1836 rating the East India Company's rupee at 2s sterling, and although Ceylon government accounts continued to be kept in sterling until 1869, the Indian rupee was formally adopted as the currency unit between 1869 and 1872, with a series of distinctive Ceylon subsidiary coins at the rate of 100 cents to the rupee, and ranging in value from fifty cents to a quarter of a cent.[17]

In Aden, annexed by Britain in 1839 and administered by the East India Company and the Government of India successively, the Indian rupee, with its fractional subsidiary pieces, became the local monetary unit. In the neighbouring imamate of Muscat and Oman the Indian rupee became the money of account shortly afterwards, and from 1894 the Imam began to issue his own one-twelfth and quarter annas.

The enterprise of Indian traders in East Africa was reflected in the adoption by the Sultan of Zanzibar of a coinage system based on 192 pysa (pies) to the Indian rupee, and the striking of copper quarter annas and silver rials equal to two Indian rupees in 1882. In 1888 the Imperial British East Africa Company put into circulation from its offices in Mombasa (Kenya) bronze quarter annas and silver rupees struck at Ralph Heaton & Sons' private mint at Birmingham, and after the declaration of East Africa as a British protectorate the striking of bronze quarter annas bearing the head of Queen Victoria began in the year of the diamond jubilee. From 1905 the Indian rupees circulating in East Africa were supplemented by distinctive fractional coins of fifty, twenty-five, ten, five, one and half cent at the rate of 100 cents to one rupee. Between 1909 and 1921 the government of Italian Somaliland formally acknowledged the fact that its territory formed part of the rupee area by striking a coinage based on 100 besa to the silver 'rupia'. To the south the German East African Company found it convenient to adopt the rupee unit in 1890 for its local currency in Tanganyika (German East Africa), coining bronze one-pesa (i.e. quarter anna) pieces from 1890 to 1892, silver one-rupee pieces of Indian standard from 1890, quarter and half rupees from 1891 and a few two-rupee pieces in 1893 and 1894. These, however, bore distinctive German legends and the portrait of the emperor Wilhelm II and were manufactured in Berlin, not in Bombay.[18] The 'Empire of the Rupee' ceased to hold sway south of Tanganyika, a fact made quite clear by a *cri de coeur* from the diary of Sergeant Pearman of the 3rd (King's Own) Light Dragoons, who sailed home from Karachi to England with his regiment in 1853. The troop-ship put in at Cape Town to take on fresh water and stores:

> I went on shore with others to change our rupees into English money; but at the Cape they were two pence less value to us than in India, but we had to lose it. In India the rupee is to the soldier 2s 0½d but at the Cape they would only give us 1s 10½d for the rupee, and in England 1s 9½d for the rupee, so they had us all ways.[19]

When the British occupied the Ile de France in the Indian Ocean in 1810 and restored its Dutch name of Mauritius they found the pre-1792 French currency system in operation and indeed in 1822, under British sovereignty, pieces of twenty-five and fifty sous were issued for the island in billon (base silver heavily alloyed with copper). In so far as the British government can be said to have had any settled policy for colonial currency immediately after the Napoleonic wars it found expression in the striking in the London mint in 1820, for circulation in Mauritius, of the so-called silver 'anchor' money, bearing the name and titles of George IV in denominations of a half, a quarter, one-eighth and one-sixteenth of a dollar, and designed to provide change for the Spanish American 'pillar' dollars or pieces-of-eight (8 reales) which circulated universally in the West Indies and north America, over wide areas in west Africa and in various places bordering on the Indian Ocean, in south-east Asia and Australia.[20] The experiment was repeated in 1822, when the same four denominations of 'anchor' money were struck for circulation in the West Indian islands. They do not appear to have been popular, and no further strikings were made.[21] The large-scale emigration of Indian labourers to Mauritius for work on the sugar plantations reinforced the already strong links with mainland India, particularly as a class of Indian traders developed, and the Indian rupee, with its subdivisions, became the everyday unit of currency. Chalmers noted in 1893 that for a time the opening up of Australia and the gold discoveries there from 1851 onwards 'threatened to make gold permanently the standard in Mauritius, but the opening of the Suez Canal in 1869, whilst dealing a heavy blow at the commerce of the colony, swept the island back into the Indian "currency area" . . .'[22] A Mauritius order-in-council and a subsequent proclamation of 12 August 1876 made the Indian rupee the only legal tender unit and, as in Ceylon, the government of Mauritius ordered fractional coins (20c, 10c, 5c, 2c and 1c) to be struck in Britain from 1877 to 1897 and from 1911 to 1924 onwards at 100 cents to the rupee. The Indian rupee also circulated in the Seychelles group of islands to the north.[23]

On the other side of the Indian Ocean the independent kings of Burma, Mindon Min (1852–78) and Thebaw (1878–85), had issued copper, silver and gold coins in anna/rupee denominations even before the country was occupied by the government of India. Their silver 'peacock' rupees (1852, 1880) were approximately of the same size, weight and fineness as the Indian rupee, and indeed their advanced workmanship suggests a product of Western technology.[24] With the annexation of Burma in 1885 and the substitution of Indian currency for King Thebaw's, the 'Empire of the Rupee' reached almost its greatest extent—from the south-western frontiers of China on the banks of the river Mekong in the east to the eastern borders of the Belgian Congo in the west, from Mauritius in the south to the borders of Afghanistan and Tibet in the north. Large quantities of Indian rupees went through the Himalayan passes into central Asia and the outlying parts of the Celestial Empire. Even inside the Chinese empire the Tibetan government issued in 1903 large numbers of silver coins struck in Szechwan which were nothing more than Chinese-style copies of the genuine rupee bearing the familiar features of the Empress of India.

THE EXTENSION OF THE STERLING AREA AND THE GOLD DISCOVERIES IN AUSTRALIA AND SOUTH AFRICA

After the failure of the 'anchor' money of 1820 and 1822 to become popular enough to create a continuing demand for further strikings, and the survival of the gold standard after the crisis of 1825, the British Treasury and mint worked to spread the use of the sterling system in various ways. One means of furthering this was by issuing small-value coins for colonial circulation which fitted into the monetary system of the mother country.[25] An early example of this method was the issue from 1827 onwards of a one-third farthing coin for Malta in substitution for the local unit of Sicilian origin known as the grano (grain), although 2·8 million silver 120-grani pieces (dollar size) struck by the defunct Kingdom of the Two Sicilies continued to circulate in Malta until they were repatriated, largely by Maltese government action, in 1885. Similarly the silver 1½d piece of 1834 for Ceylon already mentioned was exported to the West Indies, where it served as a substitute for the Spanish American silver quarter real, together with a new silver 3d piece or half real. An identical silver 3d piece was issued for Malta in 1840.

The second means was the order-in-council of 23 March 1825.[26] This had been preceded by a long and detailed Treasury minute of 11 February of the same year[27] detailing the various currency systems of the British colonies and possessions, where other ranks (but not officers) in some of the British army stations had been complaining through their paymasters that they were paid not in British sterling coin but largely in Spanish dollars at army-fixed rates which were often of long standing and therefore inequitable. This led directly to the order-in-council of 23 March 1825 approving a directive of the Lords Commissioners of His Majesty's Treasury that:

... His Majesty's troops serving in the several British colonies and possessions abroad should, in certain cases, be paid in British silver and copper money; and that, with a view of securing the circulation of such money in those colonies, it would be expedient that an Order in Council should be issued declaring that in all those colonies where the Spanish dollar is now, either by law, fact, or practice, considered as a legal tender for the discharge of debts, or where the duties to the Government are rated or collected, or the individuals have a right to pay, in that description of coin, that a tender and payment of British silver money to the amount of 4s 4d should be considered as equivalent to the tender or payment of one Spanish dollar ...

In theory the sterling system prevailed in Australia from the first landings in Botany Bay in 1788, but in practice the local media of exchange consisted of a strange medley of British and foreign coins, mutilated and countermarked Spanish American silver dollars ('holey' dollars), receipts for stores supplied to the army commissariat and bills of exchange on the British Treasury. Finally in 1822 the unmutilated Spanish American silver dollar was recognised as the ordinary standard. Rated at 5s in local sterling, it was deliberately overvalued to keep it within the colonies until 1825, when the home government insisted on the establishment of a sterling standard and called down the exchange value of the dollar to 4s 4d in current British money.[28] As the economies of the Australian colonies expanded, British currency was imported in larger quantities, but it tended to flow back to Britain whenever the Australian colonies had an unfavourable trade balance, and for a period in the mid-nineteenth century large issues of copper and bronze penny and halfpenny tokens minted in Birmingham were issued by shopkeepers and others in the rising Australian cities.[29] Not until 1910, nine years after the Act of 1901 setting up the Commonwealth of Australia, did a separate Australian silver and bronze currency (bronze pence and halfpence, silver 3d, 6d, 1s and 2s pieces) issue from the London mint.[30]

The discovery of gold in New South Wales and Victoria in 1851 and the subsequent gold rushes both transformed the monetary system of Australia and strengthened the British gold standard. Within two years of the discoveries the British government had decided to set up a branch mint at Sydney and had sent out young W. Stanley Jevons, soon to be a world-renowned economist, as one of the two deputy assay masters. Production of Sydney sovereigns began in 1855, so that diggers who had been receiving only about £3 per ounce for their produce could now receive around £4. In 1856 3 million ounces were produced; with continuing finds a second branch mint was set up at Melbourne in 1872, and a third at Perth in Western Australia in 1899. The only other branch mint which operated between 1814 and 1914 was that at Ottawa, which struck the comparatively small number of 627,834 sovereigns between 1908 and 1921.[31] Between 1855 and 1926 the Sydney mint struck over 149 million sovereigns, the Melbourne mint over 147¼ millions between 1872 and 1931, and the Perth mint over 106 millions between 1899 and 1931.[32] Although much of the Australian gold went direct to Britain, particularly before the Melbourne mint was opened, it is clear that a large number of the sovereigns found their way into the hoards, melting pots and jewellery of India. Jevons wrote in 1865:

> Asia, then, is the great reservoir and sink of the precious metals. It has saved us from a commercial revolution, and taken off our hands many millions of bullion which would be worse than useless here . . . it relieves us of the excess of Australian treasure.[33]

Professor S. B. Saul, looking at the problem from a different angle, and after remarking that Indian imports of bullion reached their height at over £16 million in the financial year 1859–60, goes on:

> These imports of bullion tended therefore to neutralise the import of capital, since to a considerable extent they were merely used for hoarding, and so made no contributions at all to economic growth.[34]

Attempts have been made to suggest that the importance of hoarding has been exaggerated, but the official figures show that net imports of gold and silver into India between 1850 and 1886 were as in table 8.1.[35]

Table 8.1.   Net imports of gold and silver into India, 1850–86

	£ million sterling		
	Gold	Silver	Total
1850–9	18	52	70
1860–9	59	101	160
1870–9	18	50	68
1880–6	28	50	78

Source. M. G. Mulhall, *The Dictionary of Statistics* (London, 4th edition, 1899), p.309.

This unproductive salting away of potential currency by India may have damped down the rise in the general level of world prices during the 'golden age of Victorian prosperity', but the process continued unabated during the world depression of prices between 1873 and 1896, and therefore must have contributed to the economic malaise felt by businessmen and farmers in the Atlantic economy, even though, as Professor Saul has stressed, they may well have been *malades imaginaires*. It is interesting to note how the critics of the British Raj in India play down these unhealthy economic habits of the Indian peasants, and fail to draw the conclusion that in this, as perhaps in other ways, the poverty of the Indian masses was largely self-induced. Britain is often accused of having operated a drain of bullion, etc, from India; it would be nearer to the truth to say that India in the nineteenth century was to a large extent parasitic as regards bullion, capital and brains on the advanced industrial nations of Western Europe, and particularly on Britain.

At the Cape of Good Hope the old Dutch rix-dollar was superseded as the unit of account by British sterling after the order-in-council of 23 March 1825. No special coins were struck, but British currency was imported into the South African colonies throughout the nineteenth century. The discovery of gold in the Transvaal and the Orange Free State from 1886 onwards assured for 'Great Britain and the gold standard world of the late nineteenth century . . . the gold supplies necessary to their economy'.[36] When the South African Republic (the Transvaal) ordered its first considerable coinage[37] from 1892 onwards the British monetary system served as the model as to the denominations, weight, fineness and size (bronze penny, silver $3d$, $6d$, $1s$, $2s$, $2\frac{1}{2}s$, $5s$ pieces, with gold $10s$ and £1 pieces).[38] The coins themselves, however, bore the stern, unsmiling effigy of President Paul Kruger, and in the denominations from $2s$ upwards the coat of arms of the republic. The imperial authorities allowed this Boer currency to remain in circulation after the peace of Vereeniging in 1902 and even extended its use to the whole of South Africa.[39] A South African branch of the Royal Mint was set up at Pretoria in 1922, and began to strike sovereigns in 1923.

THE FALL IN THE VALUE OF SILVER AFTER 1872

After 1872 the average price of silver per British standard ounce i.e. 92·5 per cent fine, began to fall from $5s$ $0\frac{5}{16}d$ to $2s$ $11\frac{5}{8}d$ in 1893, reaching a trough in 1902 at $2s$ $0\frac{1}{16}d$. A slight recovery occurred subsequently, but in 1914 its price was only $2s$ $1\frac{5}{16}d$. Never before in recorded history had the price of silver in relation to gold fallen so far and so rapidly. From time immemorial the value relationship between one ounce of silver and one ounce of gold had varied (except in Japan) between the limits of 10 : 1 and about $15\frac{1}{2}$: 1.[40] The movements had been secular ones, but now, after only three decades of sagging silver prices, the ratio was down to 39 : 1. The nations of Western Europe, valuing stability, now began to see virtues in the distrusted British gold standard, and hastened to adopt more or less similar monetary arrangements.[41] The myth of the so-called automatic gold standard began to spread.[42] The depreciation of the rupee in terms of gold-based currencies

stimulated exports of Indian manufactured goods, foods and raw
materials, particularly in cases where peasants and British planters grew
cash crops for the markets of the West, but it added greatly to the
difficulties of the government of India and the Indian railway companies, which had to acquire large amounts of sterling with which to
make payments in London. How long it took the Indian masses to find
out that their hoarded silver was rapidly losing its purchasing power
cannot be known, but the Indian money changers, merchants and
bullion dealers of Bombay must have discovered this disconcerting fact
soon enough, and switched out of silver into gold. Daniell, writing about
the Indian monetary position in the early 1880s, stated:

> The sovereigns of the Royal and of the Australian Mints are to be bought
> in every large town in the country, and are daily quoted in the exchange
> tables published in the capitals . . . Sovereigns can be said to circulate in
> India in the sense that they daily change owners . . . In times of pressure,
> French, Turkish, American, and Russian gold coins are brought to the mints
> to be melted and assayed.[43]

It is not proposed here to discuss the bimetallic controversy, except to
note that between the 1870s and 1890s the USA and France, owing to
inadequate currency arrangements, which no longer bore any relation
to the relative market prices of gold and silver, were both encumbered
with very large stocks of silver. The silver lobbies in these two countries
proved powerful enough to make possible the calling of three international monetary conferences 1878 (Paris), 1882 (Paris) and 1892
(Brussels), the basic object of which was to persuade Great Britain to
relieve France and the USA of the consequences of their own mistakes
by taking measures to support the falling price of silver. Fortunately
official opinion in Great Britain remained not only unconvinced but
actively hostile to any schemes which would clearly have placed
burdens on the British taxpayer.[44] In 1893 the government of India
closed its mints to the free coinage of silver into rupees by repealing
sections 19–26 inclusive of the Indian Coinage Act, XXIII of 1870, which
laid the obligation on its mint masters to coin all silver brought to their
mints. The rupee circulation of India was adequate and the rupee was
still legal tender. At the same time a government notification was issued
under the Indian Paper Currency Act of 1882 directing that Indian
government currency notes would be issued to all applicants in return
for gold at the rate of fifteen rupees to £1 sterling. After some fluctuations between 1893 and 1898 the rupee settled down at a sterling value
of 1s 4d,[45] and in 1899 British sovereigns were declared legal tender. A
further notification of 1906 laid it down that rupee notes would be issued
only against British sovereigns and half sovereigns.[46] These measures,
which in effect constituted a gold exchange standard with an internal

currency mainly of silver, enormously extended the area of influence of the British gold sovereign, the circulation of which was becoming more usual over wide areas of India by 1914. Notes, too, from five rupees upwards, were more widely issued. Keynes gives an account of currency flows inside India at this period which can hardly be bettered.[47]

THE FAR EASTERN POSSESSIONS, 1814–1914

The Straits Settlements to 1862. In the late eighteenth century the East India Company paid for its purchases of tea, silks and porcelain from China in silver bars, the Spanish American silver dollars to which reference has already been made, and, later, in opium. Between 1800 and 1842, however, a considerable outflow of bullion took place from China to India in payment for the increasing imports of Indian-produced opium. In 1837 the merchant William Jardine wrote from Canton, 'Without sycee [silver bullion] or gold as remittance to India we should never be able to get on'.[48] The Chinese were very particular about the kinds of Spanish American dollar they would accept. Birley Worthington & Co. of Shanghai wrote to Rathbone Bros. & Co. of Liverpool in 1854 requesting the despatch of dollars, but insisting that they must be those of Charles IV of Spain, particularly those struck in Mexico City:

> avoiding *Ferdinands or other descriptions* at any price whatever. The favourite Dollar is the one with the letters $\frac{o}{m}$ after the word Rex on the reverse side and there is also a dollar of Carolus IV with $\frac{o}{s}$ in the same place on the coin[49] which, being here at a discount of 20 per cent, must of course be avoided.[50]

From the 1820s the 'pillar' dollar was joined by the various silver dollars struck by the newly independent republics of South America, and particularly by Mexico; the Mexican mints maintained a fineness roughly equivalent to that of the old Spanish dollar until the last years of the regime of President Porfirio Diaz in 1909–10![51] These South American pieces also circulated over a wide area of south-east Asia and Oceania. The Chinese had no silver dollar-size coin until 1890; their *tael* or *liang* was a weight of pure silver, not a coin, ideally 583·3 grains.[52] As late as the 1890s Chalmers noted:

> The old 'Carolus', or 'Pillar Dollar' of Spain is to this day the standard coin in certain of the neighbouring Malay and Siamese–Malay States. In Achim and in the States of Raman, Lege, Patari and (to a less extent) Kelantan, none but pillar dollars are accepted by the natives.[53]

In the period after the end of the Napoleonic wars the British government placed the Straits Settlements (Penang, Malacca and Singapore) under the control of the East India Company, and in 1826 the company declared the heavy *sicca* rupee of Calcutta to be the official currency of these territories, but with little practical effect in view of the public faith in the Spanish American dollar. The need for small change was met after 1814 by Dutch copper doits intended for circulation in Indonesia. These doits were equal in diameter to, but thinner than, a British farthing of the period. After 1824 these tokens flooded the market places of Singapore, Pulu Penang (Prince of Wales Island) and Malacca. They were then imitated by local merchants, who placed orders in Birmingham and London and imported vast quantities of tokens of similar size known as 'kepings' or 'kapangs'. They arrived from Britain in casks, each cask containing about 100,000 kapangs and weighing about 500 lb.[54] In 1833 only fifty casks of kapangs were imported into Singapore. In 1835 the value of imported kapangs amounted to 13,754 dollars (merchandise value) and in 1842 114,030 dollars' worth was imported. After a slump from 1843 to 1845 the value of imported kapangs was back at 103,287 dollars in 1846. From 1849 only the numbers imported are known—42·4 millions in 1849, 23·7 millions in 1851. Importation ceased after 1853. The extraordinary fact emerges that there was no stable relationship between the kapang and the silver dollar: quotations for the kapang varied from as low as eighty to as high as 1,600 to the dollar: 'On the same day in the same bazaar, two different dealers would be paying and receiving tokens or doits at different rates'.[55] The ceaseless fluctuation and uncertainty associated with this wretched unofficial currency must have inflicted hardship on the inhabitants of the British settlements and their hinterlands. Attempts in 1825 and 1842 to introduce the company's copper pieces (half annas, pice, etc) failed, and the East India Company reluctantly accepted defeat in 1845 by striking its own quarter, half and one-cent pieces for the Straits Settlements, to pass at the rate of 100 cents to the Spanish and Mexican dollar. The new government of India repeated this series of coins in 1862 and, to judge by the large numbers of them which survive, the issues must have been very numerous and popular.

The Hong Kong dollar, 1866–68: the mint that failed.[56] The island of Hong Kong was ceded to Great Britain by the emperor of China in 1841, and naturally continued to feel the pull of the Chinese silver area. On 29 March 1842 the governor of Hong Kong, Sir Henry Pottinger, issued a proclamation making all the following coins legal tender for bazaar (i.e. retail) trade in the colony: Spanish, Mexican and other silver dollars, the East India Company's rupee, and Chinese brass cash at the rate of 288 cash to the British shilling; a second proclamation of 27 April 1842 made Mexican dollars and dollars of the South American republics legal tender for large-scale mercantile transactions. The home government, which wished to extend the circulation of British sterling coins, showed displeasure at Pottinger's proclamations, and the result was a third proclamation, of 28 November 1844, containing a tariff of the sterling equivalents of various pieces, e.g. the Indian rupee was to circulate as 1s 10d British, Mexican and other dollars at 4s 2d, etc. In spite of a later proclamation 27 April 1853 settling the British gold sovereign as the legal base of the currency, Mexican dollars continued to reign supreme in the local circulation, a fact recognised by another proclamation of 9 January 1863. Distinctive Hong Kong bronze cents, rated at 100 to the dollar, were struck from 1863 onwards, and a rival to the Chinese cash was prepared in the shape of a mil, or one-tenth of a cent. These mils proved unacceptable to the local Chinese and had to be largely remelted. The home government, however, accepted a proposal from the governor to set up a branch of the Royal Mint in Hong Kong, principally with the object of coining a British dollar capable of competing with Mexican and other pieces in the Far East. It was to have a weight of 416 grains and a standard of 90 per cent fine silver. Between May 1866 and May 1868 over two million dollars of this type were coined, dated 1866, 1867 and 1868, but the Hong Kong mint made a heavy loss on these and the minor coins it produced. A short-sighted home government refused to underwrite any further losses, and the mint had to close. The new Japanese government set up as a result of the restoration of 1868 bought the redundant but up-to-date Hong Kong mint machinery for its new mint at Osaka, planned as part of the westernisation of Japan.

The questions remain: given the initial losses, should the British have persevered? Or was it unreasonable when the London mint was pushing the British sterling currency, including the expensive gold sovereign, for very small direct gains on a large capital outlay, to expect the British and colonial taxpayers to underwrite the introduction of a new silver unit in competition with the Mexican mints and the prolific American silver mines?[57] It is noteworthy that after 1868, when the Hong Kong government obtained its silver five-, ten-, twenty- and fifty-cent pieces as required from the London mint, that these became very popular on the south China mainland and formed 'a standard silver currency' until after 1889, when the modernisation of the Chinese mints began,[58] with the opening of the Canton mint, equipped with machinery by Ralph Heaton & Sons of Birmingham. In this instance, as so often in the late nineteenth century, British statesmen and officials seem to have lacked the imperial vision. Additional evidence that the 1866–8 experiment should have been persevered in is provided by the second and more successful attempt in 1895 to promote a British silver dollar in the Far East as the result of a shortage of Mexican dollars and the recommendation of the Imperial Currency Committee of 1893. An imperial order-in-council of 2 February 1895 authorised the striking at the mints of Bombay and Calcutta of a dollar bearing a standing frontal figure of Britannia (weight 416 grains, 90 per cent fine). These were to be issued from Hong Kong. In the end this British dollar proved very popular and continued to be struck until 1935, by which time over 100 million had been put into circulation. The fact that the South Chinese paid the British dollar the compliment of forging it extensively in good silver suggests that these pieces filled a widespread need in south-east Asia at a time when supplies of Spanish and Mexican dollars were beginning to fail.

The Straits Settlements, 1867–1914. As from 1 April 1867 the Straits Settlements were transferred from the government of India to the Colonial Office. Up to this time the Straits Settlements government accounts had been kept in rupees, but in the year of transfer the governor issued an ordinance repealing the statutes making the rupee legal tender and declaring that as from 1 September 1867 'the dollar issued from Her Majesty's Mint at Hong Kong, the silver dollar of Spain, Mexico, Peru and Bolivia, and any other silver dollar to be specified from time to time by the Government in Council, shall be the only legal tender'.[59] In 1889 the Straits Commissioners of Currency were brought into being by ordinance No. 4 of that year. They were empowered to issue government currency notes from one dollar upwards, but their function was to economise on the use of silver dollars by printing high-value notes, and they did not in fact put out one-dollar notes until 1905.[60]

We have seen that a shortage of Mexican dollars developed in the early 1890s and ended in the issue of an imperial British silver dollar from Hong Kong. The Imperial Currency Committee of 1893 had touched briefly on the question of establishing a gold standard in the Straits Settlements, and in 1897 the Singapore chamber of commerce, unsettled by the continuing fall in the price of silver, appointed a sub-committee 'to enquire into the local currency with the view of calling the attention of the Government to the question of converting the Straits currency to a gold standard'.[61] The Straits government found that considerable differences of opinion existed among the British community, and nothing was done. In 1902 the price of silver reached its trough (the silver dollar, originally 4s 2d sterling, had by then fallen to 1s 7d). The Singapore chamber of commerce again approached the Straits government on the matter of establishing a fixed exchange rate, and the upshot was the appointment of the Straits Currency Committee, which produced a scheme for establishing a gold exchange standard on the lines of that operated by the government of India. A new Straits Settlements dollar was suggested, designed eventually to oust the Mexican and the new British dollars of 1895 from circulation, and this should be rated at a fixed number to the gold sovereign, as was the Indian rupee.

Accordingly the Straits Settlements Coinage Order of 25 June 1903 laid it down that a new Straits Settlements dollar weighing 416 grains and 90 per cent fine, to be coined in the Indian mints, should be the new unit; when supplies arrived they were to be declared the sole legal tender. The first batch of the new dollars arrived in late September 1903. They were declared legal tender on 3 October, and after that date the further import of British and Mexican dollars into the Settlements was prohibited. Conversely, the export of the new coins was prohibited.[62]

Unfortunately for the Straits Settlements government the price of silver began to improve somewhat after 1902, by which time the dollar had sunk to 1s 6⅝d sterling as against the pre-1872 norm of 4s 2d, and as the currency committee had not recommended any definite exchange value for the new dollar the government now had the task of divorcing the exchange value of the dollar vis-à-vis the gold sovereign from its bullion content. It has been estimated that by November 1904 some 35 millions of the new Straits dollar were in circulation, and all rival dollars had been demonetised. Finally, in January 1906 the government decided to fix the value of its dollar at 2s 4d sterling, and on 22 October 1906 a Straits Settlements order-in-council made the sovereign legal tender in the colony at the rate of seven sovereigns to sixty Straits dollars. This remained the rate up to 1914. In 1905 the Straits Commissioners of Currency issued one-dollar notes for the first time, although they had had the power to do so since their creation by ordinance No. 4 of 1889.

The slight improvement in the price of silver between 1902 and 1906 forced the Straits government to issue a dollar with less silver in it in order to minimise the risk of melting down. Accordingly the government announced on 11 February 1907 the issue of smaller dollars of the pattern of 1903 (312 grains weight, 90 per cent fine, i.e. 25 per cent lighter), without recalling the heavier dollars of 1903–5.

The new policy had repercussions far outside the Straits Settlements, for the new gold-exchange standard dollar became the unit not only for the Federated and Protected Malay States but also for North Borneo, where the British North Borneo Company had begun issuing subsidiary one-cent and half-cent coins in 1882–5, followed later by some cupro-nickel and silver denominations; for the sultanates of Labuan and Brunei, and for Sarawak, where Rajah James Brooke issued bronze cents, half cents and quarter cents for the first time in 1863, supplemented during the long reign of his nephew and successor Rajah Charles Brooke by silver pieces up to fifty cents (1868–1917).[63] The realm of the silver dollar had now fallen indirectly to the empire of the gold sovereign.

THE WEST INDIES AND BRITISH GUIANA

During the nineteenth century the small-scale economies of the West Indian possessions, in comparison with the large-scale economies of the East Indies, declined relatively, and in some cases absolutely, in importance in the imperial scheme. Throughout the British West Indian islands in 1814 the Spanish American silver dollar and its fractions reigned supreme, supplemented by the Spanish gold doubloon (equal to eight scudi or sixteen dollars) and the Portuguese gold johannes of 6,400 reis or four escudos. The fractions of the dollar were sometimes the original coins (often pierced or counter-stamped) of four and two reales and one, half and quarter real, the pistareen or two-real piece being particularly popular; sometimes the dollar itself was cut into segments and the segments or 'bits' counter-stamped to circulate as small change. Needless to say, great confusion could be caused to trade and finance by local methods of coin mutilation and local shortages.[64]

A device frequently adopted in order to prevent the outflow of dollars from any particular island or group of islands was to rate the Spanish dollar in a purely *local* sterling currency, e.g. the dollar would be accepted at a value of anything from 6s 8d to 10s currency in local retail transactions, when its real value in international trade was, say, 5s British sterling. This represented a form of devaluation of local goods and services which attracted merchants and specie to the particular islands and territories resorting to this device.

The order-in-council of 23 March 1825 establishing British sterling as the standard was brought into operation in Jamaica and the other Caribbean islands for the purpose of introducing British silver and copper coins into general colonial circulation. The immediate effect of this differed from colony to colony. Between 1825 and 1828, for example, the Army Commissariat Department introduced £35,000 in British silver and copper into Jamaica. The copper proved extremely unpopular and failed to circulate because the general population was in the habit of using silver and gold only; the British sterling silver was promptly revalued for everyday use in local currency terms at 1s 8d to the British shilling, which was equated with the quarter dollar or pistareen. On 7 September 1838 the order-in-council of 23 March 1825 was revoked, as far as the West Indian and the American colonies were concerned; the dollar and the doubloon were called down to 4s 2d and 64s sterling respectively and British silver coins declared legal tender to any amount. It was at this point of time that Jamaica and the Bahamas decided to adopt the British sterling system permanently—a sign, as Chalmers put it, of the 'rapidly widening "currency area" of Great Britain'.[65]

The only exception to the rule of the Spanish dollar was in British

Guiana (Berbice, Demarara and Essequibo), where the Dutch guilder standard still obtained (three guilders = sixty stivers = one dollar). Rather surprisingly, the British mint served British Guiana well, and as late as 1832–6 a complete coinage series from three guilders downwards was struck, bearing the effigy of William IV. In 1839, however, three guilders were officially rated at 4s 2d sterling. Not until 1836 did the home government begin to replace the Dutch system by introducing the imperial 'Britannia' silver 4d piece (the groat or joey) to circulate throughout the Caribbean possessions. This piece was also legal tender in Great Britain. In British Guiana it passed as a quarter guilder, and considerable quantities were struck for most years until 1856. The 'Britannia' groat was struck again in 1888, and from 1891 a distinctive British Guianan–West Indian silver 4d piece was introduced, the remains of the old guilder currency having been demonetised in the previous year. By 1914 the other British coins circulated freely, as well as the 4d piece, except that, in common with the other Caribbean colonies, the imperial bronze coins were not popular.

This unpopularity accounts for the fact that in 1869–70 the governor of Jamaica persuaded the imperial government to allow the coinage of special farthings, halfpence and pence for Jamaica in cupro-nickel, the first time that this new coinage alloy had been used in the British empire. These proved very popular.[66] Owing in part to the low standard of living, British silver 3d pieces and the curious silver $1\frac{1}{2}d$ piece originally struck for Ceylon also proved popular in Jamaica, fresh supplies of these being called for and struck in 1860 and 1862.[67]

Spanish American dollars ceased to circulate to any considerable extent after about 1850, but when the price of silver began to fall after 1872 these types of dollar, now joined by French five-franc pieces, started to flow back into circulation again and the island legislature had to pass a law, No. 8 of 1876, finally demonetising the dollar and its subdivisions. After this date pounds, shillings and pence, and particularly the shilling, became established as the standard of value in Jamaica, although in popular speech terms originating in the days of the double standard survived—a shilling was still a 'mac' or 'maccaroni' (quarter dollar or pistareen), and a 'mac and fipence' meant 1s 3d British sterling because fivepence was the Jamaican currency rating of the smallest silver coin circulating in the island, the half real, approximately equal to the British threepenny piece.

The only complete exception to the use of sterling in the British West Indies was British Honduras, where in 1855 the legislature passed an Act, 18 Vic., c. 16, whereby public accounts were to be kept in dollars and reales or rials (amended to dollars and cents in 1864), although a sample taken in 1870 revealed a strange medley of coins in actual circulation—British silver pieces, Spanish, Mexican, Colombian and

Guatemalan dollars and fractions, and United States half and quarter dollars. The gold circulation consisted of Spanish doubloons and British sovereigns.[68] Foreign silver coin flowed in after the beginning of the fall in the price of silver after 1872, and by 1876 all full-weight gold coins had been drained out of the colony. In 1885 a public meeting in Belize, the capital, decided, with two dissentients, against adopting the British sovereign as the standard; an excellent example of the non-chauvinistic character of British economic 'imperialism' is provided by a royal proclamation two years later which, issued under an order-in-council of 15 September 1887, declared the Guatemalan silver dollar to be the standard of value and allowed the circulation of six other foreign dollars. Bronze British Honduras cents bearing the head of Queen Victoria, which had been first struck in 1885, were to be legal tender up to fifty cents. In effect British Honduras was under a regime similar to that obtaining at the time in Hong Kong, i.e. silver monometallism.[69]

This state of affairs did not last for long. As Pridmore comments under the year 1894:

> This silver standard dollar was soon upset by the disturbances in the gold-price of silver and it became necessary for the colony to adopt the gold standard. Accordingly the previous legislation was repealed and by local ordinance No. 31 of 1894, the gold dollar of the United States of America was made the standard of value.[70]

It then became necessary to have a range of fractional coins, and as the coins of Canada were also subsidiary to the US gold dollar the new coins of 1894 for British Honduras (50c, 25c, 10c, 5c and 1c) were made to correspond to those of Canada in denomination, weight and fineness.[71]

A partial exception to the use of British sterling as the standard was in Trinidad, where a strange confusion reigned for most of the period from 1814 to 1914. By Governor Sir Ralph Woodford's proclamation of 14 September 1814 the Spanish American silver dollar bore the high valuation of 10s in local currency, and the gold doubloon (normally £3 4s British sterling) was rated at £8 local currency. The imperial government tried to impose the British sterling system from 1825–6 onwards, but the attempt remained fruitless for many years, since British sterling coins were bought up in exchange for dollars and doubloons, which were somewhat overrated in British sterling values at the new local valuations of 4s 4d and 69s 4d respectively. They were then shipped back to London at a small profit. The Trinidadians petitioned the Crown on three occasions for their own distinctive currency. On the final occasion in 1834, when the United States of America reformed its currency system and overvalued silver, so that neighbouring States were stripped of small silver change, the British government sent out a supply of silver 3*d* pieces, which were immediately shipped back to London as being 'unsuitable and not such as required'.[72]

Following the cheapening of gold in terms of silver after the discoveries in California (1848–9) and in New South Wales and Victoria (1851) silver dollars began to disappear from Trinidad. The way was paved for the rapid introduction of British token silver coins between 1850 and 1852, and in 1853 United States gold coins were declared legal tender; this was followed by a similar declaration with respect to Sydney sovereigns in 1866. Curiously enough, neither US gold dollars nor British sovereigns circulated to any great extent, but in practice the United States dollar was regarded as the current unit, and valued at 4*s* 2*d*. Chalmers wrote of Trinidad in 1893:

> As no ordinance has ever been passed in this island prescribing sterling denominations of account, (i) private persons continue to reckon in dollars and cents, whilst (ii) in the government offices accounts are kept both in £ *s d* and in $ currency.[73]

With the exceptions of British Honduras and Trinidad, the British possessions in the Caribbean had been brought within the sterling area by 1914, and the pieces of eight and doubloons largely relegated to the melting pots and the museums.

WEST AFRICA

The first British coinage struck for west Africa, and incidentally the first imperial decimal series, consisted of the Sierra Leone Company's silver dollar of 1791 and its subdivisions at 100 cents to the dollar, struck at Matthew Boulton's Soho mint. This dollar bears witness to the popularity of the Spanish American dollar and 'bits' down the west coast of Africa (although the Sierra Leone dollar contained 30⅔ grains less of fine silver),[74] and also owed something to the adoption of the dollar/cent system by the newly independent United States of America. North America, the West Indies and west Africa can therefore be considered as one currency area at the beginning of the nineteenth century. In Sierra Leone the Spanish American dollar was rated at 5*s* local currency. The British 'anchor money' of 1820 and 1822 seems to have been acceptable, but fifths and quarters cut from pieces of eight continued to circulate. 'Cut quarters' were even made legal tender in Sierra Leone by a proclamation of 6 December 1834. An attempt was then made to introduce British silver coins, beginning with 1½*d* and 3*d* pieces in the same year, followed by the higher denominations shortly afterwards, so that in January 1839 it proved possible to call in, demonetise and melt down the 'cut money'.[75] As in the West Indies the order-in-council of 1825 imposing the British currency system was eventually revoked in 1843, 'so far as respects Her Majesty's colonies and possessions at Sierra Leone, the River Gambia and Cape Coast, and elsewhere on the western coast of the continent of Africa', and a list of acceptable foreign coins with their British sterling equivalents was published. This reveals an almost identical state of affairs to that obtaining in the West Indies—doubloons, Spanish and Mexican dollars (4s 2d), French twenty-franc gold pieces and silver five-franc pieces (3s 10½d) were declared legal tender. As there was no legal tender limit on the French five-franc pieces, which had become undervalued in gold terms in France, these gradually ousted all the gold coins in circulation. Attempts to call the Sydney sovereign into circulation failed in 1867 and 1871. By 1879–80, with the continuing depreciation of silver, Sierra Leone and the Gambia had passed rapidly on to a silver standard. By this time, however, the French had in 1873 moved away from a simple bimetallic system, and the five-franc piece was worth a little more than its silver content. In 1874–5, too, Belgian and Swiss five-franc pieces and Italian five-lira pieces had been made legal tender in Sierra Leone by order-in-council. British gold and silver tended to be kept in hoards rather than in circulation.[76]

On the Gold Coast a somewhat similar situation obtained up to 1880, except that, as the country produced some gold, gold dust was used by weight as currency, the ounce representing £3 12s, and one-sixteenth of an ounce, or 'ackey', representing 4s 6d sterling, approximately a dollar.[77] British silver proved acceptable only if unworn and bearing the head of Queen Victoria. In 1880 the demonetisation ordinance was passed to stem the inward flood of cheapening Mexican dollars, and the same ordinance also demonetised French five-franc pieces and Dutch two-and-a-half guilder pieces. United States gold coins and Spanish American doubloons were recognised as acceptable currency at fixed prices in sterling. The foundation in 1894 of the Liverpool-based Bank of British West Africa Ltd, with a monopoly of the importation of new British silver coins from the Royal Mint, led to a rapid increase in the use of British currency.[78] Of the British coins the silver 3d piece was most extensively used in retail trade. Gold dust and nuggets were demonetised on 12 April 1899.

An unusual feature of Gold Coast currency was the use of curved copper 'manillas' as small change. They were imported from Liverpool for a century and a half, and passed as the equivalent of about 3d sterling each until withdrawn during 1948.

Finally, between 1907 and 1912 the West African Currency Board was set up to unite Nigeria, the Gold Coast, the Gambia and Sierra Leone for monetary purposes. The basic unit was the British £, but the board issued no piece of greater value than a silver 2s; silver shillings, sixpences and threepenny pieces were issued, supplemented by cupro-nickel coins for $1d$, $\frac{1}{2}d$ and $\frac{1}{10}d$, with central holes, at first issued for circulation in Nigeria only. By 1939 the normal unit of monetary calculation had become the shilling.

THE CANADAS, THE MARITIME PROVINCES AND NEWFOUNDLAND

As in the West Indies, the Spanish American dollar provided the basis of the everyday currency of British North America in 1814 and reigned unchallenged until 1825, although a few worn French silver crowns (écus) of the pre-1792 monarchical issues remained in circulation until the 1830s. The Spanish American dollar was rated at 5s local or 'Halifax', i.e. Nova Scotia,[79] currency and the British gold guinea (21s sterling) at 23s 4d in Halifax currency.[80] Small change was provided by the Spanish two-real piece (quarter dollar or 'pistareen'). After the order-in-council of 1825 the British crown piece (5s) was rated at 5s 9d Halifax currency and the British shilling at 1s 2d. This made the British sovereign worth 23s, and at this price it was eagerly bought up with local currency for re-export to Britain, via New York, where it stood at a heavy premium, in part settlement of the USA's chronic trade deficit with the United Kingdom. In 1828 it was reported that 'the circulating medium of the two provinces [of Upper and Lower Canada] is paper; British coin is never seen and except among the Canadians below Quebec, rarely a silver dollar. Specie cannot swim so near the engrossing gulf of the American paper circulation.'[81] It should be borne in mind that for the first three-quarters of the nineteenth century the United States dollar, far from being a 'hard' currency, was more often than not a 'soft' currency, partly because of this trade deficit, the existence of excessive issues of paper money and the fact that the United States mint was bound by bimetallic rules which from time to time led to monetary confusion affecting neighbouring countries.[82]

Copper change in the Canadas was supplied by large issues of private tokens for $1d$ and $\frac{1}{2}d$ ordered by shopkeepers, merchants and bankers in Upper and Lower Canada (united after 1840 as the Province of Canada), and in the Maritime Provinces. The revocation of the 1825 order-in-council in 1838 in so far as it related to the British possessions in North America and the West Indies removed one obstacle to the adoption of the United States dollar/cent system in the Canadian public accounts, which became law in 1857. The second step, again for the Province of Canada, was also taken in 1857 when the governor-in-council approved the report of a committee of the executive council on the currency question which made possible the striking, under letters patent dated 10 December 1858, of one-cent, five-cent, ten-cent and twenty-cent coins (the twenty-five-cent piece was substituted for the twenty-cent piece in 1870, in conformity with the US quarter dollar). Nova Scotia, New Brunswick and Prince Edward Island adopted the dollar/cent system for their currencies in 1859–60, 1860 and 1871 respectively, after futile attempts to enforce the order-in-council of 1825 and to secure adequate supplies of British currency.[83] About the same time these provinces put into circulation coins of various denominations in cents. Shortly after confederation in May 1867 the parliament of the new Dominion of Canada declared that it was desirable that the Canadian currency should remain of the same value as that of the United States, and two Acts passed in 1868 and 1871 translated this wish into law: United States gold coins were to circulate concurrently with the British sovereign, which was rated at $4·86⅔. Chalmers noted in 1893:

> The *metallic* currency is, therefore, on an exclusively gold basis, and consists almost entirely of eagles [$10 pieces] and other United States gold coins. British sovereigns occur at Halifax, where British troops are stationed, and an Imperial dockyard has been established. But . . . gold is rarely seen in circulation in the Dominion, its place being taken by Bank and Dominion notes . . . If gold is required (e.g. by individuals going to England) it is obtained from a bank.[84]

The establishment of a branch of the Royal Mint in Ottawa in 1908 which began to strike not only the Canadian fractional coins but also British sovereigns (from 1908), and Canadian five- and ten-dollar pieces (1912–14) marked the beginning of full Canadian monetary independence from Britain.[85]

By 1914, with the exception of Canada, Hong Kong, Trinidad and British Honduras, the countries and possessions of the British empire were firmly anchored, either directly or indirectly, to the standard of the gold sovereign, which had become, like the gold stater of Alexander the Great, the Roman silver denarius and the Maria Theresa dollar, one of the great international monetary units of history. This sterling area had come into existence by a strange mixture of accident and design, aided not only by British economic predominance in the world but also by the unpredictable and extraordinary cheapening of silver after 1872, which made this metal increasingly unreliable as a standard of value. The gold sovereign and the *Pax Britannica* had provided the twin bases for a century of unprecedented world economic expansion.

NOTES

[1] *Numismatics and History* (Historical Association, London, 1951), p.18.
[2] Notable exceptions are: F. C. Spooner, *The International Economy and Monetary Movements in France, 1493–1725* (Cambridge, Mass., 1972); J. D. Gould, *The Great Debasement: Currency and the Economy in mid-Tudor England* (London, 1970); J. K. Horsefield, *British Monetary Experiments 1650–1710* (London, 1960); M-H. Li, *The*

Great Recoinage of 1696–9 (London, 1963); Sir A. E. Feavearyear, *The Pound Sterling* (1st edition, Oxford, 1931; 2nd edition revised by E. V. Morgan, London, 1963); S. J. Butlin, *Foundations of the Australian Monetary System, 1788–1851* (Sydney, 1953).

3 The standard work on the subject, reprinted in 1972, is still Robert Chalmers, *A History of Currency in the British Colonies* (London, 1893), with three chapters by C. A. Harris of the Colonial Office. It has a chapter on India, and Chalmers, who was at the Treasury, printed many key official documents (pp.414–65). An earlier work, James Atkins, *The Coins and Tokens of the Possessions and Colonies of the British Empire* (London, 1889), is still of some value. H. W. A. Linecar, *British Commonwealth Coinage* (London, 1959), and L. V. W. Wright, *Colonial and Commonwealth Coins* (London, 1959), are also useful. In 1960 F. Pridmore issued part I of his thorough guide, *The Coins of the British Commonwealth of Nations to the end of the reign of George VI, 1952* (London). Part I lists the coins and tokens of British territories in Europe, eg. Gibraltar, Malta and Cyprus; part II (Asian Territories, excluding India) followed in 1962, and part III (Bermuda, British Guiana, British Honduras, and the British West Indies) in 1965. These are referred to in footnotes as Pridmore, parts I, II and III. Further parts are promised. For miscellaneous datings, etc, see W. D. Craig, *Coins of the World, 1750–1850* (Racine, Wis., 1st edition, 1966), and R. S. Yeoman, *A Catalog of Modern World Coins, 1850–1964* (Racine, Wis., 8th edition, 1968), will be found invaluable.

4 *op. cit.*, p.396.

5 National Bank of South Africa, Ltd., *Income Tax; Weights and Measures; Stamp Duties; Coinage* (London, 1920), p.318. In addition, Keynes reported in 1912–13 that a large proportion of the currency in Egypt and the Sudan consisted of British sovereigns.

6 E. Cannan, *The Paper Pound of 1797–1821* (London, 1919).

7 The first Lord Liverpool was a currency expert, famous for his *Treatise on the Coins of the Realm* (London, 1805, reprinted in 1880).

8 Feavearyear, *op. cit.*, 1st edition, pp.196–9. These were the 'little shillings', as distinct from previous shillings struck at 62s to the pound troy, so wrongheadedly denounced by Cobbett, whose understanding of financial matters was minimal. Silver 4d pieces (the unpopular 'Britannia' groats) were added in 1834, the silver 3d piece in 1834, and the silver florin or 2s piece in 1849.

9 *Report of the US Silver Commission* (1876), p.68, quoted in B. R. Ambedkar, *The Problem of the Rupee* (London, 1923), pp.27–8. Needless to say, once the price of silver began to fall in the 1870s, the Dutch mint, which had stopped striking silver I guilder pieces in 1866, ceased to strike silver 2½ guilder pieces (approximately 5s)— the last being coined in 1874—and in 1875 resumed the striking of gold 10 guilder pieces after an interval of twenty-two years. In 1877 the Netherlands adopted the first, rather crude, gold-exchange standard of the modern type: J. M. Keynes, *Indian Currency and Finance* (1971 edition, London), pp.22–3.

10 Evidence of Baring before the Committee for Coin (1828), *Parl. Papers*, C. 31 of 1830.

11 Section iii of 7 & 8 Vict. c. 32 (text in T. E. Gregory (ed.), *Select Statutes, Documents and Reports relating to British Banking*, vol. 1, 2nd impression (London, 1964), p.131).

12 Sir G. Duveen and H. G. Stride, *The History of the Gold Sovereign* (London, 1962), pp.92–3.

13 B. B. Misra, *The Central Administration of the East India Company, 1773–1834* (Manchester, 1959), pp.105–7, and B. R. Ambedkar, *The Problem of the Rupee* (London, 1923), pp.1–48. See also K. N. Chaudhuri (ed.), *The Economic Development of India . . . 1814–58* (Cambridge, 1971).

14 Ambedkar, *op. cit.*, p.9. Prior to the 1870s the rupee was equivalent to about 2s sterling. One rupee = 16 annas; 1 anna = 4 pice. There was also a smaller unit, the pie, of which there were three in 1 pice, twelve in 1 anna and 192 in 1 rupee.

15 Ambedkar, *op. cit.*, p.21.

16 Ambedkar, *op. cit.*, pp.55–6.

17 Pridmore, part II, 1962, pp.32–4. This early adoption of the decimal system in Ceylon was in part due to the influence of Sir Hercules Robinson, governor 1865–72, who had previously been governor of Hong Kong when the decimal system was adopted in that colony.

[18] R. S. Yeoman, *op. cit.*, pp.202–3. For later developments, including the establishment of the East African Currency Board in December 1919, see D. Vice, 'The florin coinage of British East Africa', *Numismatic Circular*, London, vol. LXXXII, May 1974, p.192.

[19] Marquess of Anglesey (ed.), *Sergeant Pearman's Memoirs* (London, 1968), p.114.

[20] Cf. the eulogy of the Spanish pillar dollar by the governor of New South Wales, Sir Thomas Brisbane, in 1822: 'that invaluable coin, which has for centuries been disseminating its benefits over every other portion of the earth . . . a coin which from the extension of its circulation over every part of the commercial globe may justly be defined as the money of the world. . . . Like the ocean that surrounds our continent, a grand circulating medium assisting to waft to every part of the world the various products of her diversified climates. Driven, indeed, from the United Kingdom by her monies of sterling denomination it still however maintains all its pre-eminence in every one of her colonies. Confined in its advantages to no faith, kindred, or government, I refer you . . . to those sterling benefits it has for ages been bestowing on the British and Protestant North American Colonies; on the French and Papal Canadas; on Mohammedan India; and on the whole world.' *Sydney Gazette*, 30 August 1822, quoted in S. J. Butlin, *op. cit.*, pp.143–4.

[21] Sir John Craig, *The Mint: a History of the London Mint from A.D. 287 to 1948* (Cambridge, 1953), p.381.

[22] Chalmers, *op. cit.*, p.360. British silver coins flowed in between 1851 and 1860 as the price of sugar rose in Europe; *ibid.*, p.367.

[23] A distinctive coinage (100 cents to the rupee) was issued for the Seychelles only from 1939 onwards. The Andaman and Nicobar Islands in the Eastern part of the Indian Ocean also used the rupee unit, as they were part of the Indian empire.

[24] It has recently been shown that they were in fact struck at the mint of Ralph Heaton & Sons at Birmingham (*Coins*, x, 7, July 1973, p.12).

[25] Craig, *op. cit.*, pp.380–2.

[26] Full text in Chalmers, *op. cit.*, p.425.

[27] Full text in Chalmers, *op. cit.*, pp.417–24.

[28] S. J. Butlin, *op. cit.*, pp.30–49 and ch. VI, 'The dollar standard'.

[29] A. Andrews, *Australian Tokens and Coins*, 1965.

[30] New Zealand currency history parallels that of Australia to some extent. At first Spanish silver dollars circulated, although New Zealand was on sterling. In the middle years of the nineteenth century there were private issues of bronze tokens for 1d and ½d as in Australia. British silver and bronze circulated in New Zealand until the issue of separate New Zealand subsidiary coins in the early 1930s; P. Blakeborough, *The Coinage of New Zealand, 1840–1967* (1966).

[31] Duveen and Stride, *op. cit.*, p.96.

[32] Morrell, *op. cit.*, pp.200–312; see Duveen and Stride, *op. cit.*, pp.94–6. For the effect of the opening of the Sydney and Melbourne mints on Australian banking policy see E. A. Boehm, *Prosperity and Depression in Australia 1887–1897* (Oxford), pp.233–4. There is a valuable table of estimates of Australian exports and imports of gold and silver coin for the years from 1885 to 1897 on p.307 of the same book. The Australian mints also issued 'gold bullion . . . for export to India in the form of gold bars of the weight of 10 oz.' (National Bank of South Africa, *Income Tax. Weights and Measures. Stamp Duties. Coinage, British, Colonial and Foreign* (London, 1920), p.244).

[33] W. S. Jevons, *Investigations in Currency and Finance*, ed. H. S. Foxwell (1884), p.137.

[34] *Studies in British Overseas Trade, 1870–1914* (Liverpool, 1960), pp.205–6. J. A. Mann (*The Cotton Trade of Great Britain* (London, 1860), pp.78–9) remarked on the heavy silver drain to India in the late 1850s and the need for a government of India note issue.

[35] C. Daniell (*The Gold Treasure of India* (London, 1884), pp.95–6) estimated that up to 1882 gold stocks in India amounted to more than £212 million, i.e. two and a half times the gold then in circulation in Great Britain. For a modern critique of the 'drain' theory, see Tapan Mukerjee, 'Theory of economic drain: impact of British rule on the Indian economy, 1840–1900', in K. E. Boulding and T. Mukerjee (eds.), *Economic Imperialism: a Book of Readings* (Ann Arbor, Mich., 1972), pp.195–212. To some extent the hunger of the Indian peoples for gold was satisfied from home production in the years before 1914. The successful exploitation of the Kolar

goldfield by the Mysore Gold Mining Company and Goldfields of Mysore Ltd from 1880 onwards using the new cyanide process, raised India from seventh among the world's gold producers in 1887 to fifth during 1889–93. In 1894 India produced 6 tons of gold worth £800,000 (Nancy Crathorne, *Tennant's Stalk* (1973), pp.138–41; M. G. Mulhall, *Dictionary of Statistics* (4th edition, 1899), p.739; *Encyclopaedia Britannica*, 1911 edition, XII, p.195).

36 D. A. Farnie, 'The mineral revolution in South Africa', *South African Journal of Economics*, XXIV, 2, 1956, p.128. See also W. P. Morrell, *The Gold Rushes* (London, 1940), ch. IX, 'The diamonds of Kimberley and the gold of the Rand'.

37 T. F. Burgers, president of the Transvaal 1872–7, had issued gold £1 pieces in 1874, but only 837 were struck.

38 A. Kaplan, *The Coins of South Africa* (3rd edition, 1965). Significantly, however, the Transvaal coins were struck in Germany.

39 It was not withdrawn and demonetised until the 1940s, even though an adequate distinct South African currency had been issued since 1923 from the Pretoria mint. The everyday circulation of the old Transvaal currency must have contributed towards keeping alive the spirit of Afrikaner nationalism.

40 Daniell, *op. cit.*, pp.83–98.

41 Ambedkar, *op. cit.*, pp.73–6.

42 Keynes was suspicious of the concept as early as 1913, when he wrote: 'To illustrate how rare a thing in Europe a perfect and automatic gold standard is, let us take the most recent occasion of stringency—November 1912'. (*Indian Currency and Finance*, 2nd edition (London, 1972), p.17). The myth of the automatic gold standard has been exposed by A. E. Bloomfield, *Monetary Policy under the International Gold Standard, 1880–1914* (New York, 1959), and A. G. Ford, *The Gold Standard, 1880–1914; Britain and Argentina* (Oxford, 1962). See also M. de Cecco *Money and Empire: the International Gold Standard, 1890–1914* (Oxford, 1975).

43 Daniell, *op. cit.*, p.102.

44 Ambedkar, *op. cit.*, pp.135–44. There had been an international monetary conference in Paris in 1867. For the whole subject of the international monetary conferences, see H. Higgs (ed.), *Palgrave's Dictionary of Political Economy*, vol. II, reprint of revised 2nd edition, 1925–6 (New York, 1963), pp.783–7.

45 Compton Mackenzie, *Realms of Silver: One Hundred Years of Banking in the East* (London, 1954), pp.184–6. The stabilisation of the rupee at 1s 4d sterling had the advantage of making one anna equal in value to one penny sterling.

46 Keynes, *op. cit.*, pp.4–8.

47 Keynes, *op. cit.*, pp.29, 36–7. H. F. Howard stated, in his *India and the Gold Standard* (Calcutta and London, 1911), p.iii, that the decision of 1893 was 'a great practical experiment in the direction of the establishment of a Gold Exchange Standard'.

48 M. Greenberg, *British Trade and the Opening of China, 1800–42* (Cambridge, 1954), p.199. See also pp.vii, 49, 141–2, 159.

49 This was the mint mark of Santiago, Chile.

50 Sheila Marriner, *Rathbones of Liverpool, 1845–73* (Liverpool, 1961), p.176. See also Greenberg, *op. cit.*, p.159, n. 2.

51 The standard Mexican dollar contained 377 grains of pure silver and was 90·27 per cent fine. A sample of 11,846 Mexican dollars assayed at the London mint in 1891 revealed that on average the silver content was 90·16 per cent (Chalmers, *op. cit.*, pp.393–4).

52 W. F. Spalding, *Eastern Exchange, Currency and Finance* (4th edition, London, 1924), pp.412–20.

53 *Op. cit.*, pp.392–3. Chalmers noted that the Malays, 'like the Arabs of North Africa . . . call these coins "*cannon* dollars", mistaking the Pillars of Hercules for the recognised pioneers of European civilisation'.

54 Most, if not all, of these kapangs were made at Boulton's Soho Mint, near Birmingham, where they were popularly known as 'cock money' from the emblem they bore on the obverse side (P. E. Razzell and R. W. Wainwright, *The Victorian Working Class: Selections from Letters to the 'Morning Chronicle'* (London, 1973), p.310). The most detailed study of the 'cock money' is to be found in F. Pridmore, *Coins and Coinages of the Straits Settlements and British Malaya . . .1828–1853* (London, 1968), pp.68–143.

206   W. H. CHALONER

55 Pridmore, part II, p.150.
56 The Hong Kong series has recently been made the subject of a monograph, R. Hamson, *Regal Coinage of Hong Kong* (Hong Kong, n.d., ? 1969). The best modern account of Hong Kong's currency in the nineteenth century is to be found in F. H. H. King, *Money and Monetary Policy in China, 1845–95* (Cambridge, Mass., 1965), pp.166–88 and *passim*.
57 The US Mint introduced a silver trade dollar for the Far East weighing 420 grains, and 90 per cent fine, in 1873 and continued to strike it until 1885. It did not prove very successful.
58 Pridmore, part II, p.277. A good summary of modern Chinese currency history is to be found in R. D. Thompson, *Coinage of Kwangtung, China* (Hong Kong, 1971), pp. 7–9.
59 Spalding, *op. cit.*, p.163. Straits Settlements subsidiary coins (bronze and silver up to 50c) were afterwards obtained from the Royal Mint in London.
60 Spalding, *op. cit.*, pp.168–9.
61 Spalding, *op. cit.*, p.165.
62 Spalding, *op. cit.*, pp.165–7.
63 Spalding, *op. cit.*, pp.165–9; Mackenzie, *op. cit.*, pp.189–91. Mackenzie's book, which is a history of the Chartered Bank of India, Australia and China, is based to an unspecified extent on the archives of the Bank, but contains no references, footnotes or bibliography. In its sections on currency history it appears to lean heavily on Spalding.
64 Chalmers (*op. cit.*, pp.46–149) gives an extremely detailed survey of the West Indian island currencies. Even in the largest island, Jamaica, the amount of silver coin in circulation in the 1890s was estimated to be only about £320,000 and that of notes about £160,000, at a time when the total population of the island was roughly 640,000, giving an active circulation of only 15s per head (Chalmers, *op. cit.*, p.113). For a contemporary account of Caribbean currency confusion in the mid-1820s (with tables), see F. W. M. Bayley, *Four Years Residence in the West Indies* (London, 1830), pp.63–5, 149, 224–6, 476–7.
65 Chalmers, *op. cit.*, p.27.
66 Chalmers, *op. cit.*, p.113. The Jamaican Assembly passed a Currency Act in 1840 formally declaring the currency to be that of the United Kingdom.
67 Chalmers, *op. cit.*, p.110, n. 5.
68 Chalmers, *op. cit.*, p.143.
69 Chalmers, *op. cit.*, pp.144–5.
70 Pridmore, part III (1965), p.57.
71 Pridmore, *op. cit.*, p.57.
72 Chalmers, *op. cit.*, p.120.
73 *Op. cit.*, p.122. Chalmers also stated that the British silver 3d piece ('six cents') was 'slowly creeping into use'. Most of the currency must have consisted of US coins, although British silver coins were legal tender to any amount.
74 Chalmers, *op. cit.*, p.208.
75 Chalmers, *op. cit.*, pp.209–10.
76 Chalmers, *op. cit.*, pp.210–11. The customary use of the dollar is reflected today in the Gambia's striking of 4s pieces (1966) and 8s pieces (1970).
77 The extent of the use of cowrie shells as currency in West Africa has been much exaggerated and declined rapidly after 1870 (Chalmers, *op. cit.*, p.213).
78 P. N. Davies, *The Trade Makers: Elder Dempster in West Africa, 1852–1972* (London, 1973), pp.117–22. For developments after 1907 see L. V. W. Wright, *Colonial and Commonwealth Coins* (London, 1959), pp.66–7.
79 Or as the tables of currency rates at the time put it: 'Sterling into Halifax currency, the dollar at 4s 6d [sterling] passing for 5s currency'.
80 Chalmers, *op. cit.*, p.183.
81 Chalmers, *op. cit.*, p.184.
82 R. Giffen, *The Case against Bimetallism* (London, 2nd edition, 1892), pp.66–7, 104.
83 The wording of the preamble to the Prince Edward Island Act of 1851 (14 Vict. c. 33) asserts that 'the orders-in-council and proclamations of 1825 and 1838 had no effect in this colony' (Chalmers, *op. cit.*, p.195).

84 *Op. cit.*, p.198. Newfoundland, where much trading continued to be by barter until well into the nineteenth century, had a local Newfoundland sterling currency (cf. 'Halifax' currency), but adopted the dollar/cent system between 1863 and 1872. Distinctive Newfoundland gold, silver and bronze coins were struck from 1865 until 1947 (Chalmers, *op. cit.*, pp.172–4).

85 Duveen and Stride, *op. cit.*, p.96. Symbolically, the Ottawa mint was transferred to Dominion ownership in 1931, the year in which Britain finally abandoned the gold standard. A branch mint had been established in 1862 at New Westminster to service the gold-fields of British Columbia. It got as far as striking a few sample coins before it was abandoned (Craig, *op. cit.*, p.387).

François Crouzet

9

Trade and empire: the British experience from the establishment of free trade until the first World War[1]

The first British empire, in the seventeenth and eighteenth centuries, was a mercantilist empire which had been conceived and built up as an economic unit, as a trading system as exclusive as possible, strictly subjugated to the interests of the mother country. Although this mercantilist edifice was shaken by the loss of the thirteen colonies and undermined by the advance of the industrial revolution in England, it survived until the middle of the nineteenth century. Between 1846 and 1860, however, it was entirely dismantled and the mercantilist empire made way for the free-trade empire that was to last until 1931. Strictly speaking, this empire did not constitute an economic unit. The English market was thrown open and was equally accessible to the goods of any other country, whether a part of the empire or not. Moreover England did not insist on favoured treatment for its own goods in its colonies. From 1859 onwards the self-governing colonies enjoyed complete freedom in tariff policy, which even enabled them to erect protective tariffs against British goods. As for the Crown colonies and India, their customs tariffs had solely fiscal ends and included no preference for goods from the mother country. Throughout the free trade era, therefore, trade between the different parts of the British empire had all the usual features of international trade, and it might appear artificial to study the commercial and financial relations between Great Britain and its empire in isolation. This study is nevertheless worth undertaking if only to determine whether, as is often claimed, the possession of a far-flung empire was an essential factor in the prosperity of Victorian and Edwardian England. Hopefully, such a study might throw light on the nature and motivations of imperialism and show whether it 'pays'.[2]

In the middle of the nineteenth century commerce within the empire was characterised by the survival of traditional trading patterns which in many respects were still those of the eighteenth century. It should not be forgotten, indeed, that the mercantilist framework which channelled empire trade survived, in the main, right up to the mid-century; the Navigation Acts were abolished only in 1849 and colonial preference for sugar and timber—two of the mainstays of the old system—disappeared only in 1854 and 1860 respectively. Besides, trade within the empire was still carried on by the traditional means of transport—that is, by sailing ships, since steam vessels were not yet competitive on long-distance routes.[3] Although freight rates had fallen since 1815, they were still too high for the long-distance carriage of heavy goods to be profitable, while the slowness of sailing ships prohibited the transport of perishable produce over great distances. Finally, the economies of many British possessions had barely changed since the eighteenth century. Thus India continued to export above all 'drugs, dyes and luxuries' and in 1858 such traditional articles—indigo, spices, drugs, saltpetre, etc—still made up 61 per cent of British imports from India.[4] Undoubtedly the emergence of the settlement colonies in temperate zones—the future dominions—was a new factor, but at this time they were only just beginning to tap their considerable natural resources.

The pattern of trade between mother country and colonies had hardly changed, then, since the eighteenth century. Textiles enjoyed a very marked predominance in British exports: in 1850 cotton goods and cotton yarn represented by value 42 per cent of British exports to the empire, and altogether textile goods made up 64 per cent, while the share of metallurgical products of all kinds was only 16 per cent. As for United Kingdom imports from the empire, they were dominated by a small number of major items—the first five alone represented 59 per cent of total imports in 1854: timber (19 per cent), sugar (18 per cent), wool (13 per cent), indigo (5 per cent) and coffee (4 per cent). Out of these five items, three—sugar from the West Indies, indigo from India, coffee, which came mostly from Ceylon—were typical of the old colonial trade, while the large-scale imports of Canadian timber can also be looked upon as a survival of mercantilism, for they resulted from the preferential duties instituted during the Continental blockade to promote timber imports from the colonies rather than from northern Europe. The only new item was Australian and New Zealand wool, imports of which had increased remarkably after about 1820. For only a small number of items—including the five just mentioned[5]—did the empire provide England with a significant proportion of its imports (rising from 55 per cent of the total for timber to 96 per cent for indigo).[6] Great Britain took from its possessions but a minute proportion of its imports of several very important articles, such as grain and flour, meat, dairy products, tea, tobacco and, above all, cotton.

As for the geographical distribution of imperial trade, during the years 1854–7 India came first, having 34 per cent of Great Britain's total trade with the empire (that is, imports plus exports). Australia was second, with 22 per cent, but this was a recent development, the consequence of the gold discoveries there in 1851.[7] British North America came third, with 13 per cent of England's trade with the empire, and the West Indies fourth with 12 per cent. The share of Africa and the remaining colonies in British trade was nominal. Here again a survival of traditional patterns can be seen, with the important role played by India and the West Indies, although this was already declining. There was, however, a new element: the growing importance of the settlement colonies, which were responsible for exactly 40 per cent of England's total trade with the empire.[8]

Altogether the colonies of white settlement took slightly under a third of British exports, excluding re-exports (31·5 per cent of the total for 1854–7), they provided a little under a quarter of Britain's imports (23·9 per cent), and their share of Great Britain's total foreign trade in 1854–7 was 25·4 per cent. The latter had hardly changed since 1815, and it remained relatively unimportant. We ought not, however, to be tempted to use this to explain the lack of interest shown by British opinion towards imperial problems in the middle of the nineteenth century, for in fact these percentages hardly altered during the following half-century, even at the height of the period of the 'new imperialism'. It is true that the situation was different from the colonies' point of view: if England had given up its legal monopoly of their trade it retained an actual monopoly because of its overwhelming industrial superiority, and remained by far their principal supplier. Only Canada and India had important trading links with foreign countries—its American neighbour for the former and China for the latter. As H. J. Habakkuk has written, from the economic point of view Britain possessed the best of all possible empires in the middle of the nineteenth century: a group of pioneer or backward countries tied to a highly industrialised country, buying its manufactured goods in return for their primary products. The division of labour between mother country and colonies that the mercantilists had desired had been accomplished despite the abolition of mercantilist constraints.[9]

From the middle of the nineteenth century until the first World War Britain's trade with the empire underwent a series of fundamental changes, whereby new elements emerged to displace the traditional features just described. These changes were brought about by three principal factors. The first of these was rising demand in Britain for foodstuffs and raw materials. As a result of the increase in the British population (from 21 million in 1851 to 41 million in 1911), of the rise in the standard of living and of the progress of industrialisation, aggregate demand for primary products greatly increased, and in addition the structure of that demand altered. Thus, from the end of the nineteenth century onwards, technical advance increased the use of new commodities like rubber, petroleum and vegetable oils, whilst at the same time British agriculture was less and less capable of meeting the country's food needs.[10] In 1907 Great Britain itself produced only 52 per cent of the non-tropical foodstuffs it consumed,[11] and for some important products its dependence on imports was considerably greater: in 1910–14 it imported 81 per cent of the wheat and cheese it consumed, 75 per cent of the butter and 42 per cent of the meat.[12] There was therefore a great increase in foodstuff imports, which rose, at constant prices, from £46 million in 1854 to £285 million in 1913.

It so happened that several areas of the empire possessed favourable natural conditions for the production on a large scale and at low cost of some of the primary products which were in rising demand in England. This was the case with the immense, fertile plains of the Canadian prairies, which were ideal for wheat cultivation, and the fine natural pastures and mild climates of Australia and New Zealand. It was the opening up of these areas in response to British demand that brought about major changes in imperial commerce. These resources, however, had only potential, and their cultivation was possible only because of the working of two other factors: the transport revolution and British investment in the empire.

In transport two vital developments affected imperial commerce: the reduction in maritime freight rates and the building of railways. The fall in freight rates was the consequence of the rapid technical changes that took place in maritime transport after 1870, particularly the gradual substitution of steel-hulled steamships for wooden sailing ships. Recent studies have confirmed that the victory of steam was speeded up by the digging of the Suez canal, which opened the Indian Ocean and Australian trade to steamers and which stimulated technical advance, especially the introduction of the compound engine.[13] At all events, competition between steam and sail, cost cutting in shipbuilding and operation, and the reduction in the duration of voyages brought a rapid fall in freight rates from 1870–3 onwards. Thus the cost of transporting wool from Australia to England fell by 50 per cent between 1873 and 1896 and that of transporting jute from India to England by 75 per cent between 1873 and 1905. Moreover, long-distance freight rates fell the most. Given this, it became feasible to transport bulky goods long distances, for example cereals from India or Australia to England. The end of the nineteenth century was marked, indeed, by the growth of trade in bulky commodities and by a tendency to operate longer routes.[14] The distant parts of the empire were thus able to exploit their natural advantages and to unload on to the British market large quantities of cheap foodstuffs and raw materials. In addition, more specific technical advances—e.g. the appearance of refrigeration in transport—enabled Australia and, above all, New Zealand to become exporters of meat and dairy produce. The revolution in maritime transport therefore played a decisive part in the economic growth of the empire and particularly of the developing economies of the future dominions.

The building of railways, however, had no less powerful an impact, for this alone permitted the opening up of the vast untapped resources by greatly reducing transport costs between the areas of production and the ports. The role of the Canadian Pacific Railway in the development of the Canadian prairies is the most striking example but far from the only one.[15] But this rapid railway construction—total mileage in the empire increased from 8,500 in 1870 to 53,000 in 1895—was possible only because of the massive investment of British capital.

This brings us to the third factor, which, S. B. Saul has asserted, was the key determinant of developments in imperial trade—as it was, moreover, of the economies of nearly all British possessions.[16] True, only a small proportion of the capital that went from England to the empire was invested directly in agriculture, industry or mining, the only important instances being investment in Australian and, above all, South African mines. The bulk of capital exported went, indeed, into the establishment of means of transport, and especially into railway building. A recent and very careful study has estimated that from 1865 to 1894 60 per cent of the funds for overseas investment raised by stock issues in London was intended to finance railways.[17] It was therefore indirectly that British investment had an impact on production in countries of the empire and on imperial trade by facilitating the establishment of an infrastructure, and, above all, of a modern transport system, which created the conditions for the internal accumulation of capital and productive investment. Local entrepreneurs and capital were responsible for the development of production proper in the various territories of the empire. The chief function of British capital was the creation of the preconditions for the 'take-off' of economic growth.[18]

It had no less profound an effect—indeed, a dual effect—on imperial trade: in the medium and long term stimulating an export-orientated agriculture and mining industry in the colonies (accompanied by a fall in the price of primary produce and an improvement in England's terms of trade) and in the short term giving rise to the export of large quantities of English capital goods, especially rails and railway rolling stock. Furthermore, fluctuations in British investment largely determined fluctuations in imperial commerce.[19]

The total of these investments was indeed considerable. Before 1850, of course, investments in the empire had been very small, but they rose sharply after this date and increased fairly regularly until 1885–8, going especially to India and Australia. There was a falling off during the 1890s, despite investments in the mines of the Rand, but from 1904 to 1914 there was another powerful upswing, and this time the chief beneficiary was Canada.[20] Total investments in the empire rose from about £270 million in 1870 to £1,780 million in 1913, which represented 47 per cent of total British foreign investments. It is often claimed that after 1873 British capitalists tended increasingly to invest in the empire in preference to independent countries,[21] but this has not been confirmed by the most recent analysis—that of Segal and Simon—according to which total flotations of 'imperial' securities on the London market between 1865 and 1894 reached 46 per cent of all flotations.[22] Indeed, these authors have shown that investments in the empire fluctuated less sharply than those that went to independent countries (chiefly in fact to the United States and South America).[23] Thus, the share of the empire in total foreign investments increased at times of depression—between 1873 and 1877, for instance—and fell during times of international prosperity (from 1868 to 1872, in 1886–90).[24] In the long run, though, the empire's share of British capital exports did not change markedly.

It may be added that the bulk of these English investments went to the settlement colonies: in 1913 the five dominions had taken almost exactly three-quarters. In contrast, the tropical countries—India, Malaya and the African colonies, including the vast territories occupied at the end of the nineteenth century—had received but a quarter,[25] a relatively minor proportion.[26] Therefore, some of the most important changes affecting imperial commerce during the free trade era were in the trade between England and the 'new countries' of the empire.

The opening up of new sources of supply for primary produce in British possessions brought about considerable changes in the pattern of British imports from the empire. Of course, the exploitation of these new resources took place in a strictly liberal framework, without government intervention; the pattern of British imports changed in response to market forces, working through the price mechanism, importers and consumers turning to suppliers whose prices were the lowest—forsaking, for instance, China tea for Indian, and West Indian cane sugar for the beet-sugar of Continental Europe.

The most important aspect of this development was undoubtedly the growth of imports of 'temperate' foodstuffs from the empire—especially wheat, meat, butter and cheese. In the middle of the nineteenth century the colonies supplied only a tiny proportion of British imports of these products, but during the following sixty years some of them greatly increased their exports and provided a rising proportion of rapidly increasing British imports (see table 9.1).

Thus in 1854 England took only 0·5 per cent of its total wheat imports from the empire. In the following years, however, significant quantities of Canadian wheat from Ontario began to be imported. This trade

proved short-lived and soon declined in the face of competition from
American wheat, Canada turning to the export of animal products.
Nevertheless, imports of wheat from the empire continued to increase
thanks to consignments from Australia and above all from India, whose
exports grew rapidly after the opening of the Suez canal and again after

Table 9.1.   Share of the empire in different United Kingdom imports (%)

	1854	1860	1870	1880	1890	1900	1913
Wheat	0·5	3·1	9·8	20·3	22·0	15·1	48·5
Total grain and flour	5·8	6·7	12·6	15·7	16·5	13·6	35·3
Coffee	76·0	86·4	73·7	62·2	33·0	22·3	18·7
Tea	0·7	3·5	11·4	26·7	71·7	91·2	87·3
Raw sugar	64·7	59·8	35·8	28·7	15·8	12·9	8·7
Meat	0·9	1·0	7·6	3·0	15·4	20·1	24·7
Butter	1·5	11·6	4·3	4·8	2·2	18·1	19·0
Cheese	–	–	5·3	15·1	39·8	58·8	81·7
Total for foodstuffs	19·1	18·2	17·5	17·4	19·1	20·9	27·0
Timber and joinery	55·2	46·1	35·2	43·1	26·7	24·9	16·2
Raw cotton	8·4	9·8	19·1	11·3	11·2	1·7	3·0
Wool	70·6	68·5	88·5	87·0	88·8	84·5	80·2
Oil seeds	26·5	47·4	37·0	42·8	42·3	34·0	53·3
Rubber	11·2	17·2	21·9	19·5	14·2	12·6	57·2
Tin	71·2	78·6	49·1	91·0	94·4	88·3	94·8
Total for raw materials	26·2	23·5	27·4	31·9	30·7	24·3	28·0
Total for British imports	22·4	20·4	21·4	22·5	22·9	21·0	24·9

Source. W. Schlote, *op. cit.*, p.99, table 40, and appendix, pp.164–5, table 21.

the completion of a direct rail link between Bombay and the grain-
growing regions of the north-west in 1881. Because of the uncertainty of
the harvest, exports of Indian wheat showed great variation from year
to year, but in 1904 India was the chief supplier of wheat to Great
Britain, and during the years 1904–13 supplied 18 per cent of total
imports. Besides, imports of Canadian wheat revived from 1890 and
rose quickly after 1900, following the opening up of the prairie provinces, which in the space of a few years became one of the granaries of
the world. Canadian wheat production quadrupled from 1901 to 1911,
and the value of English imports of Canadian wheat actually consumed
on the home market rose from £2.8 million in 1900 to £11 million in
1913, replacing US supplies and constituting 25 per cent of total wheat
imports. At the same time Australia itself greatly increased its wheat
output and exports, and provided 10 per cent of British imports between
1909 and 1914. Imports of wheat from the empire therefore made considerable progress and their share of total British imports showed a

marked increase, rising to 48·5 per cent in 1913, which represented about 40 per cent of total British consumption.[27]

The trade in meat and dairy produce shows a similar development. Before 1860 the empire provided England with practically none of these. From this date on Canada began to send salt and corned beef, bacon and hams, then, after 1875, livestock, and later refrigerated meats. At the same time dairying developed in Quebec and Ontario, where a cheese of the Cheddar type was produced. Exports of cheese and butter to England increased markedly after 1880, replacing American produce on the English market, and for a time Canada was England's major cheese supplier. But these exports fell, after 1900 for meat, after 1904–5 for dairy produce, Canada's home market taking a growing proportion of output. On the other hand, Australia and New Zealand, which had started to supply Great Britain with animal products later, continued to increase their sales and became the major suppliers. The decisive factor was the perfection of refrigeration in transport: after long experiments, the first cargo of frozen mutton from New Zealand arrived in London in 1882. Thereafter imports of meat, butter and cheese from Australasia increased very quickly, reaching £8 million in 1900 and £19 million in 1913. The New Zealand economy was profoundly changed as a result, the wool growing practised mainly on South Island declining before the dairying and mutton production of the more humid North Island. In 1913 Great Britain took 25 per cent of its meat imports (worth over £56 million, as against £1·7 million in 1854), from the empire, which was roughly a tenth of its total consumption, as well as 19 per cent of its butter and 82 per cent of its cheese imports.[28]

The rise of 'temperate' foodstuff production in the empire—in fact in Canada and later in Australasia—and the export of this produce to England is an important element in the international economic history of the period 1860–1914.[29]

However, there was also an increase in the output of and trade in tropical produce, the most important of which was tea. In the middle of the nineteenth century the tea consumed in Great Britain—in rapidly growing quantities[30]—was imported almost entirely from China, in the clippers which participated in the famous annual tea races. Around 1820, though, wild tea plants had been found in Assam, and from 1840 onwards British plantations were set up there. Output quickly increased after 1870, and after 1880 Ceylon, whose coffee plantations had been ruined by disease, also turned to tea cultivation. As a result of various advantages—greater political security and the possibility of controlling output and sales—which British merchants enjoyed, Indian tea could be sold more cheaply than the Chinese, and consumers came to prefer it. Thus the share of India and Ceylon in British imports quickly rose, and in 1888 surpassed China's for the first time. By 1913 the empire was to provide the bulk—87 per cent—of the British national drink.[31]

A further interesting trade is that in vegetable oils, which were of many different kinds—groundnuts, coconut, linseed, rape seed, cotton seed and palm oil. They were produced in many parts of the empire but first of all in India and in British colonies in West Africa, where they played a leading role in economic life. It is true that they were to be used only partly for foodstuffs (above all for the production of margarine) and that their industrial use was considerable. At all events, the value of British imports increased fivefold between 1854 and 1913, and the proportion coming from the empire rose from 27 to 53 per cent.

Changes were less spectacular for raw materials than for foodstuffs. The most important supplied by the empire (more than 80 per cent of total imports from 1870 onwards) was wool, coming primarily from Australia but also from New Zealand and South Africa, a trade which continued to grow throughout the period. The same was true for jute, of which India had a monopoly. Among the new raw materials entering trade the most striking was rubber, British demand for which increased rapidly from the end of the nineteenth century onwards as a result of the rise of the bicycle, motor car and electrical equipment industries. At first, wild rubber from the Amazon basin, plus small quantities from Sierra Leone and the Gold Coast, was used. In 1876, however, hevea plants were introduced into Malaya. Right up to the end of the nineteenth century output remained extremely small, but from 1900 onwards numerous plantations were established. Although these reached full production only during and after the first World War, as early as 1913 Malaya supplied 19 per cent of world rubber exports, whilst Ceylon supplied 10 per cent, as against Brazil's 24 per cent, and the empire was able to supply England with 57 per cent of its imports of this product.[32] From Malaya too came tin, British imports of which had been insignificant at the mid-century but were worth over £9 million by 1913.[33]

These were the principal British imports of imperial produce which increased during the half century that preceded the first World War.[34] However, there were also imports which declined or even disappeared. This was the case particularly with the four basic commodities of the old colonial trade, which in the middle of the nineteenth century still dominated imperial trade: sugar, coffee, indigo and timber. In 1854 the empire (in other words, above all, the West Indies) supplied 65 per cent of British imports of unrefined sugar, but by 1913 its share had fallen to 9 per cent, and this becomes an insignificant proportion when the imports of refined sugar—which were considerable and came entirely from outside the empire—are taken into account. What is more, imports from the West Indies had greatly fallen in absolute figures.[35]

This decline can be explained by the competition of beet sugar sold by European countries—Germany, France, Belgium and Austria—which could take place without hindrance under free trade and which forced imperial producers out of the British market.[36] In the case of coffee the ruin of Ceylon's plantations after 1877 as a result of a coffee shrub disease left the field clear for Brazilian coffee. As for indigo, it disappeared from international trade after 1890 in the face of competition from synthetic dyes. Finally, timber imports from the empire—that is, from Canada—fell in absolute terms, and fell still more in percentage terms, after 1867 under the impact of competition from Russian and Scandinavian timber, which could take place because the tariff preference enjoyed by timber from the empire was abolished in 1860 and because these countries had the advantage of shorter distances and lower transport costs.[37] The examples of sugar and timber are a good illustration of the impact of the market mechanism on the pattern of imperial commerce.

In any case, this pattern changed and in particular the range of goods imported from the empire was widened and diversified.[38] If we take empire goods that represented more than 3 per cent of total British imports from the colonies, we find only five in the middle of the nineteenth century (1854): timber, sugar, wool, indigo and coffee, in that order of importance. In 1913, however, we find nine: wool (14 per cent of the total), wheat (11 per cent), meat (7 per cent), tea (6 per cent), rubber (6 per cent), dairy products (5 per cent), tin (5 per cent) and vegetable oils (4 per cent).[39] Thus, of the five principal items in 1854, four have disappeared from the leading group (and the imports of three of these have become unimportant). Inversely, in the leading group of 1913 four items—wheat, meat, tea and dairy products—were newcomers, only negligible imports of which came from the empire in 1854. This development demonstrates some of the basic characteristics of the economic development of the empire, particularly the rise of agriculture and stock rearing in Canada and Australia and the first steps in the opening up of Malaya and the west African colonies.

At the same time, the geographical distribution of British imports from the empire altered significantly, as is shown by table 9.2.

The most remarkable change was the considerable increase in the proportion of imports from the settlement colonies, the five dominions, which rose from a third to more than a half. Australasia, supplying wool, wheat, meat, butter and cheese, was responsible for this increase, and the value of English imports from Australia and New Zealand rose more than tenfold. Imports from Canada, on the other hand, increased less spectacularly, and her share of the total remained unchanged at the end of the period. As for India, her share of British imports fell appreciably,[40] while that of the other possessions in Asia greatly increased, as a result of the rise of the trade in rubber and tin from Malaya. In contrast, imports from the African colonies barely increased, and their share of the total declined to 3 per cent in 1909–13.[41] Finally, imports from the British West Indies collapsed as a consequence of the decline of the sugar trade.

Table 9.2. Share of the principal areas in British imports from the empire (%)

	1854–7	1877–9	1898–1901	1909–13
Australia and New Zealand	13	26	31	33
South Africa	3	5	5	6
Canada and Newfoundland	16	13	20	16
Total for the five dominions	32	45	56	55
India	38	34	26	26
British Asia (excluding India)	6	10	11	13
British Africa (excluding South Africa)	6	2	2	3
West Indies	16	8	2	2
Other British possessions	2	1	2	1

Source. W. Schlote, *op. cit.*, p.168, table 23.

Altogether, Great Britain's imports from the empire increased considerably, rising from an annual average of £39 million in 1854–7 to £173 million in 1909–13; their value therefore more than quadrupled. They did not, however, grow at a faster rate than imports from foreign countries, so the proportion of total imports that came from the empire changed only slightly. It was 24 per cent in 1854–7; during the years 1861–5 it suddenly increased as a result of the American Civil War and the cutting off of supplies of American cotton, which were partly made up for by imports from India;[42] in 1864 the empire supplied as much as 34 per cent of total imports. However, its share very quickly fell again to 22 per cent for 1870–4, and until the end of the century quinquennial averages remained at between 22 and 24 per cent. After 1900 a slight increase can be seen, linked with the growth of the trade in foodstuffs and rubber, though the percentage of total imports for 1909–13 was only 25 per cent.

If the analysis is extended, we find that the greatest increase took place in foodstuffs from the empire, its share in total foodstuff imports rising from 19 per cent in 1854 to 27 per cent in 1913. (This increase, however, took place after 1900.)[43] In contrast, the empire's share of raw material imports increased only very slightly. Since, besides, British imports of manufactured goods increased faster than those of primary products, and since the empire did not supply manufactured goods, it can be understood why the empire's share of total imports remained almost unchanged.[44]

This share, then, remained small and was smaller still in reality because an appreciable proportion of imports from the empire were re-exported to other countries—29 per cent in 1913 (above all, wool, jute, rubber and tin), and in consequence the empire supplied only 20·5 per cent of net British imports at that date.[45] Moreover, for only a small number of important items did the empire, even at the end of the period, provide a high percentage of total British imports. In 1913 its share was more than 80 per cent for jute, tin, tea, cheese and wool. For vegetable oils and rubber it was slightly more than 50 per cent and nearly 50 per cent for wheat (though only 34 per cent for all grains and flour). Appreciable percentages were also to be found with meat, butter and timber. On the other hand, the empire supplied England with relatively insignificant quantities of a number of essential items, particularly sugar, cotton, tobacco, iron ore and petroleum. Any attempt at imperial autarchy would thus have been chimerical, and even the plans for the re-introduction of imperial preference put forward from the late nineteenth century onwards would have meant imposing tariffs on the greater proportion of British imports and therefore increasing the cost of living and production costs in industry. Free trade remained the best policy for England, at any rate until the first World War.

The pattern of Great Britain's exports to its overseas possessions did not undergo as radical a transformation as did that of its imports. The principal change was the decline in the proportion of total exports to the empire made up of textiles: in the middle of the nineteenth century this was nearly two-thirds (64 per cent in 1850), but in 1913 it was only 51 per cent, the proportion of cotton yarn and piece goods having fallen from 42 to 33 per cent. In contrast, the share of the various metallurgical products, a rising proportion of which consisted of capital goods, had increased appreciably, having risen from 16 to 32 per cent of total exports to the empire. This increase partly explains the relative decline in textile exports, but it ought to be added that from 1885 the growth of the latter slowed down chiefly as a result of the advance of the cotton industry in India, the leading market for English cotton goods. This slowing down heralded the sharp crisis that Lancashire exports were to face after the first World War.

Nor did the geographical distribution of British exports among the various imperial markets undergo spectacular changes (table 9.3). The share of the future dominions, which had greatly increased between 1820 and 1850 to reach 47 per cent of the total in 1854–7, fluctuated thereafter at a slightly lower level, rising a little from 1895 onwards to reach exactly 50 per cent in 1909–13. This preponderance, despite the small size of their population, resulted from their rapid economic growth and their relatively high standards of living. As with imports, Australia comes first; its share of exports to the empire fell slightly, but the figures for 1854–7 were abnormally swollen by the boom following the gold discoveries.[46] Canada's share fell markedly at the end of the nineteenth century but rose again afterwards, to return to the same level in 1909–13 as in 1854–7. Exports to South Africa, then, showed the greatest increase. India, on the other hand, remained the most important imperial market for England, its share of total exports—very nearly one-third—being unchanged. The remaining possessions in Asia and the African colonies increased their share, but it remained very small. The West Indies' share, of course, was reduced to insignificance.

Table 9.3. Share of the principal areas in the export of British goods to the empire (%)

	1854–7	1877–9	1898–1901	1909–13
Australia and New Zealand	30	28	26	25
South Africa	4	8	14	12
Canada and Newfoundland	13	10	8	13
Total for the five dominions	47	46	48	50
India	32	35	34	33
British Asia (excluding India)	6	9	8	8
British Africa (excluding South Africa)	2	2	3	5
West Indies	6	4	3	2
Other British possessions	6	3	3	2

Source. W. Schlote, *op. cit.*, p.169, table 23. Re-exports are not included in this table.

The most difficult and interesting problem, though, concerns the changes in total British exports to the empire. From 1850 to 1913 these rose from £19 million to £161 million, and this increase took place gradually, without the rather wide fluctuations that occurred in British exports to independent countries and in British exports as a whole.

This being so, the proportion of total exports that went to the empire showed quite marked fluctuations which even had a cyclical character. Thus its share increased perceptibly (if irregularly) from 1852 to 1863—from 26 to 35 per cent of the total, falling thereafter until 1871, when it was only 23 per cent, rising up to 35 per cent in 1877, falling to 32 per cent in 1879, reaching 37 per cent in 1885, and falling to 31 per cent in 1895. There was a renewed increase to 38·5 per cent in 1902, which was the peak for the entire 1850–1913 period, a fall to 32 per cent in 1906–7, and finally a rise to 37 per cent in 1913.[47]

S. B. Saul has linked these fluctuations with those of British investments in the empire, investments which stimulated British exports, especially of capital goods.[48] When there was a marked upswing in investments in the empire—as, for example, in the 1850s, following the gold discoveries in Australia, or between 1909 and 1913—there was a comparable increase in imperial trade. It also grew, however, when there was a sharp fall in capital invested outside the empire, which

brought about an increase in the empire's share of total foreign investments; at the same time sales of British goods outside the empire fell off,
whilst those to the empire increased, or at least remained stable. This is
what happened between 1873 and 1877 and between 1882 and 1885.

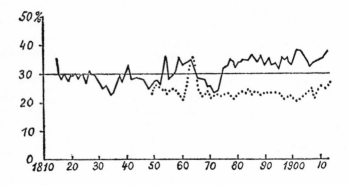

Fig. 9.1. The share of the British empire in United Kingdom trade,
1814–1914. Percentage of trade based on actual values. The solid line
represents exports and the dotted line imports.

In contrast, when there was a rapid increase in British investment in
or exports to independent countries, the Empire's share in total exports
fell, the best instance being the years 1864–72. The fluctuations in
imperial commerce were therefore in large part counter-cyclical, at least
during the period 1860–90. The empire's share in Great Britain's
exports fell during years of expansion and general prosperity (especially
in the 1868–72 boom and the upswing of 1878–9), but it increased
during depressions (1873–7 and 1882–5). Indeed, when a crisis struck
the world economy British investors forsook foreign investment, especially in the United States, and turned to the empire, where colonial
government bonds offered gilt-edged investments. This redirection of
funds helped sustain merchandise, and particularly capital-goods,
exports. The working of this mechanism to some extent insulated Great
Britain and its empire from the worst effects of general economic crises.
Thus the empire played a stabilising role in the British economy.[49]
This, however, was because the latter then held a dominant position in
the world economy.[50]

After 1890 the situation seems to have changed. Fluctuations in the
proportion of total English exports that went to the empire were no
longer counter-cyclical: its share increased during years of general
prosperity—from 1897 to 1902 and from 1909 to 1913, for example—
and fell during years of depression, such as 1893–5 and 1906–7. In short,
imperial trade tended thereafter to move in unison with the fluctuations

in world trade, and the empire was deeply affected by international depressions.[51]

This phenomenon is to be explained by the fundamental change that took place in the international position of the British economy, which lost some of its predominance and as a result was no longer able to insulate the empire from fluctuations in the world economy. In particular—and this is a point we shall return to—the United States and the new industrial powers in Europe became major purchasers of primary produce from the British empire, and in consequence when a crisis hit those powers it was passed on directly to primary producers in the empire, whose exports fell; the latter in turn reduced their purchases of English goods. And British investments were no longer capable of playing their previous role of shock absorbers, especially because the primary producing countries no longer attracted British capital when they were struck by a crisis coming from outside. In short, from the end of the nineteenth century the motor of fluctuations in imperial commerce was no longer British investment but the demand for primary produce from all the industrial countries.[52]

At all events, these fluctuations were not very great, with the exception of that between 1863 and 1873, and in the final analysis the empire's share in Great Britain's exports did not increase markedly in the long run: it stood at 31·5 per cent in 1854–7 and reached 35·4 per cent in 1909–13. It might also be noted, however, that after 1875 it settled at a slightly higher level than during the preceding decades, never falling below 31 per cent.[53] It is also true that the tendency to increase was definitely more marked for textile goods—for which the share taken by the empire rose from 31 per cent of exports in 1860 to 44 per cent in 1913—and for most metallurgical products and capital goods.[54] But if, finally, we consider British trade in its entirety—that is, the sum of exports, re-exports and imports—the headway made by the empire remained very modest: 25·4 per cent of total commerce in 1854–7 and 27·5 per cent in 1909–13.[55]

This absence of change might appear surprising, for throughout this period the empire went through considerable territorial expansion,[56] massive investments were made, and its natural resources were exploited with vigour and success. In view of this, one might even talk of a stagnation (relative, of course) in imperial trade and note that the economic results of the great imperial expansion of the late nineteenth century were very meagre. This stagnation naturally distressed the 'imperialists', who blamed foreign competition in British colonies—a charge that was not without foundation.

In the middle of the nineteenth century, as we have seen, Britain in effect retained a quasi-monopoly of the foreign trade of its colonies. This monopoly was maintained until 1870 and even beyond for some

areas. During the last quarter of the century, however, foreign manufacturers—American, German, Belgian, etc—began to infiltrate imperial markets, and competition from them went on increasing until the
first World War, with the result that England's share in its colonies'
imports tended to decline—sharply in certain instances. The intensity of
competition, indeed, varied considerably from one territory to another.

In this respect Canada and India are the two extreme cases. It was
in Canada that foreign competition was most serious—in this instance
from the United States because of its rapid industrialisation, the
geographical advantages it enjoyed (especially in western Canada) and
its technical superiority, above all in capital goods, whose share of
Canadian imports greatly increased at the expense of textiles. In consequence England's share of Canada's imports fell from 54 per cent in
1872–4 to 27 per cent in 1895–7, and to 21 per cent in 1913, whilst the
United States' share moved in the opposite direction, rising from 38 per
cent in 1872–4 to 57 per cent in 1895–9, and this despite the high level
of British investment in Canada and the latter's return to a policy of
imperial preference in 1897.[57]

The situation in India was quite different. In 1870 England supplied
85 per cent of the country's imports; her share fell slowly but it was still
70 per cent in 1890 and 66 per cent in 1913. The inroads made by
foreign competitors—Germany, Belgium and later Japan—were therefore limited, and the British defended their position well. This was
because of the predominance of textiles in India's imports, in which
Lancashire enjoyed a clear superiority, and because British firms
benefited from a quasi-monopoly of the very considerable government
orders for capital equipment.[58]

The other colonies stood between these two extremes. In New
Zealand, where the market was so small that foreign firms had no
interest in establishing themselves, there was little competition and
England still supplied 60 per cent of imports in 1913. Her share of South
Africa's imports, however, fell from 83 per cent in 1881 to 56 per cent in
1913, and of Australia's from 73 per cent to 52 per cent. Altogether the
five dominions took 38 per cent of their imports from Great Britain in
1913, while for the empire as a whole the percentage was 44 per cent.[59]

Foreign competition thus made real progress in imperial markets but,
except in Canada, it was not as severe as the protectionists claimed. And
it was not the sole cause of the relative stagnation in English exports to
the empire. This—at least at the beginning of the twentieth century—
can also be explained by the rapid expansion of British exports to Latin
America and the Far East. It can be explained equally by the fact
that British superiority was concentrated in the textile sector, which
was where demand was growing most slowly. Competition was most
intense in capital goods, world trade in which greatly increased after

1890, and it was in this sector that England's ability to compete had weakened.[60]

This shows the fallacious nature of the propaganda of protectionists and advocates of imperial preference, for the remedies they were proposing would in no way have improved the position of British industry in this critical sector.[61] It might even be maintained, indeed, that the dominant position which England retained in imperial markets had adverse consequences. The ease of access to such outlets, and especially to the unprotected market for textiles in India, dulled the sense of many exporters and turned them away from markets where there was competition. England was encouraged to continue to concentrate on its traditional export lines—textiles and railway material—where expansion was relatively slow, and to neglect new dynamic sectors—machine tools, motor cars, and the electrical equipment industry.[62]

This competition, finally, had a corollary: Britain's industrial competitors did not restrict themselves to selling manufactures to British colonies; they spent far more than they earned in purchasing primary produce, and the development of this multilateral system of trade and payments brought considerable advantages to England.

From about 1890 and especially at the beginning of the twentieth century the pattern of international trade was changing markedly. In particular, in the industrial countries of continental Europe, in the United States and later in Japan there was a rapidly growing need for raw materials, and more and more of these were bought from the British empire, whose production of various primary products had grown faster than the absorptive capacity of the English market: wool from Australia, rubber and tin from Malaya, rice, rape seed and groundnuts, jute sacking, hides and leathers and cotton from India, palm oil from west Africa. Despite their increased sales of manufactures to these areas, the balances of trade of the industrial countries went into a large (and growing) deficit, especially with India and Australia, and also with Malaya, Ceylon and British West Africa. European countries, though, easily made good their deficit with the primary producers by means of the surpluses they enjoyed in their balance of payments with the United States and Great Britain. For its part, the United States made up its deficit with Continental Europe, India and Australia by means of the growing surpluses in its transactions with England and Canada. The latter squared its deficit with the United States through the surplus it enjoyed in trade with Great Britain.

As for Britain, she had deficits in her balance of trade with Continental Europe and the United States, as well as with many areas in the empire: South Africa, east Africa, Ceylon, Malaya, New Zealand and Canada. However, Britain enjoyed large and growing surpluses in her transactions with west Africa, Australia and, most of all, India. It was as a result of these surpluses and of her considerable invisible earnings that Britain's total balance of payments was not in deficit and was even in surplus, and the circle thereby closed.[63]

England was therefore at the centre of this system of multilateral settlements which developed from 1890 onwards[64] and which she found extremely valuable. It had been possible to establish this system, moreover, only because of Britain's policy of free trade, which made her a major importer of manufactures from Europe and the United States, giving them the surpluses with which they could finance their growing imports of primary products without being obliged to increase their direct exports to primary producing countries. This system, then, clearly reduced the competition England might have faced in overseas markets. Had Britain repudiated free trade the other industrial powers would have been forced to look for new sources of supply—in their own colonies, for example—or else to increase their exports to the British empire. Again, by opening her markets to the free importation of primary produce Great Britain encouraged the growth of a number of primary producing countries and thus secured expanding markets for her own manufactured goods. British free-trade policy was therefore essential for the smooth working of the international economy, and in an apparently paradoxical way it protected England from foreign competition in overseas markets.[65]

The advocates of imperial preference, and still more those of an imperial *Zollverein*, overlooked these basic facts. They were also unaware that on the eve of the first World War the British empire was no longer a group of pioneer or underdeveloped areas, heavily dependent on an industrial mother country; from then on its different parts maintained important trading links with foreign countries which it would have been disastrous for them to sever. The idea of even a partial isolation of the empire was chimerical.[66]

Plans for imperial preference, however, were naturally attractive for those countries in the empire which were developing foodstuff exports, the sole market for which was in England—a market which seemed nearly boundless. This was the case with Canada,[67] and even more so with New Zealand, and naturally this small antipodean dominion was particularly empire-minded. Such projects were already less attractive for Australia, whose foodstuff exports were certainly heavily dependent on the British market but which sent very large quantities of wool and metals to France and the United States as well. The same was true for South Africa, whose wool and gold exports to England were in large part re-exported. And finally these projects were without interest for India or for Great Britain herself, dependent far more on foreign markets than on imperial ones.[68]

The smooth working of free trade and the system of multilateral settlements was dependent, however, on at least two conditions, neither of which was to survive the World War. The first was the proven strength of Great Britain's balance of payments, thanks to the considerable invisible earnings which made up the growing deficit on the current account. After 1918 the British balance of payments became fragile, and this put everything in jeopardy. The second condition was the continuing existence of an important surplus in the balance of payments with India; on the eve of 1914, indeed, Great Britain was more and more dependent on this surplus to make up the increasing deficit in her transactions with other countries (in fact India alone made up two-fifths of this deficit). India had thus become the keystone of the British system of payments and of the entire world network of multilateral settlements. Trade with her was thus of considerable advantage to England, all the more so as Indian exports consisted, above all, of raw materials which were in wide demand and freely admitted into most countries. This limited the vexatious effects on Great Britain of the protective tariffs which had been imposed in a number of States at the end of the nineteenth century. As for the Indian market, it was wide open to England's exports, especially her cotton goods—it was indeed the only large market in the world—outside Britain—where there was no tariff protection. This absence of protection is to be explained, of course, by Britain's political control over India. And it is here that one of the principal economic advantages which the possession of the empire conferred on England is to be found. (It is true that in the long run the effects were deleterious because of the over-concentration on cotton goods exports.) In this instance, too, the first World War, by stimulating the rise of the cotton industries of India and Japan, was to be harmful to the British economy.[69]

At all events, the empire was a source of wealth for Great Britain as an open, dynamic system, integrated into the main current of the international economy, and not as a defensive mechanism that would shelter Britain from foreign competition, as the protectionists thought.[70]

This, moreover, was the tendency of all the economic changes in the empire between the introduction of free trade and the first World War, the countries of the empire carrying on more and more of their trade with foreign countries and integrating into the international economy. Thus the tendency to decentralisation which dominated the political evolution of the empire was to be seen equally in the economic sphere.[71]

It is true that the World War and the storm of 1929–31 brought a reversal in this centrifugal tendency and enabled the protectionists to impose their views. The experience, however, showed that the dreams of imperial autarchy and isolation were chimerical. Certainly, during the inter-war period and especially after the Ottawa agreements every Commonwealth country saw a marked increase in the proportion of its foreign trade with other members of the empire. This relative increase resulted, however, from the fall in trade with foreign countries, and the practical results of the Ottawa system were disappointing. As W. K. Hancock has written, the major theme at Ottawa had been imperial *self-sufficiency*; the experience of a few years proved the *self-insufficiency* of the empire.[72]

Is it possible, finally, to perceive some causal relationships between the economic changes just sketched out and changes in British policy towards the empire? There can be no question here of an extensive analysis of this problem, and we shall restrict ourselves to a few remarks, which, however, seem to indicate that the answer is negative.

Much importance has often been attached to the fact that the proportion of British exports that went to the empire increased appreciably at the beginning of the 'great depression'—from 23 per cent in 1871 to 35 per cent in 1877. From this it has been concluded that British businessmen, driven out of foreign markets by the 1873 crisis and the revival of protection, and finding alternative markets in the empire, were promptly converted to a belief in colonial expansion, abandoning the anti-imperialist principles of Cobden and Gladstone (whose first Ministry, from 1868 to 1874, came just at the time when imperial trade was least important for Britain) for the imperialism of Disraeli and later of Chamberlain. But is not this to overestimate the importance of short-term changes in the ratio of imperial to England's total foreign trade that took place around 1870? It overlooks the fact that the ratio goes through a series of fluctuations of a cyclical kind, of which the latter is merely the most marked, that during the years 1853–63 the empire's share of British exports had already reached percentages close to 33 per cent (and even 35 per cent in 1863), that after a maximum in 1886 it fell again until 1895 at the very moment when the tide of imperialist sentiment was rising strongly. Admittedly, the proportion of total exports that went to the empire stood at a higher level after 1875 than during the preceding half century, but the difference was still small.[73] It would be rash to maintain that a change of a few percentage points could have determined or even seriously influenced the state of opinion, let alone British government attitudes. The very widely held view according to which the great depression launched Britain along the road to imperialism is in no way proved, especially since the tendency today is to regard the economic difficulties of the period as not so serious for England as has often been maintained.[74]

Far sounder seems the viewpoint defended by Gallagher and Robinson, two scholars whose recent studies have greatly altered traditional views of British imperialism, and according to whom it is useless to try to link changes in British imperial policy with fluctuations in the British economy, and in exports and terms of trade in particular.[75] Roughly speaking, the analysis we have attempted seems to reinforce the arguments of these two historians.

That trade with the empire always constituted a relatively small part of Britain's total commerce confirms the view that colonial expansion proper, the increase of what Gallagher and Robinson call the 'formal empire', was but one aspect, a function, of a much wider and multi-faceted imperialism, whereby England, the dominant economy in the nineteenth century, extended her ascendancy over, developed for her own benefit and integrated into the international economy overseas underdeveloped countries, some of which were annexed to the 'formal empire' but many of which were only part of an 'informal empire'—the rulers in London invariably showing a preference for methods of informal expansion and only reluctantly having recourse to annexation when it appeared absolutely necessary for the defence of British interests. This being so, a basic continuity can be ascertained in British imperialism all through the nineteenth century, and the traditional division into two major periods—liberal and imperialist—with a sharp break after 1870 seems no longer tenable.[76] All that can be discerned are short-term changes in imperial policy, especially in the policy followed in the various regions of British expansion, which were much more a response to local and international developments than to economic factors in Britain itself or to the promptings of pressure groups. The lack of change in trade and investments in the empire in relation to total British trade and capital exports seems to fit in with Robinson and Gallagher's arguments as well as with other recent studies which have emphasised the decisive role played by strictly political and strategic factors in British expansion in Africa during the last quarter of the nineteenth century.[77]

Several scholars have reminded us that the territories Britain annexed at this time (with the exception of the Transvaal) had but slight economic value and attracted but little investment, and that their trade constituted but an insignificant proportion of imperial trade. Gallagher and Robinson have written that in the competition between colonial powers the best finds and prizes had already been made before the end of the nineteenth century, and in Africa the imperialists 'were scraping the bottom of the barrel'.[78] For his part D. K. Fieldhouse has shown that the supposed need investors had to find outlets for their surplus capital had little to do with the partition of Africa and that the enthusiasm for imperial expansion shown by a large section of British opinion was not determined by economic factors. At the end of the nineteenth century, as during the preceding half century, financiers continued to invest their funds in profitable economic projects, generally in settlement colonies in temperate zones or in the independent 'new countries'. Statesmen, however, spurred on by a public opinion for which the possession of colonies had become a psychological necessity, continued 'to scrape the bottom of the barrel for yet more colonial burdens for the white man to carry'.[79]

Too frequently the 'extensive' annexations of marginal areas of illusory value—desert, steppe, and savanna—which took place at the end of the nineteenth century, over which English opinion enthused and which gave rise to so many disputes with rival powers, make us forget the much more important and lasting achievement of British imperialism at the time: the speeding up of development in the old colonies—Canada, Australasia and India—and of South America in the 'informal' empire.[80] It was this development, greatly stimulated by British capital, which led to a major change in imperial trade and contributed to England's growing wealth.

Note

The present paper, first published in French in 1964, has not been revised. However, several new contributions to the debate on 'imperialism' and its relationship with trade and investment have been made. The Robinson-Gallagher thesis has been criticised in Jean Stengers, 'L'Impérialisme colonial de la fin du 19ᵉ siècle, mythe ou réalité?', *Journal of African History*, III, 1962, pp.469–91; D. C. M. Platt, 'The imperialism of free trade: some reservations', *Economic History Review*, XXI, 1968, pp.296–306, and 'Further objections to an "imperialism of free trade", 1830–60', *Ibid.*, XXVI, 1973, pp.77–91; A. G. Hopkins, 'Economic imperialism in west Africa: Lagos 1880–92', *Economic History Review*, XXI, 1968, pp.580–600; and W. M. Matthew, 'The imperialism of free trade: Peru, 1820–70', *Ibid.*, XXI, 1968, pp.562–79.

The importance of economic factors has been stressed by W. J. Mommsen, 'Nationale und ökonomische Faktoren im Britischen Imperialismus vor 1917', *Historische Zeitschrift*, CCVI, 1968, pp.618–64, and especially by D. C. M. Platt: 'Economic factors in British policy during the "new imperialism" ', *Past and Present*, No. 39, 1968, pp.120–38; *Finance, Trade and Politics in British Foreign Policy, 1814–1914* (Oxford, 1968).

Fieldhouse's interpretation of Hobson, and above all Lenin, on imperialism has been criticised by Eric Stokes, 'Late nineteenth-century expansion and the attack on the theory of economic imperialism', *Historical Journal*, XII, 1969, pp.285–301. Fieldhouse has himself revised some of his views in his *Economics and Empire* (London, 1973).

NOTES

1 [This paper was translated by the editor.]

2 This paper, which arose from an *agrégation* course, has no *raison d'être* other than the absence of a general survey of this problem and is no more than a survey article. Great use has been made of the *Cambridge History of the British Empire* (hereafter abbreviated to *CHBE*), vol. II, *The Growth of the New Empire, 1783–1870* (London, 1940), pp.751–805, 'Free trade and commercial expansion, 1853–70', by H. J. Habakkuk; vol. III, *The Empire–Commonwealth, 1870–1919* (London, 1959), pp.438–89, 'Imperial finance, trade and communications, 1895–1914', by G. S. Graham; and the outstanding study by S. B. Saul, *Studies in British Overseas Trade, 1870–1914*

(Liverpool, 1960). Most of the statistical data is taken from W. Schlote, *British Overseas Trade from 1700 to the 1930s*, translated by W. O. Henderson and W. H. Chaloner (Oxford, 1952), especially tables 20–5 in the appendix; see also B. R. Mitchell and P. Deane, *Abstract of British Historical Statistics* (Cambridge, 1962). In the text the terms England, Great Britain and the United Kingdom have been used as synonymous and the word 'Colonies' applied to any British possession.

[3] *CHBE*, II, pp.759–61 and 764.

[4] *Ibid.*, p.772.

[5] As well as spices, rice, cocoa, jute and tin, though imports of these were small.

[6] The range of goods exported by each part of the empire (with the exception of India) was also very limited and generally dominated by only one item: in 1854 timber made up 82 per cent of Britain's imports from the North American colonies; wool 82 per cent of those from Australasia and 72 per cent of those from the Cape and Natal, proof that the colonial economies were still very much 'undeveloped'.

[7] *CHBE*, II, p.769.

[8] These colonies' share of England's imperial trade had greatly increased since 1830: they took 21 per cent of British exports to the empire in 1827–30, 31 per cent in 1837–40, 47 per cent in 1854–7 (Schlote, *op. cit.*, pp.91–2 and 97).

[9] *CHBE*, II, pp.754 and 780.

[10] Saul, *op. cit.*, pp.209–10.

[11] D. L. Stamp and S. H. Beaver, *The British Isles: a Geographic and Economic Survey* (London, 3rd edition, 1947), p.207.

[12] Saul, *op. cit.*, p.29. In 1909–13 the United Kingdom imported, on average, 6,060,000 tons of wheat and wheaten flour every year, 998,000 tons of meat and 212,000 tons of butter. Cf. P. Lamartine Yates, *Forty Years of Foreign Trade* (London, 1959), pp.70, 80 and 84.

[13] See, especially, M. E. Fletcher, 'The Suez canal and world shipping, 1869–1914', *Journal of Economic History*, XVIII, 4, December 1958, pp.556–73.

[14] Douglass North, 'Ocean freight rates and economic development, 1760–1913', *ibid.*, pp.537–55; *CHBE*, II, pp.762–5; Saul, *op. cit.*, pp.188 and 210.

[15] The stimulating discussion by Albert Demangeon on the role of the railway in British colonisation should be remembered (*L'Empire Britannique, étude de géographie coloniale* (Paris, 1929), pp.93, 599); also *CHBE*, III, p.466.

[16] Saul, *op. cit.*, p.208, 210; *CHBE*, II, p.754.

[17] H. H. Segal and M. Simon, 'British foreign capital issues, 1865–94', *Journal of Economic History*, vol. XXI, No. 4, December 1961, pp.566–81, 576. These investments were made, above all, through colonial government loans, which absorbed 70 per cent of funds invested in the empire during this period and which were used to establish its economic infrastructure (see also *CHBE*, II, pp.792–3, 795–6). We should not, however, overlook the article by J. D. Bailey, 'Australian borrowing in Scotland in the nineteenth century', *Economic History Review*, vol. XII, No. 2, December 1959, pp.268–79, which shows that the Australian land companies borrowed considerable funds in Scotland, through the mediation of solicitors, without using the London Stock Exchange.

[18] Saul, pp.65–6, 206, 211–13.

[19] Saul, pp.69–70; *CHBE*, II, pp.799–801, 804; A. K. Cairncross, *Home and Foreign Investment, 1870–1913. Studies in Capital Formation* (Cambridge, 1958), especially, pp.2, 225, 232–3. This author admits that foreign investment was made at the expense of home investment but he nevertheless considers it 'paying', the necessary concomitant of the economic development of England and an essential factor in the rising *per capita* income that took place during this period. To invest in countries producing primary produce was in fact to invest in the primary sector of the British economy itself; besides, it was the means whereby the powerful process of growth in Britain was transmitted to the underdeveloped countries. It might be added that British loans to the colonies were in large part used in direct purchases of English goods, though this is not trueof the capital invested in Canada on the eve of 1914, which was in fact used to purchase capital goods in the United States.

[20] *CHBE*, II, pp.787–91; Saul, pp.10 and 99; Segal and Simon, p.572.

[21] Cairncross, p.183; Saul, p.67. According to Cairncross, the empire's share of total investments rose from 34 per cent in 1870 to 52 per cent in 1885. But some of his

figures have been invalidated by the more recent calculations of A. H. Imlah, *Economic Elements of the Pax Britannica, Studies in British Foreign Trade in the Nineteenth Century* (Cambridge, Mass., 1958), pp.72–5.

[22] *Op. cit.*, pp.572, 574 and 579. See also *CHBE*, II, p.788: as early as 1850–75 the empire took 40 per cent of foreign investments. Again, between 1910 and 1913 'imperial' share issues on the London market constituted 43 per cent of total overseas issues (A. E. Kahn, *Great Britain in the World Economy* (New York, 1940, p.139). For the years 1907–13 the proportion was 48 per cent according to *CHBE*, III, p.488.

[23] The latter went through two long cycles, 1867–77 and 1877–92, with peaks in 1874 and 1889.

[24] As will be seen below, this confirms Saul's thesis (pp.110 and 112–14), according to which Great Britain succeeded in partly insulating herself and her Empire from the worst effects of economic crises during the last quarter of the nineteenth century by redirecting her foreign investments.

[25] Detailed figures in Saul, p.67; W. K. Hancock, *Survey of British Commonwealth Affairs*, vol. II, *Problems of Economic Policy, 1918–1939*, part 1 (London, 1940), p.27, n. 1. The distribution of these investments was as follows (£ million):

Canada	515	India	379
Australia	332	Malaya	28
New Zealand	84	West Africa	37
South Africa	370	Other colonies	35
Total	1,301	*Total*	479

[26] This seems to invalidate the argument that the need to invest surplus capital was the motor of British expansion at the end of the nineteenth century. It might be noted, furthermore, that the returns on colonial government bonds and on shares in railways in the empire (which took the greater part of imperial investments) were only marginally higher than those on similar stock at home. See Cairncross, pp.226–31; Imlah, p.61; *CHBE*, II, pp.802–3. See also W. J. Macpherson, 'Investment in Indian railways, 1845–75', *Economic History Review*, vol. VIII, No. 2, December 1955, pp.177–86, which shows that investors were attracted, above all, by the 5 per cent guaranteed interest that Indian railway bonds enjoyed.

[27] Saul, *op. cit.*, pp.171–2, 177, 194–5, and 210; *CHBE*, III, pp.460–1. In contrast, the empire supplied only a very tiny proportion of the large-scale imports of cheaper cereals (mostly maize from Argentina).

[28] Saul, *op. cit.*, pp.28, 172–3 and 178; *CHBE*, III, pp.209–10. In 1913 Australia and New Zealand provided 23 per cent of world trade in meat (Yates, p.81).

[29] This rise was particularly rapid following the reversal of the trend in agricultural prices in 1896.

[30] *Per capita* consumption doubled between 1847 and 1866—tea had become the chief working-class drink.

[31] Saul, *op. cit.*, p.197; *CHBE*, II, pp.772–3 and III, p.462; C. E. Carrington, *The British Overseas: Exploits of a Nation of Shopkeepers* (Cambridge, 1950), pp.460–1.

[32] Yates, *op. cit.*, pp.113–14 and 246; K. Stahl, *The Metropolitan Organisation of British Colonial Trade* (London, 1951), pp.8–9.

[33] Malaya became the world's leading tin producer in 1883 (Stahl, p.110). Large-scale smelting works were set up there from 1887 onwards. The Empire also supplied England with lead and copper, though the exploitation of the Northern Rhodesian copper belt began only in the inter-war period. Besides, Australia and Canada sold almost the whole of their zinc, silver and nickel production direct to foreign countries—the United States, Germany and Belgium (*CHBE*, III, pp.463–464).

[34] The trade in cocoa, fruit and hides and leather might also be mentioned. For cocoa the proportion of British imports provided by the empire remained steady, at about a half, but at the beginning of the twentieth century the Gold Coast replaced Ceylon and the West Indies as the chief supplier.

[35] £4,635,000 in 1875 (the peak) and £698,000 in 1913.

[36] *CHBE*, III, pp.214–15. There was also competition from foreign cane sugar—chiefly from Cuba and Java. S. B. Saul, 'The economic significance of "constructive imperialism" ', *Journal of Economic History*, XVII, 2, June 1957, pp.176–9, describes

the vain efforts of Joseph Chamberlain to revive West Indian exports to England. These, however, found alternative markets first in the United States and later in Canada, and Jamaica turned to growing bananas which the United Fruit Company exported to the United States.

[37] Saul, *op. cit.*, p.174; *CHBE*, II, p.767.

[38] Schlote, *op. cit.*, p.94. At the same time the export structure of several colonies changed radically. The clearest case is that of India, with the decline of indigo, sugar and spices and the rise of wheat, tea, jute, vegetable oils, etc.

[39] These nine items made up 64 per cent of imports from the empire (the percentages given above are rounded numbers).

[40] As a result of the growth of direct exports to foreign countries. In 1913 only 24 per cent of India's exports went to Great Britain.

[41] Although the first plantations were set up before 1914, only during the inter-war period did British East Africa begin to export significant quantities of coffee, sisal, cotton, etc.

[42] Schlote, *op. cit.*, p.89.

[43] It is estimated that the empire provided about 14 per cent of Great Britain's total foodstuff requirements at this time. If non-tropical foodstuffs only are considered, the empire supplied 36 per cent of imports in 1907, which was 19 per cent of consumption as against 33 per cent from countries outside the empire and 48 per cent from home production (Stamp and Beaver, *loc. cit.*).

[44] Saul, *op. cit.*, pp.222–3.

[45] The re-export trade in produce from the empire, considerable in the middle of the nineteenth century, had suffered from the opening of the Suez Canal which enabled European countries to open up direct trading links with the Far East. It saw a brisk expansion after 1900, however, especially to the United States which took a great deal of tin and rubber from England. From this there resulted an intensification of multilateral settlements (see below). Saul, *op. cit.*, pp.59 and 225; *CHBE*, II, pp.761–2.

[46] In fact there was a marked reduction in its share in the 1860s, then a strong recovery after 1874.

[47] Figures from Schlote, *op. cit.*, table 20b, pp.161–3; see also his graph XIII, p.91 and Saul, *op. cit.*, pp.213–15.

[48] Saul, *op. cit.*, pp.98–9, 101 and 103–5. However, he also notes the impact of harvests, especially on exports to India and Australia (p.210); and Cairncross (p. 197) asserts that India's demand for textiles depended more on harvests than investments.

[49] Saul, *op. cit.*, pp.110 and 112–14. This mechanism operated to the full during the 'great depression', after 1873, because the opening of the Suez Canal had improved the economic prospects of India and Australia, thus stimulating investment in these countries.

[50] At the time this was divided into several autonomous circuits of multilateral settlements which were linked only through England. By redirecting their investments British capitalists could prevent a crisis from spreading from one circuit to another.

[51] Saul, *op. cit.*, pp.107, 109, 114–15, 117 and 120–1.

[52] *Ibid.*, pp.129–31.

[53] Schlote, *op. cit.*, pp.89–91. Saul, moreover, points out that the increase in the empire's share on the eve of the first World War resulted solely from very high—and abnormal—cotton goods exports to India in 1912–13, without which this share would in fact have fallen.

[54] Schlote, pp.166–7, table 22 and p.104. For iron and steel products the empire's share rose from a third in the middle of the nineteenth century to nearly half in 1913. On the other hand, a marked reduction in cotton yarns, a consequence of the rise of the Indian cotton industry, should be noted. It was the rapid growth of British coal exports between 1860 and 1913, of which the empire took but an insignificant proportion, which is the chief explanation for the relatively small increase in total exports to British possessions.

[55] See Hancock, p.81, n. 1, for a continuous series of quinquennial averages which shows that the empire's share in Great Britain's total trade reaches a peak, at 28·3 per cent, in 1861–5 (as a result of imports of Indian cotton during the American

civil war), and a low, at 22·7 per cent, in 1871–5; in 1906–10 it was 26 per cent. These figures show a remarkable stability.

[56] It was increased by over two million square miles between 1880 and 1900.

[57] Saul, *op. cit.*, pp.174–6 and 180–3. After 1872, moreover, there was a stagnation and even a fall in English exports to Canada.

[58] *Ibid.*, pp.198–200 and 203.

[59] *Ibid.*, pp.215–17; *CHBE*, III, p.483; Hancock, *op. cit.*, pp.306–11.

[60] Saul, *op. cit.*, pp.218–19. In 1913, however, US exports of machinery to the empire, excluding Canada, were only a quarter of those from Britain (*ibid.*, p.36).

[61] Saul (p.22) points out that they confused the undeniable usefulness of protection for infant industries with its much more doubtful value for mature or stagnant industries.

[62] Saul, *op. cit.*, pp.220 and 229.

[63] This summarises drastically the analysis in Saul, *op. cit.*, chapters III and IV, pp.43–89 (see especially pp.43–5, 48, 50, 52–7, 60–1, 171, 186 and his very useful diagram, p.58). An earlier version of this study appeared as 'Britain and world trade, 1870–1914', *Economic History Review*, VII, 1, August 1954, pp.49–66. Other primary producers—Argentina, Brazil, Turkey and China—also played a role in this schema which is described as it functioned circa 1910.

[64] Saul considers that previously only a series of multilateral 'schemas', each rather isolated from the others, had existed (see above).

[65] Saul, *op. cit.*, pp.63 and 221; W. Ashworth, *A Short History of the International Economy, 1850–1950* (London, 1952), pp.166–7.

[66] In 1913 total exports from empire countries (including precious metals) stood at £575 million; of this Great Britain took £238 million, but as she re-exported almost all the precious metals and 29 per cent of the merchandise, her net imports of imperial goods were no more than a quarter of total imports and 20·5 per cent of her retained imports (Saul, p.225). She took 90 per cent of the exports of the Union of South Africa (though almost all the gold and all the wool were re-exported), 80 per cent of New Zealand's exports, 50 per cent of Canada's, 45 per cent of Australia's and only 24 per cent of India's.

[67] Besides, Canadians saw in such a system a means of ensuring their independence from the United States. Consequently, this dominion was the driving force behind the campaign for imperial preference.

[68] Saul, *op. cit.*, pp.185–6 and 226–9.

[69] *Ibid.*, pp.61–3, 88–9, 188, 203–6, 221 and 228. Saul considers that the growth of industry in the dominions had hardly any effect on England's trade.

[70] Saul (pp.228–9) finds that, all things considered, the empire was a source of great strength for Great Britain and that France suffered from not having a similar outlet especially for her investments, since three-quarters of those went direct to foreign governments. In any case, the greatest advantages were of an indirect kind, linked with the sale throughout the world of primary produce from the empire, which ensured the smooth working of international trade, including Great Britain's.

[71] True, as a result of the large-scale investments of British capital in the colonies, their economies were in large part permanently controlled from the offices in the City where the railway, banking, plantation, mining and other companies had their headquarters; but Habakkuk has pointed out that this partnership did not bring about any crisis between mother country and colonies, whereas the first British empire had broken up over the problem of economic relations (*CHBE*, II, pp.798–9 and 804–5).

[72] Hancock, *op. cit.*, p.266; see also my *Économie du Commonwealth* (Paris, 1950), pp. 124–9.

[73] If the different types of manufactured goods are considered, we find that between 1870 and 1880, the proportion of exports that went to the empire increased significantly only for railway material. For textiles and the remaining metallurgical products the percentages barely changed.

[74] See, especially, A. E. Musson, 'British industrial growth during the "great depression" (1873–96). Some comments', *Economic History Review*, XV, 3, April 1963, pp. 529–33. The author reconsiders some of the opinions he had earlier expressed in

'The great depression in Britain, 1873–96: a reappraisal', *Journal of Economic History*, XIX, 2, June 1959, pp.199–228.

75 R. Robinson and J. Gallagher, 'The imperialism of free trade', *Economic History Review*, VI, 1953, p.6. See also their subsequent book, *Africa and the Victorians* (London, 1961), a remarkable analysis of decision-making in the partition of Africa, based on a great deal of varied archival material.

76 O. Macdonagh, 'The anti-imperialism of free trade', *Economic History Review*, XIV, 3, April 1962, pp.489–501, suggests some slight modifications to this, for, while he admits there were clear manifestations of imperialism during the Palmerston era in the middle of the nineteenth century, he emphasises the hostility of authentic free-traders to this policy. On the other hand, Robinson and Gallagher themselves recognise changes in imperial policy after 1870.

77 Especially D. K. Fieldhouse, 'Imperialism: an historiographical revision', *Economic History Review*, XIV, 2, December 1961, pp.87–209; D. S. Landes, 'Some thoughts on the nature of economic imperialism', *Journal of Economic History*, XXI, 4, December 1961, pp.496–512; R. J. Hammond, 'Economic imperialism: sidelights on a stereotype', *Ibid.*, pp.582–98. According to Robinson and Gallagher the English government was compelled to undertake large-scale intervention in Africa as a result of the crises that broke out in Egypt and South Africa and which it was feared would endanger the safety of the route to India. It sought, therefore, not to build a new African empire or to grab Africa's trade, but simply to defend the long-standing Indian empire. Fieldhouse, in contrast, stresses the importance of inter-national rivalries in Europe and of Bismarck's decision to annex African territories. Hammond suggests that if Joseph Chamberlain laid great stress on the economic benefits of colonial expansion, it was in order to win over Birmingham businessmen (pp.594–6). His plans were, however, primarily political.

78 'The imperialism of free trade', *loc. cit.*, p.15.

79 Fieldhouse, *op. cit.*, pp.207–8 and also pp.189–90, where he points out J. A. Hobson's conjuring trick (in his famous work of 1902, *Imperialism: a study*, frequently used afterwards, notably by Lenin), where a list of territories England annexed after 1870 is placed side by side with a table showing the increase in foreign investment, without any analysis of its distribution.

80 Gallagher and Robinson, 'The imperialism of free trade', *loc. cit.*, p.15.

S. E. Katzenellenbogen

10

British businessmen and German Africa, 1885–1919

Although German interest in the profitable exploitation of Africa's commercial potential and natural resources was expressed as early as 1864, it was only when considerations of international prestige and domestic politics made it seem important for the German empire to have colonies that Bismarck decided to join the European powers in dividing Africa among themselves.[1] Germany was no different from the other major governments involved in the 'scramble' in not wanting to provide direct government support for the activities of businessmen trying to open up the interior of the continent to 'legitimate' trade, while at the same time being prepared to use those activities for political advantage. Once Germany's territorial claims had been made, no German government was prepared to allow whatever economic advantages might accrue from them to pass into foreign hands if it was at all possible to avoid this. As a latecomer to the 'scramble' Germany was able to secure only coastal areas not already specifically claimed: areas that were relatively unpromising as fields of potential development, and not attractive to cautious German investors. Foreign commercial interests, particularly from Britain and from parts of the British empire, were already well established in the German areas, and were often prepared to compete actively for the extension of their operations into the interior, or to resist the imposition of German rule. In other cases British traders were content to enjoy the advantages they had without going too far out of their way to extend them.

In the Camerouns, for example, British traders were active in parts of the interior as well as on the coast, continuing to dominate the country's trade for many years after the German annexation. British commerce was less extensive in Togoland, but continued to benefit for many years from the superior harbour facilities available in the neighbouring Gold Coast and from the customs union in force between the two colonies from 1894 to 1904.[2] It was in East and South West Africa, however, that the conflict between British and German business interests was greatest and the interaction of economic and political forces most complex.

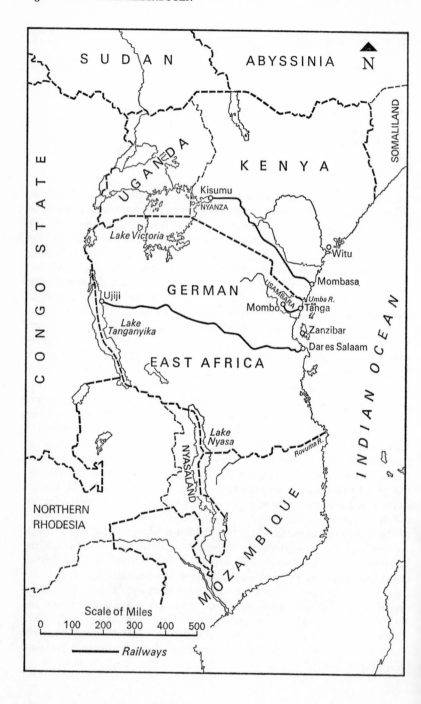

The interior of East Africa was long believed to be a source of tremendous wealth. Enthusiastic explorers spoke in glowing terms of the profit to be gained from opening the area to trade other than that carried on by the Arabs in slaves. Concrete support for this enthusiasm was conspicuously lacking. None of the men urging governments and businessmen to move into the region had carefully considered the problems of transport and other fundamental economic questions, or the many political issues involved. Baron Carl von der Decken had thought that considerable advantage would accrue to Prussia from the establishment of a colony there, but when in 1870 the Sultan of Zanzibar offered the German empire a protectorate over his country, which nominally included much of the east African mainland, the German government did not even bother to reply.[3] Official support for the colonial idea was slow to come.

In 1882 the Colonial Society (Kolonial Verein) was formed to promote interest in Germany's acquisition of colonies. Within three years it had 10,000 members. In 1884 Carl Peters went a step further, founding the Company for German Colonisation (Gesellschaft für deutsche Kolonisation) with the aim of finding money for colonial enterprises in East Africa. Rivalry between the two groups led to their amalgamation in 1887 as the German Colonial Company. (Deutsche Kolonialgesellschaft). The membership of the combined group did not rise above about 16,000 until the 1920s, when it was reorganised, increasing its membership substantially but remaining unable to 'carry colonial enthusiasm into the masses'.[4]

In November 1884 Peters arrived in East Africa with three companions and began making treaties in the interior. By the end of February 1885 he was back in Berlin, a German protectorate over the areas covered by his treaties was declared, and a charter, granting remarkably unrestricted rights, was awarded the Society for German Colonisation, which was reorganised into the German East Africa Company (Deutsch Ost-Afrika Gesellschaft).[5] The speed with which this was accomplished rather contradicted Bismarck's professed opposition to Peters's trip. The chancellor obviously considered it in his wider political interests at the time to take advantage of what Peters had done, and to establish a German claim in East Africa even more firmly by formally declaring a protectorate over the Witu district, just north of the Tana river, where the Denhardt brothers had negotiated a concession.[6] The British Foreign Office was initially stirred to give greater consideration than they had done previously to ideas put forward by William Mackinnon, a major figure in Indian trade and shipping, for the establishment of British enterprise in East Africa, but nothing concrete along these lines was done. Instead a policy of co-operation with Germany was followed, a commission being set up to delimit the two

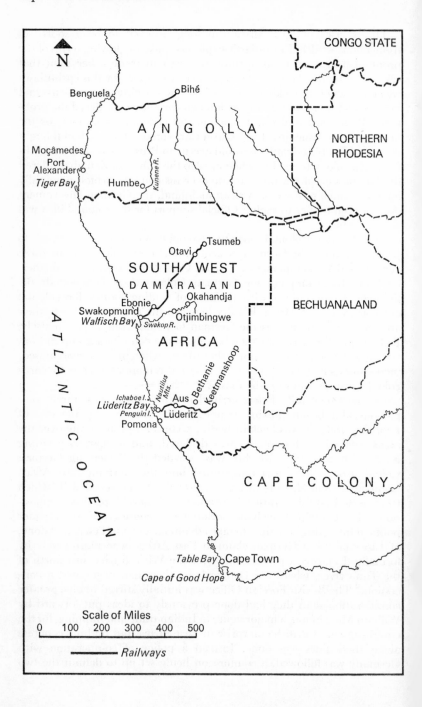

countries' respective spheres of interest. In November 1886 a British sphere was recognised north of a line drawn from the Umba river to Lake Victoria, a German sphere south of the line. The southern limit of the German sphere was set at the Rovuma river, a small area going to Germany at the expense of Portuguese territory in Mozambique. It was only when the British government felt its control of the Nile headwaters and Egypt to be threatened that Mackinnon's scheme was taken up and, in September 1888, a charter granted to his Imperial British East Africa Company. By this time Bismarck had withdrawn his support from Peters, whose 'impractical fantasies' he feared would prove very costly, and damaging to the spirit of Anglo–German co-operation.[7]

Peters was also having difficulty reaching agreement with his financial backers, Hansing & Co. and William O'Swald of Hamburg, O'Swald having been a well established trader at Zanzibar for many years. While Peters had grandiose ideas about extending the company's operations into the interior and spent much time and money trying to conclude further treaties, the hard-headed businessmen wanted to see a more solid foundation created, upon which expansion could be firmly based. This conflict delayed the final incorporation of the German East Africa Company until 1887.[8] It seems that in an attempt to retain his independence from Hansing and O'Swald Peters approached Mackinnon in 1886 to try to secure British capital for his activities. Mackinnon and his associates were not in principle unwilling to co-operate with Peters, although Mackinnon was later to become a strong Germanophobe, but they did not see that amalgamation with Peters would be any more advantageous to them than their own plans, and possibly less.[9]

With his scope for freedom of action limited by the way in which the German East Africa Company was finally organised, Peters did begin to set up stations along the coast in 1887. He and his agents rapidly acquired reputations for harsh treatment of the local residents, and of insensitivity to the feelings of those, whether African or Arab, who considered themselves worthy of some respect. In August 1888 a revolt led by Abushiri ibn Salim al-Harthi broke out and met with considerable success, being put down only in 1891 by the direct intervention of the German government. Peters was replaced as the company's representative in East Africa by Ernst Vohsen, whose approach to Africans was much more humanitarian, and the German government was forced to assume direct control of its East African colony.[10]

There was in fact very little in the way of natural resources in East Africa to attract investment, certainly not enough to generate sufficient trade and revenues to enable the German East Africa Company (or indeed the imperial British East Africa Company, operating in part of the British sphere) to cover the cost of establishing and maintaining even the most rudimentary administrative system and at the same time remain commercially viable. The economic development that did take place was limited, and was based almost entirely on tropical agricultural products, the cultivation of which was in German hands.

One exception to this was the British group of companies, already experienced in rubber production elsewhere in the world, which in 1909 began buying up rubber plantations from Germans who had enjoyed considerable benefits from the world rubber boom that had begun in 1905. The Germans sold at the right time; by 1910 the boom was ending and the new British owners found themselves in difficult financial straits. They tried to secure British government support for an approach to the German government to enable them to obtain labour more cheaply, thus reducing production costs. In view of the rather poor reputation for labour relations the Germans then had, the Foreign Office thought it best not to interfere. Even cheaper labour could not overcome the basic problem; the hevea rubber produced in Malaya was of much higher quality than East Africa's cerea variety, and was therefore in much greater demand.[11]

The greatest British impact on the economy of German East Africa was indirect and, to a certain extent, negative. The Uganda Railway, for example, by providing relatively cheap, dependable transport facilities, assisted the development of the Victoria, Nyanza and Usumbara regions, and by proving that a railway could improve trade also provided some of the greater impetus needed to bring forward German support for rail lines from Tango to Mombo and from Dar es Salaam to Lake Tanganyika. The way in which British businessmen made their presence most strongly felt in German East Africa was through the threat of the Cape-to-Cairo railway—the mythical transport route that would have enabled a person to board a train in Cairo and emerge from it some days later in Cape Town. Why anyone should have wanted to do this was never explained.

The idea of such a line was not originated by Cecil Rhodes but it was he, more than anyone else, who popularised it, mesmerised the long-suffering shareholders of the British South Africa Company (hereafter referred to as Chartered) with the prospect of the realisation of the 'dream', and convinced a number of otherwise quite sensible people that such a line could and would be built. Rhodes never gave any clear indication of why the Cape-to-Cairo railway was needed or how it could be expected to pay when the Atlantic and Indian Oceans already provided cheap north–south transport routes for Africa. What was needed, and what was more or less built, was a system of railways linking sources of traffic in the interior to coastal ports. The fact that there was no economic justification for the Cape-to-Cairo line did not prevent Rhodes and Mackinnon, who was as strong or stronger a proponent of it, from making it something of a bogy for the Germans, who were afraid, not without some justification, that if it were ever built it would drain much of the trade of the interior into British-controlled territory to the north and south, redounding to the benefit of British merchants and shippers.[12]

When the Anglo–German treaty of 1890, in which a number of outstanding questions between Germany and Britain in Africa were resolved, was being negotiated, Mackinnon urged Salisbury to provide for a Cape-to-Cairo corridor of British territory through which the railway could be built. Salisbury knew the Germans would never accept this, and, rather than jeopardise relations with Germany, refused. To pacify Mackinnon and the popular support his plans enjoyed, Salisbury said he saw no reason why Mackinnon could not come to some agreement with King Leopold for the acquisition of such a corridor through the Independent Congo State.[13] This view was not conveyed to the Germans, who thought that as the treaty recognised their western boundary as being contiguous with the eastern boundary of the Congo State, the Cape-to-Cairo threat had been eliminated. They were wrong. In 1896 Britain and the Congo State concluded an agreement which settled the boundary between the Congo State and Chartered territory, gave Leopold access to the Nile, at least in theory, and gave the British a lease on a 20 km strip of land in the Congo State connecting British territory north and south of German East Africa. Germany protested vociferously against this provision, and as neither the British nor Leopold were prepared to press the point, it was abrogated.[14]

Rhodes continued to press for permission to build the line through German territory, but without success. He was able to secure the right to construct the Cape-to-Cairo telegraph line. Negotiations on behalf of the African Transcontinental Telegraph Company began in February 1899, but were delayed for a time while von Bülow tried, unsuccessfully, to interest German capitalists in building the German section instead. By September tentative agreement had been reached, but the Germans wanted to extract as much as possible from Rhodes. They apparently asked him to use his influence to secure British support for German aspirations in Samoa, but it is not clear whether Rhodes did anything in this connection. He did bring to the attention of the Foreign Office another point the Germans wanted to settle, permission to land their submarine telegraph cable at Waterville as well as at Valentia on the west coast of Ireland.[15] The most important condition attached to the telegraph agreement was that Chartered should not link its railways in Rhodesia to the west coast of Africa north of 14° south latitude unless such a link had already been created through German South West Africa.[16]

One of the central figures in the negotiations for the telegraph agreement was Edmund (later Sir Edmund) Davis, who is one of the least-known men heavily involved in the economic development of southern and central Africa. Of French extraction, Davis was born in Australia in 1854. After being educated in England he went to Paris to study painting, until illness led him to Cape Town to work in his uncle's trading firm, Bensusan & Co. He stayed with his uncle for a number of years, but did not limit his activities to this. He was one of the first diamond buyers to reach Kimberley, where he met most of the 'Diamond Club', and came to play a major role in the development of South West Africa. His first contacts with that territory seem to have been the leases he acquired to some of the guano islands about 1874, but his close involvement in the area probably arose from his links with German financiers. In the early 1890s he moved to London, to be near the London bases of the South African diamond and gold magnates. With a German named Wertheimer he set up the firm of Jacob Picard & Co. He became a close friend of the Hamburg shipping magnate, Ballin, who in turn was very close to the emperor. Davis was also said to have had the ear of von Richthofen, through whom the telegraph negotiations had been carried on, and had the reputation of being a man of considerable influence in Germany's higher political and financial circles. Ironically, although Davis spoke English and French, he never learned German.

It is surprising that so little is known about Davis. At one time he controlled virtually all the world's principal sources of chrome through his holdings in Rhodesia, Baluchistan and New Caledonia. With Lord Gifford and George Cawston he formed the Bechuanaland Exploration Company and entered into direct competition with Cecil Rhodes in his attempts to secure a charter to administer and exploit central Africa. Rhodes absorbed this competition, but although biographies of Rhodes and histories of the region discuss the role played in those early developments by Gifford and Cawston, they generally make no mention of Davis at all. He is mentioned in connection with the development of Northern Rhodesia's mineral resources, in which his role was of prime importance, but on his activities before the first World War very little information is available. Yet Davis was definitely a man to be reckoned with: at one time a director of fifty-two companies, forty of them in the mining field, he was the most important single representative of British capital involved in the economic development of German South West Africa.[17]

Economic links between the Cape and South West Africa have roots as far back as the late seventeenth century, when the Dutch East India Company first sent ships to explore the possibility of opening up trade along the coast west of their Cape base. Nothing came of this or of the expeditions sent in the latter half of the eighteenth century in response to rumours of the existence of gold, because this section of the coast appeared to be of no value, except in so far as its harbours were useful in connection with sealing and whaling in the southern Atlantic. The fear that this might lead to annexation by other powers prompted the Dutch company to lay formal claim to all the harbours between the Cape and Walfisch Bay in 1793. When, two years later, Britain annexed the Cape for the first time, scant attention was paid these coastal claims.[18]

It was the guano islands off the coast that first attracted Cape merchants in the 1840s. The potential of this nitrate-rich fertiliser had not been appreciated when an American sealing schooner had first found them, but in 1842 a Liverpool broker, John Rae, began exploiting them. In December 1845 Benjamin Wade annexed Ichaboe, the richest of the islands, in the Queen's name, but was not acting officially. Something of a guano rush began, particularly to Ichaboe, where the deposits were between ten and forty feet deep. Up to 300 vessels were anchored around the island at the same time, and one has the rather bizarre picture of rival collectors pelting one another with rotten penguin eggs before resorting to more lethal if less odiferous weapons. Order was finally maintained by a frigate from the Cape. Although the guano found there was not as valuable as that exported from Peru, some 300,000 tons of it were removed from Ichaboe in 1844–5 and sent to Britain, where it was sold at a profit of £2 per ton. It was only after the initial clearing that Cape traders became involved in the guano trade other than as suppliers of provisions for collectors. Other islands were found, and guano remained a major export for several decades. The Cape firm most prominent in this trade was A. & E. de Pass, later De Pass Spence & Co., who for some time enjoyed monopoly rights. The island were later annexed by Britain and administered by the Cape government, which assigned leases by auction.[19]

For several decades the European presence in mainland South West Africa was maintained by small traders, and primarily by missionaries, the area, along with South Africa, having been the first field of Protestant mission activity on the continent. A German missionary founded a station at Bethanie for the London Missionary Society in 1814 and moved northwards into Damaraland. Methodists were also active, and in 1865 the Rhenish Missionary Society, which had been working in the Transvaal for some forty years, took over the LMS and Methodists' stations north of the Orange river. As was so often the case in Africa, the missionaries felt that the introduction of a trading economy was essential for introducing Africans to 'civilisation'. Missionaries themselves often engaged in commerce, trying to overcome what they considered the unscrupulous methods used by many traders. The Rhenish Missionary Society was particularly disturbed by the impact of the sale of alcohol and in 1864 began to trade on its own account. Six years later it formed the Mission Trading Company (Missionhandelgesellschaft) to carry on this enterprise separately from its spiritual pursuits. The newly formed company, which had to pay half its profits to the Society, proved quite successful.

In order to introduce the Nama and Herero peoples—two of the major groups with which the missions were in contact—to an economic system where they remained settled on the land rather than continuing their life as nomads, constantly in search of new pastures, and thereby constantly coming into conflict, the Society tried to achieve some measure of peace between them. Whatever peace it did achieve was tenuous at best, and conflict between the Herero and Nama, complicated by the presence of other, smaller groups also competing for land, remained for many decades a disruptive force in the development of trade, as well as making it very difficult for the Germans, when they took over South West Africa, to establish their authority.[20]

The period 1842–63 was one of relative calm between the Herero and Nama, making it possible for trade to flourish. De Pass Spence & Co., established several fisheries along the coast and became one of the major participants in the country's trade in ivory, ostrich feathers, cattle, hides and general merchandise. There is no way of knowing the total value of trade between the Cape and South West Africa at this time; figures are available only for goods imported and exported through Table Bay.[21] A large proportion passed overland, estimates of its extent varying widely. It is clear that this South West African trade was fairly profitable for those Cape merchants engaged in it, and that they would be loath to abandon it. Even as late as 1903, when exports from South West Africa began to find their way increasingly to Germany, some 70 per cent of exports were destined for the Cape, and a further 12·2 per cent for Britain.[22]

The discovery of copper, initially in the south—in Namaland—and later in several other areas, aroused considerable interest in the Cape and generally stimulated trade. During the 1850s and early 1860s many concessions were obtained from African chiefs and companies formed to exploit the deposits. Working expenses, particularly after the richer ores nearer the surface had been depleted, and the cost of transporting minerals to the coast or overland to the Cape were so high that all the companies operated at a loss. Trading reached a peak in 1870, and although it began thereafter to fall off sharply, it is not surprising that there was growing pressure for the British government—or the Cape government itself—to annex South West Africa rather than leave it as an unofficial part of the Cape's natural hinterland. This pressure was rather diffuse and never found sufficiently coherent expression to make the matter an important item of Cape or British government policy. The Cape government did send an envoy to the Herero in 1876 to negotiate an agreement for the declaration of a Cape protectorate over Damaraland, but this was rejected by the Cape Assembly. The British government would go no further than to annex Walfisch Bay in 1878.[23]

In the 1870s moves to develop the copper mines were once again gathering strength as traders sought new sources of income. Again it was primarily Cape-based people who showed the greatest interest, but Germans also became involved in prospecting. F. A. Hasenclever financed an expedition to search for copper and to obtain concessions if anything of value was found. By mid-1883, although a number of workable deposits had been located, it was clear that the companies formed to exploit them had neither sufficient facilities nor adequate capital to continue operations. Into what was a rather chaotic economic situation stepped Adolf Lüderitz, formerly a Bremen tobacco merchant, more recently a trader at Lagos, who was to start the chain of events leading to Germany's declaration of a protectorate over South West Africa.

Early in 1883 Lüderitz and Heinrich Vogelsang, who had previously been employed by a Cape firm, set up a trading post at Angra Pequeña (later Lüderitz Bay) and another inland at Bethanie. Vogelsang, on Lüderitz's behalf, bought the bay and a five-mile strip of land surrounding it from the Nama, who claimed ownership of it, and a twenty-mile strip of coast from the Orange river—the Cape Colony's frontier—and 26° south latitude. De Pass Spence & Co. protested vigorously against Lüderitz's action, prompting him to seek the protection of the German government. There followed a series of misunderstandings on the part of the Cape, British and German governments which ended on 22 August 1884 when Germany announced that she was establishing a protectorate over the entire South West African coast from the Orange river to the Angola border.[24] A joint commission was set up to delineate British and German interests in the area, to determine the ownership of the guano islands, only some of which Britain had formally annexed, and to settle the claims to land and mining rights put forward by De Pass Spence & Co. and several others. These questions were settled to the satisfaction of the British and German governments, if not entirely to the satisfaction of either the traders concerned or the Cape government, by July 1886, when a protocol embodying the conclusions of the commission's work and subsequent negotiations was signed.[25] Cape businessmen continued to express strong regrets to the British government that part of the heritage of the South African people had been taken from them; the eventual possibility of bringing about a union of South African territories—a very live issue at the time—had, they claimed, been seriously impaired.[26] In South West as well as in East Africa the wishes of British commerce were not allowed to interfere with Anglo-German relations.

Lüderitz and his colleagues quickly built up a thriving trade in the area they had acquired—then known as Lüderitzland—but were not financially successful, and they did not command sufficient resources to enable them to wait a long time for an improvement in their situation. After one prospecting expedition had found apparently rich copper deposits at Aus, two further parties were sent out, but found nothing of value. The copper deposits were still not worth working, and what had at first been thought to be silver ore at Penguin Island and in the Nautilus mountains turned out to be poor-quality lead and iron ore. By the end of 1884 Lüderitz claimed to have spent 500,000 marks in Lüderitzland without any return.[27] He tried to convince both the German government and German investors to buy up his holdings. Bismarck did become interested, but with few exceptions German investors were not prepared to risk their money in an area about which they knew very little, but which, from what they did know, seemed highly unlikely ever to produce profits. For them South West Africa was even less attractive than east Africa. The German capital that did find its way to Africa went not to Germany's own colonies but to those areas, generally under at least a degree of British control, whose worth had already been proved. Much of the capital brought into South African gold and diamond mines by Alfred Beit and his relatively unknown partner, Julius Wernher, for example, originated in Germany.

Pressure from Bismarck finally made a group of bankers, including Bleichröder and von Hansemann of the Discount Company (Diskonto-gesellschaft), agree to form the German Colonial Company for South West Africa (Deutsche Kolonialgesellschaft für Südwest Afrika) in April 1885. The founders stressed that patriotic, not financial, motives were primarily responsible for their willingness to do this. The amount of money they were prepared to lose was very limited. As Wilhelm Solf, one-time governor of Samoa as well as of East Africa, and for a time acting Colonial Minister, said in a similar situation, 'The good will and patriotism of our capitalists are immense . . . as long as there is no question of opening their wallets.'[28] Discouraged initially by the failure to exploit copper deposits successfully, whatever inclination the Colonial Company may have had to invest anything in the territory was almost completely dissipated by a hoax perpetrated by a group of Australians.

In June 1887 two prospectors, John and Josiah Stevens, told the German consul-general at Cape Town that their father had some years previously discovered a rich gold-bearing reef in the Colonial Company's territory. They were given permission to locate and hold claims, and had to notify the consul-general of any finds they might make. In co-operation with the Colonial Company and another Cape trader active in South West Africa, Anders Ohlsson, the Australian Diggers' Syndicate was formed. Ohlsson paid the Stevens brothers' passage to

Walfisch Bay, while the Colonial Company provided equipment. In September the imperial commissioner, Ernest Göring, was called to examine the syndicate's find at the Pot Mine. He was shown a three-mile reef in which gold was easily visible. The diggers claimed that an assay carried out in Cape Town indicated a yield of 247 grams of gold per ton of rock treated. Not unnaturally, but apparently without any independent survey of the reef, Göring thought this discovery would make it possible to put the protectorate on a sound economic footing. In March 1888 the first mining ordinance was promulgated, and from June a number of small German companies, backed by the Colonial Company, were formed to search for and mine gold. The first mining area was opened in the Swakop river valley on 31 July, and by the end of October some fifty-three claims had been registered. By then enthusiasm had abated somewhat, as nothing of value was found, but as late as February 1889 the Colonial Company's acquisition of one-eighth of the Diggers' Syndicate's rights was considered a lucrative move. It was subsequently discovered that the Stephens brothers had 'salted' the Pot Mine in the first place.[29]

The failure to begin profitable mineral exploration, as well as the fact that the Colonial Company's agent in South West Africa had been forced to withdraw to British protection at Walfisch Bay, made the Colonial Company's backers refuse to advance any more of their own money, except possibly in the form of small grants to anyone prepared to continue operations. They would have preferred a single large company, but did give Lüderitz, the only German who expressed any interest in forming any company at all, a relatively small sum. Unfortunately, he died in a sailing accident shortly after his return to South West Africa.[30]

The major source of the large amount of capital needed to develop the country was some of the British interests already involved in gold and diamond mining in the Cape and the Transvaal. The greatest single attraction for these people was the copper deposits in the Otavi region. This posed problems both for the German government and for any financial group interested, as a strong prior claim to the mines was held by a Cape trader, Robert Lewis. For many years Lewis had enjoyed the benefit of extensive trading with the Herero, whose territorial claims included Otavi, and the confidence of their chief, Samuel Maherero. In 1877 Maherero gave Lewis a twenty-one-year concession for the Ebonie Mine and in 1882 a twenty-year grant for the Otavi Mine. This was followed in September 1885 by a general mining concession over all Herero territory and a 'power of attorney' for Lewis to negotiate, on Maherero's behalf, a treaty of protection with Britain. The Germans were by this time struggling to establish their authority in South West Africa, and six weeks after giving Lewis his general concession Maherero signed a protection treaty with Göring. The chief did not seem too concerned about who gave him protection, but wanted outside support in his virtually continuous wars against the Nama.

In June 1887 Maherero, having tried unsuccessfully to invoke the protectorate treaty, issued a declaration that the Herero were not in fact under German protection, and that in future any document purporting to be signed by him but not countersigned by Lewis, his 'special commissioner for all foreign affairs', would not be recognised. In the course of a further attempt in October 1888 to secure Maherero's submission to German rule Göring asked, 'Do I understand that Lewis is the Chief?' to which the reply was 'Yes.'[31]

Advised by Europeans in the area not to arrest Lewis for fear of causing a war with the Herero, Göring withdrew. Lewis, who had been carrying on an anti-German campaign both in South West Africa and in the Cape, was clearly in a strong position. Maherero issued a further proclamation, countersigned by his special commissioner, that all prospectors had to apply to him for licences, and ordering the Rhenish missionary at Okahandja to close his church and leave. From the relative safety of his headquarters at Otjimbingwe Göring wrote to Lewis, officially informing him that he did not recognise the general concession or the power of attorney. Lewis scornfully replied that he did not recognise Göring's authority as representing the German government in South West Africa in any way. So threatened did Göring's position ultimately become that he felt compelled to withdraw to Walfisch Bay, seeking the protection of the British there, accompanied by the Colonial Company's agent. German fears in August 1889 that Lewis was trying to organise an armed force in the Cape to attack the Germans in Damaraland were considered, at least in the Cape, to be without foundation. Nonetheless, Lewis's refusal to recognise German authority was sufficient grounds to expel him from South West Africa in October 1889. His specific claims to the Otavi and Ebonie mines had not, at this point, been questioned, and could not be ignored.[32]

Lewis's position remained unsettled for several years, during which time negotiations were going on for British groups to form exploiting companies throughout South West Africa, but particularly in Damaraland. One group proposing to form the German South West African Colonisation Company entered into negotiations with the Colonial Company in 1889, and by August seemed to have reached an agreement to acquire a 120-mile strip of land along about 600 miles of coast. All that was needed was government approval, which was not at all certain to be given, strong opposition to the scheme having been aroused when news of it leaked out.[33] In response to German government demands, the agreement was modified to ensure German supremacy in the company and in the territory conceded to it. Despite the changes approval was denied.[34] It appeared to some in the British Foreign Office that the people behind the Colonisation Company hoped to amalgamate their concession with the interests Rhodes and his associates had been acquiring in Damaraland, and ultimately to push the Germans out altogether.[35] This view was not without justification.

In March 1890 Rhodes, Gifford, Davis and others connected with Chartered formed the Damaraland Syndicate, which was to work, at least initially, in conjunction with Lewis.[36] This was only one of several groups formed under Chartered's aegis. One of the others was the Upingtonia Syndicate, which in November 1889 had purchased at auction the rights in the Upingtonia district, which included Otavi, that had been granted to William W. Jordan in October 1885. This grant had been made by the Ovambo, who disputed the territory with the Herero. Jordan was also a Cape merchant, who bought up land in South West Africa, settling Boers on it to farm and raise cattle. He was murdered by Ovambos in June 1886. Göring provisionally recognised the Upingtonia Syndicate's holding, but Gifford and the other British financiers prepared to provide £10,000 for preliminary exploration would do nothing definite until that recognition had been confirmed. If preliminary work revealed anything of promise these financiers expected to form a company capitalised at £1 million in which German investors would be welcome to participate.[37] The German government at this point clearly favoured the formation of an Anglo–German company and urged the Colonial Company to be moderate in its demands. The government also tried to keep Lewis's claims out of the discussion.[38] The precise details of the progress of negotiations are not clear, but after lengthy talks agreement was reached for the formation of the South West Africa Company, which took over the interests of the Upingtonia and Damaraland syndicates, in 1892. German participation in the British company was represented by Dr Julius Scharlach, a Hamburg lawyer who played the difficult dual role of confidential adviser on colonial matters to the German government, while at the same time advising Rhodes, and by Carl Wichmann. Although Davis took an important behind-the-scenes part in bringing about this agreement, he did not join the company's board of directors until 1901, although it was felt that he should have a seat at least as early as 1895. He became chairman in 1902.[39]

Despite constant representations conveyed to the Germans through the British Foreign Office on behalf of Lewis, claiming that his rights could not be ignored, the German government refused to entertain them. As far as the government was concerned, Lewis's concessions had been basically political in nature. Rhodes and Davis had already dropped any pretence of working with him, as he had become an obstacle to the successful conclusion of any agreement. In 1899 the

South West Africa Company, in conjunction with the Discount Company and the United African and General Exploration Company, another of the syndicates set up by Chartered, formed the Otavi Mining and Railway Company, which took over the South West Africa Company's mining rights, for which they paid 1 million marks. The parent company was then free to devote itself to land and agricultural enterprises, which it has continued to do to the present day. The formation of the Otavi Company was primarily in response to pressure on Rhodes to allow a German concern, rather than a British one, to exploit the mines. Nominally German, the ordinary shares of the new company were about equally divided between Germans and British, but British interests had a slight advantage.[40] The same was true of several other companies, nominally German but British-financed. For many years the South West Africa Company, with its offshoots, was the only company operating in South West Africa that had sufficient capital at its disposal to carry out the development and exploitation of mineral resources.

In April 1908 an African, Zacharias Lewala, who had at one time worked for the De Beers mine in Kimberley but was now working in South West Africa on the section of the railway between Lüderitz Bay and Keetmanshoop, found a stone which he recognised as a rough diamond and turned it over to his employer, Herr Stauch. By this time German authority had become well established, the greatest threat to it—the Nama and Herero revolts of 1904–7—having been suppressed.[41] The feeling that non-Germans should not be allowed to gain the benefits of South West Africa's economic development had become very strong. Stauch and two colleagues immediately took out prospecting licences and pegged a large number of claims. Their attempt to gain financial backing in Berlin was unsuccessful, but within a few months news of the discovery had leaked out, and several German companies were formed to prospect for and exploit diamond deposits. The sale of all diamonds produced in the territory was exclusively in the hands of the Diamond Régie, established in February 1909 with representatives of the German government and of the Colonial Company, but not, until 1913, of the producers themselves. Substantial royalty charges were levied and export duties imposed, in some cases as high as $56\frac{1}{2}$ per cent. Shortly before the Diamond Régie was formed, the Colonial Company was granted monopoly mining rights in what was termed the 'closed territory' which, it turned out, included the richest deposits. The monopoly rights were limited by the recognition of existing rights, which once again brought British and German interests into conflict.[42]

The highest average size diamonds were found in the area around the Pomona Mine,[43] which had been included in concessions granted to De Pass Spence & Co. in 1863 and 1864. In order to enjoy the greatest advantage possible from the monopoly rights it had, the Colonial Company was in the position of having either to eliminate De Pass entirely from the field or to reach some agreement with him.[44] The concession to De Pass had included not only the Pomona Mine itself but also the land within a two-mile radius of it. This and other claims made by De Pass had been the subject of discussion by the joint commission of 1885 and of further negotiation in Berlin the following year. Although the Germans rejected much of what De Pass claimed, they did recognise 'a full title in perpetuity to the Pomona Mine with two English miles of land around the mines on every side'.[45] The Colonial Company, and the German Diamond Company it had set up in 1909 to take over its mining rights, interpreted this to mean that De Pass's mining rights were limited to the mine itself; in the two-mile area around it he had only land rights. But it was in this area that De Pass gave Ludwig Scholz prospecting rights in March 1909. Scholz had formed a syndicate with several other prospectors, and subsequently formed a German undertaking, the Pomona Mining Company, to work the field. Scholz and his colleagues were to receive $42\frac{2}{3}$ per cent of the value of the stones they found, a further $48\frac{1}{3}$ per cent being taken in taxes and charges levied by the Diamond Régie, the remaining 9 per cent going to De Pass.[46] The Colonial Company also argued that it had the exclusive right to all precious stones and that De Pass could work the Pomona Mine only for silver and lead, the metals that had attracted him to it in the first place.[47]

In the legal battle that ensued, the prospectors associated with Scholz added an additional complicating factor by claiming that any rights De Pass may have had had been invalidated by his failure to comply with regulations introduced in 1892 and 1893 regarding the registration and publication of mining claims. This point was of little force, as De Pass had enquired at the time, through the Foreign Office, and had been told the regulations did not apply to him.[48] De Pass sought British government support on the grounds that his rights as set out in the protocol of 1886 were being violated. The Foreign Office took the view that the protocol was intended to give De Pass mining rights in the entire area, and that the interpretation of the protocols was beyond the competence of a territorial mining board, which had already ruled against him. The British ambassador in Berlin was instructed to press for De Pass's rights to be upheld.[49]

By September 1910 a tentative agreement between most parties concerned appeared to have been reached.[50] Final accord was delayed by the unwillingness of the prospectors to accept the 15 per cent of the value of output allotted to them. This intransigence was most probably based on one, or both, of two points: although they had joined with Scholz in the Pomona Mining Company, they had in fact been poachers on De Pass's territory; if De Pass's claim was invalidated they would have been able to put forward their own independent claims. Also, De Beers Consolidated Mines Ltd had paid about £20,000 for some of the prospectors' rights, and were very probably delaying agreement in order to delay production, which if allowed to go unchecked would bring the world price of diamonds even lower than it then was.[51] The greatest fear of De Beers and others was that in addition to the alluvial deposits, which they thought would soon be worked out and therefore regarded as of little long-term consequence, large diamond pipes would also be found, making it possible for the Germans to put many more diamonds on the market. Buying up the prospectors' rights was only one of several possible ways for De Beers to gain a foothold in the South West African diamond fields and to attempt to limit their output.[52]

Agreement was finally reached in 1912. De Pass was to receive 8 per cent of the value of the stones produced, $1\frac{1}{2}$ per cent being taken from that to satisfy the claims of a group in the Cape, descendants of those involved in the syndicate originally formed to work the Pomona Mine in 1863. The prospectors had to be satisfied with what they received from the new German company that had been formed with a capital of 3 million marks, calling itself the Pomona Diamond Company,[53] and the working of the richest field in South West Africa resumed.

Other British interests found their way into South West Africa's diamond industry, but generally in partnership with German interests, which tended to predominate. During the 1914–18 war, following the defeat of the German forces, the Union of South Africa assumed responsibility for controlling the production and sale of South West Africa's diamonds. In 1919 the Anglo–American Corporation, formed only two years earlier, reached an agreement with the German owners for the purchase of their diamond holdings. Consolidated Diamond Mines of South West Africa Ltd took over the producing mines, while the South West Finance Corporation took over the assets and liabilities of the German Colonial Company for South West Africa.[54]

By becoming involved in the northern part of South West Africa British interests also became involved in Germany's desire to expand her colonial territories at the expense of the Portuguese. One of the instruments through which this aim was expected by many Germans to be realised was the Anglo-German treaty of 1898. According to this treaty, if Portugal were to approach either Britain or Germany for a loan secured on colonial revenues, the other would be invited to participate. A supposedly secret, but actually widely known, provision of the treaty stipulated that in the event of Portugal's defaulting on the loan the colonies would be divided between Germany and Britain. Germany was to acquire northern and southern Angola and northern Mozambique, Britain a strip in central Angola and southern Mozambique, including Delagoa Bay and the port of Lourenço Marques.

For Britain the prime object of the treaty was to eliminate the threat of German intervention in Delagoa Bay in the conflict between Britain and the Transvaal. Having tried and failed to acquire the bay herself, Britain preferred it to remain in Portuguese hands. For Germany the treaty represented, at least potentially, a respectable means by which she could expand her colonial empire, possibly moving towards an eventual linking of her territories in East and South West Africa.[55] Britain virtually nullified this aspect of the treaty by concluding a treaty with Portugal in 1899 confirming the British commitment to respect the integrity of the Portuguese colonies. This treaty was a very well kept secret, the Germans only learning about it in 1913 when the ratification of a revised treaty for the division of the Portuguese colonies was prevented by Germany's unwillingness to agree to the publication of the Anglo-Portuguese treaty. In 1898 Germany confidently expected Portugal to be forced to seek a loan for her colonies in the near future, and ultimately to default on it.[56] In the meantime attempts were made to promote German economic penetration in southern Angola, where once again German and British interests came into conflict.

The South West Africa Company in 1894 formed the Moçamedes Company, which secured a concession from the Portuguese of 23 million hectares in southern Angola adjacent to German territory.[57] Nominally the Moçamedes Company was Portuguese but financially it was under the control of Rhodes and his associates, for whom the company seems to have been part of a plan to ensure the isolation of South West Africa by surrounding it with British concessionary companies. There was still a strong feeling in the Cape and in some financial circles as well that some way should and could be found to reverse the 'blunder' Britain had committed in ever allowing Germany to take South West Africa. Rhodes's activities were seen as a possible means of accomplishing this.[58]

The Otavi Company had also acquired the right to build a railway from the mine to a port either in South West Africa itself or in Angola. The only good natural harbour on the German section of the coast was at Walfisch Bay, but not unnaturally the Germans wanted a port more under their own control. The best port facilities nearest Otavi were at either Tiger Bay or Port Alexander in Angola. The Moçamedes Company, which already had the right to build railways in its concession area, applied to the Portuguese government for permission to build a line from Tiger Bay to Humbe, making it possible for the company to develop its territory to a greater extent, and very possibly with the intention of extending it eventually to meet the Rhodesian railway system at Bulawayo. The Germans were not at all satisfied with the idea of a branch being built from this line to Otavi. They wanted a main line direct to Otavi, which they saw as part of an eventual link to the Transvaal. Nor did the Germans want a British company to become too influential in southern Angola, which they considered their own special sphere, and were most annoyed by the Moçamedes Company's intention of turning over the Humbe line concession, once acquired, to its British subsidiary, the Railway and Works Company, subsequently organised as the Trans-African Railway Syndicate Ltd, with Rhodes, Davis and Scharlach included on its board of directors.

In an attempt to reach a compromise with Rhodes, Friedrich von Lindequist, then attached to the colonial department of the German Foreign Ministry, later governor of South West Africa, put his government's demands. They wanted a concession for a direct line to Otavi from Tiger Bay, with the right to build a harbour there; the South West Africa Company was to be allowed to build an extension of the Humbe ancillary branch to this main line. The Germans also wanted Chartered to guarantee to connect its lines to all German lines leading to or crossing the Anglo–German frontier. In addition, Rhodes was to support German requests for permission to extend the Tiger Bay–Otavi line to the Transvaal. In return the East African Telegraph Agreement, already drawn up, was to be ratified immediately and permission granted for the Cape-to-Cairo railway to go through German East Africa. The German government would support Rhodes's efforts to secure further concessions from the Portuguese and would allow Chartered to undertake the building of all connections with the German lines, except for the link to Johannesburg, which was reserved to a German firm.

Von Lindequist reckoned without the Portuguese, who were well aware of the 'secret' provisions of the Anglo–German treaty and were determined not to allow the Germans to secure too great a foothold in Angola. In August 1899 they gave the Moçamedes Company permission to build the railway to Humbe, but limited the construction time to five years rather than the fifteen requested. This deprived the Germans of sufficient time to delay construction until such a time as they were in a position to exercise decisive influence in Angola. The Portuguese government also reserved to itself the right to allow the construction of branch lines.

German capitalists had generally been prepared to allow British finance to take the lead. In a surprising departure from this principle von Hansemann, entirely on his own initiative, asked the Portuguese to allow his Discount Company to build a line from Tiger Bay to the Kunene river, disregarding the rights already granted the Moçamedes Company and the Trans-African Railway Syndicate. Rhodes was understandably angered by this, not only because it would infringe these rights but also because it would deprive the syndicate of the £100,000 it was asking for relinquishing them. After delaying as long as they could, the Portuguese said they would be prepared to ignore the

Moçamedes Company's rights but would themselves build the line to the Kunene. To this von Hansemann would not agree, refusing to have anything to do with the Portuguese plan and remaining entirely unmoved by arguments that accepting their terms would fulfil the fundamental need of giving South West Africa an outlet to the coast. The Cape-to-Cairo telegraph agreement, mentioned earlier, emerged as a partial compromise between the Germans and Rhodes, neither getting what they most wanted.

Davis then proposed that the concession for the Tiger Bay–Humbe line be replaced by one for a railway from Tiger Bay to the Kunene, as envisaged by von Hansemann. This the Portuguese refused, while maintaining their willingness to build that line themselves. In the meantime the Colonial Company for South West Africa had been pressing for the abandonment of Tiger Bay or Port Alexander as the terminus of the Otavi railway in favour of Swakopmund, from which they could derive greater benefit. At that time Swakopmund was little more than an open roadstead, though from 1893 onwards it increasingly drew traffic from Walfisch Bay. Construction of a mole was begun there in 1899, and completed in 1903. The turning point in the argument came in November 1902, when the Portuguese government granted a concession for the construction of a railway from Benguela to Angola's eastern border, it being expected that part of the line would run through territory assigned to Germany by the 1898 treaty. Count von Tattenbach, German Minister in Lisbon, reacted most strongly to this and told the Portuguese that, having granted the Benguela Railway concession, they should also be prepared to meet von Hansemann's request. The Portuguese did not agree, continuing to insist that the line must go to Humbe first. In March 1903 arrangements were made for the South West Africa Company and the Otavi Company to build a narrow gauge railway from Swakopmund to Otavi, the completed line subsequently being taken over by the German government.[59]

Edmund Davis was also very much involved in a more direct attempt by the Germans to take over part of Portuguese territory, this time in Mozambique. In 1891 the Portuguese had granted a charter to the Nyassa Company (Companhia do Nyassa) to administer and exercise sovereign rights in northern Mozambique, the area adjacent to German East Africa. The capital behind this company was British, its London committee forming itself into Nyassa Consolidated Ltd in 1908. In April 1914 Davis was asked to sell the 91,400 shares his Search Syndicate held in Nyassa Consolidated. He also secured options on enough shares held by others to give whoever purchased them a controlling interest in the company, and thereby virtual control of the Portuguese parent company as well.

The offer came from a consortium of German banks, the Deutsche

Bank, the Discount Company, the Berlin Trading Company, Bleich-röder, Mendelssohn & Co. and Warburg & Co. These banks would not undertake the business without the promise of support from the German government. Negotiations were carried on by Davis, C. F. Rowsell of Nyassa Consolidated and Dr W. C. Regendanz of Warburg's. Agreement for the transfer of the desired number of shares was reached in May, with the Deutsche Bank being named in the draft as one of the contracting parties. Dr Regendanz's name was later substituted, and in the final agreement the name of Pieter Vuyk appeared instead. Vuyk was Dutch but had for some years been closely connected with German financiers.[60]

No one in Britain raised any strong objection to control of the companies being transferred to German hands. The Foreign Office was aware, though not officially, of what was going on, but did nothing to prevent it, most probably because it felt the mismanagement of the Portuguese colonies was deplorable, and could be improved, at least to some extent, with Germans in control of part of the territory. For the businessmen involved the sale represented a means of getting out of what had become a very costly enterprise. Sir Edward Grey was also, most probably, unwilling to do anything to upset the Germans, as he had tried to meet all their wishes when the revision of the 1898 treaty had been negotiated in 1913.[61] The outbreak of war altered the situation entirely.

The Nyassa Company had issued 436,000 shares, 220,000 of which were held by Nyassa Consolidated, which in turn had issued 369,000 shares, 229,590 of which were in German hands, all but 300 of them registered in Vuyk's name. The share certificates of these were held by the Deutsche Bank's London agency, which was under British government supervision under the terms of the Aliens Restriction order-in-council. The shares could not be transferred to the German banks, and no dividends paid on them could be transmitted to Germany. After some discussion of whether or not Vuyk was in fact merely a front for German interests, the shares were vested in the public trustee for the duration of the war.[62] They were then sold to a British group headed by Lord Kylsant, after lengthy negotiation, for the odd sum of £45,344 19s 11d, which was credited to the German reparations account in London. This was a small amount indeed compared with the £114,795 originally paid for them by the Germans. Attempts to revive the scheme to gain a foot-hold in Portuguese Nyassa after the war as part of Germany's wider colonial ambitions came to nothing.[63]

When Germany first embarked on her colonial career she often found herself in conflict with already established British commercial interests. In those territories whose economy was based on trade in tropical commodities this presented little difficulty, and German traders came to dominate. Where large amounts of money had to be invested—as in the telegraph line across East Africa, and the development of South West Africa's mineral resources—and a longer time had to elapse before profits, if any, could be expected, German finance was not forthcoming. Beyond investing in some colonial railways, the German generally preferred to put his money into European or American enterprises which appeared much less risky. British capital became essential for the economic development of South West Africa, at least until 1908, when German national interest was strong enough, and scepticism about returns on investment sufficiently allayed. Those British financiers who did become involved there were not, however, prepared to co-operate with the Germans any more than was absolutely necessary or advantageous to them. Germany was unable to force closer co-operation, revealing a fundamental weakness in her colonial undertaking, particularly with regard to South West Africa, her inability to exercise complete control over economic development or to use economic interests for political advantage.

NOTES

[1] The literature on this subject is extensive. Among the more recent works are: Hartmut Pogge von Strandmann, 'Domestic origins of Germany's colonial expansion under Bismarck', Past and Present, No. 42, 1969, p.140; Hans-Ulrich Wehler, 'Bismarck's imperialism', Past and Present, No. 48, 1970, p.119; Henry Ashby Turner, jr., 'Bismarck's imperialist venture: anti-British in origin?', in Prosser Gifford and Wm. Roger Louis (eds.) with the assistance of Alison Smith, Britain and Germany in Africa; Imperial Rivalry and Colonial Rule (New Haven and London, 1967), pp.47–82.

[2] W. O. Henderson, Studies in German Colonial History (London, 1962), pp.62–3.

[3] John S. Galbraith, Mackinnon and East Africa, 1878–1897; a Study in the 'New Imperialism' (Cambridge, 1972), p.23.

[4] Henderson, op. cit., pp.4–5; Wolfe W. Schmokel, Dream of Empire; German Colonialism, 1919–1945 (New Haven and London, 1964), pp.1–2.

[5] G. S. P. Freeman-Grenville, 'The German sphere, 1884–98', in Roland Oliver and Gervase Matthew (eds.), History of East Africa, vol. 1 (Oxford, 1963), pp.436–7.

[6] Galbraith, op. cit., p.146.

[7] Ibid., pp.120–1.

[8] Henderson, op. cit., pp.12–21.

[9] Galbraith, op. cit., pp.106–9, 169.

[10] R. I. Rotberg, 'Resistance and rebellion in British Nyasaland and German East Africa, 1888–1915; a tentative comparison', in Gifford and Lewis, op. cit., pp.669–70; Freeman-Grenville, op. cit., pp.438–42.

[11] Rubber Growers Association to Sir Edward Grey, 22 August 1912 and minutes thereon, and Lewa Rubber Estates Ltd. to Grey, 27 March 1912, both in F.O. 367/276, file 13107. See also W. O. Henderson, 'German East Africa, 1884–1918', in Vincent Harlow and E. M. Chilver (eds.), assisted by Alison Smith, History of East Africa, vol. II (Oxford, 1965), pp.124–62.

[12] On the Cape-to-Cairo Railway, see especially Lois A. G. Raphael, The Cape-to-Cairo Dream; a study in British Imperialism (New York, 1951). The idea did not die, and was revived, particularly after the first World War when the German obstacle in East Africa was removed; see Wm. Roger Louis, Great Britain and Germany's Lost Colonies 1914–1919 (Oxford, 1967), passim.

[13] Wm. Roger Louis, 'Great Britain and German expansion in Africa, 1884–1919', in Gifford and Louis, op. cit.; Galbraith, op. cit., 157–9.

[14] S. E. Katzenellenbogen, *Railways and the Copper Mines of Katanga* (Oxford, 1973), p.20; Ronald Robinson and John Gallagher with Alice Denny, *Africa and the Victorians; the Official Mind of Imperialism* (London, 1961), pp.339–78; Baron Pierre Van Zuylen, '*L'Échiquier Congolais ou le secret du roi* (Brussels, 1959), pp.231–5; Robert O. Collins, *King Leopold, England, and the Upper Nile, 1899–1909* (New Haven and London, 1968), *passim*.

[15] Raphael, *op. cit.*, pp.217–21; Rhodes to Francis Bentie at the Foreign Office, 21 March 1899, F.O. 2/250.

[16] Chartered was happy to agree to this condition as it seemed unlikely that their railways would be connected to the West Coast for many decades, if ever. Problems began to appear in 1909 when it seemed that the Benguela Railway, then being constructed across Angola, would create such a rail link and force the British South Africa Company either to sever the link in some way, or to build another line in the south, which by this time they had absolutely no desire to do. The matter only became urgent in 1912, but as the Benguela Railway was not in fact completed until after the first World War and the railway agreement was nullified by the war, none of the difficulties envisaged actually materialised. See Katzenellengboen, *op. cit.*, pp.67–9, 79–81. The Foreign and Colonial Offices took no part in negotiating this agreement, but gave it tacit approval.

[17] This brief account of Davis's life and the discussion below of his involvement in South West Africa is based on the obituary of him that appeared in *The Times* on 21 February 1939 and an anonymous appreciation of him that appeared the following day, on R. Murray-Hughes, 'Edmund Davis (1854–1939)', *Northern Rhodesia Journal*, VI (1965), p.645, and on Horst Drechsler, 'Germany and S. Angola', *Actas do Congresso International de Historia dos Descobrimentos* (Lisbon, 1961), p.73. See also J. Wernher to Francis Bertie at the Foreign Office, 23 February 1899, F.O. 800/160.

[18] Eric A. Walker, *A History of Southern Africa*, 3rd edition (London, 1957), pp.124–33.

[19] J. H. Esterhuyse, *South West Africa, 1889–94; the Establishment of German authority in South West Africa* (Cape Town, 1968), p.9, G. McColl Theal, *History of South Africa, 1834–54* (London, 1893), pp.227–9.

[20] John H. Wellington, *South West Africa and its Human Issues* (Oxford, 1967), pp.129–73.

[21] Esterhuyse, *op. cit.*, p.13, gives the following figures:

	Imports (Rand)	Exports (Rand)
1850	532	4,496
1860	19,290	14,292
1870	18,824	40,982
1880	48,940	68,206

[22] Henderson, *Studies*, p.52.

[23] Walker, *op. cit.*, p.372.

[24] Jeffrey Butler, 'The German factor in Anglo–Transvaal relations', in Gifford and Louis, *op. cit.*, pp.183–4; Robinson and Gallagher, *op. cit.*, pp.172–5.

[25] 'Further correspondence respecting the claims of British subjects in the German protectorate on the south west coast of Africa', British Parl. Papers, 1887, C. 5180.

[26] Merchant's memorial in F.O. 84/2085.

[27] Esterhuyse, *op. cit.*, pp.89–90.

[28] *Ibid.*, pp.91–5, 130; Drechsler, *op. cit.*, p.75; Pierre Décharme, *Compagnies et sociétés coloniales allemandes* (Paris, 1903), pp.163–4, 167; and Solf to Rosen, 7 November 1913, cited in Willequet, *Le Congo Belge et la Weltpolitik (1894–1914)* (Brussels, 1962), p.391.

[29] Esterhuyse, *op. cit.*, pp.123–5, 129–34; Beauclerk to Foreign Office, No. 49 Africa, 22 February 1889, F.O. 84/1956.

[30] Décharme, *op. cit.*, p.170; Esterhuyse, *op. cit.*, pp.122–3.

[31] Esterhuyse, *op. cit.*, pp.104–7, 124–8, 135–8; note from Count Leyden, 10 May 1889, and minutes thereon, F.O. 84/1960.

[32] Esterhuyse, *op. cit.*, p.137; Malet to Foreign Office, No. 94 Africa, 10 May 1889, F.O. 84/1957; minute by Sir Gordon Sprigg, Prime Minister of the Cape, No. 1/55, copy in Colonial Office to Foreign Office, 7 May 1889, F.O. 84/1994, and Acting Commissioner Nels to Lewis, 15 October 1889, copy in Colonial Office to Foreign Office, 26 February 1891.

[33] Beauclerk to Salisbury, No. 114 Africa, confidential, 2 August 1889 and No. 116 Africa, very confidential, 9 August 1889, F.O. 84/1957.

[34] Malet to Salisbury, No. 179 Africa, secret, 11 December 1889, F.O. 84/1958 and No. 16 Africa, confidential, 1 March 1890, F.O. 84/2031.

[35] Minutes on Malet to Salisbury, No. 179 Africa, secret, 11 December 1889, F.O. 84/1958.

[36] Hollams, Sons, Coward and Hawksley (Chartered's solicitors) to Salisbury, 5 May 1890, F.O. 84/2085.

[37] Esterhuyse, *op. cit.*, pp.110–11; Davis to Salisbury, 31 July 1891, F.O. 84/2170.

[38] Malet (for Sir Percy Anderson) to Foreign Office, telegram, 24 June 1890, F.O. 84/2035.

[39] Murray-Hughes, *op. cit.*, p.646; Wernher, Beit & Co. to George Cawston, 3 April 1895, Cawston papers, Rhodes House Library, Oxford, vol. v.

[40] Henderson, *Studies*, p.64; Drechsler, *op. cit.*, p.77.

[41] Helmut Bley, 'Social discord in South West Africa, 1894–1904', in Gifford and Louis, *op. cit.*, pp.607–30.

[42] Percy Albert Wagner, *The Diamond Fields of Southern Africa* (Cape Town, 2nd impression, 1971), pp.290–1; Theodore Gregory, *Ernest Oppenheimer and the Economic Development of Southern Africa* (Cape Town, 1962), pp.64–5.

[43] Wagner, *op. cit.*, pp.297–300.

[44] The sole partner in De Pass Spence & Co. by this time was Daniel De Pass. John Spence had withdrawn from the partnership in 1873 and became bankrupt in 1886 when De Pass bought up his share in the Pomona mine: De Pass to Colonial Office, 30 December 1909, copy in Colonial Office to Foreign Office, No. 645, 7 [?] January 1910, F.O. 367/180, file 293.

[45] C. 5180, *op. cit.*, and opinion given by a German barrister, translation of which can be found in F.O. 367/180, file 293.

[46] De Pass to Colonial Office, 19 March 1909, copy in Colonial Office to Foreign Office, No. 9847, 29 March 1909, F.O. 367/134, file 1222.

[47] Legal opinion cited above and Muller, British Consul in South West Africa, to Foreign Office, No. 8 Africa, confidential, 10 September 1910, F.O. 367/180, file 293.

[48] Legal opinion cited above.

[49] Foreign Office minute on conversation with De Pass, 20 January 1910, Foreign Office to Goschen, No. 11 Africa, 28 January 1910 and minute on Colonial Office to Foreign Office, No. 2226, 2 February 1910, F.O. 367/180, file 293.

[50] Muller to Foreign Office, No. 9 Africa, 14 September 1910, F.O. 367/180, file 293.

[51] Foreign Office minute on talk with Charles Hess of De Pass Spence & Co., and De Pass to Foreign Office 1 February 1911, F.O. 367/228, file 410.

[52] Gregory, *op. cit.*, pp.65–74.

[53] De Pass to Foreign Office, 7 March 1912, F.O. 367/275, file 6293.

[54] Gregory, *op. cit.*, pp.115–16.

South West African diamond production, 1908–13

Year	Carats	Value (£)	Value per carat	Average number of stones per carat
1908*	39,762	53,842	27s 1d	n.a.
1909	519,190	704,123	29s 0·5d	5·0
1910	792,642 3/16	1,015,779	25s 7d	5·96
1911	766,465 3/16	968,418	25s 3·1d	6·48
1912	992,380	1,408,500	28s 4·7d	6·09
1913	1,470,000	2,953,500	40s 1·9d	n.a.
Total	4,580,439 3/8	7,104,162	–	–

*August–December only
Source. Wagner, *op. cit.*, p.340.

[55] This idea of a Mittelafrika was strongly supported by many influential Germans, and by members of the Government, but enjoyed little widespread support among the German people or in the Reichstag.

[56] See, for example, W. L. Langer, *The Diplomacy of Imperialism 1890–1902*, 2nd edition (New York, 1951), pp.523–9; P. R. Warhurst, *Anglo-Portuguese Relations in*

South-Central Africa 1890–1900 (London, 1962), pp.129–46; R. J. Hammond, *Portugal and Africa: a Study in Uneconomic Imperialism* (Stanford, 1966), pp.245–71; Robinson and Gallagher, *op. cit.*, pp.369–70, 447–8.

[57] Except as otherwise noted, the following paragraphs are based on Drechsler, *op. cit.*

[58] See, for example, Sir Gordon Sprigg to Lord Knutsford, Colonial Secretary, 22 January 1891, copy in Colonial Office to Foreign Office, 30 January 1891, F.O. 84/2155 and Sir John Kirk to George Cawston, 21 January 1895, Cawston papers, vol. v.

[59] Henderson, *Studies*, p.66; Katzenellenbogen, *op. cit.*, pp.41–3. On the eve of the first World War other German attempts to gain a foothold in Angola included a move to acquire control of the Benguela Railway, and another to invest in the Ambaca–Malenge line in the northern part of the country. No British capital was involved in supporting either of these moves.

[60] 'Statement by C. F. Rowsell as to the true ownership of Mr Pieter Vuyk's shares in Nyassa Consolidated Limited', 23 May 1917, C.O. 525/77.

[61] Willequest, *op. cit.*, pp.379–99; P. H. S. Hatton, 'Harcourt and Solf: the search for an Anglo–German understanding through Africa, 1912–14', *European Studies Review*, i, 1971, p.123.

[62] Colonial Office memo to Sir J. Anderson, C.O. 525/59 and 'Note on Nyassa Company' by the Hon. H. C. Hull, 16 January 1918, C.O. 525/81.

[63] *Ibid.* and 'Nyassa Consolidated Limited, shares acquired by Pieter Vuyk, C.O. 525/76, and F. W. Pick, *Searchlight on German Africa: the Diaries and Papers of Dr W. Ch. Regendanz; a Study in Colonial Ambitions* (London, 1939), pp.115–58. On Germany's intentions regarding the Portuguese colonies during the inter-war period see also Schmokel, *op. cit.*, pp.112–13, 119–20, 138.

Francis E. Hyde

11

Cunard and North Atlantic steamship agreements, 1850–1914

I

The operation of agreements between rival steamship companies on North Atlantic routes can be divided chronologically into three distinct phases. The first and earliest consisted of simple arrangements between two companies designed to offset the harmful effects of competition between specified ships on a particular voyage pattern. The second, consequent upon the growth of emigrant business after 1860, was that concluded between a number of British (in this case mainly Liverpool) lines principally as a means of regulating levels of traffic during periods of fluctuation. Finally there was the extension of all such agreements embodying pooling arrangements between Continental, American and British companies. This latter and more complicated type of agreement was called into being by two factors: the swing of the emigrant trade away from Liverpool to Continental ports, and the rise of a powerful German mercantile marine in alliance with an equally powerful American combine of shipping interests. As a result, it became necessary to construct a Conference system regulating traffic across the North Atlantic on a wider international plane.[1]

The British and North American Royal Mail Steam Packet Company (later known as the Cunard Steam Ship Company) was established in 1840. Samuel Cunard, who had negotiated a contract for the conveyance of mails from Liverpool to Halifax and Boston and, later, New York, entered into agreement with Robert Napier and John Wood of Glasgow to build the first four steamships for the new company.[2] The former provided side-lever engines generating an i.h.p. of 740, the latter supplying stout wooden hulls.[3] The company was capitalised at £270,000 (raised to £300,000 in the following year), and Samuel Cunard paid over the £55,000 received from the Admiralty for the mail contract as his share of the original capital. The remaining £215,000 was provided by Glasgow and Manchester businessmen within the legal entity of what was known as the Glasgow Proprietory.[4]

Having arranged for the provision of funds and having secured the services of first-class shipbuilders, Samuel Cunard returned to Halifax, where, with his son Edward, he occupied himself in organising the Canadian and American side of this shipping venture. The brothers George and James Burns took over the Glasgow agency and conducted the negotiations for the building of the ships, while in Liverpool, the British terminal of the line, David and Charles MacIver acted as agents for the management and running of the ships.[5] In essence, this threefold management worked extremely well, the Burns brothers taking over responsibility for liaison with government departments, the MacIver brothers assuming control of the commercial side of the business and Samuel Cunard developing contacts along the North American seabord. After 1848 New York became a chief port of call, and branches of the mail service were extended from Quebec in the north to Bermuda in the south. After David MacIver's death in 1845 his brother Charles assumed a dominant role in the company's affairs, and for a period of more than thirty years his forceful personality virtually controlled the expansive direction of the company's interests. He was not only responsible for the discipline and regulation on board ship but was also active in the ordering of cargo, the transport of passengers and the commercial arrangements of the company as a whole.[6] He entered the Mediterranean produce trade on his own account in 1852 and, with the help of his partners, turned this trade into a most profitable venture for the company; he persuaded the company to embark on the carriage of emigrants in 1860 and he was active in the promotion of iron screw ships fitted with compound engines after 1870.[7] In short, Charles MacIver was a driving force, and to his energy and skill the early successful expansion of Cunard's interests may be attributed.

Secure in the monopoly of the carriage of mails, Cunard directors felt that they had little to fear from rival British steamship lines. The Great Western Company, for example, with its service between Bristol and New York, had added a remarkable ship to the fleet in the early 1840s. This was the *Great Britain*, which under Brunel's supervision had been constructed in accordance with the latest technical improvements. Her hull was made of iron instead of wood and she was fitted with a screw propeller instead of paddle wheels; she was some 300 ft long, and of 3,200 tons—nearly three times larger than Cunard's first ship, the *Britannia*. When the Cunard managers proposed sending their ships to New York the directors of the Great Western Company complained bitterly that such action was an encroachment upon their legitimate interests.[8] As events turned out the *Great Britain* proved to be uneconomical in operation, but her presence in 1845 aroused the hopes of her directors that the government might be persuaded to grant a mail subsidy to their company.[9] This did not happen, and subsequently the Great Western Steamship Company foundered on the rock of bankruptcy.

Apart from British shipping companies Cunard had to meet competition in its formative years from American- and French-owned shipping lines, all of which were in receipt of congressional or government support. In particular American opinion was becoming insistent that the country's mercantile marine should be revitalised in order to regain the supremacy which its shipping companies had held before the coming of the steamship. The first expression of this desire was evident in the construction of two steamships, the *Washington* and *Hermann*, which were put on to the route between New York and Bremen.[10] A second line out of New York began in 1849 under the title of the New York and Havre Steam Navigation Company. This company, also aided by a subsidy, ran two ships, the *Franklin* and *Humboldt*.[11] These vessels, however, did not offer any serious competition to Cunard's regular mail services, and Samuel Cunard was not perturbed by their presence on the North Atlantic. He was, however, much more concerned about the efforts of certain American shipping interests to build up a powerful steamship fleet, in particular, those of a remarkable man of enterprise, Edward Knight Collins.[12] The struggle between the ships of Collins's company and the Cunarders is the first real manifestation of competition between rival steamship companies on the North Atlantic. Though the essential historical elements in the development of this competition are known in general terms, the details about the working of the respective ships have never been properly investigated. Out of the ensuing conflict to obtain a division of the trade the first agreement between steamship companies on the North Atlantic was negotiated and put into operation.

II

The career of Edward Knight Collins is reasonably well known. For some twenty years he had operated sailing packets first to Vera Cruz, then to New Orleans and, until 1847, with his Dramatic Line, to Liverpool. His services commanded a high reputation, mainly because of the provision of excellent accommodation and good food on board ship. It is likely that the aura of success enabled him to win a subsidy contract from the US Postmaster General on 1 November 1847. In return for an annual payment of $385,000, Collins agreed to build four fast ships capable of beating the Cunarders.[13] Supported by the financial backing of James and Stewart Brown, he organised the United States Mail Steamship Company, known from its inception as the Collins Line.

The new Collins Line ships *Atlantic*, *Pacific*, *Arctic* and *Baltic* offered a potential threat to Cunard's position. Of some 2,800 tons, they were approximately 1,000 tons larger than the average Cunarder; they were also equipped for speed, making the crossing at least a day faster than the crack ships in Cunard's fleet. The impact of such vessels was instantaneous, so much so that Charles MacIver was shortly estimating a prospective loss of some £30,000 worth of business from his company to the new American line.[14] When Collins, by a master stroke of lobbying, managed to persuade Congress to increase his mail subsidy to $853,000, the apparent threat to Cunard's traffic in passengers, freight and mails was given added strength. The prospect that increased resources in Collins's hands would inevitably lead to more intensive competition from larger and faster American ships undoubtedly spurred the Cunard Company into an acceptance of iron screw ships and to many modifications in the building of their large paddle ship, the *Persia*. The fact remains, however, that following their first flush of success the Collins Line did not overwhelm Cunard. The latter company continued to carry more mail, though the speed and comfort of the Collins liners attracted more passengers.[15] Competition was therefore finely balanced, and it appeared that the strict instructions to all Cunard captains to couple speed with safety might yet prove to be an inhibition on comparative profitability in the face of Collins's avowed intention of driving the Cunarders off the Atlantic.

In the last resort, however, Collins's insistence on speed led to heavy fuel consumption, with consequential high running costs, and to the overstraining of boilers followed by large maintenance and repair charges. By contrast, the regularity of the Cunard services, which continued throughout the year, produced dividends. Cunard made profits, Collins did not. In the eight years of the Collins Line's history not a single dollar was returned to shareholders. Finally, the financial consequences of the tragic losses of the *Arctic* and *Pacific*, coupled with the reduction of the mail subsidy, involved the company in bankruptcy, the new large ship *Adriatic* having to be sold to meet the claims of creditors.

There was, however, another side to this struggle between Cunard and the Collins Line. New information concerning the two companies shows that, far from engaging in a life-and-death struggle, they had a secret working arrangement for the pooling of earnings on the carriage of passengers and cargo.[16] This did not obviate the possibility of competition in service, though it helped in maintaining levels of rates and in ironing out fluctuations in earning capacity.

By the beginning of 1850 Charles MacIver realised that it was not possible for Cunarders to match the technical superiority of the Collins ships *Atlantic* and *Pacific*. He had, therefore, to resort to other methods in order to ameliorate the sharpness of competition. Accordingly, an agreement was signed on 29 May 1850 (to operate as from 25 May) between Charles MacIver, representing Cunard, and Messrs Brown Shipley & Co., representing the Collins Line.[17] Minimum rates were fixed on the carriage of both passengers and cargo: £35 for adult first-class cabin passengers and £20 for second-class from Liverpool to America and $120 and $70 respectively from America to Liverpool. Each company was permitted to charge higher rates and retain the difference, the prohibition applying only to the charging of a lower rate than that agreed. The rate for cargo was fixed at £7 7s per ton, including primage. Individual parcels not paying less than 10s and all parcels paying less than 21s had to be pre-paid. The most interesting part of the agreement, however, was that concerned with the pooling of earnings in order that subsequent allocations might be adjusted equitably in accordance with variations in the earning capacity of the steamships.[18]

As the American ships possessed greater capacity for the carriage of passengers and cargo than the Cunarders, it was agreed that some balancing of advantage and disadvantage was necessary. The British ships, because of their high reputation in Liverpool, were likely to carry more and consequently earn more on westbound passages, whereas the Collins ships, because of their reputation in New York, had an advantage on eastbound voyages. For these reasons a pooling arrangement, based on a triple-voyage pattern, was established. On the westward route the earnings from the carriage of cargo and passengers of one Collins ship were set against those of two paddle-wheel Cunarders. On the eastbound route the agreement applied only to the carriage of passengers. If the gross annual earnings of the American ships were less than one-third of the aggregate of all the voyages of the two companies, Cunard was required to pay to the Collins Line 'such sum as shall increase the gross receipts of the American company to one-third of such aggregate'.[19] On the other hand, if the American ships earned more than one-third of the aggregate receipts the Collins Line would pay to Cunard 'such sum as shall increase the gross receipts of the British company to two-thirds of the aggregate'.[20] The receipts from the carriage of specie and other goods paying an *ad valorem* freight were to be simply divided, one-third to the Collins Line and two-thirds to Cunard.

Finally, it was agreed that any transhipment cargoes from MacIver's Havre steamers, carried westwards in American ships, should be so carried free from managerial charge. The freight collected on such cargoes was to be placed to the credit of the Havre steamers. As a *quid pro quo* the Cunard company agreed to credit its transhipment of Havre cargoes in the same way and add the receipts from this trade to those collected on cargo from Havre to Liverpool. '. . . If any profit shall appear thereon [after charging the current expenses of working] such net profit shall be divided between the American company and the British company rateably and in proportion to the number of voyages performed.'[21] In case of any loss being incurred in the operation of the Havre steamers, it was agreed that Cunard should be solely responsible for coverage. In other words, the agreement provided for a semi-pooling arrangement on the working of the Havre steamers as well as upon the working of the transatlantic ships.

The initial agreement was operative from 25 May 1850 to 1 January 1852. It was renewed and lasted until 24 February 1853, when it was again renewed and revised. The last settlement was made on 31 March 1855. By the following year the loss of the *Pacific* made it difficult for Collins to implement the terms of the agreement, and Charles MacIver, on behalf of the British company, agreed to a suspension until the new Collins liner *Adriatic* could be put upon the berth.[22] In fact the agreement never again became operative, for, as we have seen, Collins was shortly to be engulfed in bankruptcy. Nevertheless, for a period of five years the two supposedly rival steamship companies worked in reasonable harmony, agreeing freight and passenger rates and ironing out inequalities arising from differences in service and discrepancies in tonnage. The annual financial settlements between Collins and Cunard will be published elsewhere.[23] It is relevant in this context to mention only that, in historical terms, the agreement is of considerable importance. It overturns previously conceived ideas about the nature of the competition thought to exist between Cunard and the Collins Line. Furthermore, if this agreement is considered as an *ad hoc* arrangement and therefore, in a strict sense, not a Conference device, the details of its operation were certainly embodied in many later Conference agreements. The conclusion must therefore be that some early steamship owners were alive to the means by which competition might be alleviated by agreement and that the Cunard management, in particular, was prepared to put these ideas into practice.

So ended an exciting and, as events proved, a not unprofitable chapter in Cunard's history. For Collins the story had an unhappy ending. Cunard, on the other hand, had greatly strengthened its position on the North Atlantic. The company was secure in the monopoly of its mail contract and, because of the implied threat from Collins, had greatly improved the technological direction of its shipbuilding policy. Its prestige, based on safety and regularity of service, had been fortified. It remained for management to direct resources into new and lucrative trades in order that earning capacity might be increased with the growth of new opportunities. In this context it was a logical step for Cunard to lay down iron screw ships and take the company into the emigrant business.

III

From 1860 onwards the increasing flood of emigrants from the United Kingdom and the Continent westwards to Canada and the United

States attracted resources into the creation of facilities by both established and newly created steamship companies. The level of competition
in the carriage of emigrants was precisely determined (as far as Liverpool shipping companies were concerned) by three factors. The first
was the seasonal nature of the trade, the second was fluctuations caused
by the ebb and flow of the trade cycle, and the third was changes in the
source of emigration away from the United Kingdom and northern
Europe to central and southern Europe. These changes, in turn, affected
the relative importance of ports and shipping services provided; Liverpool, for example, lost its pre-eminent status as a port of embarkation in
the face of the growing volume of traffic through Hamburg, Fiume and
Trieste.

In this process of change there developed a series of short-term
devices, mutually agreed between rival shipping companies and designed to offset the adverse effects of fluctuations in the trade. The first
of these was formed in 1868 by British companies and was representative of Liverpool and Glasgow shipping interests. The second
series was the result of a change in the direction and composition of the
trade under conditions in which British companies found themselves in
competition with Continental lines, principally North German Lloyd
and Hamburg–Amerika. The third phase involved a bitter struggle
between Cunard and the Morgan combine of American shipping
interests after 1902 and culminated in the creation of a North Atlantic
Conference in 1908. This conference provided a protective umbrella for
all the principal lines, British, German and American, running services
across the North Atlantic.

Leadership in a successful development of the steerage trade had
come from William Inman. Recognising the strength of the Cunard
Company in such services as mails and cabin class, he had concentrated
his resources in the provision of adequate accommodation for the large
and growing numbers of emigrants. With the foundation of his Liverpool New York and Philadelphia Steamship Company in 1850, he not
only had a head start in this kind of business but was, by the nature of
his experience, in a strong competitive position. He accepted technological innovations, being one of the first shipowners to use iron screw
ships on regular crossings. He was also among the pioneers of compound
engines.[24] By 1870 his company was carrying an average of 40,000
emigrants a year. The real strength of operation, however, was tested in
the relationship between total capacity and traffic available. Though
Cunard did not enter the trade until some ten years after Inman, these
two companies were the main contenders for emigrant business during
the greater part of the 1860s. Their rivalry at this precise time was not
mutually restrictive, as it was conducted under conditions of increasing
traffic, though this simple division of enterprise was shortly broken by

the incursion of three new Liverpool lines: National, Guion and White Star. The dual balance of interests was accordingly upset, and competition between rival British companies became an established feature of the passenger trade as a whole.

At first the National and Guion companies were content to allow Cunard and Inman to compete for the express cabin-class traffic while they concentrated on the carriage of emigrants. By the early 1870s, however, National and Guion had built up fleets with a combined total of some 60,000 tons, an expansion which seemed to be justified by the rapidly rising tide of emigration. It was in such optimistic circumstances that the White Star Line had been created by T. H. Ismay in 1869. As a result of these foundations the tonnage of steamships on the North Atlantic was more than doubled within the space of a decade.

The initial overcrowding of the North Atlantic sea lanes by so many companies and so much tonnage could be sustained only in profitable operation under conditions of increasing trade. Even so, there were difficulties arising from relative competitive strengths during boom periods such as that existing before 1874. Well established lines, such as Cunard, experienced short periods of acute embarrassment, while the newcomers had to face a whole variety of inhibitions on the free use of resources. It became extremely difficult, for example, to find adequate berths for the increasing number of ships within the Liverpool dock system.[25] For Cunard there was the ever-present fear that competition from so many new companies might not only reduce the volume of its traffic but that the government might be induced to transfer the mail contract.[26] In fact, the claims of the new steamships for a share in the mail contract became so persistent that Cunard was forced into a programme of modernisation.

It was, however, the assertion that Cunard's mail subsidy enabled the company to undercut freight rates and so obtain an unfair advantage that brought to light the existence of a steamship Conference. John Burns, one of Cunard's managing agents, denied the charge, though he admitted that Cunard and Inman had been working a private arrangement for the equalisation of rates. Further, he went on to announce what must then have been one of the earliest forms of steamship Conference on record.

> To show the necessity for people to look for self-preservation [he stated] there is at the moment in Liverpool what they call a steam Conference of all the British steamship owners in Liverpool and Glasgow whereby all the rates of freight are regulated at that Conference whether by subsided or by non-subsidised lines. The National and Guion companies are parties with Mr Inman and my own company to this arrangement. Therefore, the question of subsidised companies being able to carry at less rates of freight is a gross fallacy.[27]

The interesting question which arises from such a disclosure is why such an early Conference was called into being, for, operating as it did in 1869, it must have had antecedents and pre-dates other known steamship Conferences by several years.

In late 1867 or early in 1868 Cunard and Inman had entered into a working agreement fixing rates of freight.[28] They were joined by the National, Guion, Allan and Anchor lines.[29] Besides cargo rates the arrangement also covered minimum passenger fares. It is obvious that this was not a protective device against foreign competition, for in 1870 the four Liverpool companies, Cunard, Inman, National and Guion, carried 96 per cent of the passenger traffic to America.[30] This being so, it is pertinent to enquire further into the nature of this type of agreement.

The need for a shipping Conference amongst British shipping lines at this time was made clear during the depression in the Liverpool–American trade between 1874 and 1878. For more than five years the Conference had worked reasonably well because, under the terms of the agreement, the lines had been placed on a relatively equal footing in competing with each other for the trade available, though there had been considerable differentiation in frequency of sailings and in quality of service. With the onset of falling traffic and falling receipts, however, strains and weakness in the Conference structure began to appear. On 1 May 1874 the National Line left the Conference, supposedly in protest against a refusal by the other lines to allow National to charge lower rates in compensation for that company's slower ships.[31] In strictly legal terms this was a valid protest, because the principle had been admitted (even as early as 1850) that older and slower ships should be allowed to charge a lower rate than newer, faster ones. There were two other causes of dissension. National complained bitterly that the government subvention paid to Cunard made it impossible for its own ships to offer, under the agreed rates, the same kind and quality of service as the other lines were able to provide.[32] Furthermore, when National began despatching ships to Boston, Massachusetts—a port which Cunard had always maintained as a particular preserve—the rift between Conference members became wider, and the whole agreement was brought to an end. There followed a fierce rate war, not only between Cunard and National but involving all the other companies, and for a period of thirteen months there was severe competition for both passengers and cargo. Steerage fares fell as low as £2, freight rates were halved, receipts fell sharply and all the lines suffered financial loss.[33]

It became a matter of urgency for the agreement to be renewed, and negotiations between the Liverpool lines were opened to that end. By September 1874 some form of compromise seems to have been reached, but this was made null by National and Guion, who claimed that the differential rates allowed them were not sufficient.[34] William Lamport, himself a shipowner and a member of the Liverpool Steamship Owners' Association, was brought in as mediator but his task was made virtually impossible by Cunard's bitter resentment over the National Line's incursion into the Boston trade. By May 1875 Charles MacIver had become so perturbed by the worsening trade conditions that he turned to mediation in his company's best interests.[35] He was even less successful than William Lamport, and the whole problem seemed to be intractible of solution.

It was therefore surprising and unexpected that harmony was able to be restored on 4 June 1875. All the lines agreed to accept differential rates, steerage fares being fixed at £5 5s on fast ships and £5 on certain slower ships owned by National and Guion. On the carriage of cargo the fast ships were to charge a tariff of 40s per ton for fine goods, with the slower ships paying 5 per cent primage instead of 10 per cent.[36] It is interesting that these new rates were lower than those ruling under the first Conference. Another source of irritation was removed by a general agreement that no line should henceforth have a preserve in any trade or port.

Unfortunately, compromise and good intentions were no proof against adverse fluctuations in trade. The depression in America got worse, and as a consequence there was a drastic reduction in the flow of emigrants from Europe. Average numbers of passengers carried per ship fell from 340 in 1874 to 210 in 1875.[37] Worse was to follow. In 1876 the chairman of the National Line reported that 'all the steerage passengers that we took from Liverpool in 1876 could have been taken over in three steamers. The falling off has been nearly from 40,000 to 6,000 and the resultant loss of profit to the company on that one item alone exceeds £100,000.'[38] It thus became obvious that, in order to tide over a period of such adverse fluctuations, drastic remedies would have to be applied outside the operation of rate-fixing agreements. Economies were effected by a reduction in expenditure through the suspension of building programmes, by the laying up of ships and in the curtailment of services. Cunard and Inman adopted a stern policy of retrenchment, selling off their old and less efficient ships and adopting various expedients for the diversification of their business. White Star sent some of its ships to the Pacific, and Cunard diverted a few of its larger ships to the Mediterranean trade; but for those ships, built especially for the carriage of passengers, these measures were not appropriate. There was no real substitute for the emigrant traffic.

The financial losses suffered by the Liverpool lines were proof of this fact. With the recovery of the emigrant trade in the early 1880s, however, the threat of competition came mainly from sources external to those hitherto within the power of British companies to control. The first threat came from incursions into the trade by the two powerful German companies, Hamburg–Amerika and North German Lloyd; the second from an attempt to revive an American mercantile marine. Henceforth the North Atlantic ceased to be an ocean predominantly in the control of Britain's maritime power and became instead the scene of bitter international rivalry.

IV

Before entering upon a discussion of competition and passenger agreements after 1886 it is necessary to mention the relative importance of cargo. Cunard, in common with other passenger lines, depended at certain times on freight earnings to cover operating costs. In periods of declining passenger revenue the carriage of cargo provided a relatively important source of income. Between 1860 and 1914, for example, there were years in which Cunard's freight earnings accounted for some 30 per cent of total voyage receipts.[39] In this respect, therefore, the adjustment of freight rates was of concern to management. In general, cargo liner agreements were subjected to the pressures of outside competition in much the same way as were passenger liner agreements. On the whole, however, the former (apart from those confined to the North Atlantic trade) were more permanent in operation and worked in the interests of harmony amongst shipowners.

As the trend in freight rates was steadily downwards from 1870 to 1908, volume became important. Thus in gross terms it was more lucrative to carry bulk cargoes of wheat, cotton, linseed and sugar. Though passenger liners were designed to carry cargo, they normally transported high-value, low-volume merchandise. If bulk cargoes were dealt in, they were usually accommodated under charters; but at times when high-value, low-volume cargoes were scarce bulk shipments such as wheat were carried. Furthermore, the possibility of creating a separate Atlantic Conference for cargo was inhibited by the simple fact that the severity of competition on the various Atlantic routes ruled out the use of a rebate system. Without a rebate shippers had little incentive to send bulk cargo in ships belonging to passenger lines. There was, as a consequence, a greater incentive to rate cutting. Although most passenger agreements contained clauses relating to cargo, these proved to be much less effective in preventing rate warfare than did the agreements entirely devoted to the carriage of freight on other routes.[40]

The most serious upheaval in the Atlantic cargo trade occurred in 1889. The *Liverpool Journal of Commerce* reported on the intransigence of Liverpool companies in the following terms:

Advices from New York state that the White Star Company has made a sensation in commercial circles by a cut of 50 per cent in freight rates. They assert that all the other lines have been secretly cutting rates and that it is better to have a sharp rate war than to do a cut-throat business. The Cunard Company says it can do business as low as, if not lower than, any other line and will meet and beat the White Star cut.[41]

In short, the cargo agreements among the Liverpool companies trading on the North Atlantic were no whit less uncertain than passenger rate agreements. Unlike cargo agreements on other routes, they disintegrated as soon as trading conditions began to worsen, and, accordingly, freight capacity was adversely affected. As a result a large proportion of a company's earning capacity and ultimate level of profitability was jeopardised.

The impact of changing emphases in the carriage of passengers and cargo across the Atlantic seemed only to demonstrate the need for more precise forms of protection. The introduction of larger and faster ships by all companies created higher degrees of competitive services which, in times of adverse fluctuation in the levels of traffic, led to a wasteful and unprofitable use of resources.

As long as the bulk of the emigrant trade had passed through Britain, Continental shipping lines had very little chance of breaking into a trade almost wholly served by British companies. In the 1880s, however, the passage of emigrants from Germany, Austria and eastern Europe through Hamburg and Bremen provided the North German Lloyd and Hamburg–Amerika shipping companies with the same basic financial springboard as that from which the strength of Liverpool companies had stemmed after the 1860s. This was given greater significance as the source of emigration shifted to central, eastern and southern Europe, thus providing the German lines with a geographical advantage, apart from their control of the frontier stations after 1894.

The further fact that German shipyards were ill equipped to provide the right types of vessel was no real deterrent to their entry into the emigrant business, for the majority of German ships were built on the Clyde. Undoubtedly, however, the real driving force behind the growth of a German mercantile marine came from the inspiration and organisational skills of such managers as Albert Ballin of Hamburg–Amerika and Herr Lohmann of North German Lloyd. If one accepts the assertion by D. H. Aldcroft that 'German shipowners had few marked economic advantages over their rivals' the implication must be that success was achieved by dynamic management.[42] These men exploited every opportunity likely to yield a high return on capital. North German Lloyd had carried British mails since the late 1860s, and in 1886 made a successful bid to capture the contract for the carriage of mails from Southampton for a short period.[43] As a means of overcoming seasonal fluctuations in the emigrant trade Hamburg–Amerika instituted winter cruises in 1891.[44] There is no doubt at all (as D. H. Aldcroft has proved) that they made deep inroads into Britain's privileged position in the North Atlantic trade in the years before 1900.[45]

Both German lines used the conference system merely as a device to undermine the power of British companies. There were three principal methods by which the latter could combat the growth of such overseas competition. The first was counter-amalgamation. Several tentative attempts had been made in the 1890s to explore the possibility of Cunard and White Star joining forces; but these attempts had always foundered on the rock of personal antipathy and pride in family achievement.[46] At a somewhat later date an abortive attempt by Sir John Ellerman was made to secure control of Cunard.[47] It was an age in which larger and larger units of shipping capital were brought together in an endeavour to secure greater power. Cunard alone resisted the temptation to be drawn into such a combination. The second recourse was inducing a competitor to take his services elsewhere. This was the successful plan agreed upon by Cunard and White Star in 1891, persuading Clement Griscom, president of Inman and International, to make Antwerp rather than Liverpool their European terminal. To offset this, Southampton was made the British port of call for American ships, and John Burns of Cunard and T. H. Ismay of White Star agreed to indemnify the American line for this change, White Star paying £20,000 and Cunard £10,000 per annum for a period of five years.[48]

The third method of alleviating competition was through the reorganisation and redevelopment of Conference agreements and procedures. This, however, was not easily achieved; for, although most North Atlantic shipping companies had by 1900 accepted the need for some sort of agreement, the Liverpool lines in particular had always resisted the idea of pooling or sharing out passenger revenue. This attitude was based on the contention that the more efficient lines would continuously subsidise the less efficient. As a consequence the agreements which eventually found acceptance were usually based on complex systems of differential rates for the various lines within the ring. The whole situation was further complicated by the fact that some Liverpool lines were carrying passengers and freight from German, Scandinavian and American ports as well as from Liverpool. The control of so disparate a business involved a wide range of agreement and participation in various short-lived Conferences. Of these the most important for Cunard were those concerned with the carriage of emigrants from Liverpool to Boston and New York.

In general, passenger Conference agreements were brought into being at times when the destructive effects of rate wars demanded common action. Between 1884 and 1885, for example, emigration from the United Kingdom dropped by as much as 60,000 on the figure for the previous year.[49] Steerage rates were cut to £3 and, following this collapse, unrestricted competition caused the break-up of existing agreements, based on the principles of the 1875 compromise. In fact, Cunard was the first to withdraw from agreed commitments.[50] Rate cutting was widespread, though on this occasion White Star would seem to have been under less pressure than Cunard in reducing fares. The result was that Cunard not only undercut White Star but captured an appreciable amount of the rival company's traffic. To Ismay's incredulity, Cunard cut rates to a figure which he believed to be well below cost.[51] In the event, it was not possible for any line, however well managed, to hold such a position for more than a few months. By the end of August 1885 the steerage rate had been restored to £5 5s, but it came too late to catch the peak-of-season traffic.[52] It was, therefore, no inducement for complete and loyal adherence to the maintenance of agreements, especially during the winter months when seasonal shortages of emigrants led to reduced sailings and the laying up of ships. Consequently, fresh agreements had to be negotiated to adjust rates, sailing schedules and agents' commissions. For the next ten years this pattern of dissension, agreement, negotiation and companies opting out became a common phenomenon. It was not a happy atmosphere in which to conduct steamship operations. 'Mr Ismay has of late years assumed the rights of a freelance,' complained Vernon Brown to Cunard; '. . . the White Star people seem disposed to rule or ruin.'[53] Thus it was that lack of any consistent policy between British passenger lines meant that there was very little real resistance to the determined and united opposition from American and Continental lines.

By contrast, the agreements between Continental companies were formidable in their effect, being designed primarily to give the German companies the greatest possible advantage over their rivals. The general background from which such agreements sprang was that they should cease competing with British services in British ports in return for a like restriction on the activities of British companies in Continental ports. The first attempt to negotiate an agreement between British and Continental lines occurred in 1885.[54] Two Conferences were formed in that year. The first was a North Atlantic Conference composed of British lines with headquarters in New York, entitled the North Atlantic Passenger Conference (NAPC). The second was a Conference of North European Steamship Lines and was the result of a meeting held at Cologne in April 1885. The European lines invited the British lines to participate in joint discussions about the regulation of rates. It is possible that the approach was prompted by Albert Ballin's attack on the British lines' monopoly of the Scandinavian traffic to New York. This was to be effected by the establishment of a line between Stettin and the USA. In the event of this project failing, Ballin made it clear that Hamburg-

Amerika would invade British ports and carry steerage passengers from Liverpool via Le Havre and from Plymouth via Hamburg.[55]

Cunard's directors were greatly perturbed by this threat of competition in their home port, and in 1886 an agreement was signed under which Ballin withdrew the Scandinavian service, though as a *quid pro quo* his company was given access to certain British ports for the carriage of steerage passengers. D. H. Aldcroft has given full particulars concerning the establishment of this agreement.[56] Minimum steerage rates were approved and a clearing house was set up in Hamburg for the distribution of passengers between British and German lines. Aldcroft asserts that, for a time, this agreement worked reasonably well. This was probably true of British lines apart from Cunard. The directors of that company had given but a grudging acceptance to membership and they were highly suspicious of Ballin's motives.[57] In a particular sense they had been outwitted, for having been forced to enter the Conference it became extremely difficult to lower rates as and when occasion demanded. Furthermore, it soon became clear that Cunard was becoming apprehensive about the operation of the agreement as a whole. The directors complained that their company was not receiving the share of the traffic to which it was legally entitled. They also had grave doubts whether Hamburg–Amerika had really withdrawn from the Scandinavian trade.[58] Cunard was the first to withdraw from the agreement, an action which undoubtedly induced other British lines to follow suit.

The break-up of this first European Conference was greatly resented by Ballin. Having been thwarted in his first encounter with Cunard, he tried a different tactic. He had cherished the idea of pooling the North Atlantic steerage traffic and of bringing all lines engaged in it under one cover. This was a proposition which, as already stated, had been previously rejected by both Cunard and White Star. Ballin's chance, however, came unexpectedly with the prospect of a depletion in the trade, caused by cholera in Europe and depression in America. It became obvious that a desperate struggle for passengers would follow, rates would tumble, ships would be laid up and heavy losses of revenue would be sustained by every line. The future seemed to be so foreboding that it was enough to bring a pool into being. This creation was within the framework of the Nordatlantischer Dampfer Linien Verband (NDLV) and included the North German Lloyd, Hamburg–Amerika, Holland America and Red Star lines.[59] Provision was made for British and American lines to join, but no great enthusiasm was shown by such companies in the initial stages of the operation. Again, D. H. Aldcroft, using German archives, has given an excellent account of the arrangements.[60] Briefly, the participants received a share of the westbound steerage traffic from northern European ports, plus or minus movements in a line's tonnage or passengers being met by compensatory adjust-ments in the levels of quotas and fares. Though British companies were invited to join, they eventually refused on being informed that their share of the Continental traffic would be only 14 per cent. So fragile was the state of negotiation that it needed only the effect of a falling market to spark off a damaging rate war with the German lines. Once again the steerage fare from Liverpool to New York slumped to £3, a rate which persisted through 1893. 'The low rate of steerage', com-plained a Cunard director bitterly, 'has so far not increased the numbers outwards ... It is very mortifying to have to carry them for such miserable pay.'[61] Conditions remained depressed throughout the first half of the following year, and by August 1895 fresh approaches from the Continental lines resulted in yet another form of agreement to which British, American and Continental lines subscribed.

Under the provisions of the 1895 Declaration of Intent (signed in September) the main levels of proposals were that the Continental lines should withdraw from the Finnish and Scandinavian berths, and that the British lines (apart from Anchor) should retire from the Italian trade both outwards and homewards while retaining 6 per cent of out-ward passages from Libau to Le Havre. Finally, the Continental lines agreed to retire from the British traffic outwards and homewards.[62] The significant difference between this agreement (which was to last for about three years) and the 1892 proposal was that British lines were allocated 6 per cent instead of 14 per cent of Continental traffic. Other consequential arrangements were to follow. In 1896 minimum cabin fares were fixed on both fast and slow ships; the summer season was defined as running from 1 May to 31 October.[63] In 1898 agreement was reached by fourteen lines allocating eastbound and westbound steam-ship routes across the North Atlantic.[64] Within the terms of this agree-ment the German lines undertook to leave the Scandinavian traffic to the British lines and to the Danish Thingvalla line. It appeared that at last common sense was prevailing and that internecine strife between rival companies engaged in the North Atlantic passenger trade would become no more than an unhappy memory.

Alas for such hopes! At the very time these apparently co-operative meetings were taking place Cunard and other British companies were becoming more and more dissatisfied with their small share of Con-tinental business. Their resentment was further exacerbated by the methods employed by foreign lines to capture their trade. The whole structure so laboriously built up became subject to recrimination and strife. With yet another adverse fluctuation in the level of emigration in 1898–9 a rate war broke out and the joint Conference began to dis-integrate, though in fact Cunard did not break all ties with it until 1903.[65]

So far this review of the many attempts to find a solution of the bitter rivalry which characterised passenger carrying between 1868 and 1900 does not make edifying reading. The fact that the trade became increasingly volatile and that solutions, when found, proved to be ephemeral undoubtedly caused a vast waste of resources. Too much capital was poured into what proved to be an unstable and at times an unprofitable venture. Mistrust led to rate wars and increasingly to low return on capital employed. By the beginning of the twentieth century these difficulties were magnified through a change in emphasis. The amalgamation of shipping companies into powerful competitive units raised the strength of competition from a purely local and individualistic plane to one of international dimensions. The struggle became a matter for government intervention in the maintenance of a British mercantile marine.

V

In 1902 the formation of Morgan's combine, the International Mercantile Marine, greatly accelerated the competitive pressure against Cunard. This combine not only brought together certain powerful American companies but added to its power by taking over White Star's share capital, together with the capital and the ships of other companies in the Ellerman group.[66] The threat to Cunard became more pronounced when it was made known that the two German shipping lines had entered into an alliance with the American combine for the purpose of waging both a defensive and an offensive war against Cunard.

In the face of this array of rival shipping interests Cunard was forced to seek help from government sources in order to build bigger and faster ships to beat off competitors. The details of the negotiations leading to the granting of a government loan to build the *Lusitania* and *Mauretania*, together with an operational subsidy, are published elsewhere.[67] It is sufficient to state here that, until the new ships could be put upon the berth, Cunard had to meet and overcome determined attempts to drive its ships from their established trades on the Atlantic and from the Mediterranean.

By the middle of 1904 the rate war against Cunard was intensified. Ships in the Morgan combine began carrying westbound emigrants from London for as little as £2. At a board meeting on 11 June 1904 the Cunard directors agreed that as from 13 June the following rates would be charged on westbound third-class traffic: *Campania* and *Lucania*, £3; *Umbria*, *Ivernia*, *Etruria* and *Saxonia*, £2 15s 0d; all Continental westbound rates £3 off, and first-class rates from Rotterdam, Paris, Antwerp and Bremen to be the same as those from London. Eastbound rates were left at the discretion of their New York agents to reduce as circumstances should dictate. The Morgan group replied by reducing their rate for steerage passengers to something less than 30*s*.[68] As a result Cunard was forced in August to instruct the New York office to lower immediately the eastbound cash minimum to £12 for saloon fares and to £8 for second-class cabin on the *Campania* and *Lucania*, and on all other ships to £10 for saloon and £6 for second-class accommodation.[69] Thus originated one of the fiercest rate wars in the history of the North Atlantic.

This state of affairs could not be long maintained by either side. Though, in the course of the struggle, Cunard had managed to carry more passengers and increase gross earnings by £50,000, total direct running costs increased by £217,000, thus reducing net income by approximately £160,000 in 1904.[70] It is true that a small part of the £217,000 cost was devoted to the inauguration of the New York–Fiume service and that this was, therefore, a development charge; but the general position was that marginal revenue was not increasing at a rate sufficient to cover increasing costs. There is also evidence that constituents of the Morgan combine were making comparable losses.[71] Not least among these were the German lines, and as a consequence a Conference was called at Frankfurt at which Cunard and the Continental lines were represented.

In order to understand the significance of this Frankfurt Conference to Cunard it must be made clear that the company had recently built up a profitable business in the carriage of Hungarian and Austrian emigrants from Fiume to New York. This was a trade in which the German lines also participated. The rate war had affected the German companies adversely in this trade, and Albert Ballin, on their behalf, suggested to the Conference that Cunard should, in respect of the Hungarian business, become a member of the Continental pool.[72] This was in the nature of an olive branch, as by implication it would have given Cunard a share of other Continental business. In practice, however, the share of the traffic was to be based on the ratio between the number of Cunard sailings from Fiume and that of the other Continental lines. This worked out at twenty-six sailings per annum, or 5·27 per cent of the total Continental business. For any number of emigrants carried in excess of this percentage Cunard would be required to pay a specified sum per head into the pool. Conversely, the company would be paid *pro rata* for any number under that percentage.[73]

Such an arrangement was not acceptable to Cunard, as it would have involved a loss on every sailing. As a counter-proposal the company put forward a new percentage designed to give it a minimum of 40,000 passengers per annum. This in turn was subjected to further amendment by the chairman of the Conference to the effect that Cunard should be entitled to carry from Fiume and Liverpool a number of passengers equivalent to two-thirds of the Hungarian emigration; but if such numbers should be less than 26,000 the Continental lines should pay to Cunard on such shortage a fixed rate per head.[74] If the number exceeded 40,000, however, Cunard should pay to the Continental lines the same rate on the excess. Also, if the total number of Continental passengers should be reduced in any year below 300,000 the minimum above mentioned should be *pro rata* reduced.[75] If the total number in any one year exceeded 400,000 the maximum of 40,000 allowed to Cunard should be proportionately increased.[76] This offer, which was somewhat more to Cunard's advantage, was, however, rejected by the Continental lines.

Nevertheless, despite frustrations, some progress towards a settlement was made, and it was reported to the Cunard board on 17 November 1904 that provisional agreement had been reached with the German companies. This agreement was approved by the Hungarian Government in December. Accordingly, the rate war was given a tentative termination in January 1905 and passenger rates were maintained at agreed levels.[77] By March Lord Inverclyde, chairman of Cunard, was able to make a full report on the negotiations during the past year and indicate the agreed rates to be charged for first- and second-class passengers in addition to those for steerage.[78] It was a somewhat uneasy truce. On 13 April Lord Inverclyde made a further statement informing his fellow directors that, in his opinion, better terms could have been arranged had the company fought longer and 'if there had not been so great a desire to make peace'.[79] He also accused the International Mercantile Marine of breaking agreements made between themselves and Cunard on 14 January—agreements on which all the other contracts were contingent. Cunard therefore informed Albert Ballin and J. P. Morgan that they considered themselves 'absolutely free both in regard to rates and in every other respect'.[80]

It was, to say the least, an unfortunate moment to adopt so unconciliatory an attitude. The rate war continued in a desultory way, and the regularity of service from Mediterranean ports was seriously affected—so much so that the Hungarian Government put forward proposals in December 1905 to form a national shipping line to take over the agreement with Cunard for the carriage of new emigrants to the United States. This proposal, however, proved abortive, as the Hungarian Government could not raise the necessary capital to purchase the Mediterranean ships and goodwill of Cunard's fleet.[81]

In essence, the prolongation of the struggle was a direct consequence of the alliance between Morgan's combine and the German lines. As already stated, this alliance was both defensive and offensive in operation and was mainly directed against Cunard's control of the carriage of emigrants from Mediterranean ports.

It is true [stated Cunard's chairman] that the Continental companies were annoyed with the arrangements which we had made with the Hungarian Government for a service between Fiume and New York, but as I said last year, it was a simple matter of business, which we or anyone else were quite free to enter into. The Continental companies have no right to object to our opening up a new route or developing new business just as they themselves have done.[82]

Furthermore, when it became known that the German lines had sought the active assistance of companies in the Morgan combine to bring competitive pressure against Cunard the rift widened.

Opposition to Cunard took various forms. There was political pressure on the Hungarian Government to terminate the agreement with the company; there was intimidation of Cunard's agents in Fiume and threats to agents in the United States by a prospective boycott of their services should they continue to book passages on Cunard ships, 'with the result', declared Cunard's chairman, 'that, in many instances, agents have been alienated from us and we have been obliged to find and appoint new ones'.[83]

Against this background must be set both the cyclical pattern and the declining trend in emigration from British ports across the Atlantic. Such adverse influences, however, were sometimes subject to mitigation, as in 1907, for example, by the maintenance of westbound freight rates.[84] Nevertheless, if such ameliorating factors are discounted, there is no doubt that the earning capacity (particularly that in relation to tonnage employed) of most passenger lines was seriously curtailed by purely economic pressures. The wasteful effects of cut-throat competition aggravated the decline in business caused by worsening conditions. By the beginning of 1908 it had become clear to Cunard's competitors that an agreement on steerage and other rates was vital to the continuation of all services. The German emperor himself took a hand in bringing the two sides together. 'The emperor', stated William Watson, Cunard's chairman, 'had said that he was going to tell Mr Ballin that he must settle things with the Cunard; that it was absurd this fighting and cutting of rates and throwing away money.'[85] Accordingly, the fierce and unnecessary rivalry was stopped and, by agreement, all rates were restored. 'This agreement, we hope', stated William Watson on 23 April 1908, 'will work satisfactorily for the next few years.'[86] The advent of peace was given added significance through the putting into operation of the *Lusitania* and *Mauretania*. These fast ships were run in conjunction with either the *Lucania* or the *Campania* on a three-ship weekly service, leaving Liverpool on Saturdays. This enabled the company to inaugurate a further service with four ships leaving Liverpool on Wednesdays. This, indeed, was wise and economical management designed to make the best and most efficient use of resources. It was also a sign of Cunard's technical superiority over its rivals. With such superiority the company could adopt a less intractible attitude towards the Continental lines.

The Conference referred to by Cunard's chairman met on 31 January 1908. The meeting was held in London and was representative of all lines engaged in the North Atlantic trade. The agenda included consideration of agreements on rates for first and second-class passengers and a pooling arrangement for third-class emigrants. In tracing the course of events over the past five years Albert Ballin referred specifically to the difficulties caused by the agreement between the Hungarian government and Cunard 'by which a service was formed which seriously interfered with the business of the Continental lines'.[87] He also referred to the volume of passengers carried by British lines over and above the 6 per cent which they had accepted in the agreement of 1898. The first-class rates were then examined, those for the *Mauretania* and *Lusitania* being taken as a basis for the fixing of a graduated tariff for various classes of ship. A minimum of £25 for first class and £12 for second class was agreed.[88] The proposals relating to the third-class pooling scheme met with considerable difficulty, though it was agreed that Cunard should carry some 13·75 per cent of both eastbound and westbound traffic, with complete freedom for its Fiume service westbound.[89] All non-Hungarian passengers carried on Cunard's Fiume service, however, had to pay compensation to the general pool. On eastbound sailings Cunard was required to enter the pool in respect of non-Italian passengers to Trieste, on the basis of the company's average carryings for 1906 and 1907.[90] As an overall measure of commitment Cunard agreed to limit its westbound Continental ships to twenty-six regular and four extra crossings. Should this number be increased, the company would compensate the pool for the additional numbers carried.[91] All the above proposals were to take effect from 1 March 1908.

It is sufficient in this present context to note that peace in the competitive struggle was achieved for a period of approximately three years, adjustments to rates being made by general consent in accordance with the levels of demand for service. After 1911 the competitive pressures were contained by a series of short-term extensions of existing agreements. In the six months before the outbreak of war in 1914, however, the German lines came into conflict with one another, Ballin and Heineken of North German Lloyd quarrelling openly over the control of the Austrian frontier stations.[92] This quarrel was carried to a bitter conclusion by the German lines withdrawing from the Conference, and a short but sharp renewal of rate warfare took place during the spring and summer months previous to the outbreak of world war in August.

Thus from 1850 to 1914 Cunard had been involved in a constantly changing pattern of agreement in the control of its North Atlantic trade. The evolution of procedures had been inherent in a developing policy to maintain the company's strength under conditions of fluctuating demand and changes in the patterns of the trade. From the first pooling agreement with the Collins Line in 1850 to the regulation of competition for the emigrant business in the 1860s and 1870s the control had come within the scope of a Liverpool agreement. This had subsequently extended to a more comprehensive arrangement with Continental and American lines and the institution of an Atlantic pool. With the advent of the Morgan combine, however, the emphasis had changed, and the fierceness of the ensuing struggle had underlined the necessity of applying agreements to all categories of passenger traffic. The 1908 Conference was probably a most successful attempt to secure agreement among so wide and disparate a body of competitors. If by 1914 the structure of agreement was once again beginning to disintegrate, the lesson which such co-operation had taught undoubtedly proved to be a basis for future action. It is difficult to make any assessment of the advantages which Cunard might have enjoyed by being party to successive agreements over a period of sixty-four years. It is probably true that what advantage accrued came not so much from Conference regulation as from the efforts of its own management in attempting to secure the maximum revenue at the lowest possible cost.[93]

NOTES

[1] The primary sources of evidence for this chapter are drawn from the shipping archives of the Cunard, White Star, Guion, National and Inman lines. In addition, much reference has been made to the MacIver papers, kindly presented to the author by Mrs Lois Rae, granddaughter of Charles MacIver. The Cunard papers are used by permission of the Cunard Steam Ship Company. The citations are as follows: MacIver papers, MIP; Cunard papers, CP; Cunard board minutes, BM; minutes of Cunard annual ordinary general meetings, OGM; verbatim reports of such meetings, VR.

[2] CP, copy of contract of the British and North American Royal Mail Steam Packet Company and relative deeds, 1839–45, document dated 18 March 1839; J. Napier, *Life of Robert Napier* (1904), p.93.

[3] CP, ships' specifications for the *Britannia, Acadia, Columbia* and *Caledonia*.

[4] CP, agreement dated 4, 6, 7, 18 and 25 June, 23 July 1839.

[5] Edwin Hodder, *Sir George Burns, Bart.* (1890); F. L. Babcock, *Spanning the Atlantic*, (date) pp.44–9; MIP, mss of a short history of the MacIver family.

[6] MIP, Charles MacIver correspondence with Samuel Cunard and the Burns brothers; ships' day books and instructions, 1848–60.

[7] MIP, Charles MacIver correspondence with his son, David MacIver, and with A. Squarey.

[8] Parl. Papers, 464 (1846), p.37; *Report of Select Committee on Halifax and Boston Mails* (1849), pp.1–5.

[9] *Ibid.*

[10] R. G. Albion, *The Rise of New York, 1815–60* (1970), p.324.

[11] *Ibid.*, p.325.

[12] MIP, Samuel Cunard to Charles MacIver, 1 May 1847.

[13] Albion, *op. cit.*, p.327.

[14] MIP, memo from Charles MacIver to his partners, 1 March 1850.

15 Albion, *op. cit.*, p.328.
16 MIP, accounts and papers relating to the agreement between the British and North American Royal Mail Steam Packet Company and the United States Mail Steam Ship Company, 1850–6.
17 *Ibid.*
18 The financial details of the annual settlements are contained in MIP as cited. These details are published by F. E. Hyde in his business history of Cunard (see note 93 below).
19 MIP, papers and accounts relating to the agreement as cited, 29 May 1850.
20 *Ibid.*
21 *Ibid.*
22 MIP, suspension of the agreement, 11 November 1856.
23 See n. 18.
24 *Liverpool Journal of Commerce*, 8 January 1875, and F. C. Bowen, *A Century of Atlantic Travel* (1932), p.105.
25 CP, secretaries' letter books, 1875–95, *passim*; there is much correspondence on this subject with the Mersey Docks and Harbour Board.
26 MIP, *British and North American Mail Contracts and Relative Papers 1869*.
27 Parl. Papers, Select Committee on mail contracts, 1868–9 (106), VI, p.116.
28 MIP, *British and North American Mail Contracts and Relative Papers 1869*.
29 Select Committee on mails, *op. cit.*, evidence of William Inman, p.130.
30 Parl. Papers, *Progress of British Merchant Shipping*, 1882, LXII, 22.
31 National Steamship Company papers, report of chairman for 1874; also *Liverpool Journal of Commerce*, 26 February, 1875.
32 *Ibid.*
33 Chairman's reports to annual meetings of Cunard, Guion, National and White Star lines, 1875–6.
34 MIP, Charles MacIver correspondence, September 1874.
35 *Liverpool Journal of Commerce*, 14 May 1875.
36 MIP, Charles MacIver correspondence, 1–10 June 1875.
37 *Ibid.*, 31 December 1875.
38 Report of chairman of National line published in *Liverpool Journal of Commerce*, 23 February 1877.
39 CP, statements and accounts 1880–1900.
40 From information supplied by Mr T. Laird, former general manager of Cunard Steam Ship Co. Ltd.
41 *Liverpool Journal of Commerce*, 16 February 1889.
42 D. H. Aldcroft, *The Development of British Industry and Foreign Competition 1875–1914* under the chapter 'Mercantile Marine', p.361.
43 CP, OGM report for 1886.
44 R. Bastin, 'Cunard and the Liverpool emigrant traffic 1860–1900' (University of Liverpool, M.A. thesis), p.88.
45 D. H. Aldcroft, *op. cit.*, p.357.
46 White Star papers, Cunard file, January 1889, memo from Sir William Forwood to T. H. Ismay.
47 CP, correspondence, J. Ellerman to Lord Inverclyde, 5 and 8 July, 26 August 1899, 22 March 1900.
48 White Star papers, correspondence between T. H. Ismay, J. Burns and Clement Griscom, August 1891 to March 1892.
49 BM, 10 March 1884.
50 *Ibid.*
51 CP, T. H. Ismay to John Burns, 3 February 1885.
52 CP, directors' letters, file 1; J. Houmphrey to Vernon Brown & Co., 1885.
53 CP, directors' letters, *loc. cit.*, Vernon Brown & Co. to D. Jardine, 23 February 1888.
54 CP, statements and accounts for 1885.
55 D. H. Aldcroft, *op. cit.*
56 *Ibid.*
57 BM, for 1886 and 1887, *passim*.
58 *Ibid.*
59 W. H. Roper, *The Atlantic Conference 1921–1939*, privately printed, p.5.

[60] D. H. Aldcroft, *op. cit.*

[61] CP, directors' letters, *loc. cit.*, D. Jardine to Vernon Brown & Co., 25 July 1894.

[62] CP, directors' letter, *loc. cit.*, memo from D. Jardine to E. Taylor, 1895.

[63] BM, 27 October 1896; *Shipping World*, 16 December 1896, p.719.

[64] CP, agreements and related papers for 1898.

[65] VR, OGM, 29 March 1899.

[66] CP, documents relating to the Cunard Steam Ship Co. and the Government, 1905, pp.15 ff.

[67] In F. E. Hyde's business history on the Cunard Steam Ship Company (see note 93 below).

[68] CP, minutes of evidence of the US Commission of Enquiry into the operation of agreement AA, 1912.

[69] BM, 18 August 1904.

[70] CP, accounts for the year 1904.

[71] BM, 31 August 1904.

[72] *Ibid.*

[73] *Ibid.*

[74] *Ibid.*

[75] *Ibid.*

[76] *Ibid.*

[77] BM, 16 March 1905.

[78] *Ibid.*, also 15 June and 20 July 1905.

[79] BM, 13 April 1905; also VR, OGM, 13 April 1905.

[80] *Ibid.*

[81] BM, 7 December 1905.

[82] VR, OGM, 13 April 1905.

[83] *Ibid.*

[84] VR, OGM, 23 April 1908.

[85] CP, chairmen and directors' letters, William Watson to V. H. Brown, 24 December 1907.

[86] VR, OGM, 23 April 1908.

[87] CP, reports of meetings leading to 1908 agreement on rates; particularly correspondence from William Watson; see William Watson to V. H. Brown, 7 February 1908.

[88] *Ibid.*

[89] CP, correspondence and agreement, January 1908.

[90] *Ibid.*

[91] *Ibid.*

[92] CP, chairmen and directors' letters, A. A. Booth to Charles P. Sumner, 14 January 1914.

[93] The author is indebted to Messrs Macmillan & Company for permission to use material in this chapter, as some part of it is taken from the author's *Cunard and the North Atlantic 1840–1973* (Macmillan, 1975).

D. H. Aldcroft

12

Investment in and utilisation of manpower: Great Britain and her rivals, 1870–1914

It has frequently been suggested that many British industries were technically backward compared with their nearest overseas rivals in the latter half of the nineteenth century. The causes of this technical lag have been much debated by economic historians, but a consensus of opinion has not yet been reached. Whether the failings of the entrepreneur make him the villain of the piece or whether his actions were based on a logical economic rationale remains the subject of dispute for the moment.[1]

Be that as it may, it is a fact that this backwardness was not confined to the strictly technological field—that is, to the adoption of new processes, new machines or better methods of production. Indeed, it would appear that the deficiencies extended further than this, to the question of investment in human capital, and it is less easy to find sound economic arguments to explain the lag on this front.

In recent years the subject has attracted a considerable amount of attention from economists, and although it is difficult to formulate precise relationships between rates of growth and investment in human resources, it is none the less apparent that inadequate investment in this field will in the long run limit the possibilities of economic growth.[2] Since the acquisition and spread of new techniques is dependent to a large extent on the rate at which knowledge about them is disseminated, it follows that investment in human resources or talent has an important part to play in establishing the foundations on which further growth can take place. Without a reservoir of human talent able to comprehend and utilise, or for that matter even produce, new techniques, economic growth in the long term would stagnate. In fact it has been suggested that the rate of return on investment in human capital may well be at least as large as that on physical capital. Denison, in a recent study,[3] concludes that education and research have made the most important contribution to the growth of the American economy in the period 1929–57, while Kendrick has shown[4] that there is a positive association between productivity changes and outlays on research and development.

Obviously, investment in manpower is a more important factor in growth today than it was in the nineteenth century. The complex and sophisticated nature of the modern industrial economy requires a sizeable outlay on educational and developmental work, and most mature economies devote a far higher proportion of their total national product to investment in training manpower than they did in the nineteenth century. Nevertheless, the importance of investment in human resources at that time should not be underestimated, since at least one country, Germany, was spending over $2\frac{1}{2}$ per cent of her national product on education by 1914.[5] It was in this period that the basis of industrial production was becoming increasingly complex from both a scientific and a managerial point of view, and therefore it required the services of an ever-increasing number of scientists, production engineers and other qualified personnel. In such industries as steel, chemicals and many branches of engineering new advances were being determined by the scientist or the production engineer rather than by the 'practical tinkerer' of the classical industrial revolution.[6] The former multifunctional entrepreneur was being replaced by specialists trained in various fields of management, production techniques and scientific research. Similarly, marketing and distribution methods were changing, especially on the export side, where trained salesmen and trade representatives were becoming increasingly important. Finally, improvements were being made in worker–management relationships and in systems of wage payments designed to improve productivity.

Attention to detail in all three respects involved investment in human capital, or investment in a better educated labour force. International comparisons are difficult to make in this field, and the fragmentary data available for Britain cannot be used to formulate precise relationships between investment in human resources and economic growth. However, much of the evidence we have does suggest that British industrialists were falling behind their American and German counterparts on all three counts.

One of the reasons for the relatively slow rate of technical progress in some British industries was the reluctance of many industrialists to recruit properly trained workers—hence the lack of fundamental scientific research. British manufacturers were generally reluctant to depart from the rule-of-thumb methods which had proved successful in the past, and many seemed even proud of the fact that they carried out little original research or employed few qualified technicians and scientists. 'The only research British entrepreneurs would readily sponsor was that which led quickly to immediate and practical results. They thought in terms of training clever mechanics rather than engineers, and laboratory analysists instead of chemists.'[7] As late as

1904 a leading Sheffield steel-maker was saying that there was a feeling in the industry that young men with engineering and science degrees had spent too much time in theory to have the necessary workshop experience and that degrees stood in the way of obtaining good positions in the industry.[8] This attitude was fairly typical of many British firms, and it stands out in sharp contrast to that adopted abroad, particularly Germany, where '. . . one of the most fundamental and important causes of the present prosperity of the German nation is the close relations which exist in that country between science and practical affairs'.[9] In fact much of the success of Germany (and to a lesser extent America), especially in the newer industries, can be attributed to the systematic and organised application of science to industry, the thorough system of technical education under State auspices and the co-operation between academic institutions and industry. The Germans made every effort to break down the basic raw materials in order to find new derivatives which could be utilised for the manufacture of new products. Painstaking and persistent research by qualified technologists and scientists enabled Germany to exploit her resources fully and to acquire superiority in a wide range of industries, including engineering, chemicals and precision instruments.

The lack of properly trained personnel was particularly acute in science-based industries such as iron and steel, chemicals and electrical manufacturing, where progress was dependent to a large extent upon scientific and technical expertise. Opportunities were certainly lost in steel because of this. The most obvious case is in the mass production of steel, where the scope for the employment of scientific knowledge in solving the problems was considerable.[10] Similarly the technical lags in fuel conservation, in the recovery of by-products and in the exploitation of phosphoric ores can be attributed in part to the same cause. Scientists and trained technicians and engineers were a rarity in British steelworks, whereas on the Continent it was common practice to employ such workers. By the 1890s most of the major European steelworks had a university-trained engineer continually present in each of the main-shops. There was nothing comparable in the British steel industry, and in many works not one member of the engineering staff had a scientific training.[11] Many German firms, moreover, had impressive lists of trained staff at various levels of the managerial hierarchy. As one director of a German iron and steel works pointed out, 'We can compete and make profits because of the scientific basis of our manufacture and the technical education of our workpeople . . . every one of our foremen and managers has had two years' special education at the cost of the firm—a technical and scientific education.'[12] In Britain it was unusual for the managers and directors to have had a good grounding in science subjects. By 1914 fewer than 10 per cent of the steel industry's leaders had received either a technical school training or university education in science.[13]

For the operative there was even less training. 'Any healthy adult who could find employment could enter the industry; by a system of gradually taking byeshifts he found his way on to a team in one department or another and was then promoted by seniority, gaining his training on the job.' No iron and steel company had a special education and training scheme before 1902 for junior operatives, and even after this date progress was slow and patchy.[14]

The contrast between British and German achievements in this respect is brought out even more sharply in the chemical industry. This industry more than any other depended upon an adequate supply of scientifically trained manpower, yet by comparison with Germany British chemical works were seriously understaffed. In 1910 there were fewer than 1,500 trained chemists employed in the British chemical industry, compared with about 5,500 in Germany, while the ratio of university graduates in German and British chemical works was four to one. Moreover, German chemists were generally superior in training and quality to their British counterparts.[15] That Germany's investment in trained manpower produced results is borne out by the report of an informed contemporary witness:

> The sums expended by the German states upon chemical instruction have been amply repaid by the creation and rapid growth of the most important chemical industries and the addition of large sums to the sum total of national wealth. Germany has been enabled by means of the thorough chemical instruction afforded by her universities and technical high schools, and the sound preliminary scholastic education of her students, to rise within the last fifty years to the front rank in chemical industries, and not only to render herself independent of many imports from foreign countries, but also to deprive the latter of many lucrative branches of chemical manufacture and to substitute her own in their stead.[16]

Germany's outstanding success in the dyestuffs trade, and the concomitant decline of the industry in Britain, can be largely attributed to the different attitudes towards science and research. Initially Britain had held the lead in dyes but after the 1860s Germany rapidly established an almost unrivalled supremacy. By 1880 the German industry was substantially larger than the British, while by 1913 it was more than twenty-five times as large. It then produced 85 per cent of world output of dyestuffs, exported four-fifths of its production and supplied Britain with 80 per cent of her total domestic consumption of dyestuffs.[17]

There are a number of reasons to explain the differing fortunes of the British and German dyestuffs trades in this period, but undoubtedly the most important factor was the contrasting approaches to the question of scientific research. Professor Sir James Dewar, addressing the British

Association in 1902, attributed Britain's weakness in chemicals and dyestuffs to the lack of an adequately educated work force, and he reckoned that it would take Britain two generations to catch up with the Germans in general training and specialised equipment.[18] It is significant that nearly all the major discoveries in dyestuffs in the later nineteenth century were developed as a result of painstaking scientific research carried out in chemical laboratories. Given the neglect of research and the scarcity of trained chemists in British chemical works, it is not surprising that the majority of the discoveries were made in Germany, where a premium was placed on applied science. Britain had little to compare with Germany's enormous chemical laboratories and the army of trained scientists which they employed. The Bayer company, for example, completed a laboratory in 1891 costing $1\frac{1}{2}$ million marks and the firm employed a staff of over 100 trained chemists at the end of the nineteenth century (as against fifteen in 1881), nearly a fifth of them engaged on work into the search for new dyes.[19] The big chemical firms in Germany were prepared to spend large sums and years of research in perfecting new products. The Badische chemical works of Ludwigshafen spent no less than £1 million over a period of some seventeen years in order to bring the discovery of artificial indigo to commercial perfection. Another large firm at Höchst was testing (*circa* 1900) some 3,500 new colours annually, of which only eighteen eventually reached the market.[20] As Beer has observed, it was this:

> ... tedious, meticulous, endless experimental work carried on in the coloristic division [that] best illustrates the method and spirit with which the German dye industry overwhelmed all foreign competitors. It won its ascendancy in the dye and chemical field by wrenching thousands of little facts from nature by massed assault. The whole color-testing enterprise during the late 1890s came to be set up like a military operation.[21]

Iron and steel and chemicals were not the only British industries to suffer from a shortage of trained manpower. Many others have been criticised for their unscientific approach to production and failure to recruit the right people. By the end of the nineteenth century the machine tool trade, for example, had degenerated into the most unscientific of the mechanical engineering trades, while the new electrical engineering industry 'took on a tinkering character; many of its leaders were telegraph and telephone men, inventors, wiring contractors, good enough in their fields but rarely engineers in the broad sense.'[22] The cycle trade was no better.

> The deliberate employment of technically educated managerial personnel ... was ... the exception rather than the rule. Many of the leading entrepreneurs in the industry were 'commercial men' with no engineering training of any

sort. Others received only an elementary education supplemented by an engineering apprenticeship.[23]

The slow development of a home demand (and hence production) for chrome-tanned leather has been attributed to the weakness in British industrial chemistry.[24] Even the hosiery industry has been criticised for its slowness to realise 'that the old rule-of-thumb methods that had served well enough in the past were quite inadequate for the age of science and system that was beginning in industry'.[25] Moreover, the deficiency was not simply one of pure scientists. What was particularly needed was a generation of commercial engineers and chemists, that is, men who could combine science and business. The lack of people with such qualifications was a serious deficiency in British industry, especially in such fields as engineering and motor car manufacturing, where modern mass-production methods were applicable. As Saul has pointed out, the vital absentees from the British motor industry

> were the men with a deep knowledge of modern machine tools and the production methods that went with them. The American industry, in marked contrast, had many such engineers, Leland, Flanders, Wills and all those who learned the essentials of automobile manufacturing at the Old works come immediately to mind. In Britain the engineers were obsessed by the technical product rather than by the technique of production.[26]

Some industries were even short of skilled workmen or craftsmen. Habakkuk has noted how the lack of a highly intelligent class of work-men to carry out the practical details was responsible for the fact that many valuable inventions in the steel industry were abandoned in England.[27]

The failure of British industry to recruit sufficient trained personnel can be attributed in part to the fact that they were in short supply owing to the defects of the country's educational system. At times the dearth of good scientists, especially chemists, was so acute that the more enlightened British firms were forced to recruit staff from Germany.[28] Britain had little to compare with the scale and provision of university, technical and elementary education in Germany which ultimately provided an army of technicians and scientists for the science-based industries of that country. Until the middle of the nineteenth century there was little in the way of formal science teaching other than that provided by the new University of London, the mechanics' institutes, occasional evening classes and a few courses in elementary science in the more enlightened grammar schools. During the latter half of the century improvements were made at all levels, the most notable advances being the establishment of new science-oriented universities in the provinces and the beginnings of technical education by local authorities. But developments were slow and patchy, especially in technical education, and by 1914 the British system of scientific and technical education was still far behind that of Germany, particularly from the point of view of providing trained recruits for industry.[29] At that time Britain had only about 9,000 full-time university students, compared with around 58,000 in Germany—a figure not reached in this country until 1938. In addition, Germany had 16,000 polytechnic students, whereas there were only 4,000 taking comparable courses in Great Britain.[30] It has been estimated that in 1912 eleven polytechnic schools—they were granted degree status in 1899—were supplying German industry with 3,000 engineers per annum. By contrast, the annual number of students graduating with first- and second-class honours degrees in science and in technology (including mathematics) from universities in England and Wales was only 530, and but a small proportion of these had received any training in research.[31] Yet even this was probably an improvement on what had gone before. In 1872 a British deputation visiting Germany and Switzerland found that all the universities and colleges in England contained fewer students taking up research and the higher branches of chemistry than a single German university, that of Munich.[32]

Comparative statistical data for other branches of education are unfortunately not available for this period. But nearly all the contemporary observations made on the subject by official committees and informed authorities testify to the fact that in elementary, secondary and technical education Britain lagged some way behind Germany. Alfred Marshall, for example, reckoned that apart from Scotland, Britain's educational system lagged behind the German by more than a generation.[33] When one recalls that it was not until the last decades of the nineteenth century that any properly organised system of State education really got under way it is not difficult to accept the accuracy of this judgement. Compulsory primary education was not introduced in Britain until 1880, and before this most education had been dispensed by the private schools. Thus by the 1860s probably no more than half the children of school age received a formal education of some sort, whereas in many parts of Germany, where compulsory education was established much earlier, attendance was almost 100 per cent.[34] Organised technical and secondary education did not appear until the 1890s and the early twentieth century, and even then it was but a pale image of that provided in Germany. Furthermore, many of the schools established tended to concentrate on classical and cultural subjects to the neglect of scientific and vocational studies. And in any case, since for much of the nineteenth century the basic educational system in Britain left much to be desired, it is probable that there were relatively few industrial workers who had received sufficient elementary education to enable them to benefit from the more advanced secondary and educational facilities when they became available.

Conversely, it can be argued that the rather slow development of technical and scientific instruction in schools and other educational institutions was a product of the lack of support for it on the part of industrialists. The Board of Education maintained in one of its reports that

> the slow growth of technical institutions is in the main to be ascribed to the small demand in this country for the services of young men well trained in the theoretical side of industrial operations and in the sciences underlying them. There still exists among the generality of employers a strong preference for the man trained from an early age in the works, and a prejudice against the so-called 'college-trained' man.[35]

Many trades put a premium on the 'mystique of practical experience', and workers trained in technical schools were rarely given a rapturous welcome. Even when employers recognised the need for properly trained workers they did little to encourage them. Job and promotion opportunities and conditions of service were relatively poor compared with those in Germany, and this in turn discouraged students from seeking to improve their educational performance.

> The underpaid 'scientists' were put in sheds, reclaimed workrooms and other improvised quarters that hardly permitted controlled conditions and accurate tests. Their work was one cut above the rule-of-thumb techniques of the skilled workman; it was far below that of the German laboratory researcher.[36]

The ironworks chemist was considered to be in a dead-end job. Salaries were low and compared unfavourably with those of works foremen. Even as late as 1910 the War Office was offering a salary of only £100 for a chemist for the Woolwich Arsenal, and its chemists 'technically were placed on the same footing as ordinary workmen, and they could have been required, had the regulations been enforced, to join and queue every Saturday morning to take their £2 at the pay office'.[37]

In view of the lowly status accorded to scientists and engineers it is not surprising that, few as they were in numbers, many of them tended to drift into the professions or teaching rather than into industry. On the other hand, the argument can be switched the other way round. It may well have been that the widespread indifference among British manufacturers to the advantages to be derived from employing properly trained personnel can be attributed to the fact they themselves had received, for the most part, no more than a smattering of scientific and technical instruction. In other words, the neglect of scientific studies in public schools and elementary schools and the failure to organise a system of secondary education until the turn of the century produced generations of employers who were in no position to appreciate the importance of qualified men. Thus the stock of trained manpower available, small though it was, was sufficient to satisfy the limited needs of British industry.

Whatever the line of causation in this matter, there can be little doubt that poor educational facilities coupled with the indifferent response from employers were ultimately responsible for the paucity of properly qualified men in British industry. Certainly down to 1914 investment in trained manpower was not generally considered to be a profitable or worthwhile objective by industrialists. This explains why relatively little basic industrial research was carried out in this country compared with Germany, where 'the mutual interaction between research and manufacture became extraordinarily close.'[38] Despite the development of research units by some well known firms from 1890 onwards[39] the gap between science and industry still remained very wide, whereas in other advanced economies there was a much closer affinity between the two.[40] This neglect naturally limited the range of opportunities open to British businessmen in both a productive and a technical sense; for, given the technical incompetence of many captains of industry, the British industrialist had few if any qualified staff on whom he could call for advice. The system was in fact a vicious circle. The amateur status of business leadership discouraged the employment of scientists and trained workers and this in turn meant that British firms were less likely to be successful innovators.[41] It is difficult to escape the conclusion, therefore, that one of the most vulnerable features of British industry was its lack of properly trained personnel.[42] As Sir William Armstrong, one of the few more enlightened employers, remarked:

> The ignorance of the great masses of persons engaged in industry as regards natural science and technical knowledge is a bar to the progress of the individual, as well as a loss for the nation. Almost every branch of skilled labour could be developed if the persons engaged in it were trained in the elements of natural science, which come into account in the labour.[43]

British firms were also reluctant to adapt their marketing methods to changing conditions. 'In marketing, as in manufacturing, England was clinging, in a changing world, to methods and types of organisation which had been formed in the days of her supremacy.'[44] Some would argue that in this department British business was even further behind then in techniques and methods of production. Certainly British firms still relied heavily on the traditional merchanting system which served its purpose well in the days of iron and cotton, but, as Lewis has pointed out, it was less suited to selling sophisticated capital equipment to industrial countries.[45]

There were obvious drawbacks in a system whereby selling and production organisations were separated. Many merchant houses acted as agents to a number of firms, and this inevitably produced a certain conflict of interest between competing lines. All too frequently the system of indirect selling provided an inadequate reflection of the needs and requirements of customers, both at home and broad, partly because of the poor system of communications between firm and agency. Moreover, many merchants were accustomed to selling relatively simple consumer goods and were not equipped to promote sales of the technically complex products of the later nineteenth century. Even for fairly simple consumer articles the merchanting system was apparently becoming unsatisfactory. By the 1890s C. & J. Clark, the footwear specialists, admitted that they had lost a good deal of business by their reliance on agents and were slowly coming to the conclusion that direct selling was necessary.

> The sequence of events in Australia illustrates the difficulty faced by a manufacturer when sales through merchants become unsatisfactory. Direct selling was an obvious remedy but difficult to accomplish, half measures were of little value, and the intimate contact with the market that was required if information was to be entirely reliable was precluded by the merchant system. That a final break was the only solution was only obvious after the event. [46]

Furthermore, as Kindleberger suggests, [47] it might well be that the merchant system must bear a significant share of the blame for the slowing down of technical change. The division of functions between producing and selling agents interposes barriers of communication between producer and consumer, and may render external to the firm the benefits of any technical change. He cites the case of the cotton textile trade, where the merchant was partly responsible for the large number of separate qualities of product because he lacked the incentive or ability to induce customers to standardise their requirements. [48] Similarly, in the machine tool trade the lack of close liaison between producer and customer because of the interposition of the merchant restricted both the standardisation of tool design and the development of new tools.

The obvious answer to the defects of the merchant system was to switch to direct selling methods. Both the Americans and Germans found that with widening markets, increasing competition and more complex products, the agency or merchant system was becoming unsatisfactory and the only real solution was to invest capital in establishing their own sales networks, staffed with trained personnel. This was true of both the home and the export markets. Originally, in the 1870s, the majority of American industrial concerns only manufactured, and they purchased their supplies and sold the finished products through the wholesale and commercial agents. But by 1900 many of the major industrial concerns were integrated enterprises which did much more than just manufacture. They handled their own purchasing and controlled their own raw materials. Through their own nation-wide distribution networks they carried on wholesaling and retailing and established agency offices abroad. The building up of extensive sales organisations often required more in terms of capital, employment and entrepreneurial skills than did the expansion of production facilities.[49] Extensive advertising was employed throughout; in marketing breakfast cereals, for example, W. K. Kellogg is said at times to have spent nearly one-third of his company's working capital on advertising.[50] The pattern of development was somewhat similar in Germany, though here greater attention was paid to the promotion of exports. By organising foreign commerce, establishing direct selling agencies and sending highly qualified travellers all over the world to ferret out openings for business German industry virtually created its own markets.[51] The country's whole commercial policy was said to be directed towards the enlargement and extension of foreign trade. There were a number of collective organisations such as the Commerce Defence League and the export bureau of the German Export Bank which sent agents abroad and supplied information about foreign markets to member firms.

By contrast the British approach appeared singularly undynamic, and at times even old-fashioned. There were important exceptions, of course—Lever and Beecham were as advanced as any American firm in sales techniques—but, generally speaking, British firms seem to have been very reluctant to adopt more intensive and dynamic selling methods. This is particularly true of the export trade. From all over the world came complaints that British firms were inadequately represented by trained salesmen or direct selling agencies.[52] The frequency with which this question was raised in consular reports strongly suggests that it was of no small importance. In many areas, it was said, the British commercial traveller was conspicuous by his absence. In Spain the *bona fide* traveller was almost unknown,[53] and from Rumania it was reported by the consul that trade opportunities were being lost through inadequate representation.

> There is no doubt, were proper representation to be secured, that British merchants would increase, instead of losing the trade they already do with the country in machinery, textiles, ironwork, paints, chemicals, tea, clothing, hats, boots, machine and other tools, etc . . . Merchants might do worse than pay a personal visit to the country.[54]

The Italian market was also neglected by British salesmen. 'No efforts appear to be made by British manufacturers to recapture the trade by sending out practical persons to inquire about German prices and to study the means of adapting themselves, if possible, to the ways and conditions of the country.'[55] The number of travellers representing Britain in some countries was derisory by comparison with her main competitors. Apparently Switzerland was honoured by visits from only twenty-eight salesmen in 1899, as against 3,828 German, 1,176 French and even 350 from Italy.[56] Worse still, it was frequently the case that British representatives, though few in number, were ignorant of the customs and languages of the countries they represented.

The investigation of selling methods has been comparatively neglected by historians and so our knowledge of the subject is still very incomplete. Present indications are that British firms were weak in this field, especially on the export side. Even where dependence on the agency system was small, deficiencies in sales techniques still remained. As Harrison has shown in the case of the cycle trade, British selling methods compared unfavourably with American, the latter employing extensive advertising and technically competent salesmen.[57] There is little evidence to suggest that much attention or effort was devoted to improving or adapting existing sales techniques, despite the pressure exerted by American and German firms,[58] and certainly one hears little about the recruitment of trained manpower in this department or, for that matter, the in-firm training of new recruits in selling and distribution methods. In fact technical expertise in distribution was thinner on the ground than in the laboratory and one's guess is that the occupation remained very much the cult of the amateur.

It is by no means easy to say exactly why British industrialists were reluctant to alter or adapt their methods of selling. Possibly the small scale of the typical firm, together with the apparent lack of co-operation among firms for marketing purposes, made it difficult to establish viable direct selling organisations or to maintain staffs of qualified salesmen. Possibly, too, innate satisfaction with existing arrangements and an apparent ignorance regarding the deficiencies of the merchant system go some way towards explaining the situation. In this context it perhaps hardly needs to be mentioned that the supply of trained recruits was virtually non-existent. But whatever the reasons may be, one thing is certain: British firms could have increased their sales had they been more willing to adapt their selling techniques. There is much evidence of British firms losing export orders through weak selling methods,[59] and in so far as exports were lower than they might have been this could have lessened the urge to make technical improvements.

Moreover, reliance on the merchant system did nothing to encourage technical progress, and if anything it helped to slow down the rate of advance. The system was geared to selling traditional goods in traditional markets and less suited to selling new and sophisticated goods in the rich and expanding markets of Europe and America. By 1914 nearly 70 per cent of Britain's exports went to primary producers, but exports to these markets did not provide the same kind of incentive to adopt sophisticated techniques as those to America and Europe. Thus the merchant system tended to intensify a relative over-commitment to traditional products and traditional markets, and indirectly reduced or at best gave little encouragement to technical change. Given that technical change is an important element in productivity growth, it follows that the above factor contributed to the productivity lag. It is unlikely that this factor is of major importance, but nevertheless it is another example of delayed innovation which must have affected the economy adversely in the long run.

A further field in which British manufacturers were slow to make advances was in the utilisation and management of their work forces. This is an important subject but one which has been inadequately explored by British scholars. The literature is too limited to allow us to undertake a detailed examination of the subject, but an attempt will be made to make a few comments directly relevant to the question of productivity.

It is generally agreed that in the latter half of the nineteenth century there was considerable scope for securing economies and productivity advances in British industry by utilising the labour force more effectively. In most industries there was slack to be taken up, for as a result of bursts of technical innovation in the first half of the nineteenth century manufacturers had tended to neglect the possibilities of economising in the use of labour.

> The increase in output due to technical innovation was so vast that it was easy to forget how much greater it might have been with efficient exploitation... It seemed not to matter that they might have turned out more, because few entrepreneurs realised the potential economies of really efficient labour exploitation.[60]

There was, as Hobsbawm points out, an extraordinary neglect of the problem of productivity and efficient labour utilisation. Little attention was given to the question of labour management, and handbooks for industrialists and managers neglected the problem entirely. Generally speaking, employers assumed that the lowest wage bill for the longest hours meant the lowest labour costs per unit of time. Productivity was conceived largely as a function of mechanisation and discipline of the labour force, and little regard was paid to how it might be increased by adopting more efficient work methods or incentive payments.

Obviously this is a rather simplified description of the situation, though not an inaccurate one. It is suggested that these attitudes and practices continued to prevail during the latter half of the nineteenth century. But not without some modification, of course. It would be wrong to assume that industrialists made no effort at all to use labour more intensively in this period. Indeed, the pressure on profit margins, increasing competition and the limited possibilities of cutting costs by extending the hours of work, forced employers to find other ways of reducing costs. But the advances which were made in this direction were never commensurate with the degree of slack which prevailed in the system. The slowness with which more rationalised and mechanised methods of production were adopted in various trades is evidence enough that labour was not exploited to its fullest extent. Even in America, where much greater emphasis was placed on efficient man-power utilisation, evidence of under-utilisation was still common even by the early twentieth century. The author of *The Economics of Efficiency* was told[61] by a number of prominent business manufacturers that they were getting only 50–60 per cent of the possible output from their workers. Needless to say, American methods of labour management, work and time studies were given short shrift by manufacturers in this country. By 1914 both rationalised methods of production and scientific management of the labour force were still in their infancy in Great Britain.[62]

Improvements in methods of industrial remuneration were not readily adopted by British industrialists. It is generally agreed that labour makes its best effort when payment is by results.[63] Indeed, the increase in productivity which can be derived from a change-over from time to piece or premium wages has often been quite impressive. The Belgium glass industry, for example, found that productivity rose by 100 per cent in six years (1903–9) with the introduction of payment by results.[64] Similarly, after collective piece wages were instituted in the Admiralty dockyards in 1887 ships were built on average in 25 per cent less time and at 25 per cent less cost than formerly.[65] Although it is difficult to state the position precisely, it seems unlikely that the system of payment by results was used extensively in British industry, at least not before 1900. An inquiry made in 1894 reported that 'Taken as a whole the system of time-work appears to be the most extensive method of wage-payment in the United Kingdom'.[66] Although after the turn of the century a number of employers began to introduce incentive payments, progress tended to be rather slow, and they were never used as exten-sively as in America. Nor was it always very apparent whether the switch to incentive wage schemes was accompanied by worthwhile gains in productivity. In part this was no doubt due to the fact that payment by results and scientific management tended to go hand in hand, and in so far as the latter was slow to make headway the progress of the former was retarded.[67]

That industrial manpower was used less effectively in this country as compared with America few would deny, though the reason for the difference is open to debate. Possibly the attitude of the British worker is one reason for the comparative indifference of manufacturers to making more effective use of their manpower. This was a popular explanation at the time and gained wide support when Pratt published a book in 1904 denouncing the restrictive practices of the trade unions.[68] Most modern historians of the labour movement have been unwilling to attribute much importance to this factor,[69] yet it is clear that the trade unions were not prepared to accept changes without question. One American scholar has suggested that before 1914

> any application of Taylor's principles . . . had to be modified to fit English tradition and labour opposition. Output and time studies, piece or bonus rates were usually found undesirable. Even American time-clocks did not speed up production as anticipated. A hearty reception for American shop methods from Nottingham as early as 1901 appeared unique to the *American Machinist*.[70]

Even Hobsbawm, a writer by no means unsympathetic to the labour movement, has acknowledged the existence of workers' restrictions on output.[71]

It is difficult to say exactly how extensive and effective such restrictive practices were. Certainly the opinion held by contemporaries was that British workers were far less willing than their American counterparts to aid and abet the process of industrial change.[72] The Mosely Industrial Commission which visited America in 1902 came to the conclusion that the American manufacturer had in his workmen a more efficient instrument of production than generally fell to the lot of the British employer.[73] Attempts to promote the efficiency of labour were often regarded with open hostility, especially if they involved the rearrangement of work loads and a change in the method of remuneration. The lace manufacturers, for example, frequently claimed that they could not reorganise their factories on more efficient lines, since the men were immediately called out on strike if any action occurred contrary to the 'customs of the trade'.[74] In the footwear trade 'the labour problems accompanying mechanisation were recognised to be formidable in the organised centres'. Here the great bone of contention was the negotiation of the new piece rates, and it was not until the operatives had been defeated in the great lock-out of 1895 that the problem was finally settled and the employers were given a freer hand to introduce new machinery.[75] Similar difficulties in the engineering trade resulted in a series of strikes in the 1890s.[76] In a number of other industries, e.g. coal, light engineering, shipbuilding and cotton, it was reported that the workers were prejudiced against labour-saving machinery and new methods.[77] The extent of such opposition was no doubt exaggerated, but it existed all the same. Moreover, deliberate restriction of output, a practice which was hardly conducive to the most efficient utilisation of labour, was present in a number of trades, such as glass making, engineering and printing and publishing. The effect of these practices was brought to light during the war, when it was found that unskilled munitions workers could turn out 100 per cent more work than skilled mechanics at the same machines.[78] One reason why workers adopted such practices arose from the mistaken belief that there was a lump of labour, that is, a fixed amount of work to be done, and the more work performed by any one man the less there was for his fellow workmen. The Bradford Lodge of the Labourers' Union had a rule to the effect that its members were 'strictly cautioned not to overstep good rules by doing double the work you are required by the society, and causing others to do the same, in order to get a smile from the master. Such fool-hardy and deceitful actions leave a great portion of good workers out of employment.'[79]

Union opposition to work study, piece rates and the whole idea of scientific analysis of work methods was partly based on the belief that the 'system' was inhuman in its approach to the treatment of workers. This prejudice in turn sprang from a misunderstanding of the principles of Taylorism, fostered, no doubt, by the fact that British union leaders relied mainly on unfavourable reports on the matter despatched by their American counterparts. Though the unions certainly took an active interest in such things as workshop planning and piece-work schemes, Urwick doubts whether the trade union movement ever really understood or acquainted itself fully with Taylor's teachings in this period. The conviction grew that the 'sytem' was bad in principle; hence the outright condemnation by the Trades Union Congress in 1908–9:

> The Congress strongly condemns the modern method of increasing output by the introduction of the premium bonus system of working, regarding it as utterly opposed to the principles of trade unionism, in as much as it creates a form of sweated labour, and acts as a factor in increasing the number of unemployed, and hereby recommends that societies should use every effort to stop the further development of the system, also to take steps to abolish it wherever it has been introduced.[80]

Such obscurantist attitudes were not helped by the fact that few manu-facturers were in a position to expound the teachings of Taylor in a way which would have reconciled organised labour. Taylorism was as much misunderstood or misinterpreted by the managerial hierarchy as by the lower-order rank and file. For the most part scientific management got a 'vague, cool and distant' reception from British businessmen (there were some notable exceptions, and more interest was shown in the subject in the last years before the war), whose notions about business were still very much of a technical nature. 'The industrial milieu presented an infertile soil because of scepticism and apathy—an incapacity to understand that anything other than technology was of consequence—rather than because of any active opposition or obstructive ignorance.'[81]

Although manufacturers' attempts to improve labour performance were not always greeted with outright approval, union opposition can scarcely be considered as a major factor inhibiting technical progress, for it rarely delayed the introduction of new methods for more than a decade.[82] On the other hand, manufacturers were no doubt less inclined to introduce improvements if opposition was expected or if, as they maintained, the benefits were likely to be nullified by the men refusing to allow a reduction in labour or an increase in output or an adjustment in wage rates commensurate with the changes in productivity. Habakkuk has suggested that the lack of enthusiasm and the difficulty which manufacturers met in reducing piece rates to the extent warranted by the increased productivity due to labour-saving machinery made British manufacturers less willing than their counterparts across the Atlantic to introduce new machinery and methods.[83] The delay in speeding up productivity in the boot and shoe industry, for example, was in part due to the protracted negotiation over piece rates consequent upon mechanisation; in this case the manufacturers were not unjustified in asserting that the union's aim was to keep deductions so small as to render the machines uneconomic and thus slow down the displacement of labour.[84] Similarly, those restrictions on output which were designed to share out the work load were obviously inimical to maximum labour utilisation, since such practices could nullify the effect of any improvements made. It should be recognised, however, that the workers often had a legitimate cause for grievance, and in adopting such tactics they were merely trying to preserve their standards in the face of pressure from employers. As a rule the men resisted change only when there was a danger of their own interests being sacrificed in the process. The four-loom convention of the cotton weavers, for instance, was not simply a feather-bedding device but a serious attempt to preserve their established position. That the weavers were not opposed to technical change as such is confirmed by their ready acceptance of the automatic loom so long as it was 'not a success at the expense of their wages'.[85]

In any case it could be argued that the employers themselves were partly to blame for the attitude of their workers. Manufacturers at this time were facing severe competition from abroad and they were all too ready to find scapegoats to hide their own deficiencies. As Fox points out, 'Trade unionism, restrictive practices, and the incorrigible laziness

of the British working class as compared with its Continental and trans-
atlantic counterparts were, then as now, stimulating talking points.'[86]
When profit margins were under pressure manufacturers sought to
reduce the cost of the most variable factor, labour, not by economising
in its use but by reducing wages. In this respect things had not altered
very much from the early nineteenth century. The general impression
one gets is that manufacturers were preoccupied with the question of
wage costs, and if these could be kept as low as possible in money terms
things would be all right. Wage cost reduction was the short-term
alternative to long-term technical economies and as such provided an
easy way out for manufacturers in difficulties.[87] The policy of wage
cutting was resorted to frequently in times of stringency, but it was one
hardly designed to allay the workers' suspicions of their masters when
confronted by proposals for improving working methods. The employers, moreover, can be criticised for not taking the workers into their
confidence in matters which affected both sides.[88] This cavalier attitude
obviously engendered a feeling of suspicion and mistrust. Had British
employers shown the capacity of their American counterparts for
mutual co-operation and a greater willingness to encourage their men
to share in the benefits and profits of improved methods and new
machinery the unions might have been far more receptive to new ideas.
Even Pratt, who was an ardent critic of the unions and their restrictive
practices, admitted that British employers had much to learn from
American methods of labour management.[89] As it was, the estranged
relations between management and men acted as a barrier to progress
and, as one scholar has concluded, did much to retard the development
of more modern manufacturing methods.[90]

Essentially this essay has been concerned with questions of investment
in, and management of, manpower in British industry. It is no more
than a preliminary survey of some aspects of manpower recruitment and
utilisation. The general conclusion which emerges is that British firms
neither employed enough trained personnel nor utilised their work
forces in the most productive fashion. Generally speaking, the management of labour was badly handled before 1914, and only a few attempts
were made to emulate American and German practice. It is difficult to
explain the pattern of business behaviour in these matters by recourse
to economic rationality. The reasons for inaction are varied but for the
most part they pre-empt a defence based simply on the grounds of
economic logic. Though as yet it is not possible to make any precise
quantification of the extent of the neglect or its effects on economic
growth, there is every reason to suppose that had more attention been
paid to such matters further advances in technique and productivity
could have been secured. The subject may defy quantitative assessment

but this does not mean that it is of no importance. Research in depth, more particularly at the industry and firm level, may well yield handsome dividends.

NOTES

1 Donald McCloskey in particular is making every effort to rescue the entrepreneur from disrepute, though many more detailed case studies are required before a final judgement can be made. See D. N. McCloskey and L. G. Sandberg, 'From damnation to redemption: judgements on the late Victorian entrepreneur', *Explorations in Economic History*, IX, 1971.
2 T. W. Schulz, 'Investment in human beings', *Journal of Political Economy*, 1962.
3 E. F. Denison, *The Sources of Economic Growth in the United States and the Alternatives Before Us* (1962), p.266.
4 J. W. Kendrick, *Productivity Trends in the United States* (1961), p.152.
5 W. G. Hoffmann, 'Expenditure on education and research in the process of economic growth', *The German Economic Review*, III, 1964, p.207. The British proportion was around 1·3–1·5 per cent.
6 Though A. E. Musson would have reservations about this latter point. See A. E. Musson and Eric Robinson, *Science and Technology in the Industrial Revolution* (1969), and A. E. Musson (ed.), *Science, Technology, and Economic Growth in the Eighteenth century* (1972).
7 J. J. Beer, *The Emergence of the German Dye Industry* (1959), p.20.
8 C. Erickson, *British Industrialists: Steel and Hosiery, 1850–1950* (1959), p.36.
9 E. D. Howard, *The Cause and Extent of the Recent Industrial Progress of Germany* (1907), p.145.
10 D. Burn, *The Economic History of Steelmaking, 1867–1939* (1940), p.214.
11 *Ibid*, p.215.
12 S. J. Chapman, 'Work and wages', part I, *Foreign Competition* (1904), p.78.
13 Erickson, *op. cit.*, p.390.
14 P. W. Musgrave, *Technical Change, the Labour Force and Education: a Study of the British and German Iron and Steel Industries 1860–1964* (1967), pp.89, 157.
15 See Chapman, *op. cit.*, I, pp.227–9; W. M. Gardner, *The British Coal-Tar Industry* (1915), pp.222–3 and *Report on the Chemical Industry in Germany*, Cd. 430, 1901, pp.38 ff.
16 *Report on the Chemical Industry in Germany*, Cd. 430, 1901, quoted in Chapman, *op. cit.*, I, p.229.
17 H. W. Richardson, 'The development of the British dyestuffs industry before 1939', *Scottish Journal of Political Economy*, IX, 1962, pp.110–11.
18 L. F. Haber, *The Chemical Industry 1900–30: International Growth and Technological Change* (1971), p.53.
19 Beer, *op. cit.*, p.84.
20 *Ibid.*, p.89; L. F. Haber, *The Chemical Industry during the Nineteenth Century* (1958), p.84.
21 Beer, *op. cit.*, p.90.
22 S. B. Saul, 'The American impact on British industry, 1895–1914', *Business History*, III, 1960, pp.24, 30.
23 A. E. Harrison, 'The competitiveness of the British cycle industry, 1890–1914', *Economic History Review*, XXII, 1969, p.302.
24 Rather than to lack of enterprise, which implies that the burden of guilt lies elsewhere. See R. A. Church, 'The British leather industry and foreign competition, 1870–1914', *Economic History Review*, XXIV, 1971, p.568.
25 F. A. Wells, *The British Hosiery Trade: its History and Organisation* (1935), p.182.
26 S. B. Saul, 'The motor Industry in Britain to 1914', *Business History*, V, 1962, p.42. Cf. I. C. R. Byatt, 'The British electrical industry, 1875–1914' (University of Oxford, D.Phil. thesis, 1962), pp.392–3, and W. H. G. Armytage, *A Social History of Engineering* (1961), p.214.
27 H. J. Habakkuk, *American and British Technology in the Nineteenth Century* (1962), p.154.

[28] See A. E. Musson, *Enterprise in Soap and Chemicals: Joseph Crosfield and Sons Limited, 1815–1965* (1965).

[29] See D. S. Landes in *Cambridge Economic History of Europe*, vol. VI, part I, p.571, and *The Unbound Prometheus: Technological Change and Industrial Development in Western Europe from 1750 to the Present* (1969), pp.339–45.

[30] In 1900 the number of day students per 10,000 population was 5·0 in Britain, 7·9 in Germany and 12·8 in the US; D. S. Cardswell, *The Organisation of Science in England* (1957), p.156.

[31] H. Hauser, *Les Méthodes allemandes d'expansion économique* (Paris, 1915), p.43.

[32] A. Marshall, *Industry and Trade* (1919), p.97, n. 1.

[33] *Ibid.*, p.97.

[34] Landes, *Cambridge Economic History of Europe*, loc. cit., p. 569.

[35] Cardswell, *op. cit.*, p.167; S. F. Cotgrove, *Technical Education and Social Change* (1958), p.28.

[36] Landes, *The Unbound Prometheus*, pp.345 ff.

[37] As a result of a debate in the House of Commons the salary was actually raised to £150. See Musgrave, *op. cit.*, pp.102, 144.

[38] R. A. Brady, 'The economic impact of imperial Germany: industrial policy', *Journal of Economic History*, supplement, 1943, p.117.

[39] The picture is certainly not completely barren. There are several examples of industrial research in the larger firms and activity on this front speeded up after 1890, but the total effort compared with, say Germany, remained small. For a useful corrective see M. Sanderson, 'Research and the firm in British industry, 1919–39', *Science Studies*, II, 1972, pp.108–12.

[40] J. D. Bernal, *Science and Industry in the Nineteenth Century* (1953), p.158.

[41] The reluctance to employ statistical analysis had a similar effect. See *Departmental Committee on Railway Accounts and Statistical Returns*, Cd. 5052, 1910, Evidence, pp. 326–7.

[42] Though for the opposite view see Habakkuk, *op. cit.*, pp.216–17 and E. G. West, *Education and the State: a Study in Political Economy* (1970), pp.107–8.

[43] Quoted in G. von Schulze-Gaevernitz, *The Cotton Trade in England and on the Continent* (1895), p.140.

[44] G. C. Allen, *British Industries and their Organisation* (1935 edition), p.19.

[45] W. A. Lewis, 'International competition in manufactures', *American Economic Review*, XLVII, 1957, p.578.

[46] G. B. Sutton, 'The marketing of ready made footwear in the nineteenth century: a study of the firm of C. & J. Clark', *Business History*, 1964, p.11.

[47] C. P. Kindleberger, *Economic Growth in France and Britain, 1851–1950* (1964), pp. 148–9.

[48] *Ibid.*

[49] A. D. Chandler, 'Entrepreneurial opportunity in nineteenth century America' *Explorations in Entrepreneurial History*, fall 1963, p.118.

[50] A. J. Silk and L. W. Stern, 'The changing nature of innovation in marketing: a study of selected business leaders, 1852–1958', *Business History Review*, autumn 1963, p.190.

[51] Aggressive selling methods were a prominent feature of Germany's chemical firms. From the 1880s onwards the major firms launched a massive attack on foreign markets by establishing direct sales agencies and sending out trained salesmen and consultants to foreign countries. By 1914 the Baeyer Chemical Company had no less than forty-four sales branches and 123 agent companies selling its products abroad; Beer, *op. cit.*, pp.95–6.

[52] See *Opinions of H.M. Diplomatic and Consular Officers on British Trade Methods Abroad*, Cd. 9078, 1899.

[53] *Ibid.*, p.6.

[54] *Diplomatic and Consular Reports: Rumania*, No. 5102, Cd. 6665, 1913, pp.7–8.

[55] *Diplomatic and Consular Reports: Italy, Report for 1909–10*. No. 4635, Cd. 5465, 1911.

[56] Chapman, *op. cit.*, I, p.253.

[57] Though some of the large firms did have their staffs of travellers, some of whom were drawn from the racing fraternity; A. E. Harrison, 'The competitiveness of the British cycle industry, 1890–1914', *Economic History Review*, XXII, 1969, p.294.

[58] For a brief comment on the American impact on British selling methods in the footwear trade see R. A. Church, 'The effect of the American export invasion on the British boot and shoe industry, 1885–1914', *Journal of Economic History*, XXVIII, 1968, p.253.

[59] See D. H. Aldcroft, 'The entrepreneur and the British economy, 1870–1914', *Economic History Review*, XVII, 1964, pp.123–7.

[60] E. J. Hobsbawm, *Labouring Men: Studies in the History of Labour* (1964), p.354.

[61] N. A. Brisco, *The Economics of Efficiency* (New York, 1914), pp.5–6.

[62] A. L. Levine, *Industrial Retardation in Britain 1880–1914* (1967), pp.60 ff.

[63] P. W. S. Andrews and E. Brunner, 'Productivity and the business man', *Oxford Economic Papers*, June 1950, p.219; for a general discussion see R. Marriot, *Incentive Payment Systems* (1957), and J. P. Davison et al., *Productivity and Economic Incentives* (1958).

[64] Hobsbawm, *op. cit.*, p.362.

[65] D. F. Schloss, *Methods of Industrial Remuneration* (1898), p.120.

[66] *Report on Wages and Hours of Labour*, 1894, part III, p.vi.

[67] The practice of making payment by results was given a considerable boost in the first World War and, according to an official report in 1921, a fairly high proportion of skilled operatives in British industry were paid on this basis: *Report of the Departmental Committee on the High Cost of Building Working Class Dwellings*, Cmd. 1447, 1921, p.35.

[68] E. A. Pratt, *Trade Unions and British Industry* (1904).

[69] Cf. H. A. Clegg, A. Fox and A. F. Thompson, *A History of British Trade Unions since 1889*, vol. I, *1889–1910* (1964), p.475.

[70] R. H. Heindel, *The American Impact on Great Britain* (1940), pp.195–6.

[71] Hobsbawm, *op. cit.*, p.351.

[72] Chapman, *op. cit.*, I, pp.176–7 and W. P. Strassmann, *Risk and Technological Innovation: American Manufacturing Methods During the Nineteenth Century* (1958), p.186.

[73] *The Times*, 26 December 1902.

[74] N. C. Cuthbert, *The Lace Makers Society* (1960), p.50.

[75] A. Fox, *A History of the National Union of Boot and Shoe Operatives 1874–1957* (1958), pp.90, 246.

[76] J. B. Jeffreys, *The Story of the Engineers, 1800–1945* (1946), pp.142, 143, 146, 156–7.

[77] See Pratt, *op. cit.*, pp.51–3; A. R. Griffen, *The Miners of Nottinghamshire*, vol. I, *1881–1914* (?1955), p.158; W. H. Chaloner, 'The British miners and the coal industry between the wars', *History Today*, June 1964, p.422; S. Pollard, *A History of Labour in Sheffield* (1959), pp.127, 129; H. A. Turner, *Trade Union Growth, Structure and Policy; a Comparative Study of the Cotton Unions* (1962), pp.257–9.

[78] See the very informative article in *The Times*, 27 March 1919 and *Report of the Tariff Commission*, vol. 6, *The Glass Industry* (1907), paras. 7, 73.

[79] Schloss, *op. cit.*, p.83.

[80] L. Urwick, *The Making of Scientific Management*, vol. 2, *Management in British Industry* (1949), pp.104–5.

[81] *Ibid.*, pp.88–92.

[82] See Levine, *op. cit.*, ch. 5, on this issue.

[83] H. J. Habakkuk, *American and British Technology in the Nineteenth Century* (1962), p.136.

[84] Fox, *op. cit.*, p.91.

[85] Turner, *op. cit.*, p.272.

[86] Fox, *op. cit.*, p.272.

[87] See D. H. Aldcroft, 'Technical progress and British enterprise, 1875–1914', *Business History*, VIII, 1966, p.134: '. . . the manufacturer who could not afford to scrap his plant and yet must compete with up-to-date firms was tempted to cut his costs at the workers' expense'. F. A. Wells, *The British Hosiery Trade: its History and Organisation* (1935), p.198.

[88] The Tariff Commission felt that management could do more to convince workers that mechanisation would not create redundancy or lead to a reduction in wages. *Report of the Tariff Commission*, vol. 2, *The Textile Trades*, part 2, *Evidence on the Woollen Industry* (1905), para. 1483; cf. vol. 4, *Engineering Industries* (1909), para. 481.

[89] Pratt, *op. cit.*, p.186.

[90] Saul, *Business History*, 1960, p.27.

A. J. Marrison

13

Great Britain and her rivals in the Latin American cotton piece-goods market, 1880–1914

Whilst contemporary observers differed over the degree of competition that rose to face British cotton exporters in the period 1880–1914, few failed to regard that period as one in which the old order was changing. The growth of domestic cotton industries in markets previously dominated by Britain was well documented in the trade press. The emergence of rival exporters was reported, often over-reported, by the consular service.

In searching for reactions, both theoretical and observed, to the changing world situation, contemporaries developed a belief in the 'fine counts' theory, arguing that the proportion of finer yarns and cloth in total British output and exports increased,[1] thus moving the British exporter to a position less liable to erosion by less advanced overseas industries[2] and by tariffs specifically geared to weigh more heavily on the importation of coarser goods. Such a response would seem well suited to higher-income countries, as Copeland observed of the US market in 1912.[3] In lower-income markets, however, effective demand for higher-quality lines would have been much smaller; the demand for goods of a quality high enough to remove Britain not only from native competition but also from that of (more advanced) rival exporters would necessarily be limited, and dependent to a large extent on income inequalities in those markets. The gain in avoiding such competition would stand in danger of being greatly outweighed by the losses involved in a self-imposed reduction in the size of the market available to British shippers. As it is hoped to show in this essay, successful importation into lower-income markets involved the acceptance of and compliance with strict 'income constraints' imposed by the nature of those markets.

Two recent studies have looked to a broader definition of quality than the count element emphasised in the 1890s and 1900s. Sandberg derives a quality index, for total piece-good exports, that is defined as 'the real value per yard of cloth . . . exported.'[4] This index declined until 1898, the fall being due to the net effect of an increase in export quality to high-income countries and a decline in quality to low-income countries, though without the inclusion of India the situation in the latter would have evinced little change. But after 1898:

> ... there was little or no change in the quality of British cotton cloth exports. Interestingly enough, quality to the HI [high-income] countries, especially Canada, Australia and New Zealand, did somewhat less well than quality to the LI [low-income] countries. There was also a slight increase in the percentage of cloth exports going to the HI countries.[5]

Even in India the period after 1890 saw an improvement in the quality of imports from Britain, a change which Sandberg ascribes to the growth of Indian output, which by 1913 was equivalent to 70 per cent or more of total imports of cotton cloth.[6]

Sandberg notes that his 'real unit value' definition of quality was composed of two main constituent parts, an increase in the proportion of higher-count cloths exported, and an increase in the proportion of more highly finished (e.g. printed or dyed) cloths exported. Tyson tends to emphasise the degree of finish, pointing to Lancashire's increasing concentration on exporting dyed and printed cloths:

> Where colour, design and finish were important, French and German cottons were able to compete and sometimes surpass those of Britain, while Italy with dyed cloths and the USA, in coarse and lightly sized fabrics, were successful in a few limited markets. But none of these countries were in a position to compete with the great staple products of British manufacturers, dyed and bleached piece goods. Grey goods, however, faced some competition from India and Japan, which was partly responsible for their diminishing role in exports from the 1890s onwards. Dyed piece goods increased from 12·3 per cent of total cloth exports in 1890–94 to 20·4 per cent in 1910–13, while grey goods fell from 43·5 per cent to 32·4 per cent.[7]

It is the intention of this essay to examine British export performance during the period 1880–1914 with reference to Latin America, an area which took consistently well over 10 per cent of British cotton exports. The variety of Latin American market conditions make the region interesting for the purposes of a case study. There were present two, perhaps three, economies which could boast healthy and growing cotton industries; there were also smaller economies which had none at all. The area was also the field of competition between the major industrial exporters of a degree scarcely experienced in other neutral markets, yet in most of the region Britain retained a more than substantial lead in market shares down to 1914. In the main, Latin America was a low-income market, yet unequal income distribution, sometimes sizable colonies of foreign residents, and the existence of high-productivity export enclaves gave rise to demands for higher-quality goods which, whilst small in relation to total imports, were nevertheless considerable in absolute terms.

Much of what is to follow bears implicitly but perhaps indirectly upon the long-standing debate on British entrepreneurial ability in the years after 1870. The great staple export industries, in particular, have been much criticised for their performance in the new and perhaps trying era that followed the mid-Victorian boom. In some senses this criticism may have been particularly short-sighted; certainly the record of cotton piece-good exports to Latin America would have been considerably less favourable but for the development of new lines of good, a development that was a response not only to the new forces of foreign competition but also to changing demand structures in that region.

It will be argued that the Latin American case does show a movement towards higher quality, as is shown by a growing concentration on dyed goods, but that the emphasis remained, down to 1914, on the marketing of cheaper qualities of goods. Thus, given a change in the broad classifications of cloths exported, we must look at the policies of different exporters and national manufacturers towards quality *within* these broad classifications. Such trends would tend to be hidden by an index of quality based on Sandberg's 'real unit value' criterion. Whilst fineness of weave and degree of finish were to some extent interrelated, marketing considerations in Latin America made finish a more important variable than count in quality manipulation.

The change towards dyed goods did indeed partly reflect growing competition, not only in grey goods from some indigenous South American industries but also in prints from rival exporters. But, as is shown by the existence of the trend even where there was no development of home manufacturing, it reflected more than this—a response to changing demand conditions in favour of dyed goods, occasioned most probably by rising *per capita* incomes and by changes in consumer tastes. Though competition was an element in the change in the British piece-good export mix, therefore, the existence of the other element, demand, dictated the direction and the magnitude (through income constraints) of the change, and consequently Britain was still to experience competition from foreign rivals and some native producers. The consequence of ignoring essential demand considerations will be illustrated by the shortcomings of US export policy. The view that British supply functions changed to adapt to new conditions of increasing competition from indigenous industry and from foreign rivals—a view which formed the backbone of the belief in the 'fine counts' theory, and which Sandberg, some seventy to eighty years later, still found useful to explain the improvement in quality of exports to India after 1890—must, in the Latin American case, be modified.[8]

Piece-good exports, overwhelmingly predominant in total British cotton exports to Latin America throughout the period 1880–1914, are separated in the Board of Trade returns, after 1888, into four categories —'Unbleached grey', 'Bleached white', 'Printed' and 'Dyed or manufactured of dyed yarns'.[9] There was no separate classification of goods according to 'count' or number of threads per square inch warp and weft.

An examination of the official returns for the period 1885–1914 shows clearly that goods 'dyed or manufactured of dyed yarns' were the growth sector of British piece-good exports to Latin America in the decades before the Great War. Furthermore, the product mix of exports to this region altered much more dramatically than did the product mix of similar exports to the rest of the world. The results of this examination are summarised in table 13.1. It can be seen that one of the outstanding

Table 13.1.   Total British (home-produced) piece-good exports (percentage volume)

	Unbleached grey	Bleached white	Printed	DMDY*
To the world				
1889	45·68	23·61	18·96	11·74
1894	42·70	26·35	18·48	12·45
1899	39·78	24·92	19·47	15·81
1904	36·37	27·32	18·54	17·75
1909	36·55	27·69	17·70	18·04
1913	33·32	28·90	17·39	20·37
To Latin America				
1889	14·96	32·27	37·51	15·25
1894	13·62	32·29	37·04	16·93
1899	11·26	31·74	36·08	20·90
1904	12·24	26·37	33·02	28·35
1909	9·04	31·99	24·41	34·54
1913	6·53	32·68	20·22	40·55

* Piece goods 'dyed or manufactured of dyed yarns'.

Source. Annual Statement of Trade of the United Kingdom, 1889–1913.

features of changes in the composition of British piece-good exports to Latin America in the period was the increase in the proportion of dyed goods exported, the relative gain of this category being offset by a relative, and absolute, decline in the importance of unbleached grey and printed goods. This change was much more marked than for British cotton exports as a whole.[10] The increase in world purchases of British dyed goods, by volume, was considerable in absolute terms, though the percentage increase was rather below the Latin American figure, especially after 1899. In terms of their proportionate gain in the product mix, however, dyed-good exports to Latin America far outstripped those to the world.[11] This differential movement was largely due to the fact that, as a whole, the world did not experience the large absolute decline in its imports of British unbleached and printed goods that occurred in Latin America. Now we must consider whether this changing emphasis towards dyed goods in the southern continent's imports did indeed represent an upward movement in quality.

Descriptions of the general characteristics of the Latin American market for imported cottons are not hard to find. The area presents us with a classic example of underdeveloped and developing countries being drawn increasingly into a world trading system dominated by the industrial powers bordering the North Atlantic. The coexistence of export-oriented and domestic sectors, of high- and low-productivity sectors, of high- and low-income groups within the same country was commonplace. Dual economies were the order of the day, with the consequent inequalities of income that such structures imply. But, as is in the nature of dual economies, the high-income groups tended to be small. By example, McGreevey uses a census figure for 1870 to show that less than one per cent of the Colombian population described themselves as *commerciantes* and remarks that the great majority of these must have been clerical workers rather than leading merchants.[12] In consequence of generally low income levels, contemporary observers stressed the importance of supplying cheap goods. A member of the US government's commercial commission to South America (1885) stressed the importance of price in exporting unbleached drills to Argentina and Uruguay.[13] Reports from Haiti in the 1880s and early 1890s emphasised the unimportance of fine goods in total demand,[14] whilst HM Consul Gosling, of Guatemala City, found that British goods were suffering from the introduction of inferior goods at lower prices by her rival exporters.[15] After 1900 the need to concentrate on cheap goods had, according to trade comment, not diminished. A British consular report of 1906 emphasised the importance of supplying cheap goods with a high finish, since it was for this type that the largest market existed.[16] Mr William Whittam junior remarked in 1900 that the bulk of South American demand was for cheap and heavily sized cloths. Seven years later he made the point that to poorer customers price, and marginal variations in it, were critically important. He was familiar with the view that as native incomes rose the demand for sized goods might fall; indeed, this *might* even have been happening very slowly in the 1900s. But, he concluded, it would be many years before sized goods lost their position of great importance in the cotton-good requirements of the less developed countries.[17] In Mexico in 1889 one suggested reason for the high demand for cheap qualities was that the retailer added the amount payable under the tariff[18] to his buying price, and doubled it to obtain his selling price. Thus the consumer often paid four times the 'simple value' of the cloth.[19] This was supported by a statement in the *Textile Mercury* to the effect that the absolutely heavier duties on higher-quality goods, though in Mexico representing a lower *ad valorem* rate, were sufficient, when combined with the higher initial cost of these goods, to maintain the demand for cheaper qualities. Consequently the major part of British piece-good exports to Mexico at this time consisted of cheap calicoes and prints not exceeding thirty threads per square centimetre.[20] Such a view throws doubt on the orthodox picture of high protective tariffs and low-quality import-substitutes inducing an increase in overall quality of imports from Britain.

Cheapness appears, therefore, to have been one of the dominant requirements of the Latin American demand for imported cloth down to 1914. The extent to which rival exporting nations catered for it will be examined later.[21] But this continued emphasis on price does not preclude an increase in export counts, or more generally an improvement in export quality, of British cloth. The static condition of the South American market in requiring cheap goods was not incompatible with the dynamic possibility that demand for finer or higher-quality goods increased, even though the market remained one for relatively cheap goods throughout the period. It must make us doubtful, however, of expecting this dynamic shift to have been large.

It could, of course, be argued that the increase in the proportion of dyed goods exported from Britain to Latin America did not involve an improvement in overall quality. In particular we might postulate a reduction in average count great enough to equal or outweigh the higher degree of finishing, in a value-added sense. Such a view might gain strength from the knowledge that the larger part of the relative advance of dyed goods was made at the expense of prints, the category that we might, intuitively, think to place at least on a par with dyed cloth in terms of value added. HM Vice-consul Dickinson's remarks on the Colombian market in 1902 might tend to confirm the impression that unit values of prints and dyed goods were not very different:

> Of course, in woven zephyrs, Oxfords and Harvards, the effects of the roller cannot be produced, but designs can be woven that would suit very well for dresses. There has always been a demand for zephyrs, but now importers and retailers are comparing the difference in prices, *quality for quality*, between woven zephyrs and prints, and are trying to order zephyrs . . . They ought to try to give the best designs possible consistent with a low quality.[22]

Unfortunately, information on count in piece-good exports is very limited. The relative movement out of grey goods to dyed goods would certainly have involved an upward shift in average count. Grey cloth exports were commonly of 30s and considerably less. Dyed goods varied widely, but a range from 35s to 65s probably covers them adequately. Thus even if all the dyed-good expansion was comparatively coarse, average count would improve. But with the relative shift out of prints one would expect the effect on count to be much less certain, and to be influenced by whether the shift was from 'common' or fine prints to coarse or fine dyed goods. Here we could have four basic types of shift as limiting cases, with an infinite number of intermediate cases. Professor Saul notes:

> The distinction between plain and printed cloths is really a technical one. Plain cloth is 'in the loom state'; printed cloth has undergone further finishing processes. On the whole, however, it is justifiable to think of plain goods as the coarser, cheaper cloths which were sent to the markets of low individual purchasing power . . . Printed cottons were generally finer and dearer although some coarse printed cloths were exported, mainly to the Middle East. The point is perhaps best made by comparing British and American prices. Their printed cloths sold abroad on average at about the same prices, but American plain cottons, which consisted almost entirely of fine cloth, averaged over 3d a yard compared with British plain cottons which were on the whole coarser and sold at an average of 2d a yard . . . We must use these not entirely satisfactory measures, as the trade returns give us no further useful information.[23]

The range of piece-good exports to Latin America was huge; the range of unit values of both prints and dyed goods varied widely between markets and, almost certainly, within markets. In general, however, we can largely resolve the problem of the relative positions of different classifications of goods within the range of unit values by deriving current unit values of British piece-good exports within the same year and comparing the differentials obtained with those in different years. These unit values, and their differentials, should contain both 'count' and 'finish' elements. Whilst the figures given in table 13.2 are in no sense *real* unit values, it is warrantable to compare relative current unit values of the different classifications within a given year, especially over large market areas. It might be argued that changes in national income levels in the recipient countries would affect the unit value differentials between unbleached, bleached, printed and dyed goods according to the nature of the demand changes induced by those income movements. Such an approach, however, would require detailed knowledge of disposable incomes, changes in income distribution, and price and income elasticities of demand for importables (and import-substitutes), none of which we possess. Fortunately, the derived unit values for given years summarised in table 13.2 exhibit a stability and predictability great enough for us to doubt the realism of such subtle analysis. Table 13.2 shows that, in both the South American and world cases, average unit prices of bleached goods were in all years considered higher than those of unbleached goods, average unit prices of printed goods higher than those of bleached goods, and average unit prices of dyed goods higher than those of prints.[24] It will thus be seen that the classification adopted by the Board of Trade in 1889, that of 'Unbleached grey', Bleached white', 'Printed' and 'Dyed or manufactured of dyed yarns', in that order, does indeed represent a progression from lower to higher unit values in current terms. Making one or two very plausible assumptions about demand conditions, and about the cost and pricing policies of manufacturers and merchants, it is warrantable to see the official classification as reflecting a spectrum of increasing 'value added' in production, with unbleached goods at the bottom of this spectrum and dyed goods at the top.

Table 13.2. Current unit values of British piece-good exports to world and South America (£ per yard)

	1889	1894	1899	1904	1909	1913
Unbleached grey						
South America	0·0089	0·0074	0·0068	0·0085	0·0092	0·0110
World	0·0087	0·0077	0·0075	0·0092	0·0096	0·0116
Bleached white						
South America	0·0104	0·0090	0·0087	0·0109	0·0114	0·0136
World	0·0104	0·0092	0·0092	0·0109	0·0116	0·0132
Printed						
South America	0·0112	0·0108	0·0090	0·0106	0·0110*	0·0125*
World	0·0115	0·0109	0·0101	0·0121	0·0122*	0·0136*
DMDY						
South America	0·0129	0·0121	0·0109	0·0130	0·0136*	0·0159*
World	0·0138	0·0133	0·0131	0·0159	0·0166*	0·0184*

* From 1908, the 'Printed' and 'DMDY' classifications were each split into two further classifications. This is considered below, pp.317–18. In table 13.2 the unit values for DMDY are given as a weighted average of the two components. The difference is unimportant for the 'Printed' category, and only the major component is included.

Source. Annual Statement of Trade of the United Kingdom, 1889–1913.

If, therefore, there was any autonomous deterioration in average count of British exports over time it would have had to be large enough to outweigh the probable increase in count due to a shift towards dyed goods, and the upward influence of a greater degree of finish upon unit values. No evidence for such a long-term deterioration exists in the Latin American case, whereas the shift to dyed goods and the ranking of these at the top of the unit value spectrum are indisputable. The increased emphasis on dyed goods over time would therefore point to an improvement in the 'quality', in Sandberg's sense, of British piece-good exports to Latin America in 1880–1914. It is hoped, however, to show that count was of minor importance in Latin American sales before 1914. The critical element was that highlighted above—improvements in finish. This factor was intimately related to the willingness and ability to meet consumer requirements. Manufacturers and merchants sought constantly to improve one element of quality, that of finish, whilst at the same time avoiding parallel improvements in other elements, notably in fineness, which were not in accord with the market's income constraints.

.   .   .

Before going further it will be well to point out a feature, perhaps a trend, which table 13.2 conceals. From 1908 onwards there is a change in the classifications of printed and dyed goods in the British returns. The change in the 'Printed' category is unimportant.[25] With dyed cloth, however, it is more significant. Piece goods 'dyed or manu-factured of dyed yarns' were split up into goods 'dyed in the piece' and goods 'manufactured wholly or partly of dyed yarns, commonly known as coloured cottons'. Goods 'dyed in the piece' were on average more expensive and were exported in greater quantity, but in this case the minority classification was large enough to affect the general picture when the two are summated. In table 13.2 the figures for dyed goods in 1909 and 1913 are given as a weighted average of the two components. A more detailed breakdown is given in table 13.3. Table 13.2 shows that

Table 13.3. Composition of British dyed piece-good exports in 1909 and 1913

	1909			1913		
	% yards	% value	Unit value	% yards	% value	Unit value
DMDY (i)[a]						
South America	59·7	63·5	0·0145	64·9	68·0	0·0168
World	78·0	80·1	0·0170	79·7	81·5	0·0188
DMDY (ii) *b*						
South America	40·2	36·5	0·0124	35·1	32·0	0·0143
World	22·0	19·9	0·0151	20·7	18·0	0·0165
ΣDMDY[c]						
South America	100·0	100·0	0·0136	100·0	100·0	0·0159
World	100·0	100·0	0·0166	100·0	100·0	0·0184

Notes [a] Piece-goods classified as 'dyed in the piece'.
   [b] Piece-goods classified as 'manufactured wholly or partly of dyed yarn, commonly known as coloured cottons'.
   [c] Summation of *DMDY* (i) and *DMDY* (ii), weighted by volume or value as appropriate.

Source. Annual Statement of Trade of the United Kingdom, 1909–13 (volume and value figures rounded).

current unit values of South American imports of unbleached grey and bleached white piece goods from the UK were far more consistent with world[26] unit values than were current unit values of South American imports of printed and dyed goods. With bleached goods, for instance, average world and South American values actually coincided to the nearest farthing (one-thousandth of £1) in 1889 and 1904. With printed goods, however, the close relationship holds only in the early years. With dyed goods the differential was even more marked. The differentials between South American and world average unit values are given in table 13.4, which shows not only that exports to Latin America were of lower unit value than those to the world as a whole,[27] but also that the differential between them shows some tendency to increase down to 1914. This result must be partially ascribed to the unusually large proportion of 'coloured cottons' in British shipments to South America, these being the cheaper of the two broad types of dyed piece goods. Unfortunately, since the separation in the trade returns occurs only in 1908, we cannot say with certainty that the importance of

Table 13.4.   Percentage difference of current unit values of British piece-good exports to South America from current unit values of total such exports.

	1889	1894	1899	1904	1909	1913
Unbleached grey	+2·2	−3·8	−9·3	−7·5	−4·0	−5·1
Bleached white	0	−2·1	−5·4	0	−1·8	+3·0
Printed	−2·6	−0·9	−11·0	−12·4	−9·8*	−8·0*
DMDY (i)	} −6·5	−9·0	−16·7	−18·2	{ −14·7	−10·7
DMDY (ii)					−17·9	−13·4

* Only 'Printed—other' category shown.

Source. Derived from tables 13.2 and 13.3.

'coloured cottons' within the dyed category increased during the period 1880–1914. But, as table 13.3 shows, we can say that 'coloured cottons' were unusually important in South American imports of British dyed goods, and that dyed goods were the growth sector of British cloth exports to that region. Furthermore, as is shown in table 13.5, South American imports of British 'coloured cottons' constituted a very high proportion of total world imports of these goods. It must also be remembered that unit values of South American imports of goods 'dyed in the piece' were also considerably below the world average.

Table 13.5. British piece-good exports to South America and the world, 1909 and 1913

	1909	1913
(a) DMDY (i) to South America (million yards)	145·2	188·8
(b) DMDY (i) to world (million yards)	804·6	1151·4
(a) as percentage of (b)	18·0	16·4
(c) DMDY (ii) to South America (million yards)	97·7	102·6
(d) DMDY (ii) to world (million yards)	227·7	290·4
(c) as percentage of (d)	41·9	35·2
(e) All other piece-goods to South America (million yards)	460·6	427·0
(f) All other piece-goods to world (million yards)	4689·8	5663·5
(e) as percentage of (f)	9·8	7·5
(g) Total piece-goods to South America (million yards)	703·7	718·4
(h) Total piece-goods to world (million yards)	5722·1	7075·3
(g) as percentage of (h)	12·3	11·5

Note. If this table were to be presented in value terms instead of volume, exports to South America as a percentage of exports to the whole world would be slightly lower. This would be true to a greater extent for 'DMDY (i)' and, especially, 'DMDY (ii)' than it would be for 'All other piece-goods' and 'total piece-goods'.

Source. Annual Statement of Trade of the United Kingdom, 1909–13.

The reasons behind the increasing differentials between South American and world unit values as we pass up the finish spectrum are perhaps not obscure. By the turn of the century British exports of unbleached cottons to higher-income countries had largely ceased; indeed, even Mexico had exhibited the same feature in her import structure. Thus average world unit values could be expected to have been close to those of one particular underdeveloped or developing country. But in the new 'growth' lines—dyed goods—one would also expect to find that unit values of Latin American imports of British cloth lay below a world average which included the imports of much higher-income countries such as the USA and those of Western Europe, since the British manufacturer had long experience of developing special export lines for less affluent areas. As earlier in the century Britain had developed unbleached cloth of coarse quality—Indians, Mexicans, T cloths, etc.—for specific and narrowly defined markets, so too in the period after 1870 did she develop similar special lines in dyed goods. These represented more highly finished goods; they probably represented also a limited upward movement in count, though examples of exceptionally coarse dyed goods were exported as well. But the principal reason for developing these export lines—as indeed for the introduction of the speciality trade three-quarters of a century earlier—was not so much to escape competition by exporting goods similar to those which could still leap tariff barriers into advanced manufacturing countries as to supply the dynamic sector of the Latin American piece goods market at prices and in qualities which would meet the overriding requirement of the low-paid consumer. Always, in Latin America, the consumer was king.

There is no direct way of estimating changes in average count of British piece-good exports to Latin America before 1914. The shift towards dyed goods over time possibly involved some upward movement in fineness, but in the absence of any large geographical distribution changes (from lower- to higher-income markets)[28] the probability of its being large is small. The main efforts of British exporters were to supply dyed goods which suited the requirements of the market. Prevailing low incomes in Latin American countries and increasing demand for more highly finished goods left the exporter in something of a dilemma, and led to a conflict between finish and count. But in this finish was regarded as overwhelmingly important; count remained a secondary consideration. The disproportionate importance of 'coloured cottons' in the British export mix testifies to the substantial trade that was carried on in relatively cheap, relatively coarse coloured goods.

In Mexico and Brazil, more than in any other Latin American country, we might expect the British exporter to develop the classical response suggested by Sandberg and the 'fine counts' advocates. An approximate measure of the growth of the Mexican cotton industry can be gained from an increase in spindlage from 249,570 in 1885 to 762,149 in 1911–12, and an increase in loomage from 8,758 to 27,019 in the same period. Employment rose from 12,728 in 1885 to 34,500 in 1908–9. The number of establishments in operation increased from eighty-seven in 1885 to 148 in 1911–12.[29] In accord with its close watch on the development of capacity overseas, the British trade press reported closely the growth of the Mexican industry, and its comments reflect the generally coarse products of national manufacturers. In 1884 the *Textile Recorder* gave details of four mills producing coarse yarn on (at least in two cases) ring spindles. Production was wholly for the domestic market and consisted overwhelmingly of *lona*, 'a loosely woven coarse article about the weight of our duck', and *manta*, 'resembling our unbleached muslins'.[30] L. L. C. Hamilton's *Mexican Handbook* (London, 1884) further confirmed the emphasis on coarse goods. In 1886 it was reported that the coarse grey shirtings called *manta*, sold in pieces 31–32½ in. wide and 30 yards long, fetched high prices in the Mexican market, but were nevertheless so favourably priced compared with other lines as to constitute the sole clothing of some three-fifths of the population.[31] The concentration of the home industry on coarser goods explains the government's policy, in the 1880s, of imposing higher *ad valorem* (equivalent) duties on these qualities.[32] By the early 1890s home coarse-good production had gained sufficient strength to allow President Diaz to reduce protective levels more on lower- than on higher-quality goods. Duties on piece goods under thirty threads per half centimetre square were reduced from nine to seven cents per yard, those on goods over thirty threads from eleven to ten cents per yard.[33] Annual output around 1896–8 (a somewhat dubious figure of 7·116 million pieces of thirty-two *varas* – one *vara* = thirty-three inches—each) was described as 'comparatively coarse,' the major part being cloths of thirty-three threads warp *and* weft per half centimetre square or less, whilst the industry was now deemed sufficiently advanced to bear the burden of a 5 per cent tax on value of output. Attempts had been made to develop production of higher-quality goods—for instance, sateens—but plain, coarse, low-quality goods remained the staple product.[34]

It does appear, however, that the Mexican industry was attempting by the late nineteenth century to introduce higher-quality lines into its product range. In 1902 the US *Textile World* reported that the expansion of Mexican cotton manufacturing in the previous ten years had introduced a tendency towards overproduction, which was inducing the adoption of better machinery for producing higher-quality goods.[35] By 1908 the *Textile Recorder* could report considerable progress, particularly on the part of the large, up-to-date mills of Orizaba, though it laid stress on the increasing diversity of products rather than on fineness. Sheetings and shirtings were turned out with an increasing range of

accompanying lines—tickings, linings, drills, printed percales, etc—
many of them coloured goods. Manufactured cotton goods such as table-
cloths, quilts and hosiery were present, though in their infancy.[36] But the
movement to higher-grade goods must be seen as a limited one. As late as
1912 E. Enever Todd stressed that the principal piece-good product of
Mexico was a 24 in. wide cloth counting from 20 to 30. Only a few of the
country's 140–150 mills span up to 70s, and then from imported yarn.[37]

In Brazil, too, the development of the industry before 1914 was
mainly along the path of increased production of lower qualities.
Reporting from the province of Bahia in 1884, Mr Consul Stevens
counted ten factories, the four largest of which[38] boasted a combined
loomage of 407 and employed around 800 people. Output was coarse
cloth for working-class clothing and sacking.[39] In 1887 Minas Province
produced an estimated 6·2 million metres of cloth per year, mainly
'coarse regattas and domestics, Americans and such like'.[40] In 1891 the
Board of Trade Journal could remark that, notwithstanding rapid growth
and government encouragement in the 1880s, attempts to produce
finer qualities had not been very successful, and that Brazilian production still concentrated on coarser stuffs. In 1903, whilst giving details of
a newly opened mill owned by Messrs. E. Zschoeckel & Co. at São
Paulo, the Textile Recorder noted that the spinning machinery, by
Hetherington's of Manchester, was capable of spinning only from 6s to
28s, such goods being 'suitable for the requirements of the district'.[41] In
1908 the secretary of HM legation in Rio de Janeiro (Mr M. Cheetham)
estimated Brazilian cotton consumption per spindle as over 100 lb per
annum. He described native production as 'practically all coarse, little
if any being over 30s'.[42] By 1909 the Textile Recorder could point to a
few cotton factories which produced cloth up to 60s, and in these concerns only a few looms were at work on such yarns. The 'great majority'
of work was carried on with yarns less than 30s.[43]

The increasing emphasis on dyed piece goods in British exports to
Mexico and Brazil can perhaps, therefore, be properly regarded as a
movement to escape native competition in coarse goods. Unit values of
dyed goods shipments were amongst the highest in Latin America,
especially after 1900, though it is important to note that Argentina,
Chile and Uruguay (where domestic production was comparatively
insignificant) paid similar or higher prices for their imports of British
dyed goods. But even if this was the reason, the shift could not prevent a
considerable decline in export volumes to Brazil and Mexico.[44] This
was because these countries were fast developing their own lines of cheap
coloured goods, thus to a certain extent limiting British exporters to
supplying those high-quality coloured goods which accounted for only
a minor part of the market.

In the case of Brazil we can trace the development of cheap coloured goods from the 1880s. The Ampara, the largest mill in Bahia province, was equipped with dyeing machinery perhaps earlier than the 1880s, yet the concern span only coarse cloth at the time of Consul Stevens's report. In 1885 Mr Andrews, US Consul General in Rio, gave details of an 800 loom mill in the city which produced not only unbleached and white stuffs but also coloured and mixed cloths for cheap men's clothing.[45] By the mid-1890s another report from Bahia mentioned one of the mills of the Emporio Industrial do Norte concern as having in current operation 470 looms for grey cloth and 250 for coloured. The mill was equipped with a complete plant of finishing machinery for coloured goods, output at that time being given as 125,000 yards of grey and 35,000 yards of coloured cloth per sixty-hour week.[46] A year later the establishment produced ginghams, dappled cloths, drills, cassinettes and about a thousand patterns of zephyrs, whilst another Bahian concern, the Fabrica Conceição, produced 2 million metres of coloured ginghams and drills per annum.[47] In 1899 the British consul at Pernambuco, pointing to the great difficulty in exporting grey domestics to Brazil, mentioned also the gradual 'ousting' of madapolams, Oxford shirtings and coarse coloured cloths by domestic producers.[48] Similar reports came from the consul at Porto Alegre two years later.[49] In 1902 the US consul at Santos gave a possibly exaggerated report that the fourteen mills in São Paulo province devoted the larger part of their output to coloured goods, mentioning specifically Oxfords and zephyrs, not as well finished as British or other imports but 'apparently as durable'.[50] Zschoeckel's mill, mentioned earlier, may have been equipped for spinning only 6s to 28s, but it was fully equipped with a printing and dyeing house. According to the recent and comprehensive researches of S. J. Stein, a survey of Rio mills in 1894 showed that, though concentrating mainly on coarse goods:

> ... eight of eleven mills were producing small quantities of fine and medium grey goods. A few also offered coloured goods and white shirtings; only one could handle prints ... Now favoured by tariff protection, Rio mills were spreading their distribution wider than the regional market. Their gray goods, drills, denims and regattas drove from the Porto Alegre market in southern Brazil all similar British goods in 1897 and seriously threatened imported oxfords, ginghams and shirtings. The following year there were reports of successful production in Rio mills of shirtings, grays, simple prints, ginghams, oxfords, trouserings, zephyrs, and blue drills. Even the Bahian mills had supplemented their bagging and coarse cloth with calicoes, striped checks, and blue drills, completely eliminating grays and domestics once imported, and making serious inroads upon Manchester dry goods in general—madapolams, oxford shirtings, and coarse coloured goods.[51]

In the early years of coloured goods development it is evident that selling price was something of a barrier to expansion. The directors of the Petropolitana, facing a decline in the price of plain and checked ginghams in the latter half of the 1880s due to local competition and disturbed financial and trading conditions, considered marketing a very low-priced gingham because of 'competition from other mills and customers' preference for cheaper qualities' in an attempt to meet the purchasing power of workers who were 'spending a large part of their low earnings on clothing'.[52]

Development of the Brazilian industry can thus be seen to have involved a movement into cheap coloured goods. Significantly, it appears that progress was perhaps most marked in woven cottons. Stein mentions briefly that dyeing—presumably dyeing cloth in the piece, though he is not clear on this point—and printing advanced more slowly in the 1880s and 1890s.[53] For the period 1890–1920, which he dubs the 'golden years', Stein says little of changes in product mix within the Brazilian industry. Probably developments and improvements in manufacture and finishing proceeded along the lines of the 1870s and 1880s—certainly Stein regards the industry as 'emerging from infant-industry status in the 'nineties'.[54] Again, some increase in average count probably went hand in hand with greater diversity and more widespread finishing, especially in the Rio area, which was shortly to emerge as the national pace-setter, but in 1900 and 1910 national output still 'consisted chiefly of coarse and medium goods in narrow widths'.[55] Coarse and medium grey and coloured goods were the sole output of the Confiança Industrial, a Rio mill, in 1910.[56]

It is a commonly accepted view that the British export trade in cottons before 1914 suffered more from the rise of national industry than from foreign competition in neutral markets.[57] In Latin American the greatest pre-war developments in cotton manufacture took place in Mexico and Brazil, with Colombia lying third. Certainly, in Mexico and Brazil, the decline in British export values can be traced to this as the principal cause. Elsewhere, because of the prevalence of cottage industry, it is difficult to judge. With factory industry proper, the *Textile Recorder*'s survey of late 1898 probably underestimates the extent of development.[58] Certainly it is clear that Argentina, Britain's single most important Latin American market in 1913, had pursued economic policies from the 1860s onwards that had effectively destroyed the chance of a significant import-substitute cotton industry emerging.[59] Furthermore, the history of the Colombian cottage industry in the nineteenth century was one of decline in the face of competition from imports.[60] E. Enever Todd found only two cotton factories in Chile in 1913.[61] Board of Trade Commissioner Milne's reports from central America in the same year implied by omission a lack of factory production in Costa Rica, Salvador, Honduras and Panama. In Nicaragua, the largest of the six central American republics, sugar was the only manufacturing industry of any consequence.[62] Information on product quality is scarce, but such as there is indicates the embryonic stage of what development there was. Milne reported that the most important mill in Colombia, owned by Messrs Obregon of Barranquilla and employing 400–500 hands, used yarn mainly in the range 16s to 24s and entirely imported from Britain. A smaller mill at Cartagena, with 105 looms and 160 workers, span and wove 11s to 16s. Two mills at Medellin concentrated on cheap grey domestics and drills:

> ... although the textile industries of the country are as yet imperfectly developed, they tend to increase in the direction of supplying those fabrics which are in general use among the labouring classes, and ... they restrict the sale of import goods.[63]

Except in Brazil and Mexico, therefore, and compelled as we are to underplay the role of cottage industry, we must see the relative importance of rival exporters as being of greater concern to the British exporter of cotton goods to Latin America than it was elsewhere.

The huge British cotton textile export machine, and no less the piece goods sector of it, possessed great diversity of product quality and finish in the mid-nineteenth century.[64] After 1870 diversity tended to increase. In 1900–1 Elijah Helm was able to tell the Manchester Statistical Society that the variety of textures, lengths, widths, weights, colours and finishes of piece goods was 'many hundreds of times' greater than it had been twenty or thirty years previously.[65] In Latin America the generally coarse nature of local piece-good production, and the fact that it made such large localised inroads on imports from Britain, tell us much about the prevalent nature of demand in that market. The difficulties experienced by the USA in expanding her high quality home market-oriented surpluses to her sister republics provide supportive evidence.[66] Though Britain found that rising Latin American incomes and domestic competition tended to push her towards higher-quality exports, the movement was necessarily limited by very definite price (and therefore quality) constraints.

The principal British adaptation came in the form of a shift towards coloured goods at the relative expense of unbleached goods and prints. The shift out of unbleached grey goods, unfortunately of the lesser magnitude of the two, probably involved an improvement in count. The shift out of prints is less certain in its effect in this respect.

Except in Mexico, which could boast some nine printing machines in 1896 and fifty in 1911–12,[67] native production was a minor reason for Britain's large absolute and relative decline in the Latin American print trade. To some extent the decline may be seen as a rational response to the general difficulties besetting world trade in prints, especially in the 1890s. Not only in Britain did the technical supply-side advantages of long runs result in overproduction and attempts at combination to restrict output and maintain prices. But it must be remembered that elsewhere in the world British print exports exhibited none of the huge decline that took place in Latin America after 1890. There are two possible explanations for this. One is that intense British, German and US competition caused an aversion to the Latin American market on the part of British printers and shippers of prints that had still not worked itself out by 1914. The other is a shift in tastes away from prints in that market.

Turnbull estimates that the output and capital employed in British printing increased some threefold during the period 1850–80, so that by the latter date producers were confronted with over-supply in foreign markets. At the same time changes in home demand to woollens and worsteds and the rise of foreign competition resulted in dramatic falls in prices. The dismal 'eighties culminated in twenty-five failures among British printing firms in 1889–92 alone.[68] Attempts at defensive combination in the early 1890s were unsuccessful. Even the initial results achieved by the three large combines of 1897–8[69] were far from encouraging. After 1900 the market situation improved somewhat, and the export trade gradually revived.[70]

After sharing in the world situation of the trade in printed goods in the 'eighties and 'nineties, the Latin American market, taken as a whole, experienced a singular failure to revive after 1900. The general situation of overproduction was aggravated by the rise of serious competition from advanced rivals. Turnbull regards this market as being the only one in which Britain encountered severe harassment by alternative suppliers:

> Virtually the only markets in which there was direct conflict were those of South America, where it would appear that there was little to choose between the rivals in their capabilities to supply the requirements.[71]

The principal supply-side characteristic peculiar to the print trade appears to have been the technological feasibility of great variations in output over very short periods. The tendency of US printers to overproduce is indicated by the relative output of Britain's 900 and the US's 300 printing machines in 1891. Output per machine/day in that year averaged 3,500 yards in the UK and 12,200 yards in the US. But such large-scale output on the part of American producers was possible only by standardisation of pattern and long runs:

> In England the printing business is conducted mainly on orders, and for any number of pieces a buyer may require. Such small quantities as 300 yards to a colouring, and only two colourings to a design, are nearly the rule of the

trade. In such cases the loss of time in changing the pattern—that is, taking the rollers out of the machine and putting in another pattern—is far greater than the whole time spent in actually printing the goods . . . In addition to the inevitable delays arising from what are called 'short runs', English printers do a great deal of sampling; that is, new patterns are sampled in many varieties of colourings in short fents only, from two to six yards in length. The pattern is then taken out of the machine, and is not put in again until the arrival of the order, which may only be for the two short runs before mentioned of 300 yards each in two combinations. In many English concerns 30 per cent of the machines are engaged all the year round in sampling only. The system in the States is totally different. There sampling fents is unknown. The American printer receives his orders from the merchant in large quantities to a pattern. A new design will be ordered in quantities ranging from 800 to 1,000 pieces of 50 yards each. These are printed right off to eight or nine colourings, and the merchant takes the risk of the sale of them.[72]

Whilst the American methods possessed obvious cost advantages in production, their effect on final market price appears to have been more questionable. Mr T. W. Worthington, Special Commissioner of the Board of Trade, wrote from Argentina in 1898 that, whilst US printed cloths were of good quality, they were sold only in large lots of a limited assortment of patterns, a circumstance which had the effect of depressing realised prices.[73] Furthermore, customer behaviour was not necessarily strictly rational in the narrow economic sense. In the early 1890s the *Textile Recorder* had observed that the US policy of selling large quantities of similar designs at cheaper prices, quality for quality, than her rivals was not one which guaranteed success in South American markets, since it neglected the adverse reaction of consumer taste to standardised patterns.[74] Certainly it seems that British methods of production and distribution suited large parts of the South American market as late as 1900 and well beyond. Chilean consumers, for instance, regarded price as more important than quality, and tastes worked in favour of British products. German shippers experienced the same loyalty to Lancashire prints as the Americans did, for the great variety of British patterns, offered at prices closely geared to the Chilean market, hampered German attempts to sell higher-priced goods whose 'designs and finish [were] not so distinctly superior as to greatly damage the sale of the English product'. US prints, by their nature surplus to home requirements, presented little threat.[75] Similar conditions obtained in Venezuela, Peru and Paraguay.[76] In Mexico, the only important print producer in the region,[77] the rise of domestic production and the tariff structure hit British prints harder than American, since they were of lower *average* count, whilst the quicker delivery, superior styles and patterns, and lower *relative* price of US fine prints meant that British exporters could gain little respite from competition by shifting to the higher reaches of the quality range.[78] Nevertheless, a cyclical revival of Mexican imports in 1898–9 showed British printers still to be in a strong position. The expansion was strongest in imports of printed goods counting under 30s, these accounting for 200 per cent of the total increase in piece-good imports during these two years. In the fiscal year 1898–9 coarse prints and cretonnes from the UK held 63 per cent of the import market, whilst the US held second place, with 23½ per cent.[79] Some years earlier a report to the US State Department from Piedras Negras had suggested reasons for Britain's continued ascendancy over the US in print shipments to Mexico. Buyers could obtain US goods only from stock, thus having to take the fixed assortment of colours and designs in the original package as given. Under the British system, however:

> . . . the manufacturer sends out patterns, designs and colours, together with samples of all the different grades of grey cloths. The buyer first selects a grey cloth of a quality and width suited to his local trade, and then chooses the designs and colours to be printed from this cloth.[80]

Furthermore, British shippers would cater more for short orders (as low as 200 yards) of *special* designs, a departure from economy in production that the American manufacturer would not contemplate, and would, when required, produce coarser printed cloths to lower their rating under the Mexican tariff classification and supply reduced widths to enable the Mexican dealer to undersell his rivals. In Colombia, too, British predominance in 1890 was held to be due to close attention to the styles, patterns and qualities dictated by the rigid tastes of *peon* women in respect of 'hideous purple prints'.[81]

Perhaps because of the declining importance of prints in British cotton exports to Latin America, or perhaps because of the general revival of world exports of prints in the early twentieth century, we are left uninformed on the state of print exports to the southern continent after 1900. Even if, however, British printers were able to compete effectively with their rivals, there is enough evidence of the world print trade situation to suggest that victory would have been phyrric. The level of capacity amongst the three great exporting powers was such as to make prices unattractive to producers even when demand was active.[82]

Turnbull suggests that the reason for British malaise in the South American printed shirting market was twofold, being due to the increasing intensity of import competition and also to a great improvement in the attractiveness of woven fabrics.[83] With regard to competition, Milne's report of 1913 from Central America, previously a very important market for British printers, showed that by that time the US had achieved a surprising degree of penetration. In Guatemala British exports had fallen, over the three years 1908–10, from 60 per cent of total print imports to 40 per cent, compared with a rise in the American figure from 34 to 38 per cent, and the German from 6 to 12 per cent. A similar report came from El Salvador. In Honduras Milne found the US printer to hold 66 per cent of the market, compared with the 28 per cent held by his British counterpart. Everywhere the reasons given were the same: US exporters were able to deliver more quickly, to supply more designs from stock, and to provide a better quality of dye on ordinary grades of cloth.[84] Even in Nicaragua, where Britain held 49 per cent of the market for ordinary prints, her lead had been eroded by intensive American sales drives. New York commission houses had increased pattern assortments in shipments to Panama by opening bales received from the manufacturers and rearranging them. Only in Venezuela was the US printer unable to make inroads into British business, a situation which Milne ascribed to his unwillingness to conform to the Venezuelan consumer's idea of 'customary prices':

> The paying of so much only for a certain type of cloth is so much established as a custom that, in order to comply with the buyer's demands in t his respect, importers have found it necessary to introduce narrower widths and lower grades.

However, it is probably of greater significance in assessing the reasons for US absence in the Venezuelan print market that:

> Demand has fallen off of late in Caracas and the larger centres, cheap cretonnes and zephyrs of British manufacture having taken their place.[85]

Turnbull's second suggestion, that of an increase in the attractiveness of coloured woven goods, is itself attractive, since it accords with the observed changes in the British piece goods export mix to Latin America after 1880. We must, of course, remember that the observed pattern does not necessarily support Turnbull's line of causation: the causal sequence could have been in the reverse direction, the expansion of dyed goods being consequent upon the decline of prints. But this would neglect the fact that the expansion of dyed goods was not only relative but also absolute and on a greater absolute scale than was the decline in prints. Furthermore, we can find evidence to suggest that contemporary opinion was in accord with Turnbull's suggestion. Vice-consul Dickinson observed in 1902 that such forces were at work in the Colombian market.[86] On a general level, the *Manchester City News* had commented in 1896:

> A feature of our exports in cotton piece goods . . . is the growth of demand for cotton fabrics which have undergone some manipulation beyond the grey state. The value of the four classes of cotton piece goods tabulated by the Board of Trade may be roughly stated as follows: Grey goods, $1\frac{7}{8}d$ per yard; bleached goods, $2\frac{1}{4}d$ per yard; printed goods, $2\frac{5}{8}d$ per yard; and dyed goods

$3\frac{1}{4}d$ per yard. As cotton is the basis for all classes and about the same weight of cotton is used in a given number of yards, it follows that the difference in values has been distributed in this country in the shape of wages and interest on capital.[87]

Whilst, on a world scale, changes in the British export mix more nearly accorded with this view of a straightforward increase in the degree of finishing than they did in the South American case, Manchester Chamber of Commerce was ready by 1907 to concede that the pattern we have observed in the less prosperous parts of the western hemisphere had a wider applicability:

> Is the immense increases in dyed goods due to the marvellous productions of the loom, assisted by the increased skill of our dyers, and, on the other hand, has the closing of so many print works, and the concentration of so many under one management, killed individuality and enterprise, and thus stopped the increase in printed fabrics? . . . In any case it is a subject of congratulation that those goods show the highest rate of expansion on which the largest quantity of labour per length is expended.[88]

It will be useful at this moment to digress into the reasons why the US failed, by and large, to gain a strong build-up of trade in the southern continent, since this illustrates the market constraints under which cotton exporters to that region had to operate. Faced with the post-Civil War rise of coarse goods production in the south, northern manufacturers looked outwards. After rapid expansion of both northern and southern capacity early in the 1880s[89] stagnant markets and mill closures caused the industry to look with greater interest at overseas markets. Reports were coming in of the US industry's vastly inferior position in Latin America:

> These southern nations purchase all kinds of fine and coarse goods from Europe. We endeavour to push our products of skilled labour upon the countries which produce already the surplus which supplies our southern continent, Mexico and the West Indies, from a double distance, at what ought to be a greater cost in freight. We also, with the balance of trade greatly against us in those southern countries, furnish through that paid-up annual balance the money that pays for those purchases of European goods.[90]

With regard to Mexican imports, the US consul at San Blas maintained that shortcomings in US performance were in no way due to the inferiority of American cottons ('. . . on the contrary, its superiority amongst consumers is universally admitted . . .') but to the long entrenchment of foreigners in the mercantile community and, more important, the subtle prejudices against American intervention in that country:

> We have been largely prevented from competition in a contest where we had the natural right of a fair hearing and the geographical advantage of

closer proximity. That day has passed . . . It is honourable and manly now to openly assert that we enter the field to stay as competitors for a fair share of the profits of the imports and exports of our neighbouring sister republic.[91]

The *Textile Recorder*'s American correspondent, of course, put all his opinions with colour, but his vehemence in advocating greater efforts in Latin America was a reflection of wider viewpoints than his own. In 1884 the President appointed a commission to ascertain the best methods of securing more intimate commercial relations with the various Latin American countries. At the same time American manu-facturers looked to the forthcoming New Orleans exposition to en-courage South American importers to switch to US suppliers. That the threat was taken with at least some seriousness in Lancashire was reflected in the *Textile Recorder*'s fears over Britain's lack of representation at the exhibition:

> Not only will visitors from all parts of the world be present, but it will be specially attractive to the nations in South America, who have hitherto been good customers of Lancashire, and whose custom the manufacturers and merchants of the US desire to secure for themselves . . . it is not well that Lancashire productions should be unavailable for inspection at the exhibition, while those of the States are to the front for examination and approval.[92]

The organisers of the New Orleans exhibition[93] sent their own com-missioner to South America.[94] Shortly afterwards came news of a dual US export drive into Brazil and Colombia. By May 1886 the American correspondent was reporting successes in Latin America by southern US coarse good producers.[95] The brief export boom, perhaps main-tained by price reductions, had allowed manufacturers of brown and bleached goods to increase prices by $2\frac{1}{2}$ per cent in January, and by the summer output was up to 'full standard' for the first time in two years, though prices remained low.[96] There followed a period of comparative silence. Reports came to Britain of US advances in Costa Rica, but they were discounted in view of the overwhelming importance of Britain as an absorber of Costa Rican coffee.[97] By early 1887 it was felt that the federal commissioner sent south of the Rio Grande had achieved little success.[98] Even in Mexico congressional rejection of Mexican overtures for reciprocity had resulted in a coolness towards further attempts at closer commercial relations.[99] The US export boom to South America, born in the depression of 1884–6, seems to have lost much of its force by the late 1880s. *Bradstreet's Journal* reported an increase in the volume of (total) US cotton exports from 135·2 million yards in 1884 to 204·6 million yards in 1887. Mexico had not quite fully shared in the general expansion, but nevertheless the increase in exports to Latin America between the financial years 1885–6 and 1886–7 was from 35·39 million to 53·40 million yards, an overall 51 per cent increase.[100] In January 1889 the *Textile Recorder* noted an increase in the number of southern mills from 154 in 1879 to 235 in 1889, with fifty-seven more nearing readiness.[101] Northern manufacturers feared that southern competition would push them involuntarily into the production of finer classes of good.[102]

Whilst showing considerable expansion in percentage terms, US exports to Latin America during the boom of the second half of the 1880s remained miniscule when compared with British.[103] Moreover the boom burnt itself out in the late 'eighties. In 1889 the State Department was sufficiently concerned with the stagnation in piece-good exports to circularise consular officials, asking why.[104] By mid-1891 *Bradstreet's Journal* was again noticing accumulation for stock and output reductions in the US industry. Southern mill expansion had not brought with it a concomitant increase in exports. Contraction was especially marked in the print trade, and in the important outlets of Brazil, Argentina and Mexico.[105] The cycle began again and US interest in South America revived. The US press hoped that new reciprocal treaties with Brazil and Cuba, giving American manufacturers a preference of 25–50 per cent on the amount of duty, would double trade volumes.[106] Mr Curtiss, director of the Bureau of American Republics, circulated an elaborate list of Latin American tariff schedules on cotton goods. The McKinley tariff was followed by a rash of negotiations with Latin American countries, mostly in Central America, but the reciprocal treaties which came into force during 1891–2 were in the short term more effective in increasing US imports than in developing her overseas outlets.[107] By the autumn of 1894 the Fall River Cotton Manufacturers' Association was considering reducing wages to combat low prices, especially of prints, and a quarter of eastern mill capacity had been shut down.[108] Again came the familiar reports of US intentions of capturing larger shares of South American markets,[109] the despatch of special commissioners to seek to increase trade avenues in Venezuela and Mexico by a newly formed National Association of Manufacturers,[110] and numerous attempts and plans to set up sample warehouses, 'commercial museums' and 'bureaux of commercial information' in South American cities, including that actually set up under a Mr Dolge in Caracas.[111] By the mid-1890s increased efforts in export markets were showing results in all except Latin America, where overstocking of prints left prices at a very dismal level.[112] Even the settlement of sovereignty over Cuba and Puerto Rico in July 1898 did not have the immediate effects hoped for by US exporters. In 1900 the British consul-general in Cuba could report that depression and dislocation were still preventing trade revival.[113] Elsewhere, in Argentina, US attempts to obtain reciprocity had, as in the earlier negotiations with

Mexico, been floored by the Senate refusal to ratify, again with a loss of goodwill in the other country.[114]

Nevertheless, US exporters did achieve some increase in the size of their export trade towards the end of the period. The depression of the home market initiated by the panic of 1893 led to a sustained increase in the total value of cotton-good exports. Average annual export values, fluctuating narrowly between $10·0 million and $13·3 million between 1876–80 and 1891–5, rose to $20·4 million in 1896–1900, $31·3 million in 1901–5, and $35·1 million in 1906–10.[115] Central America took its share of this general expansion, but South America proper fared less well. Exports to the area declined from an annual average of $3·0 million in 1891–5 to $2·6 million in 1896–1900, rose to only $3·6 million in 1901–4, then fell again to $3·3 million in 1905–10.[116]

The US's main successes in the western hemisphere occurred in Central America, where by 1913 considerable penetration had taken place. US suppliers provided 34–9 per cent of Guatemalan imports of printed piece goods in the years 1908–11, and 24–41 per cent of her dyed piece good imports, whilst in grey goods the figure was much higher—some 60–73 per cent. In Salvador the US had nearly 30 per cent of the market for imports in 1906–11, second only to Britain (with consistently over 50 per cent) and far outstripping France and Germany, who in combination never managed to supply more than 9 per cent of the market in any one year. US shippers possessed 38 per cent of Nicaragua's market for unbleached shirtings (compared with Britain's 55 per cent), 89 per cent of her market for drills and sheetings, and 42 per cent of that for common prints. In Costa Rica the US share of cottons stayed steady at 30 per cent, whilst the British share rose from 35 to 40 per cent. Whilst British piece-good exports to Colombia were nearly three times those of the USA, those of the latter were nevertheless five times those of Germany, in third place; in prints the UK lead was considerably narrower, and during the three years 1909–11 the US shipped more unbleached piece goods to this market than did Lancashire. Venezuela was the only Central American country where Germany, not the USA, held second place to Britain.[117]

However, Central America was a relatively minor market for cottons compared with South America proper. US observers saw with some concern the failure to make large inroads on British trade in this area. By 1913 the US held only 8·3 per cent of all Latin American import markets for cotton goods, compared with a figure of 53·6 per cent for Britain, 15·6 per cent for Germany, and 8·6 per cent for Italy.[118]

One important reason for this relatively poor performance was the American cotton exporter's neglect of competitive price as a predominant requirement of the Latin American market. In many cases the US export product was of too high a quality. This was to a large extent the direct result of a situation in which the US producer concentrated on home sales during years of good trade and only became really concerned with expanding export outlets in years when the home market was unable to absorb all his product. The different Latin American markets displayed great variety in consumer requirements, not only between nations but also within nations. Perhaps more important, requirements of taste, pattern, style and quality were not well satisfied by a US product range which was basically determined by surpluses in the (higher-income) home market. In the mid-1880s the *Textile Recorder*'s American correspondent pointed to America's inability to make serious inroads on Britain's trade in Mexico and elsewhere in Latin America because of her lack of familiarity with local tastes:

> On the other hand, your [British] manufacturers know what sort of goods to send to every country under the sun, and I am told that the same mills manufacture entirely different classes of goods for China, India, South America, and elsewhere. Well, we don't.[119]

The American correspondent believed fervently in the superiority of American cloth, price for price, and used consular reports on occasion to affirm the truth of this.[120] In November 1885 he commented that, whereas a common price for British drills in South America was five cents (US) and one for American products seven cents, the latter were superior in quality, and Britain could not have put a similar line on the market for less. The cheaper British product was described as two-thirds cotton and one-third starch. Its popularity was ascribed not only to price but also to its superior 'look' and its glossy appearance. Such goods were fairly durable as long as they were not washed. According to the American correspondent, British exporters were fortunate that the *peon* did not wash!

> He buys so many yards of the pipeclay stuff, makes it up . . . and wears it until it hangs in tatters about his legs, never stopping to consider that a better class of goods would last longer. It would be useless for the American manufacturers to educate him in economy, but it would be profitable for them to produce what he wants, and sell it to him at the same price he pays for English goods.[121]

This commentator realised that, although Brazil, Argentina, Uruguay, Chile, Peru, Ecuador, Bolivia, Paraguay, Venezuela, Colombia, Central America and the West Indies took some $100 million worth of these 'bogus cottons' every year, US manufacturers might not be willing to furnish new lines if the result might only be a small increase in market shares. The American consul at Medellin supported this view. British shippers knew better those market requirements of finish, dimensions, quality and taste. US manufacturers would accept only orders which could be supplied from stock, because advices from Medellin were never large enough to enable them to embark upon 'strange' lines of production. English producers had for many years accepted very small orders, and provided a special 'light' finish to secure the fullest advantages under national, state and district tariffs structured according to weight.[122] Mr Baker, British consul at Vera Cruz, stressed the regressive nature of the Mexican tariff in pressing hard on British goods, especially 'common calicoes and prints', because they were so cheap, being of a quality generally lower than US imports.[123] According to *Bradstreet's Journal*, the accumulation of stocks prevalent in the US in 1891, especially in printing, had been less felt across the Atlantic because Lancashire production was in large measure a special trade for foreign markets, whilst the US product was essentially that left unsold at home. US trade with Brazil, Argentina and Mexico had declined and left the printer no alternative but to sell his cloth at a loss at home. Furthermore, since Lancashire worked far more to order only, it had an in-built preventative to overproduction.[124] In 1906 it was the opinion of one consular official that the situation had changed little, at least in Venezuela:

> Occasionally a consignment of 'remnants' from the American season is brought over from the United States and is sold at a very low figure, but so far no serious rival to British goods has appeared in this field.[125]

In the spring of 1900 William Whittam junior produced for the New England Cotton Manufacturers' Association some thirty-four samples of European (predominantly British) piece goods that he had collected in Venezuela, Colombia, Puerto Rico and Curaçao. Thirteen grey and bleached samples had been 'scoured' to ascertain the loss in weight when the 'size' was removed. It varied from 12 per cent for a grey Loneta to 61·5 per cent for a grey Loneta Cruda. Whittam observed that:

> If the amount of size found in the grey sample had been shown in the original weight of the warp only, one would wonder how so little cotton could possibly be made to retain such a weight of sizing materials.[126]

Whittam intended no moral censure on the ethics of the large British trade in sized goods. He argued that, in Latin America, the bulk demand was for cheap and showy goods, and that successful exporters had to meet this demand. The preference was for the 'full appearance' and 'clothy feel' that heavy sizing gave. Furthermore, sizing allowed price to be maintained at levels necessary to obtain sales amongst the '*peon* class', especially in view of heavy tariffs:

> While in the office of a very large South America [importing] house, a young man came in who represented an American exporting firm . . . when the customer talked of ordering hundreds of pieces, the salesman replied that they only had possibly twenty or thirty pieces of that pattern for sale . . . no business was done. Shortly afterwards the representative of a Manchester

[exporting] house was announced . . . The customer remarked on one sample, 'Mr B., this fabric is too expensive; can you give me one something similar in appearance at . . . [a lower price] . . . ?' Out came a pick glass, pencil and notebook, and in a short time the seller answered in the affirmative. All in all the British representative got $20,000 orders from the house.[127]

A slightly later paper read before the same Association reflected a similar preoccupation with American inability to meet price and taste requirements. In most overseas markets US cloth was seen to be too highly priced, partly because most of it was 'pure-sized'.[128] The paper advocated the installation of apparatus for mixing and storing size in those mills producing coarse goods. The goods in greatest demand in low-income countries were given to be those which possessed a maximum content of raw material and size, and a minimum content of labour. To produce such cloth the American process of 'hard twisting' the warp would have to be replaced, since 'oozy, little twisted' warps took size better.[129] In September 1905 Whittam, now spreading his gospel in the southern states, pointed to the US's 'minute share' in world trade in cotton textiles and to the reasons for this, 'nearly all of them discreditable to the business acumen of the managers of our industry'.[130] He gave as his main reason that US exporters would 'offer to sell a customer a buggy when he wanted to purchase a farm wagon', and lamented that cheap export lines such as shirtings (often 30s warp and 36s weft with 50–125 per cent size in the warp) like Indian cloths, Mexicans, T cloths, madopollams and domestics were manufactured almost exclusively by Lancashire firms. In 1907 Whittam, now a commercial agent of the federal government, was writing a report on finishing.[131]

In the years before the Great War there were many reports from Latin America that the feel and appearance of a cloth were more important marketing considerations than were durability and 'intrinsic' value, at least amongst the major part of the consuming public. In 1906 we hear that a 'smart, showy appearance' was essential to export success in Venezuela. What happened to cloth after washing was a minor consideration. Durability and texture took second place to cheapness and 'look':

> This 'faible' of the Venezuelan public is, then, the chief factor . . . and such material as 'filled shirtings' and similar stuffs which, whilst surviving but a few applications of soap and water, possess a smart appearance when they are first worn, are imported in very large quantities.[132]

Vice-consul Dickinson had reported similarly from Colombia in 1902, remarking that importers stressed the importance of finish in atisfying consumer tastes.[133] The Buenos Aires correspondent of the *British Trade Journal* was tempted to ask whether heavy starching was not of 'doubtful expediency', but nevertheless admitted that imports of such goods were large, even in the relatively high-income market of Argentina.[134] Such illustrations could be multiplied, and accord well with the observations of the *Warehouseman and Draper's Journal* that the neglect of 'getting up' and outward appearance at the expense of intrinsic quality could be a mistake.[135]

The use of size and other finishing materials is thus seen to have been a critical and widely accepted method, especially amongst Lancashire firms, of producing a cheap export cloth with an appearance usually only associated with higher quality goods. Basically, the rationale was to substitute a cheaper raw material input—at its simplest, starch or China clay—for a more expensive one, cotton, during a period when, at least until 1905–7, margins between raw cotton and product selling prices were unfavourable.[136] Whittam saw the sizing question as relating primarily to grey goods. He remarked that whereas in 1907 virtually all US cloth was 'pure-sized' most British cloth of this kind was bleached, printed or dyed *after* it had left the loom, since the further processes removed the size and it was not economical to reapply it.[137] This, however, conflicts with the result obtained earlier when he scoured samples of grey and bleached goods to ascertain the loss in weight that resulted. Only two out of the six bleached cloths examined could be said to reasonably fit the definition 'pure-sized', and even then their size content was a little high, being 15·2 and 15·4 per cent. Three of the remaining four lost over 20 per cent of their weight, including one which lost 28·6 per cent.[138] Though the average amount of size was probably greater in British grey goods exports, therefore, it does appear that more highly finished goods were exported sized.[139] Furthermore, it is of great importance to remember here that one very significant class of more highly finished piece goods underwent its dyeing and bleaching processes *before* being woven into cloth. This was none other than the class which held an unusually significant position in the growth sector of British exports to Latin America after 1880, 'goods manufactured wholly or partly from dyed yarn, commonly known as coloured cottons'. Such goods could be subjected to bleaching and dyeing and *then* to sizing *before* being woven into cloth. Also, it must be remembered that finishing processes other than sizing could be applied to coloured cottons, printed cottons and cottons dyed in the piece, to render a finish superior to that usually associated with cloth of a given quality of count, construction, weight and raw cotton type. There is much technical information on this subject in the trade press, but one article published in the *Textile Recorder* in 1908 is of great significance:

> There can be no doubt that the sale of coloured cottons depends upon the
> finish, well-finished goods attracting customers and badly-finished goods

repelling them; and for this reason the finishing process is of the utmost importance. At one time goods fetched a sufficiently high price to allow of the best yarn being used, and then extraneous methods were not necessary to give handle and weight to the material. But nowadays this happy state of affairs does not generally exist, and the finisher is called into being. His business is to give a heavy appearance to light goods, both in handle and weight, and the question how best to do this in the cheapest manner possible is one for consideration.[140]

The article shows that, in addition to certain coloured goods (i.e. 'coloured cottons') being sizable before weaving, there was a considerable range of subsequent operations designed to increase the weight, finish and appearance of the final product without increasing the selling price. Such methods included 'the proper use of Epsom salts', solutions of magnesium sulphate, magnesium chloride, glycerine, potassium sulphate and even lard. Magnesium sulphate on its own was considered the cheapest finishing solution, but it gave a somewhat harsh feel, which could be countered by softening agents such as starch, dextrine, syrup or castor oil.

A Cuban merchant, writing in 1906, gave useful intelligence into the types of goods 'most largely employed' in that market, emphasising as he did so the importance of a high degree of finish throughout the whole range of imports in low-income markets. For 25 in. wide Lienzo Crudo (sheetings) it was essential to deliver these finished to render them acceptable. Goods '3½ cents finished' were preferable to those '4 cents unfinished'. With Listados (ginghams) it was remarked that:

> A beginning has been made to consume this cloth from the United States in preference to others, since it counts more to the threads, viz. 60 by 54, instead of 52 by 48, and has 1 in. more of width (26 in.), and whose quality and weight are better. There ought to be made a cloth that counts 52 by 48 threads in 25 in width of 6¼ yds to the pound with special finish, since otherwise it would have the appearance of inferior quality.[141]

So far we have seen that Britain's relative shift out of grey goods may be said to have been a reaction to the rise of domestic industry only in Brazil, Mexico, and perhaps in Colombia. With regard to the shift out of prints, the larger of the two adaptations, this reason is less tenable, except perhaps in Mexico. The movement towards dyed goods must be seen as a response to different factors—firstly a large degree of external competition in the print trade, and secondly an autonomous increase in the attractiveness of dyed cloth, coupled probably with changing consumption patterns as Latin American incomes rose.

But though incomes per head were rising, South America remained largely a low-income market. Consequently, it cannot be considered that the shift towards dyed goods effectively insulated British exporters from competition. Much of the growing dyed goods trade was, by the nature of the market, in relatively cheap, relatively coarse coloured products. We have seen above that Mexican and Brazilian production of such goods was by no means absent. More widespread in its effect was the ability of the German and Italian industries to effect strong rivalries in the cheap coloured goods markets of Latin America. By 1913 Germany's total cotton exports to Latin America were nearly twice those of the USA by value, though the ratio of other cotton manufacturers, such as hosiery, to piece goods was probably higher in the case of German exports. US export problems centred around the nature of its products, these being determined by home surpluses. The German industry, on the other hand, achieved some considerable success in producing low-quality export goods with a high degree of finishing.

The rise of the German artificial dyestuffs industry had been, of course, intimately associated with German economic progress ever since the discovery of alizarene by Bayer, Perkin and others in 1869. According to Howard, writing in 1907, Germany produced four-fifths of world dyestuffs output in that year.[142] Of course, German superiority over Britain in dyestuffs for application to cottons was perhaps less than her overall lead in the dyestuffs industry,[143] and in any case her large exports of dyes[144] would have lessened the relative advantages possessed by German cotton colourers. Furthermore, superiority in producing chemicals would not necessarily indicate superiority in applying them to cotton fabrics. Nevertheless, Germany's strong position in the anciliary industry undoubtedly had considerable spin-off in cotton goods production. That writer of exemplary consular reports, Mr Oppenheimer, of Frankfurt, stressed that the German industry's strength lay in the finishing of yarn and cloth. Exports of dyed and printed cloth were far greater than exports of unbleached and bleached cloth.[145] Other observers used Germany's strength in more finished lines as an indictment of the British manufacturer. In 1892 the *Textile Recorder* published an article which argued a German superiority in calico printing.[146] Ten years later the same journal remarked on the superior quality of German dyeing, a state of affairs which had resulted in British merchants sending unbleached goods to Germany for finishing.[147] The famous spectre raised by the *Dyer* in 1883 had not yet been laid to rest:

> We cannot help deploring the sleepiness which seems to be spreading over many of our industries . . . foreigners are daily shortening the distance which separates English perfection from their crudeness . . . We see this very plainly in the dyeing trade . . . there appears to be a taste springing up in England to employ foreign foremen and dyers. Only the past few days we have been asked by an English dyer to find him a German foreman. The reason he gives

is disgust of 'rule of thumb' men, and his desire to have about him a man who understands thoroughly his business.[148]

Whilst such reports evidently contain much exaggeration and over-generalisation, it is evident also that one of the main strengths of the German industry did indeed lie in the finishing processes.[149] But at the same time it would seem that German sales efforts in Latin America concentrated predominantly on low qualities of cloth, often with high degrees of finishing. Doubtless such evidence must be used carefully, but the frequent observations of the German role as the 'Chinese of Europe' are indicative of the prices at which Germany was able to offer goods suitable for the requirements of low-income neutral markets.[150] In 1885 the French chamber of commerce in Mexico pointed to German advances in poor-quality, cheap lines. In Chile pattern and finish were regarded as more important than other aspects of quality, and German printed handkerchieves were consequently displacing imports from Britain and Switzerland.[151] The secretary of HM legation at Rio de Janeiro wrote home:

> Of trade there is plenty, but it does not pay. Not so with German goods. They are produced at far less cost than British manufactures; they are not so good or as durable, but they are more showy, and catch the Brazilian eye.[152]

At the same time a report from San Domingo observed:

> When the British manufacturers realise the fact—and they are beginning to do so, too—that they must produce cheap and tawdry goods to suit the tastes and pockets of their far-off customers, then will they derive larger profits, and surpass their German and French rivals.[153]

In Haiti in the early 'nineties Germany was reported to be making inroads on the French trade in fancy goods by supplying cheap and inferior articles, whilst a similar trend in Mexico was concealed by German shippers sending goods via French ports and even through French commission houses.[154] In 1896 the London correspondent of the *Manchester Guardian* commented on the cheapness and unpleasantness of German goods,[155] but intelligence from Brazil again emphasised that German cottons, far more than British, suited income levels and quality requirements in that market.[156]

British opinion on German competition was thus somewhat ambivalent. On one hand, German goods were described as 'inferior', 'showy' and 'tawdry'; on the other, writers accepted the nature of demand and urged manufacturers and exporters to conform to market requirements by supplying goods of poor quality and low price, but of a finish, pattern and taste that would render them popular. The Germans were not the only ones who directed their efforts to supplying the low-quality markets of Latin America; the Italians, too, were making strong progress in coloured goods, especially where there were communities of

Italian residents. The Italian chamber of commerce in Montevideo sent home detailed recommendations for exporters to the La Plata states in 1885, urging the shipment of striped and checked cotton cloths in 'lively, varying and well-combined colours.'[157] In 1886 exports of coloured cottons from Genoa to the Latin Americas were reported to be flourishing.[158] By the turn of the century Worthington's findings showed strongly that the area in which Britain was expanding her exports most rapidly, coloured and dyed goods, was one in which competition was fierce, perhaps less so than in printed goods but certainly more so than in grey and bleached cottons. Of course, the picture varied considerably. In Chile Britain possessed the 'great bulk' of the market in 'Oxfords, Tickings, etc.', but in other woven cottons, such as trouserings, Germany was said to prevail. In Argentina imports of German wove coloured trouserings had 'for years had the largest sale', but in general the Italians were 'making the largest progress' in such goods. The Italian goods were found to be superior in design, and the Italian practice of producing samples to requests for specific designs and quoting for them on the spot, by running up the sample on a hand loom, suited the variety and flux of the Argentinian market, where fashions could be 'as capricious as in Europe'. In Brazil Worthington's impression was that national manufacturers supplied the bulk of Oxfords, wove coloured trouserings and zephyrs on the market, so that it was difficult for importers to compete. In wove coloured flannelettes, however, where domestic production was insignificant, Germany was very strong. Italy also figured prominently in Uruguay, lying second to Britain in supplying ginghams and Oxfords, whilst even in the better class of trouserings, such as imitation cashmeres, she had largely replaced Germany and Britain.[159] Worthington sent home samples of foreign piece goods which were subsequently put on display in Manchester City Art Gallery by the Chamber of Commerce. The *Textile Recorder* noted that amongst the coloured woven good samples German and Italian were most prominent, and hoped that the display would prove useful to British manufacturers, since it was frequently said that Lancashire producers of such coloured goods did not take enough care in the design, shading, pattern and specification asked for by the importer.[160]

By Milne's report of conditions in Central America in 1913 US influence was manifest not only in unbleached goods (in Central America sizing was less expedient than elsewhere in Latin America because of the deleterious effects of a moist climate on sized cloth) and prints, but also in one or two lines of dyed good, especially denims. Rapid US advances in dyed cottons in Guatemala resulted in that country taking over from Britain as the chief supplier in 1910. The situation in Salvador was similar, though the American position was less advanced, except in denims, and Italian imports of drills were gaining ground. In Honduras, in addition to controlling the denim trade, the US could boast of supplying 73 per cent of cotton drill imports, compared with Britain's 15 per cent. In Nicaragua British shippers stood in greater favour, holding 86 per cent of the market for goods dyed in the piece and more than two-thirds of that for ginghams and zephyrs. In other wove coloured goods, however, such as drills and the higher-quality imitation cashmeres, the British lead over Italy and the US was only a marginal 5 per cent. In 1910 Italy took the lead from Britain in supplying coloured drills by supplying higher qualities, but Britain maintained the great share of the market in ginghams, Oxfords (Listados) and zephyrs.[161]

The main change in the British piece-good export mix to Latin America in the late nineteenth and early twentieth centuries was an increase in the importance of dyed goods and a decrease in that of unbleached and printed goods, both absolutely and relatively. Exports of bleached white cloths, unlike those to the rest of the world, exhibited stagnancy on both criteria. The absolute increase in dyed cloth occurred more at the expense of prints than of grey cloth.

Though we might expect great variations in realised unit values of all categories of piece goods, *average* unit values of the four categories maintain a sufficiently steady relationship to allow us to use them as a very crude spectrum of value added, unbleached goods being lowest on the scale and dyed goods being highest. But it is significant that, the further we progress up this spectrum, the more did Latin American unit values diverge from world unit values. Furthermore, this progressive divergence tended to grow wider with time.

There was probably some correlation between the count of piece-good exports and their position in this rough value-added spectrum. But since the main shift was from prints, themselves fairly high up the spectrum, the validity of regarding it as a pronounced movement towards finer counts must be doubtful.

The bulk of demand in Latin American markets was exerted by low-income consumers, as is shown by the nature of the products of indigenous industry, where it existed. This is further evidenced by the US's difficulties in expanding South American outlets for the high-quality cloths which were periodically surplus to her home market. This low-income restraint induced a price constraint which could be ignored only by sacrificing market shares.

To avoid losing its large trade outlets in the region Lancashire had therefore to avoid large increases in product quality. The classical response to indigenous development of cotton manufacturing and rival exporters had necessarily to be avoided. Sizing had for long been a method of keeping Britain ahead of her competitors. With the great growth of dyed goods the acuteness of this problem was not alleviated. Sizing and other cost-reducing processes were extended to the dyed cloth sector. Intrinsic quality and count were subordinated to finish, appearance and market requirements in matters of consumer tastes. Considerable emphasis was put upon 'coloured cottons', goods woven of dyed yarn and on average coarser than goods dyed in the piece, and amenable to heavy sizing.

Because the upward shift in quality could not be very great, Britain could not exploit her full technical superiority over Germany and Italy in the production of fine goods. The effective, though limited and to a certain extent localised, competition in Latin American coloured goods markets shows that Britain's product mix could be changed only within certain constraints imposed by purchasing power in those markets.

Thus the movement to dyed goods did indeed represent an upward shift in quality, since there is no evidence of a long-term deterioration in average count. The effect of the shift in ridding the British exporter of competition was, however, thwarted by the need to retain price-competitiveness. Even national producers could show progress in the production of coarse coloured goods. But whilst British exporters did not lose their rivals in the shift, they did retain a larger share of Latin American piece-good imports than they would have done if they had either made no change in their export product mix, or had markedly improved elements in quality other than finish and appearance.

Lastly, examination of the changing product mix shows us that the generalised assertion that quality changes were of the form of a progressive movement up the spectrum from unbleached to dyed goods is less true of Latin America than of the world as a whole. Prints occupy a relatively high position in the spectrum, yet they experienced severe decline in Latin America before 1914, whilst bleached goods did not. This trend is not paralleled by the world pattern. Furthermore, goods 'dyed in the piece' occupied a position higher in the spectrum than 'coloured cottons', yet it is doubtful whether they were expanding as fast in this period. The key element in South America's imports of British piece goods in the few decades before 1914 was the rapid growth of the cheap 'coloured cottons' sector.

NOTES

[1] See, inter alia, 'Finer counts in Oldham, and what they are indicative of', Textile Mercury, III, 69, 16 August 1890, p. 104; Textile Recorder, x, 117, 14 January 1893, p.239; XIII, 153, 15 January 1896, p.321; E. Enever Todd in Manchester Guardian, reprinted in Textile Recorder, XXIX, 341, 15 September 1911, p.143.
[2] See S. L. Bresso's remarks on British ascendancy in fine spinning, The Cotton Industry in Switzerland, Vorarlberg and Italy (Manchester, 1910), pp.10–11, 19.
[3] M. T. Copeland, The Cotton Manufacturing Industry of the United States (Cambridge. Mass., 1912), p.240.

[4] Lars G. Sandberg, 'Movements in the quality of British cotton textile exports, 1815–1913', *Journal of Economic History*, XXVIII, 1968, p.1–27. Sandberg's study includes a consideration of yarn quality which lies beyond the scope of this essay, in view of the general unimportance of yarn in total British cotton exports to Latin America. As Sandberg points out, his task would be relatively simple if actual types of cloth exported had been delineated in the Board of Trade Returns. Since they were not, he is forced into an 'indirect' method of adjusting indexes of current unit prices of piece-goods (derived from the official returns) by indexes of the f.o.b. selling prices of certain types of those goods for which information is available. He is satisfied that, especially after 1845, the selection of those cloths chosen on which to base the f.o.b. selling-price index does in fact reflect general movements in selling prices.

[5] *Ibid.*, p.9.

[6] *Ibid.*, p.19.

[7] R. E. Tyson, 'The cotton industry', in D. H. Aldcroft (ed.), *The Development of British Industry and Foreign Competition, 1875–1914* (London, 1968), pp.100–27; see especially pp.117, 126.

[8] Lars G. Sandberg, *loc. cit.*, p.19.

[9] Towards the end of the period two of these categories were broken down further; see below, pp.317–19.

[10] In view of year-to-year fluctuations, absolute export figures within particular years should, in the Latin American case, be treated with caution:

British (home-produced) piece-good exports (million yards)

	Unbleached grey	Bleached white	Printed	DMDY
To Latin America				
1889	117·527	253·570	294·699	119·806
1894	108·206	257·156	294·067	134·484
1899	85·207	240·060	272·834	158·080
1904	97·272	209·636	262·457	225·314
1909	63·654	225·120	171·838	243·089
1913	46·948	234·791	145·289	291·366
To the world				
1889	2284·601	1180·863	948·293	587·394
1894	2268·329	1400·057	981·979	661·863
1899	2163·770	1355·562	1059·399	860·106
1904	2033·983	1528·116	1036·733	992·988
1909	2091·930	1584·988	1012·899	1032·301
1913	2357·492	2045·252	1230·754	1441·753

Source. Derived from *Annual Statement of Trade of the United Kingdom*, 1889–1913.

[11] Exports to the world, of course, include those to Latin America. The difference between the two in terms of product-mix changes would be shown to be even greater if we removed Latin America from the world figures.

[12] W. P. McGreevey, *An Economic History of Colombia, 1845–1930* (London, 1971), p.164.

[13] *Textile Recorder*, III, 31, 14 November 1885, p.160.

[14] *Textile Recorder*, III, 29, 15 September 1885, p.111; IX, 98, 15 June 1891, p.43.

[15] Cited in *Textile Recorder*, IX, 107, 15 March 1892, p.258.

[16] *Diplomatic and Consular Reports, Annual Series*, No. 3657 (1906), from Venezuela.

[17] Whittam's view on cloth quality requirements in Latin America are considered in greater detail below, pp.334–5.

[18] At this time the average duty paid on all cloth imported into Mexico was 133 per cent *ad valorem*.

[19] *Diplomatic and Consular Reports, Annual Series*, No. 786 (1890); see also Manchester Chamber of Commerce, *Monthly Record*, I, 11, 24 November 1890, p.257. It should also be remembered that the depreciation of silver and paper currencies, and ever rising gold premiums, would have had a corresponding effect in increasing the real cost of imports into Latin America.

[20] *Textile Mercury*, I, 19, 31 August 1889, p.334.

[21] In 1912 E. Enever Todd cited figures given to the Washington Commercial

Conference which gave yearly cotton goods imports into Latin America as being divided up as follows: from the UK 53·6 per cent; from Germany 15·6 per cent; from Italy 8·6 per cent; from the US 8·3 per cent; from France 6·4 per cent; from Spain 3·6 per cent; from Belgium 1·7 per cent; from elsewhere 4·3 per cent (by value—percentages approximate). See 'The cotton trade of South and Central America: British and American competition', *Textile Recorder*, xxx, 351, 15 July 1912, p.71. Such figures must be regarded very cautiously. Apart from the general question of the comparability of different countries' official returns (see Y. Don, 'Comparability of international trade statistics: Great Britain and Austria–Hungary before World War I', *Economic History Review*, second series, xxi, 1968, pp. 78–92; B. Ellinger, 'Value and comparability of English and German foreign trade statistics', *Transactions of Manchester Statistical Society*, 1903–4, pp.139–58), it appears that some British dry goods exports to Latin America went via Hamburg or Belgium, and some from Germany via Belgium. See Board of Trade Commercial Intelligence Department, *Reports to the Board of Trade on the Condition and Prospects of British Trade in Central America, Colombia and Venezuela, Parl. Papers*, LXVIII, 1913, Cd 6969, p.11.

[22] *Diplomatic and Consular Reports, Annual Series*, No. 2747 (1902) (my italics).

[23] S. B. Saul, *Studies in British Overseas Trade, 1870–1914* (Liverpool, 1960), p.101 n.

[24] Separate calculations have shown this also to be the case for Colombia. These findings can be reconciled with Vice-consul Dickinson's remarks (p.314) if we admit the presence of overlap between higher qualities of one category and lower qualities of the category above it. The accompanying schematic diagram illustrates this situation. The shapes of the distributions *DD* and *PP* are not the only ones possible. It is likely, however, that *DD* at least was skewed in a manner similar to that depicted. *DD* and *PP* represent the quantities of dyed and printed goods actually sold at various prices measured on the *x* axis. The arithmetic means of *DD* and *PP* (i.e. the observed actual values as given in the official returns) are *Od* and *Op* respectively. British official figures show that *Od* is greater than *Op*. However, much dyed cloth is in a price range directly competitive with printed cloth. This could be true irrespective of the shape of *DD*. But the greater the degree of skew of *DD* towards the origin, the larger will be the volume of dyed goods sold in the price range associated with prints. It is even possible, if overlap is big enough, for some dyed cloth to be sold at prices below the *minimum* price at which prints can be purchased. This possibility is represented by the dotted section of *DD*.

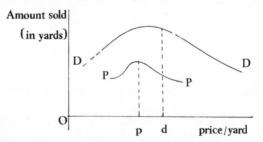

[25] The 'Printed' category is split up into two—'Printed . . . flags, handkerchieves and shawls in the piece' and 'Printed—other'. In table 13.2 only the second category is shown. Since the first accounted for only £24,456 (1,597,000 yards) out of total British printed piece-good exports to Latin America of £1,830,604 (145,289,400 yards) in 1913, and this proportion was correspondingly small throughout the period 1908–13, its inclusion would increase the unit value figures in table 13.2 from £0·0110 per yard to only £0·0111 per yard in 1909 and from £0·0125 per yard to only £0·0126 per yard in 1913. Since the proportion of this category in the world figure was similarly small, the corresponding world values would change from £0·0122 per yard to only £0·0123 per yard in 1909 and from £0·0136 to only £0·0137 per yard in 1913. The divergence between South American unit values

and average world unit values can thus be seen to remain virtually unchanged in percentage terms.

[26] Again it should be remembered that the South American figures have not been removed from the world total figures in these calculations.

[27] In the years considered, this was true for all but two cases—grey goods in 1889 and bleached goods in 1913. Table 13.4 understates the actual difference between South American and world average figures, since the former have not been extracted from the latter.

[28] It must, however, be remembered that the relative decline of Brazil and the relative rise of Argentina as markets within South America proper did possibly represent a limited step in this direction.

[29] *Textile Recorder*, II, 24, 15 April 1885, p.285; XXVI, 307, 15 November 1908, pp. 234–5; XXVIII, 330, 15 October 1910, p.228; XXXI, 362, 14 June 1913, p.62.

[30] *Textile Recorder*, II, 2(14), 14 June 1884, p.42.

[31] *Textile Recorder*, IV, 40, 14 August 1886, p.88.

[32] *Textile Recorder*, VII, 78, 15 October 1889, p.137.

[33] *Textile Recorder*, X, 115, 15 November 1892, p.185; 116, 15 December 1892, p.213.

[34] *Textile Recorder*, XVI, 181, 14 May 1898, pp.1–2.

[35] *Textile World*, quoted in 'The textile industry in Mexico', *Textile Recorder*, XIX, 226, 15 February 1902, p.291.

[36] 'The Mexican cotton industry', *Textile Recorder*, XXVI, 307, 15 November 1908, pp. 234–5.

[37] E. Enever Todd, 'The cotton trade of South and Central America: British and American competition', *Textile Recorder*, XXX, 351, 15 July 1912, pp.70–1.

[38] The Amparo and the Fodos os Santos at Valença, the Tororó at Cachoeira, and the San Salvador in Bahia City.

[39] Cited in *Textile Recorder*, II, 19, 15 November 1884, p.161.

[40] 'Cotton factories in Brazil', *Textile Recorder*, V, 53, 15 September 1887, p.105.

[41] *Textile Recorder*, XXI, 247, 14 November 1903, p.216.

[42] *Diplomatic and Consular Reports, Annual Series*, No. 4358 (1909).

[43] *Textile Recorder*, XXVII, 322, 15 February 1910, p.337.

[44] *Volume of British piece-good exports 1889–1913 ('000 yds)*

	1889	1894	1899	1904	1909	1913
To Mexico						
Unbleached grey	683	–	282	–	–	–
Bleached white	17,860	15,680	22,944	9,561	8,371	8,826
Printed	20,703	9,749	16,547	5,181	2,998	2,697
DMDY	4,453	3,787	8,595	5,589	4,223	11,246
Total	43,699	29,216	48,368	20,331	15,593	22,769
To Brazil						
Unbleached grey	17,360	12,280	7,931	6,928	833	3,442
Bleached white	48,448	68,934	32,435	30,540	22,376	25,439
Printed	79,898	100,351	58,110	49,815	27,067	9,871
DMDY	32,296	46,254	34,086	47,558	40,335	57,786
Total	178,001	227,819	132,562	134,841	90,611	96,538

Source. Annual Statement of Trade of the United Kingdom, 1889–1913.

[45] *Commercial Relations of the United States with Foreign Countries* (1884–5), p.736.

[46] *Diplomatic and Consular Reports, Annual Series*, No. 1764 (1896).

[47] 'Textile mills in Brazil', *Textile Recorder*, XV, 172, 14 August 1897, p.115. For an indication of Brazilian diversity in cheap coloured goods, see also, *inter alia*, the descriptions of the Empreza Valença and the Italian-owned Fabrica São Roque in São Paulo.

[48] *Textile Recorder*, XVII, 195, 15 July 1899, p.74.

[49] *Diplomatic and Consular Reports, Annual Series*, No. 2602 (1901).

[50] Quoted in *Textile Recorder*, XIX, 226, 15 February 1902, p.315.

[51] S. J. Stein, *The Brazilian Cotton Manufacture* (Cambridge, Mass., 1957), pp.68–9.

[52] Petropolitana, Directoría, 29 December 1887; 30 August 1888, quoted in Stein, *op. cit.*, p.74.

[53] *Ibid.*, p.79.

[54] *Ibid.*, p.77.

[55] *Ibid.*, p.100.

[56] *Ibid.*, p.101.

[57] See, for example, R. Tyson, *op. cit.*, p.126.

[58] Except in Brazil and Mexico, and in Cauca, Cundimanca, Boyaca, Bolivar, Antioquia and Santander in Colombia, factory industry in Latin America was largely discounted. Peru was credited with two establishments, the largest situated at Vitante and producing three million yards of cloth per annum. In Argentina, the Textile industries had 'scarcely a foothold'. Production in Ecuador was carried on entirely in private houses and small workshops. Elsewhere, in Venezuela, Uruguay, Paraguay, Chile and Bolivia, no details of local production were given. See 'Textile industries in Spanish America', *Textile Recorder*, xvi, 188, 15 December 1898, p.299.

[59] A. Ferrer, *The Argentine Economy* (Berkeley, Calif., 1967), pp.115, 128–9.

[60] W. McGreevey, *op. cit.*, pp.81–2.

[61] E. Enever Todd, 'The cotton trade of South and Central America', *loc. cit.*

[62] Board of Trade, Commercial Intelligence Department, *Reports on British Trade in Central America*, Cd 6969, lxviii, pp.4–5, 29–30, 51–3, 69, 86–7.

[63] *Ibid.*, pp.132–3. Milne gives details of three Venezuelan mills, two owned by the Telares de Caracas Valencia and one by the Hilanderias de Oriente. Yarns used were in the range 8s to 40s, and the products principally grey and coloured yarn, coarse grey piece-goods, drills and plain and coloured undervests. See Board of Trade, Commercial Intelligence Department, *op. cit.*, pp.160–1. According to Enever Todd, these mills would seem to have been the whole extent of the Venezuelan industry. See 'The cotton trade of South and Central America', *loc. cit.*

[64] See, for instance, the range of goods offered for auction by a Brazil dry goods importing house, J. Dalglish Thompson & Co., in 1855, in R. Graham, *Britain and the Onset of Modernisation in Brazil, 1850–1914* (Cambridge, 1968), p.83.

[65] E. Helm, 'The middleman in commerce', *Transactions of the Manchester Statistical Society*, session 1900–1, p.62.

[66] See below, pp.329–37.

[67] This compares with a British total of 900 machines and a US total of 300. See 'English v. American calico printing', *Textile Mercury*, iv, 107, 9 May 1891, p.323.

[68] G. Turnbull, *A History of the Calico Printing Industry of Great Britain* (Altrincham, 1951), pp.117–23.

[69] F. Steiner & Co. Ltd., the United Turkey Red Co. Ltd., and the Calico Printers' Association.

[70] G. Turnbull, *op. cit.*, pp.124, 327, 330.

[71] *Ibid.*, pp.335–6.

[72] 'English v. American calico printing', *loc. cit.*

[73] *Reports Received from Mr. T. Worthington, Special Commissioner to the Board of Trade, to inquire into the Conditions and Prospects of British Trade in Certain South American Countries (Parl. Papers, Reports of Commissioners, xcvi, Cd 9100, 1898)* (hereafter cited as *Worthington*), pp.496–7 (cumulative).

[74] 'Central and South American trade', *Textile Recorder*, ix, 102, 15 October 1891, p.123.

[75] 'The export business in textile manufactures', *Textile Recorder*, iii, 30, 15 October 1885, p.122.

[76] *Diplomatic and Consular Reports, Annual Series*, No. 3657 (1906); No. 1963 (1897).

[77] Brazil's print capacity seems to have lagged markedly behind other sections of the industry. See *Worthington*, pp.540–2 (cumulative).

[78] *Textile Recorder*, vii, 78, 15 October 1889, p.137; viii, 91, 15 November 1890, p.146.

[79] *Textile Recorder*, xviii, 214, 15 February 1901, p.335.

[80] 'English textiles in Mexico: grey cloths and prints', *Textile Mercury*, vii, 193, 31 December 1892, p.467.

[81] 'Hideous purple prints for South America', *Textile Mercury*, ii, 61, 21 June 1890, p.419.

[82] *Textile Recorder*, xxiii, 271, 15 November 1905, p.217; xxviii 320, 15 December 1909, p.246; G. Turnbull, *op. cit.*, p.330.

[83] G. Turnbull, *op. cit.*, p.271.

[84] Board of Trade, Commercial Intelligence Department, *op. cit.*, pp.12–13, 36–7, 58. See also Milne's remarks on the Costa Rican trade (p.93), where a preference for British designs had been rendered ineffective because of the disadvantages otherwise connected with British print imports.

[85] *Ibid.*, pp.75, 112, 172.

[86] See above, p.314.

[87] *Manchester City News*, 13 June 1896, p.6.

[88] Manchester Chamber of Commerce, *Monthly Record*, XVIII, 2, 28 February 1907, pp.48–9.

[89] *Textile Recorder*, I, 12, 15 April 1884, pp.277, 280; II, 1 (13), 15 May 1884, pp.1, 18.

[90] *Textile Recorder* (American correspondent), II, 2 (14), 14 June 1884, p.42.

[91] US consul at San Blas, cited by *Textile Recorder*'s American correspondent, *ibid.* Quotation from American correspondent.

[92] *Textile Recorder*, II, 20, 15 December 1884, p.171.

[93] Significantly called in full the North, Central and Southern American Exhibition.

[94] *Textile Recorder*, III, 29, 15 September 1885, p.106.

[95] *Textile Recorder*, III, 33, 15 January 1886, pp.193, 208–9; (American correspondent) IV, 37, 15 May 1886, p.17.

[96] *Textile Recorder* (American correspondent), IV, 40, 14 August 1886, p.89.

[97] *Textile Recorder*, IV, 41, 15 September 1886, p.114.

[98] 'Central and South American trade', *Textile Recorder*, IV, 45, 15 January 1887, p.194

[99] 'American trade with Mexico', *Textile Recorder*, V, 53, 15 September 1887, p.98.

[100] *Textile Recorder*, V, 56, 15 December 1887, p.186.

[101] *Textile Recorder*, VI, 69, 15 January 1889, p.194: see also VII, 73, 15 May 1889, p.20.

[102] *Textile Recorder*, VI, 77, 14 September 1889, p.98.

[103] In the first eleven months of 1888 US piece-good exports to Colombia of £47,000 compared with a British figure of over £565,000. In Argentina the corresponding figures for 1888 were, for all US cottons, $106,000 (Argentine) and for all UK cottons, $5 million (Argentine): see *Textile Recorder*, VI, 70, 15 February 1889, p.217; VIII, 87, 15 July 1890, p.50.

[104] *Textile Recorder*, VIII, 87, 15 July 1890, p.50.

[105] *Textile Recorder*, IX, 100, 15 August 1891, p.74.

[106] *Textile Recorder*, IX, 102, 15 October 1891, p.123.

[107] *Textile Recorder*, X, 120, 15 April 1893, p.335.

[108] *Textile Recorder*, XII, 135, 14 July 1894, p.122.

[109] Mr Warner Mitchell, in *Boston Journal of Commerce*, 30 November 1895, quoted in *Textile Recorder*, XIII, 152, 14 December 1895, p.255.

[110] *Textile Recorder*, XIV, 158, 15 June 1896, p.34.

[111] *Textile Recorder*, XV, 176, 15 December 1897, p.246; XVIII, 211, 15 November 1900, p.249.

[112] *Textile Recorder*, XIV, 167, 15 March 1897, p.341.

[113] *Diplomatic and Consular Reports, Annual Series*, No. 2473 (1900).

[114] *Textile Recorder*, XVIII, 211, 15 November 1900, p.249.

[115] M. T. Copeland, *The Cotton Manufacturing Industry of the United States* (Cambridge, Mass., 1912), pp.220–1.

[116] *Ibid.*, derived from table on p.222.

[117] Board of Trade, Commercial Intelligence Department, *op. cit.*, pp.11–15, 36, 57–60, 75–7, 93, 145–7, 171–2. Such figures should be treated with extreme caution, but they do give an impression of relative market shares.

[118] E. Enever Todd, 'Cotton trade of South and Central America', *loc. cit.*

[119] *Textile Recorder*, II, 20, 15 December 1884, p.184.

[120] Tyson argues that in this period the US was Britain's nearest rival in terms of economic efficiency—*loc. cit.*, p.121.

[121] *Textile Recorder*, III, 31, 14 November 1885, pp.160–1.

[122] Cited in *Textile Recorder*, III, 32, 15 December 1885, p.184.

[123] In 1889 British cotton imports into Vera Cruz paid an average of 133 per cent *ad valorem* compared with a figure of 83 per cent for US goods. See *Diplomatic and Consular Reports, Annual Series*, No. 786 (1890).

[124] *Bradstreet's Journal*, cited in *Textile Recorder*, IX, 100, 15 August 1891, p.74.

[125] *Diplomatic and Consular Reports, Annual Series*, No. 3657 (1906).

[126] Whittam's paper is reprinted as 'The Latin American trade in cotton fabrics', *Textile Recorder*, XVIII, 205, 15 May 1900, pp.20–2.

[127] *Ibid.*, p.20.

[128] To improve the quality of weaving and to make the operation more trouble-free, even 'pure-sized' cloth contained some 15 per cent of size.

[129] Paper (author unspecified) read before North-East Cotton Manufacturers' Association, reported in *Textile Recorder*, XIX, 222, 15 October 1901, p.195.

[130] Wm. Whittam jr., 'Consumers of export goods and their requirements', a paper read before the Southern Manufacturers' Association, reported in *Textile Recorder*, XXIII, 269, 15 September 1905, p.150.

[131] *Textile Recorder*, XXV, 293, 14 September 1907, p.145.

[132] *Diplomatic and Consular Reports, Annual Series*, No. 3657 (1906).

[133] *Diplomatic and Consular Reports, Annual Series*, No. 2747 (1902).

[134] *British Trade Journal*, cited in *Textile Recorder*, XIX, 222, 15 October 1901, p.195.

[135] *Warehouseman and Draper's Journal*, cited in *Textile Mercury*, VII, 176, 3 September 1892, p.176.

[136] R. Tyson, *loc. cit.*, p.101–2.

[137] *Textile Recorder*, XXV, 293, 14 September 1907, p.145.

[138] 'The Latin American trade in cotton fabrics', *loc. cit.*

[139] According to the *Textile Recorder*, South America was one of the markets for which a cheap 'sized and filled' cloth was especially manufactured. Such goods were 'practically devoid of wearing properties, but of striking and effective design, or grey, bleached or dyed'. Lancashire was stated to be pre-eminent in this trade. Significantly, printed cloth is the only type not mentioned. See *Textile Recorder*, XVI, 189, 14 January 1899, p.329.

[140] 'Finishing coloured cottons', *Textile Recorder*, XXV, 297, 15 January 1908, pp.284–5.

[141] 'Markets for cotton goods in Cuba', *Textile Recorder*, XXIII, 274, 15 February 1906, p.290.

[142] E. D. Howard, *The Cause and Extent of the Recent Industrial Progress of Germany* (Boston, 1907), pp.58–62.

[143] Though the *Textile Mercury* thought otherwise; see IV, 73, 13 September 1890, p.174.

[144] By 1900, some 100 million marks' worth per annum; see Howard, *op. cit.*

[145] *Diplomatic and Consular Reports, Annual Series*, No. 1082 (1892).

[146] *Textile Recorder*, X, 114, 15 October 1892, p.134.

[147] *Textile Recorder*, XX, 235, 15 November 1902, p.205.

[148] *The Dyer, Calico Printer and Colour Trades Review*, IV, 30, 15 January 1884, pp.1–2.

[149] See, for example, S. J. Chapman, *Work and Wages*, Part I, *Foreign Competition* (London, 1904), p.167.

[150] *Textile Recorder*, XIII, 151, 15 November 1895, p.239.

[151] German consular report from Valparaiso 1885, cited in *Textile Recorder*, III, 30, 15 October 1885, p.122.

[152] Quoted in *Textile Recorder*, IV, 45, 15 January 1887, p.195.

[153] *Diplomatic and Consular Reports, Annual Series*, No. 87 (1887).

[154] *Textile Recorder*, IX, 98, 15 June 1891, p.43; 106, 15 February 1892, p.233.

[155] Cited in *Textile Recorder*, XIV, 163, 14 November 1896, p.191.

[156] *Textile Recorder*, XVII, 197, 15 September 1899, p.146.

[157] *Textile Recorder*, III, 27, 15 July 1885, p.49.

[158] *Textile Recorder*, III, 35, 15 March 1886, p.241.

[159] *Worthington, First Report* (Chile), p.453; *Third Report* (Argentina), pp.495–9; *Fourth Report* (Brazil—Rio de Janiero), pp.540–3; *Sixth Report* (Uruguay), pp.595–6.

[160] 'Exhibition of foreign manufactures from South America', *Textile Recorder*, XVI, 192, 15 April 1899, p.435.

[161] Board of Trade, Commercial Intelligence Department, *op. cit.*, pp.12–14, 36, 57–9, 75–7, 93.

Index